Caesar in Gaul and Rome

CAESAR in Gaul and Rome

WAR IN WORDS

by Andrew M. Riggsby

University of Texas Press, Austin

*Publication of this book was aided by a generous subsidy
from Peter and Ashley Larkin.*

*This book has been supported by an endowment dedicated
to classics and the ancient world and funded by the Areté
Foundation; the Gladys Krieble Delmas Foundation; the
Dougherty Foundation; the James R. Dougherty, Jr.
Foundation; the Rachael and Ben Vaughan Foundation;
and the National Endowment for the Humanities. The
endowment has also benefited from gifts by Mark and
Jo Ann Finley, Lucy Shoe Meritt, the late Anne Byrd
Nalle, and other individual donors.*

Requests for permission to reproduce material from
this work should be sent to:
 Permissions
 University of Texas Press
 P.O. Box 7819
 Austin, TX 78713-7819
 www.utexas.edu/utpress/about/bpermission.html

∞ The paper used in this book meets the minimum
requirements of ANSI/NISO Z39.48-1992 (R1997)
(Permanence of Paper).

 Library of Congress Cataloging-in-Publication Data

Riggsby, Andrew M.
 Caesar in Gaul and Rome : war in words /
 by Andrew M. Riggsby.
  p. cm.
 Includes bibliographical references and index.
 ISBN-13: 978-0-292-72617-8

 1. Caesar, Julius—Military leadership. 2. Caesar,
Julius—Political activity. 3. Gaul—History—Gallic
Wars, 58–51 B.C.—Political aspects. 4. Rome—
History, Military—265–30 B.C. I. Title.
 DG264.C333R54 2006
 936.4′02—dc22
         2006006554

D.M.

Katherine Tate Riggsby

Contents

Acknowledgments

Thank you to the several people who read the entire manuscript at some stage: Cynthia Damon, Erik Gunderson (who revealed himself as an excellent Press reader), Chris Kraus (twice!), Gwyn Morgan, Matt Roller, and the University of Texas Press's other, extremely professional, anonymous reader.

Many others (some of whom I fear I have omitted in the long gestation of the book) helped by reading extended segments and/or providing crucial discussion: Jim Burr, Penelope Davies, Michael Dewar, Bryan James, Lisa Kallet, Eric Orlin, Michael Peachin, Miriam Pittenger, Margaret Woodhull, David Woodward, and the members of my Caesar seminar at the University of Texas at Austin.

Alexa Jervis, Aislinn Melchior, and Miriam Pittenger were kind enough to provide me with pre-publication texts of their own work on Caesar and related topics.

Several chapters of this book were delivered to gracious audiences at the New York Classical Club, and at the Classical Association of the Mid-West and South (Southern section) and the Universities of Tennessee, Texas (Austin), Texas (Arlington), Toronto, and Wisconsin.

Most of the research and much of the writing of this work were carried out during the tenure of a Solmsen Fellowship at the Institute for Research in the Humanities at the University of Wisconsin, Madison. I thank the director and senior fellows for the Fellowship, and the entire membership (especially Paul Boyer, Heather Dubrow, and David Woodward), for a very pleasant and profitable stay. I was also welcomed most hospitably by the Department of Classics (most notably Laura McClure and Patricia Rosenmeyer).

Last, I have gotten invaluable practical assistance from Christina Schlegel, who made the line drawings, and Beth Orr, who provided photographs.

Caesar in Gaul and Rome

Introduction

This book is a study of what is—in many senses—an already well-known historical event: Julius Caesar's *De Bello Gallico*, or *Gallic War*.[1] To think of texts as events is certainly in line with various historicist tendencies in the field of Classics in general, but it is also an approach that has come to be seen as particularly appropriate to this work.[2] For one thing, the direct evidence for *De Bello Gallico* is incomparably better than that for the Gallic War fought in the 50's B.C.[3] We have the former actually before us (though not its prior composition nor its subsequent circulation). Slightly less obviously, however, we have much better controls for the *War* than for the War. After a long period in which Caesar was largely taken at his word, it became popular in the middle of the last century to try to find deceptions on the evidence of Caesar's own text.[4] It is by now notoriously difficult to confirm or refute anything Caesar says.[5] There are few other sources for the Gallic War, and none can be shown to be substantially independent of Caesar's account. Consequently, even disagreement with Caesar may be more a sign of invention or error in the historical tradition than of independent testimony.[6]

For the text, on the other hand, many things can be brought to bear. Not only are there a few direct testimonia to its reception, but we also have a variety of different sources for how Romans might talk about the war and about the other topics of *De Bello Gallico*. Here it is enough to note the existence of contemporary texts such as Cicero's oration *On the Consular Provinces*, which treats Caesar's conduct of the war at some length, and Posidonius' anthropology (preserved only in fragments) of the Gauls whom Caesar was both fighting and describing.

This study has two roughly equal parts. The first, "external" part looks outward and considers the kind of Roman identity postulated by Caesar's work, particularly how it is constituted in the context of various non-Roman others. Here Caesar prefigures in small but important ways the coming Imperial order, establishing a link between empire and Empire. The second, "internal" part treats Caesar's political self-fashioning and the potential ends of his writing and publishing such a work. Of particular interest here is how (and why) Caesar persuades in a work that on its surface is so lacking in argumentation. Each part comprises case studies on key topics (spatial representation, ethnography, *virtus* and technology, genre, the just war) that are followed by a more broadly synthetic conclusion, filling out a broader picture of the part's topic (national identity; Caesar's self-presentation) and setting these results in the context of other current scholarly work. Thus, while I focus on the single work, I hope to provide conclusions about the *interaction* of that work with its cultural and political environments.

The Social Life of Texts

None of the case-study topics is entirely new, and two of them (ethnography and genre) are arguably mainstays of writing on Caesar. Substantively, however, their specific conclusions are largely new and gain by combination into the two parts just described; they are mutually illuminating in ways not possible in previous (often very insightful) studies on those topics individually. Moreover, all seven chapters share a methodological coherence, and, I think, a methodological advance. The key notion here is "intertextuality," the idea that texts ultimately and necessarily take on their meanings by comparison and contrast with other texts. (The following account of intertextuality is, I think, important to ground the study as a whole and to justify several lines of argument. However, I do not introduce any special vocabulary or the like that would be necessary to the understanding of the rest of the work. Some readers might find it more useful to skip now to the next section of the Introduction, and return to this theoretical discussion after the rest of the book.)

Specific definitions and extensive theorization about "intertextuality" have taken many forms over time and across scholarly disciplines.[7] Many of those understandings of the term are dependent on fairly specific linguistic and philosophical commitments, many of which are in turn debatable and are at any rate hardly shared by all theorists of intertextuality. I here rely mainly on three propositions that, though hardly novel, I hope will be largely uncontroversial.

The first proposition is that the meaning of words is constrained by the fact that they are common property; they are known through usage, and no stipulation can entirely free them from that history.[8] To take an extreme example, some older dictionaries offer "holocaust" as a translation for Greek ἔμπυρα, "burnt sacrifice." Yet this is almost impossible for contemporary students who have heard much more about Nazi Germany than about animal sacrifice, even if the term is explained to them. Description of a ballistic missile defense system as "Star Wars" effectively conveyed the ambition of the program (by comparison to the movie's epic character), but also made it hard to avoid a sense of mockery (since the movie was overtly fictional).

The second proposition is that the reciprocity of language production and learning will produce a considerable degree of intersubjectivity among actual communities without requiring us to posit any ideal form of language. Different speakers of a language operate with slightly different rules (most obviously slightly different vocabularies), which linguists call their individual "ideolects." These ideolects arise in roughly similar circumstances; English speakers grow up hearing English sentences. Moreover, speakers implicitly compare and test their individual versions every time they attempt to communicate with others. Thus, although two different speakers almost necessarily have different primary linguistic experiences (in detail), they will over time tend to share more and more background, at least indirectly. Thus there are many different "Englishes," each material and at least potentially well-ordered as part of the neurophysiology of various speakers. To assert the existence of English in general is then shorthand for an essentially sociological claim about the potential for communication between these speakers.

A similar argument about acquisition could be made for many other kinds of cultural knowledge (e.g., greeting rituals),[9] and that leads to the third proposition: constraint of language by shared history occurs not just at the level of words, but also at higher levels of organization. Minimally, speakers share fixed phrases, some with idiomatic ("hit the showers") or technical ("malice aforethought") meanings, others not ("animal instinct"). The phrase "this space intentionally left blank" not only comes as a unit, but also suggests the whole world of bureaucracy. Audiences recognize verse forms, so that, for instance, a reader of this stanza—

> Thales' theory, to quickly review it,
> Is that everything's made from a fluid.
> How it's done, he'd not venture,
> Though he'd say, facing censure:
> Don't forget steam and ice somehow do it.[10]

—is likely to view the information it contains with some suspicion, since the limerick form is typically used for jokes.

The verbal complexes with which I am most concerned in this book are particularly large ones, which I describe as "discourses" and (to a lesser extent) "genres." I intend "discourse" here in a fairly general way: a way of talking about some subject matter.[11] That would include characteristic vocabulary, metaphors, themes or parameters, omissions, or procedures for assessing individual statements.[12] A "genre" will be a pattern of associations between features of form, content, and context/occasion of verbal production.[13] This includes both "literary" genres (e.g., epic, the novel) and nonliterary ones (newspaper story, conversation).

Both discourses and genres share a number of features. First, they have the same dual character as languages in general. For individuals, they are concrete and can (though need not) be stable. In the abstract, they are sociological fictions. All versions of "epic" are likely to be similar; no two will be exactly alike. Second, both genres and discourses can overlap and/or encompass other genres and discourses, respectively. For instance, a discourse on "war" might contain discourses on "tactics," "courage," or "divine favor." The latter might additionally be part of a discourse on "philosophy." That in turn might be cross-cut by "Stoicism," "Epicureanism," etc. Discourse and genre can also overlap/encompass each other in the same ways. War discourse would appear not only in military manuals and actual commands, but also in epic and history.[14] Third, both are in principle subject to a producer's conscious control. It is well established that, say, an Ovid can carry out elaborate manipulations of his readers' generic expectations. Similarly, one could choose to discuss "war" in nonstandard terms. Such variation, however, is constrained by intelligibility. Too great a variation has the same effect as making up one's own words.[15] So, for instance, I argue that Caesar's text is largely typical "war" discourse, but that it redefines one of its key terms, *virtus* (Chap. 3 below; contrast Chaps. 6 and 7). Here the modification depends on exploiting a contradiction already existing within the tradition. Conversely, Caesar pointedly avoids the discourse traditionally surrounding northern "barbarians" (Chaps. 2 and 4 below).

Though the term "intertextuality" has been in vogue for some time now, and is perhaps already losing favor, the idea remains underexploited, as argued by Fowler.[16] (In fact, I suspect recognition of the gap between awareness and use has itself become something of a topos, though without producing much change.) Far the most common case in which classicists invoke the notion of intertextuality remains allusion in some passage of poetry (say, the opening phrase of the *Aeneid*) to an earlier passage in a similar context (say, the opening of the *Odyssey*).[17] My plan is to exploit the broader range of the term in three ways, albeit with some overlap.

First, in probably the most common extension of the prototypical procedure, many of the relationships discussed here cross genre boundaries. Of course, it is legitimate, sometimes even necessary, to compare Caesar's work to that of other "historians" (though see Chap. 5 below on the sense of that term), but there is much to be gained from looking further afield to oratory, geography, surveying manuals, and others.

Second, since intertextuality is a general property of language rather than of literature, it can be just as important for prose as for poetry. Now, it is perhaps increasingly common to recognize prose influences on poetic texts; see, for example, Thomas 1988 on Vergil's use of agricultural texts in the *Georgics*. And historians are known to have responded to their predecessors in ways beyond mere collection of source materials.[18] Nonetheless, both instances tend to be treated as isolated, artistic phenomena rather than as a normal feature of prose texts.

Third, and most important, I am interested here not in Caesar's reference to specific passages of specific works, but in his relationship to entire discourses.[19] The existence of a discourse on some topic creates what might be called a "field of positions," a set of distinctions, contrasts, axes, and/or spectra with respect to which terms are defined and positions taken.[20] Segments of Caesar's text (or any other) take on meaning by their locations in one or more of these fields. In one sense, such an appeal to a broader "interdiscursivity" is a common move.[21] It is not, after all, entirely unlike appeals commonly made to "the (ancient) context" of a work. Yet this conventional formulation has unnecessary limitations. While not denying the theoretical possibility of multiple or multivocal intertexts, it tends to fix on one. Take, as an example of skillful application of the traditional method, the philosophical contextualization of the end of the *Aeneid*. Galinsky starts by detailing the diversity of ancient philosophical opinions on anger (and Vergil's incomplete adherence to any of them). Yet, in the end, the effect of Galinsky's interpretation is to downplay the "pessimistic," Stoicizing reading that Aeneas should not have lost control at the end of the poem.[22] More generally, this kind of "contextualization" is usually used to limit meaning: "This passage must mean A, not B, because the latter is anachronistic." Modern theory would suggest that appeal to intertexts can open up readings, but not close them off.

More positively, a modern notion of intertextuality makes it easier to account for three phenomena that will be observed in the course of this study.

One is a style of naturalization. A text (or passage) that is written according to the standard rules of some recognized form is more likely to gain at least provisional acceptance, since it will be at least formally plausible. To give a non-Caesarian instance, consider Mader's recent (2000) reading of Josephus' *Jewish War* in the light of classical historiographical intertexts (primarily Thucydides). On this reading, Josephus is "concerned to dissociate the rebels from the traditions of Jewish piety [and] plays down, refracts, and filters out this religious dimension by applying the political and psychological categories of Greco-Roman historiography."[23] That is, classical historiography favors (and leads readers to expect) certain explanatory gestures and categories of analysis. Hence, faction/stasis, demagoguery, and tyranny easily replace eschatology and religious traditionalism, without the need actually to argue for the former set of descriptions. Similarly, I here argue (Chap. 5) that Caesar's choice of the *commentarius* form and perhaps the appearance of "Gallic War" in its title make natural the exclusion of much contemporary material (politics back at Rome, Caesar's nonmilitary activities in Gaul). This allows him to omit much that would potentially have been controversial, and to focus on circumstances in which he is opposed by armed foreigners, maximizing sympathy for himself.

Another phenomenon is the possibility of feedback among several texts, absent a text/context distinction. For instance, the Latin literary letter took on a number of forms and self-definitions from the time of Cicero and Caesar to that of Pliny. Starting from Fronto, however, the genre began to see its origin and model in the collection of Cicero's letters.[24] For some of these later letter-writers, the Ciceronian model must have been immediately useful, but, as far as we can tell, it ceased to become a choice. Even writers who were anti-Ciceronian in one sense or another had to deal with the "fact" that they were now writing in a Ciceronian genre. This fact was created by the accumulation of individual, increasingly constrained choices until non-Ciceronian readings were driven from the field. Moreover, Seneca's and Pliny's letters were retroactively read into this tradition. The meaning of these texts was shifted by the creation of subsequent intertexts. Conversely, I argue below (Chaps. 6 and 7) that *De Bello Gallico* and other generals' narratives gained authority by their mutual reinforcement.

Interdiscursivity is also important to *De Bello Gallico* because it creates covert argumentation. The narrator of *De Bello Gallico* does not make arguments. He rarely even offers explicit judgments of the sort, "This was treachery," or "Caesar's decision proved to be wise." Outside of a few speeches by characters, the text is narrative and (to a lesser extent) descriptive. It is punctuated only by rare and quite general *sententiae* ("sound bites").[25] But by their location in a field of positions created by other texts, descriptions and narratives can become argumentative.

Let me give non-Caesarian examples of both cases. Roman literature is very familiar with the embedded narrative form of the exemplum. For instance, Cicero asserts that suicide is normally a moral error, but can be correct or even an obligation for persons who have led a particularly rigorous life (*Off.* 1.112):

> Since nature had given Cato an incredible gravity and he himself had fortified it with perpetual self-consistency and had always held to whatever course of action he had taken up, he had to die rather than look on the face of a tyrant.

Cicero here assumes that suicide is contrary to human nature and therefore wrong. But Cato, he claims, is an exceptional case because of his long history of self-consistency; he may and even must violate the normal rules with respect to suicide. Does his past life really explain this exception? Surely the serial killer is not ipso facto licensed to murder. Cicero has no philosophical argument how past life could create exceptions to more general rules. Rather, the conventions of exemplary discourse provide the justification. Cato did it, so it must be right. Sometimes, there is not only no argument, but also no explicit moral, as when Cato is also cited for rigor in making sure that his son was properly and personally enrolled in the army before joining combat with an enemy (*Off.* 1.37). The Roman reader of exempla knows not only that Cato's actions are normative, but that their salient aspect will have to do with moral punctiliousness.

The same is true of descriptions. So, for instance, Cicero frequently explains his enemy Piso's political success by reference to his eyebrows.[26] Sometimes he explains that Piso's brow gave him a grave and serious appearance; sometimes he does not. General knowledge of Roman physiognomic discourse is what allows the omission; most of the audience could fill in the blanks.[27] Similarly, when Cicero remarks that Catiline's followers wore "sails rather than togas," he has no need to fill out the syllogism: therefore they were effeminate, therefore they were politically and socially untrustworthy.[28]

I have chosen the above examples of "covert" argumentation from overtly argumentative contexts: philosophy and oratory. We know from the broader context that these descriptions and narratives should have an argumentative point. To recover what that point is, we need to refer to other texts. (The texts we have today are, of course, just a small fraction of the oral and written discourses available to the original audience, but the mechanism is the same.) Hence we can be sure that such interdiscursivity was one means for Roman authors to generate argument. But nothing prevents the same mechanisms from working in less overtly argumentative texts.

Given that such arguments only come into being via the contact of at least two texts (or discourses), it is probably easiest to think of intertextuality in general as an element of the reading process, as part of interpretation. There are, however, two caveats that should be offered. First, the author (here Caesar) is himself a reader. Presumably, one part of deciding what is to be written is weighing, at various levels of consciousness, how it might play against various intertexts. Second, as I suggested above, knowing the language means sharing intertexts with the author to a significant extent. And to the extent that a reader is closer culturally to the author (as Roman aristocrats would have been to Caesar), they will share more. Still, perfect unanimity of readings is unlikely. It hardly needs pointing out that no two readers will have precisely the same previous experience. On the other hand, actual intention may cause potentially salient intertexts to escape an author's notice.

Caesar's famed *celeritas* may provide a quick example. I argue in Chapter 1 that Caesar tends to depict Gaul as a series of unconnected spatial "islands," and that this has certain consequences in the context of the more general Roman spatial imagination. One textual feature that emphasizes this depiction is the lack of detail in narrating Caesar's journeys from one point to another. This feature of the text is perfectly well motivated as an advertisement of Caesar's swiftness and decisiveness, and one could easily imagine that it was so written for precisely that reason.[29] Yet it also plays into the scheme of division, which is otherwise visible in the text. For at least some readers, then, that lack of detail is likely to emphasize that spatial scheme even if such emphasis played no part in the author's intention.

On the whole, I am inclined to suspect that most of the effects I argue for in *De Bello Gallico* were part of Caesar's intention (whether that amounts to elaborate planning or just an intuition of what "sounded right"), but I will not generally be arguing in those terms. In part, this is because I do not find "intention" a useful explanatory term.[30] Even if it were, however, *my* intentions in this book are ultimately historical. I am concerned with the likely or possible effects of *De Bello Gallico* rather than its meaning in some potentially pure sense. Thus a reader-oriented focus, though not required on general theoretical grounds, is appropriate here.

The Composition of De Bello Gallico

Many basic questions about the composition of *De Bello Gallico* have remained open despite extended scholarly discussion. As for the time of composition of *De Bello Gallico*, one camp has maintained that it was composed and circulated book by book, that is, year by year, presumably having been written in the midst of Caesar's other administrative duties in the winter after each campaigning season.[31] The other camp holds that it was written all at once (though probably incorporating earlier material, such as dispatches to the Senate).[32] Various specific times have been suggested, but a date between very late 52 and sometime in 50 is generally accepted. Though a few core arguments have been advanced on either side, interpretation of the evidence continues to be problematic.

Purported anachronisms and self-contradictions have been used to demonstrate unitary and serial composition, respectively. A small number of clear examples might be decisive, but surprisingly few candidates have been proposed in either direction, and none is obviously dispositive. On the one hand, for instance, Caesar refers to the near-total destruction of the Nervii in 57 (2.28.1: *prope ad internecionem*), but three years later he had to confront a force of (allegedly) 60,000 men led by the Nervii in their own territory (5.49.1; cf. 5.39.3, 7.75.3). There is certainly a prima facie contradiction, but, even if we ignore the question of how many actual Nervii were in the force they led, we cannot be sure that the earlier claim was not meant as hyperbole for political or literary reasons.[33] On the other hand, some have pointed to 1.28.5, "[The Boii] to whom [the Aedui] give lands and whom they afterward accepted into the same state legal equality and freedom as themselves." The "afterward," it is alleged, refers to a time outside 58, and therefore suggests composition after the fact. Some have questioned the authenticity of the "and whom ... " clause (see below on interpolation), but, perhaps more important, the temporal reference of that clause is still unclear. The Boii are still dependents of the Aedui early in the last book of *De Bello Gallico* (7.10.1), and it is only plausible that they are liberated at some point later in 52; the later references are not explicit (7.17.2, 7.75.4). Anachronism in the first book is certainly a possibility, but it could also be that the legal equality of the Boii came early, yet did not give them practical political equality.

Most readers of *De Bello Gallico* sense stylistic and substantive development over the course of the work. Most objectively, the quantity and importance of direct discourse grow over the second half. Additionally, Görler has argued that the narration becomes less character-focalized and more "Olympian." It is often claimed that what starts out as a *commentarius* ("commentary"?) becomes more like "true" history (see Chap. 5 below on questions of genre). Such stylistic development is taken to support serial composition.[34]

Those who argue for unitary composition have two responses. One is to quibble with the premise of development.[35] It is often possible to show that Caesar's changes in style are not entirely smooth or regular, but little has been done to shake the basic claim that many parameters vary in fairly predictable ways as the work goes on. Alternatively (and this strikes me as the more powerful argument), the developments can be seen as having literary aims. Thus, if von Albrecht (1997, 332–333) is right that the changes in direct discourse in *De Bello Gallico* are replayed over the course of Caesar's later Civil War commentary, it is hard to attribute either development individually to mere change over time. Mutschler has made the same argument for a number of other features.[36] Similarly, I argue below (Chap. 3) that some kinds of "progression" in Caesar's knowledge of the Gauls are thematically significant. Moreover, since the reader of a continuous text would learn and change by virtue of the reading, Caesar might well have made adjustments to the texture of his text accordingly.

Caesar's continuator, Aulus Hirtius, makes two remarks that are sometimes taken as evidence for the composition of *De Bello Gallico*. Unfortunately, neither is very explicit, and the inferences conventionally drawn from them are opposed. In the prefatory letter to Book 8, he remarks to Balbus (8.pr.6) that only they really know how great a writer Caesar was: "Others know how well and correctly he wrote; we also know how easily and swiftly he finished those books." This has suggested to some that all of Books 1–7 were composed together in a fairly short period of time in 51, but obviously Hirtius could just as well be referring to the composition of individual books in, say, just a few days per year each. Later he justifies the inclusion of two different years in one book (8.48.10): "I know that Caesar produced individual *commentarii* of individual years. I thought I ought not to do that because nothing important happened in the next year." Now, it is possible that the individual years (*singulorum annorum*) to which he refers here are actual years, and so Hirtius is alluding to serial composition. However, both the construction and the general sense of the passage require that he be talking about years primarily as units of composition—separate campaigning seasons. Not only is neither passage decisive, but it is far from clear that either bears on the question at all.

Finally, advocates of unitary composition point to the absence of testimonia to the existence of the *commentarii* before Cicero's *Brutus*, from the year 46. In particular, neither Cicero's speech *On the Consular Provinces* (in large part about the war) nor his letters to members of Caesar's staff make explicit reference to books of *De Bello Gallico* appearing during the war. The facts here seem not to be in question, but the interpretation is more problematic. We have substantial evidence of regular dispatches from Gaul to keep Caesar in the public eye.[37] Does it matter that we are not told explicitly that *commentarii* were involved?

To my mind, then, the question of the timing of composition of *De Bello Gallico* is one where we are left assessing comparative probability, not established fact. Moreover, we must keep in mind that at least some of the purported evidence (for instance, Hirtius' two statements) can only be shown to support a particular position if we presuppose that it is salient to the debate at all (unlikely in those cases). This kind of information should probably not be allowed at all in the weighing. Nonetheless, I am inclined to accept the theory of serial composition, simply because of the obvious value to Caesar in keeping the public aware of his deeds throughout the war. This historical consideration seems to me to tip the scales where the philological arguments are roughly equal and quite weak on both sides. This weakness is also the subject of one further observation. I argue in Chapter 5 that, for strategic and generic reasons, Caesar wants to give the impression (whether true or not) of writing as he goes, not just year by year, but almost line by line.[38] (More precisely, I will suggest that the choice of genre is in part a way of advancing those strategic aims.) If this is the case, then Caesar may be deliberately writing in a fashion that would (perhaps less deliberately) neutralize internal evidence for a distinction between serial and unitary composition.

Another of the much-debated traditional questions about the composition of *De Bello Gallico* has to do with interpolation.[39] All classical texts handed down in manuscript traditions are vulnerable to addition to some extent. "Corrections" can be made deliberately, or, perhaps more commonly, marginal and interlinear notes can be incorporated into the main text by an incautious scribe. In the case of *De Bello Gallico*, however, it has been suggested that long passages were deliberately composed and inserted in the text in (perhaps) late antiquity. There is considerable variation in just which passages are suspect, but what is essentially at issue is the authenticity of the various geographic/ethnographic excursuses throughout the work.[40]

In part, the question arose from a hyper-skepticism common to textual critics in general in the late nineteenth and early twentieth centuries and should perhaps simply be ignored today.[41] Moreover, even on its own terms, the interpolation theory was never fully worked out.[42] How and why were additional passages composed and inserted in the tradition? Take the "double" description of Gaul in 1.1 (to be treated at length in Chap. 1 below). The versions are similar enough that it is not clear why an interpolator would feel the need to insert material, but too far apart to suggest the intrusion of a marginal gloss. Contrast the case of interpolations in the legal texts that make up the *Digest* of Justinian. Mechanisms (including a known redaction) and a motivation (keeping law current) are clear; yet even so, scholars are much more cautious today in identifying interpolations in the *Digest* than they once were.[43] Nonetheless, the idea of interpolation in *De Bello Gallico* may not be quite dead yet, and I make considerable use of some of the allegedly interpolated passages (especially in Chaps. 2 and 3), so it may be worthwhile to say a few words about their authenticity.

There have been both stylistic and structural arguments for interpolation.[44] The geographic and ethnographic passages are unquestionably different from the rest of *De Bello Gallico* in, say, vocabulary, but these differences are simply those of content or genre, not of authorship.[45] Any author switching from narrating battles to describing giant, kneeless elk will show changes in style. The structural argument is that these passages break up the narrative. Not only are they "interruptions" in the general sense of being descriptions in the midst of a mainly narrative text, but, it is alleged, they would leave behind a seamless narrative if they were removed. For instance, in Book 5 we read a description of Britain and its inhabitants (5.12–14) just after being told that Cassivellaunus was put in charge of the entire war effort against the Romans (5.10.9). Immediately after the excursus, we are on the battlefield, getting a description of the disposition of the British forces (5.15.1). On the one hand, it is probably true that the excursus would not be missed if it were removed. On the other hand, it is well motivated at the opening, and not hard to follow at the close. Where there is a potential problem, as at the opening of the Gallic ethnography (6.11.1), the reader is warned about what is going on. If the "digressions" are arranged so as to minimize narrative disruptions, it is not clear why that should be attributed to interpolators rather than to Caesar himself. Recall, moreover, the write-as-you-go style I suggested that Caesar had adopted in *De Bello Gallico*. Given that choice, Caesar would have been forced either to incorporate visible narrative breaks to provide these descriptions or to forego them altogether.[46] The latter solution would not have been surprising, but the former is hardly so incredible that we should suspect tampering with the text instead.

The third compositional question, and a more recent one at least as a matter of overt debate, has to do with audience. Most scholars seem to have assumed an elite audience for *De Bello Gallico*, perhaps senators and *equites* for the most part.[47] Wiseman has recently challenged this view, suggesting a popular audience not only in addition to but instead of the elite one.[48] We would then have to imagine large-scale oral performances of *De Bello Gallico*. Although Wiseman has not proven his case, the question deserves consideration. The crucial, if general, passage purportedly illustrating popular interest in such works comes from Cicero (*Fin.* 5.52): "What about the fact that men of the lowest station, with no hope of a public career, even craftsmen take delight in history?" Wiseman reasonably argues that Cicero's off-hand tone shows that he expected the proposition to be uncontroversial, but problems remain.[49]

First, while Cicero may be sincere, we do not know whether he was expert in popular culture. Moreover, although Cicero's *historia* is less ambiguous than the "history" I have used to translate it, it is not entirely clear whether in this passage it refers to the literary genre or to any knowledge of the past.[50] This raises two questions. First, how did ordinary fans of history like their history delivered? Readings of literary historians? Plays? Art? Stories told round the campfire or hearth? All of these forms are substantially better attested than full-scale historical narrative, whether read to oneself or to a group.[51] Second, and more fundamentally, would the audience envisioned by Cicero, even if they did have a taste for Roman history, have found *De Bello Gallico* satisfying, given that for them it was a narrative on current affairs? In modern American terms, are Caesar's potential audience members Civil War buffs or CNN junkies (or something in between)? The (again limited) evidence appears to argue for the former.[52] This is not necessarily to deny political interests to the masses. Some significant (if not necessarily representative) fraction must have been keenly interested.[53] Rather, the point is that there is no evidence that popular taste in literature and popular interest in politics had any connection.

Wiseman also finds internal evidence for a popular audience, both in the respectful treatment of soldiers in the ranks (as opposed, in some cases, to aristocratic staff officers) and in the "talismanic" repetition of the phrase *populus Romanus*.[54] Yet, as Welch's careful study (1998) has shown, the officer class is on the whole treated reasonably well. As she puts it, "No legate, with the exception of the dead Sabinus, could complain about what Caesar says about him."[55] Even the soldiers could be questioned (2.8.1–2), or publicly reprimanded if necessary (7.52). If officers are slightly more often criticized, it may well be for internal reasons. As I argue in Chapters 3 and 4 below, Roman generals traditionally distanced themselves from the worth of their troops (mostly to deny responsibility for their failures). Caesar, however, presents a picture of battle in which the soldiers are dependent on their general for their prowess. Since one of Caesar's implicit claims to distinction lies (unusually) in the virtue of the ranks, he has good reason to praise them, whoever the audience may be.

The repetition of the phrase "Roman people" raises some interesting questions. It might be suggested that the crucial word here is "Roman" rather than "people," and that Caesar is merely aligning himself with national as opposed to personal interests (cf. Chap. 5 on how many of his narrative choices are directed at a similar effect). It would probably be incautious to throw out the other word entirely, but we might inquire further as to the meaning of the phrase as a whole. If the whole nation comprises the "Senate and People of Rome," then the people are in principle everyone but the Senate, that is, a group that extends across all meaningful class (if not juridical) boundaries in Roman society. So, for instance, even on the most conservative estimates of literacy, the vast majority of the reading population of Italy would have been part of the "Roman people" in this sense.[56] This group (literate nonsenators) could easily have had more political clout than the urban proletariat audience Wiseman imagines. They would have been better spread out throughout the voting units of the Roman assemblies. They would also have been largely well-to-do, and thus in a better position than most to go to Rome to vote. Moreover, this group may well have been not just *part* of the Roman *populus*, but the whole of what many members of the elite meant by that group. Mouritsen points out that the term could be used of any number of official and semi-official gatherings of potentially highly unrepresentative fractions of the populace. We might reasonably accept Hall's view of a substantially "middle-brow" "middle Ital[ian]" audience if we keep in mind that, due to extreme inequalities in social condition, a group in the "middle" in terms of juridical strata (senators, knights, … slaves) was part of a cluster of very small absolute numbers at the top of the pyramid.[57] It is possible that Caesar had in mind a universal, or even a strictly non-elite, audience, but the evidence is not compelling. For the time being, it seems best to retain the assumption that Caesar is aiming at the top of Roman society, though perhaps at a slightly larger segment of that top than is sometimes implied.[58]

In addition to their social location, we should also consider the level of sympathy of Caesar's target audience. This can only be inferred from internal evidence, and in particular by working back and forth between interpretation and potential audience. Thus I will be developing my answers in the course of the book. However, it may be helpful if I briefly sketch some positions here.

Let me distinguish two parameters: strong commitment for or against Caesar vs. more malleable attitudes, and sympathy for Caesar vs. that for the general project of a Gallic War. Regarding the first distinction, Hall is surely right to point out that there is nothing Caesar could have written that would have won over a committed enemy like Cato.[59] We might add that there would be just as little reason to target firm allies. I argue in Chapter 7 that Caesar has in mind a public that is not automatically committed to him, but would like to be given a reason to believe he was acting well and correctly. As for the second point, Chapter 5 below will show that Caesar was taking steps to emphasize the Gallic War (even beyond his own actions) over his personal career (beyond this war). This suggests (probably not surprisingly) a larger audience that wants to root for the Romans against the Gauls than for Caesar against his political rivals. This is not, of course, to suggest that Caesar is not trying to sell himself, only that patriotism is a crucial part of his strategy for doing so.

Reality and Representation

In the first words of this chapter I appealed to the notion of the *De Bello Gallico* as a historical event. Some readers will, quite reasonably, be reminded of the distinction commonly drawn today between the study of real events and the study of representations. Even if we take that distinction at face value, it is hard to apply here. On the one hand, this is a study of reality, as the production and circulation of objects—including representations—are real events. On the other, much of that history will be inferred from the character of this and other representations. Given that complication, it may be worthwhile to take a closer look at the original distinction through examination of a case whose themes will recur in the chapters below.

Diodorus reports that the Celts were very fond of wine. They drank it unmixed and in excessive quantities (5.26.3). The Greeks and Romans generally drank their wine mixed with water, so to drink it straight could be seen as just another, more indirect way of expressing barbarian excess above and beyond explicit reference to sheer quantity. Posidonius (preserved in Athenaeus) similarly claims that Celts normally drink their wine unmixed (4.152c). Both authors also stress that the wine had to be imported from Italy, or at least from Marseilles.[60] One might expect under these circumstances that wine would be relatively more expensive in Gaul than in Greece or Italy, and this is precisely what Diodorus claims. Delighted Italian wine merchants, he says, can trade a slave for a single *keramion* of wine. Nor is distance necessarily the only factor in pricing. While it is probably meaningless to try to establish a "normal" ratio of wine to water in the Greco-Roman world, recorded figures tend to fall between 1:3 and 1:1.[61] Drinking unmixed wine in full quantities would be proportionately more expensive. The combination could make wine a vastly more expensive beverage for the Gauls, and this in turn might give it the status of a luxury item, not the ordinary drink it was along the Mediterranean. In fact, Posidonius says it was served in the houses of the rich, while the poor drank wheat-beer. He also describes "gifts" of wine (along with gold and silver), apparently a means by which the elite secured the allegiance of followers (Ath. 4.154c). On these grounds, Celticists have seen wine as a "prestige good," that is, one of a set of items that "[do] not move so much along commercial lines, but along those determined by social and political relations," and especially serve as "status indicators among the elite."[62]

Wine plays a somewhat different role in Caesar's ethnography. The Suebi reject its importation entirely. So do the Nervii, fierce among the Belgae, already the nearest of the Gauls to the Germans (BG 2.15.4, 1.1.3). In both cases this is part of a broader rejection of commerce (4.2.1, 2.15.4), and in both cases the reasoning is similar:

> [The Nervii] allowed no wine or other luxury goods to be brought into their territory, because they judged that by these things their spirits were relaxed and their virtue (*virtutem*) lessened; they, on the other hand, were fierce folk of great virtue (*virtutis*). (2.15.4)

> [The Suebi] do not permit wine to be imported to themselves at all, because they think that by this thing people grow soft and effeminate in putting up with labor. (4.2.6)

Drinking unmixed wine is merely barbaric; it means you are doing civilization wrong. To reject wine entirely is to reject human civilization altogether. Prohibiting wine is thus emblematic of the supposed "nomad" attempt to maintain primitive (manly) virtue intact by avoiding all civilization.

That Caesar is cribbing from himself in writing these passages, that he is talking about an item (wine) with such clear symbolic value in the ancient world, and that he is doing so in a way that lends support to his much broader argument might suggest that we read these little stories about wine as purely literary devices. Similar arguments might suggest that the accounts of wine-drinking in Diodorus and Posidonius as well are simply a (different) ethnographic trope. This is certainly possible, but let me suggest that there is at least one other plausible interpretation. The details of unmixed wine, transport difficulties, and elite consumption in Diodorus and Posidonius co-here very neatly, without either account clearly being derived from the other. Furthermore, the latter two points do not seem to have nearly the motivation in terms of broad ethnographic thematics as the first. Finally, we should keep in mind that at least Posidonius had direct experience of some of these Celtic peoples. Perhaps the story we can reconstruct from the Greek accounts is essentially true. It may then either have been completely unaffected by the tradition, or perhaps it was particularly interesting to Posidonius (and others) because of its partial implication of categories that were of standing importance to Greek culture.

What, then, of Caesar's account? Let us imagine that it, too, contains at least a kernel of truth, and that at least some of these tribes, perhaps the more remote ones (where wine was the most expensive?), actually prohibited or restricted the importation of wine. Understood, with Caesar, as the rejection of the "virtues" of civilization, this account is rightly suspect; let us instead begin with the Posidonian/Diodoran understanding of wine. If it was in fact an expensive luxury good, and perhaps one particularly symbolic for being imported, then such prohibition or restriction makes sense as a sumptuary law, a type common in Roman and other societies.[63] Consider what we know of the contemporary Celtic political context. It is widely (though not universally) held that the century or so before the Roman conquest saw a move in Gaul from political organization based largely on "tribes" or "chiefdoms" to more state-like arrangements.[64] Among the purported causes of this shift is increased trade with the Mediterranean area (including wine). These transformations would have

> opened a new channel of access to obtaining the means necessary to operate in one of the important traditional arenas for status competition: that is, the "commensal politics" of feasting.... An escalation of competition played out in feasting activities was likely to have occurred between those with privileged access to the traditional forms of drink ... and those with newly advantageous access to the exotic form.[65]

Sumptuary legislation, whether or not literally effective, delegitimizes the "luxuries" at which it is directed by appeal to morality and/or tradition.[66] This, in the present context, would be a sensible strategy for the old Celtic aristocracy in the face of opponents who were attempting to establish novel authoritative symbols. Such a conservative strategy seems particularly plausible among the Suebi and Nervii, who seem, archeologically, far from Roman influence.[67]

One can then imagine Caesar grasping the truth (if that is what it is), but rejecting it so as to make the bare facts serve his immediate purposes better. Or, perhaps just as likely, it might genuinely never have occurred to Caesar that impoverished "barbarians" such as these would have felt any need for sumptuary laws as he knew them. Especially if he knew nothing but the bare fact of the regulations, the explanation he offers in *De Bello Gallico* may well have been the one he felt was most reasonable.

My interpretation of the Greek tradition is, of course, speculative; my reading of Caesar, doubly so. I would not claim that I was myself totally persuaded by either. Nonetheless, I think the attempt makes two important methodological points. First, recent years have seen an increased awareness of the rhetoric of ancient historians.[68] On the whole, this must be taken as a positive development, but it has had some unfortunate side effects. In particular, it is now easy to find claims that a particular passage, because it invokes an identifiable topos, has no evidentiary value, except perhaps for the attitude of the author (particularly the case for invective or for "tyrannical" stereotypes directed at "bad emperors").[69] The present example suggests that, even when discourse is shaped by common topoi, those topoi may signify something other than their own presence. Second, in Chapter 1 I consider the claim that Caesar's account of Gaul was distinctive because of autopsy; he had been there, so his information was allegedly better than earlier, quasi-mythical stories. That claim can be rejected, at least as a complete explanation, on several grounds. Here we see another case where the other sources may well be closer to the truth (perhaps, admittedly, with the aid of autopsy themselves). We may even have a case where Caesar has had direct experience but has still refused (or been unable) to arrive at an interpretation that has a claim to being the better one.

It has been fashionable in the last couple of decades to speak of the "textuality of history," that is, the fact that our access to history is always textually mediated.[70] Brunt has responded to essentially this challenge by arguing that the problem is not a new one, and furthermore, that we negotiate it successfully every day:

> There is no distinction in principle between the propositions that Caesar was killed by Brutus and Cassius and that Smith has just been injured by a golf ball.... In ascertaining what we need to know (in the loose sense of that term applicable in daily life), we draw not only on our own perceptions

but on those of others. We accept what they tell us, provided that experience has not seemed to show that they are generally mendacious, at
any rate in the kind of report that is our immediate concern, or faulty in
their recollections, or incapable of giving accurate accounts of their own
perceptions.[71]

It is tempting simply to say that Brunt is right. It *is* an old problem, and the
method he suggests has long been (and must be?) the response.[72] Yet, the
question of the wine shows how many things could go wrong in a fairly ordinary exchange of understanding (whether or not they have actually gone
wrong in this particular case), especially if we are translating across many
centuries and between multiple cultures. Even though the processes of day-
to-day and historical reconstruction are not different in principle, there are
huge differences in practice; in matters near to us we have vastly more background information about the habits of our informants (and *their* informants
and *their* informants ...), as well as the opportunity to cross-check information in various ways.

The situation is actually worse than this. The hypothesis that I have
advanced so far claims that in some sense the Greek version is better than
Caesar's. Suppose that Caesar is "right" as well. Sumptuary legislation often lends itself to the kind of moralizing, macho language in which Caesar
casts the barbarians' refusal of wine. Perhaps he has represented their original
claims accurately in this respect. It might be objected that he still erred out
of naivete, that he (and conceivably the Nervii and Suebi themselves) did not
"really" understand what was going on. We have then (at least) two incompatible representations—one "sociological," one "moralizing"—neither of
which is clearly false.[73] The distinction between the two is not so much one of
truth value, but of appropriateness to different circumstances. Actually, Brunt
almost admits that this is the historian's usual dilemma, though he cannot
quite bring himself to do so. Note his phrases "what we need to know" and
"the kind of report that is our immediate concern." These are not epistemo-
logical categories, but pragmatic ones; the criterion here is utility, not truth.
I adopt here a viewpoint that (like skepticism) questions whether language
(and thought more generally) can even in principle be said to "represent" reality, but that nonetheless (unlike skepticism) does not object to the existence of
a real world that could have some kind of *causal* relationship to language (and
thought). As a result, the utility of narratives is constrained (though never absolutely) by factors other than coherence with other narratives. Thus Brunt's
dismissal of "Pyrrhonists" on pragmatic grounds is valid, but not salient

to the point he claims to be making. The position that his arguments seem to me actually to support (and that I myself favor) is more like Rorty's neopragmatism or Lakoff's "experiential realism."[74] This leaves little left of the distinction between the history "of representations" and the history of anything else.

The point here is not, of course, to condemn any particular traditional historical practice (and certainly not to do so categorically); historians are good at telling stories that meet their shared needs, and there is no generalized reason to stop doing so now. In fact, historians have also been fairly good about allowing new types of story when new needs demand them—the rise of family history is an example.[75] Rather, the point is to keep in mind that just as we ourselves work on shifting sands, so do our sources.[76] But in the latter case, we rarely see the motion itself, only traces of its results. Hence, a more or less deductive mode of historiography cannot be uniquely valuable.[77] Room should be made for other modes in addition, such as model-building or quasi-fictionalization.[78] Responsible theorizing, then, calls for more histories, not fewer.

1. Where Was the Gallic War?

In 56 B.C., the orator Cicero gave a speech, *On the Consular Provinces*, that, among other things, favorably contrasted Caesar's conduct of the Gallic War with the work of other provincial governors.[1] In the speech, Cicero took a strong position on how to resolve the proximity of hostile Gauls on Rome's northern frontier. His solution to the problem was not to establish a buffer zone, nor even to annihilate the Gauls, but to absorb them. He assumed that if the Gauls were reduced to a position of legal subordination (*in nostram dicionem*, 32), the problem would be solved. As it happened, he was largely right. But given the history with the Gauls he had just described and the long-term difficulties in the subjugation of, say, Spain, his assessment was optimistic at the time. This was, however, not just the exaggeration of a politician trying to sell a controversial policy. Cicero's strategic thinking here reflects a deep-rooted aspect of the Roman ideology of empire, which we can see more clearly earlier in the speech—a model of an empire with a peaceful interior rigidly distinguished from a dangerous exterior. It also reflects a tendency to individualize political questions.

Near the beginning of the speech, Cicero makes the case for removing other governors from their provinces. He offers to pass over Piso's alleged misdeeds while consul in Rome, though they "have done more harm than Hannibal ever hoped." Instead he will speak only on the immediate issue—the results of Piso's failure as governor of Macedonia. This he does at some length:

> Macedonia, which had previously been fortified not by generals' towers, but by their victory monuments, which had long ago been pacified by a series of victories, is so hard pressed by barbarians (whose opportunity for peace has been snatched away by [Piso's] greed) that the Thessalonians, though seated in the very lap of our empire, have abandoned their city and are forced to fortify a citadel, and that that military road of ours

which passes through Macedonia is not only filled even to the Hellespont by barbarian raiders, but is dotted with Thracian military camps. (*Prov. cons.* 4)

Here both success and failure are personalized. Hannibal wanted one thing, but Piso and Gabinius have done another. What has been overturned is not a policy so much as the work of many individual "generals." Why has this come about? Because of individual "greed."

It is important to note that this motivation is advanced at the beginning. In succeeding sections, Cicero criticizes a number of exactions that Piso demanded of his subjects. In principle, this might be seen as an argument about policy, but given the opening of the attack, they are better read as examples of greed. Similarly, Piso's corrupt administration of justice is eventually seen to be aimed at profit (§7). Finally, we should recall what Cicero claimed was Piso's greatest shame: that "very noble virgins cast themselves into pits and escaped inescapable violation only by suicide" (§6). What Cicero puts at stake are not Piso's skills or his policy, but his duty and moral character.

And what is the result? Of what, exactly, is Piso guilty? He has allowed the simple inside/outside scheme of empire to become confused. The enemy is in the very "lap" of the empire, traveling along Roman roads. Where once there was peace, even relatively loyal subjects are now forced to fortify their cities. What should be a tranquil part of the empire is once again a war zone. But that possibility cannot, as we shall see even more clearly below, be treated as an ordinary political development. It is important that dangers to the state lie only on the outside. Hence the need to describe the governor in terms that are resolutely moral (not political) and pathological.[2]

A system that insists so strongly on a particular worldview is liable eventually to the appearance of self-contradiction, or at least arbitrariness. This occurs later in *On the Consular Provinces*, and the problem can be phrased in terms of the same basic inside/outside scheme. Immediately before the direct discussion of the Gallic wars, Cicero offers Pompey as an example of a proper commander (§31). He refers to Pompey's campaigns against the pirates in 67 and his land campaigns in the east from 66 to 62. The result of the latter is particularly relevant here. Cicero says that under Pompey's command:

Those nations which, by the very number and multitude of their population, could have poured over into our provinces were cut back or crushed to the point that Asia, which previously marked the end of our empire, is now itself girded by three new provinces. (*Prov. cons.* 31)

That is, Pompey had faced some of the same problems that were still present in Gaul.[3] The enemy were numerous and therefore dangerous. They (i.e., Mithradates) were perched just outside the borders of the Roman province of Asia, waiting to spill in. Pompey's solution is the one Cicero claims Caesar will achieve in Gaul. He reduced the troublesome peoples to subject status, bringing them within the empire. But when the matter is put in such bare terms, one is tempted to ask what has really been accomplished. Pompey has not eliminated the border of the empire, he has merely moved it east. The problem has been displaced rather than solved. The process could continue indefinitely until and unless it reaches the end Cicero actually suggests two sections later: that the borders of the empire and of the world should be the same. That is, if it is a given that all danger lies outside, it is easy to fall into thinking that anything outside is ipso facto a danger. On the other hand, world conquest guarantees peace and security.

This reasoning can be seen more clearly in Cicero's discussion of Caesar's campaigns. We will soon see (chapter 2) a list of adjectives Cicero uses to describe the Gauls and explain why they present a danger (§33), words like "hostile," "unfriendly," and "barbarian." These are all more or less self-explanatory. What is striking is the inclusion in the middle of the list of the word "unknown." The preceding *and* succeeding terms all give reasons to fear the Gauls, so we have every expectation that this one is meant to do the same. The implication is that Gallic tribes that live outside of Rome's sphere of influence are inherently suspect. Two sentences earlier, Cicero had praised Caesar for mastering the Germans and Helvetii, and then for the conquest of regions and peoples "which no letter, no voice, no rumor had before made known to us." Here we can see in action the procedure that Pompey's conquests only suggested. The defeat of one set of enemies gives rise to war with new ones that Rome had not previously realized she had. Nor does Cicero stop to claim that a second and novel threat had arisen (though presumably most of the ethnic arguments he makes are as valid here as anywhere). The new, unknown tribes seem to be a danger mainly by virtue of being next in line. Again we see the slippage from "all dangers are outside" to "all outside is dangerous." Thus not only is absorption guaranteed to be a sufficient solution to the Gallic problem (inside is safe), it is the necessary one (outside is dangerous).

Lakoff has shown that much of cognition is structured by a set of simple physical schemes (e.g., container, path) and composites of those.[4] It is hardly surprising, then, that space itself can be so represented and understood. In Cicero's speech, we see the use of the container schema as a rough and ready way of understanding the empire for certain purposes. But such a scheme is obviously too simple for many purposes. Perhaps less obviously, the empire is so large that one's experience of it could often be reducible to "in" or "out." At other scales, there are more forms of representation and individually more complex ones. In the rest of this chapter, I examine how this works in *De Bello Gallico*. To that end, I need to introduce some terminology from Rambaud's essay, "Space in Caesarian Narrative."[5] Rambaud shows that Caesar tends to organize space in three different ways—"geographic," "strategic," and "tactical"—each characteristic of a different scale. The largest-scale representations make up "geographic space."[6] This is "the ideal place of a synthetic vision of the most vast regions. Most often, its descriptions are presented as digressions." From a modern point of view, they would be quite unhelpful for almost any practical purpose—partly because of some geographical errors, but primarily because of their marked vagueness. At the intermediate level of representation, we find "strategic space." "[Caesar] conceived of strategic space directly before himself, essentially along a line of sight, in the sense of a movement which carries the army from one point to another....One sees ... that the space is not felt as a continuous surface but as a network of lines." When we move from the scale represented by "strategic space" to a smaller one, we encounter "tactical space." In direct contrast to strategic space, "this vision of space, embracing a much wider field, is more precise, making us no longer see a simple line, but a surface, and that even in relief."[7] Rambaud's essay raises a number of questions, both theoretical and empirical, about cognition and representation of space, which I hope to treat in another context. For present purposes, however, his framework is more than adequate as a descriptive typology, and I use his terminology throughout.

Types of Space

All the cases discussed to this point involve characteristics—dimensionality, divisibility, mutual compatibility—in which modern Western modes of representation are more advanced than Roman. By this I mean that so far, one can easily describe Roman spatial models in modern terms, but not the other way around. One can, for instance, draw cartographic plane representations of what "between" or "near" mean in a linear context. By contrast, the Romans simply did not have the means to express a modern, mathematicized view of space. There is one respect in which Caesar's spatial imagination is perhaps more advanced than modern cartographic representation, however. Though he does not make the same quantitative distinctions we have available, he makes qualitative ones that are rare today.[8]

An example from the representation of time may help explain the quantitative/qualitative distinction I am trying to draw here. We can divide time into many different units: seconds, minutes, hours, days, weeks, years, as well as multiples and subdivisions of these. When spans of time are divided into so many minutes or years, a purely quantitative distinction is (generally) being made.[9] One year is the same as the next, or even as one much later; two years differ from one year by being twice as long. The numerical comparisons can be made because the individual units are identical for most purposes. There are, however, a few cultural contexts in which units of time take on a qualitative aspect. Within the cyclical pattern of the week, different days take on different values. "I have to go to work tomorrow [i.e., Tuesday]" has quite a different force than "I have to go to work tomorrow [i.e., Sunday]." This is because weekends are seen as a different kind of time than weekdays. Different activities are appropriate at different times. Similarly, *De Bello Gallico* assumes the existence of different kinds of space.

The most obvious kinds of space are precisely Rambaud's tactical, strategic, and geographic spaces. These are not simply different in scale. They are, rather, incommensurable; representations at one of the smaller scales cannot be added together to form one at a larger scale. First, there are gaps in the hierarchy of scales. As I noted early on, even the subunits of geographic representation tend to be larger than what is mapped by any single strategic representation. Similarly, the elements of strategic space seem to be larger than whole tactical spaces. Second, even at a single level, representations are given sometimes an absolute orientation, sometimes a relative one, and most often none at all. There is no universal standard and hence no principle of combination. Third, there are the basic differences of type. Even in principle, how could one-dimensional spaces be composed into a two-dimensional one or (even more difficult) vice versa? Finally, there are differences in use. People fight in tactical space, move through strategic space, and inhabit geographic space. In practice, Caesar does not describe enough areas to compose several representations into a single one of higher order. If I am right about the qualitative distinctions between levels, then the very idea of such composition is incoherent.

There are also types of space that are not tied to scale. The most different from "normal" space are the marsh (*palus*) and the forest (*silva*). In a few cases, "marsh" seems to mean a marshy area small enough to be seen across. Generally, though, marshes and forests seem to be functionally equivalent, suggesting that the former is usually a large area of marshland. The formula "marshes and forests" appears (with minor variations) nine times in *De Bello*

Gallico.[10] Both marshes and forests are commonly cited as places of refuge for Gauls, especially when mentioned together. (See also the next chapter on connections between lands and people.) Other combinations show, not surprisingly, that marshes but not forests are also thought of as water features. Nonetheless, for purposes of the arguments below, the two types appear to be essentially equivalent.

Sometimes access to marshes and forests is described as merely difficult for the Romans (2.28.2), but more often it seems to be entirely impossible (2.16.5), even if Gauls have entered the same place.[11] In fact, the Romans can hardly even see into these areas. This is shown in practice by the frequent surprise attacks launched against the Romans from forest and marsh.[12] The problem of visibility also affects Caesar's language. When Gauls and Germans enter such an area, they are commonly said to "hide" (*abdere, occultare*) themselves.[13] In practice, the asymmetry between Romans and Gauls would have been due to the difficulty of marching massed formations over irregular terrain (a difficulty Caesar himself points out once).[14] Yet in Caesar's version, the Gauls can draw up battle formations (*aciem ordinesque*) in forests (2.19.6), and the British can find "roads and paths" in them (5.19.2). Neither marshes nor forests slow the Germans, "born to banditry" (6.25.7). Practically speaking, both sides would have been somewhat impeded, the Romans merely to a greater degree. In *De Bello Gallico*, Caesar converts this difference of degree to a difference of kind.

Another type of space is represented by the Latin noun *angustiae*, "defile." Like a "forest" or "marsh," a "defile" could in principle have been treated as just another slight variation on "normal" space that might happen to be more easily navigated by one side than the other. Again, Roman dependence on close-order formations would have made them less able to fight from or into such a feature. Yet, again like forests and marshes, that is not how Caesar in fact treats defiles. They are space through which Romans can move, but in which the Romans are always in danger. So, for instance, the troops who threatened mutiny at Vesontio were worried that Caesar wanted them to attempt a march through forest and *angustiae* (1.39.6). Caesar responded by picking a much longer path (fifty miles) through "open spaces" (1.41.4). Rambaud has pointed out in another context that "the use of the word *angustiae* is nearly always reserved to the situation of the enemy."[15] That one exception is, significantly, at the tactical level (see below). There is no mention of Romans even attempting to catch their enemies in such a place at any scale. And even when the word itself is not used of a narrow place, the same rules apply: one party is always in an advantageous position, and it is never the Romans.[16] Again, this represents the literary exaggeration and essentialization of what in practice would have been a more subtle effect. Romans never march safely through *angustiae*. It seems unlikely that this could be literally true; would they not be most likely to pass through defiles precisely when it was known that the enemy was not present? Rather, *angustiae* are not simply narrow spaces; they become, in *De Bello Gallico*'s definition, *dangerous* narrow spaces.

A third type of space represented in *De Bello Gallico* is the "mountain." To see this we need to make a distinction between what Caesar calls mere "hills" (*colles*) and what he labels "mountains" (*montes*). One might hesitate to do so, given that Caesar seems occasionally to call the same formation by both names.[17] Rambaud, however, has shown that in most of these cases, the "hills" are lower parts of a large, complex relief feature, whose totality or highest part is called a "mountain."[18] We can add further evidence that Caesar understood a significant distinction between the two. Mountains, but not hills, are marked for their sheer height (usually with the superlative *altissimus*).[19] Hills, but not mountains, are described in terms of their (modest) slope.[20] Finally, mountains, but not hills, can be regarded as places of refuge for non-Romans, rather like forests and marshes.[21] These considerations confirm the intuition that a "mountain" is a much more formidable thing than a "hill." Mountains have a different structural role than forests and marshes. Instead of being geographically indistinct, they commonly serve as boundaries between two other areas.[22]

Rambaud argues that the conventional treatment of forests and *angustiae* shows an ambivalence between strategic and tactical space. Such obstacles, he thinks, could not have been imagined in linear, strategic space. Passages in which they appear to do so show at least traces of interest in a second dimension, the open width of the path perpendicular to the direction of travel.[23] This, I would suggest, is not precisely what is going on. First of all, forests appear within clearly tactical descriptions and remain just as indefinite in form and extent there as they are at the strategic level; they do not show clear dimensionality at any level. No specifics of the various *angustiae* are given at the strategic level.[24] Defiles lose their dimensionality at the larger scale, if they ever had it. Nor is there ever a hint that any marsh, forest, or defile has a limited capacity.[25] They have no size or shape and thus no dimensionality. Caesar the general presumably had some sense of the two-dimensional topography of these areas, but Caesar the writer has taken a different approach. He has abstracted the average effects of various types of terrain, even exaggerated them, and, most important, essentialized them. Thus, while the facts of two-dimensional space give the ultimate explanation of Caesar's attitude toward special types of terrain, his descriptions of them are not themselves two-dimensional.

Geographic Space in De Bello Gallico

The description of Gaul that opens *De Bello Gallico* is the most famous and clearest example of geographical space in the work.

> Gallia est omnis divisa in partes tres, quarum unam incolunt Belgae, aliam Aquitani, tertiam qui ipsorum lingua Celtae, nostra Galli appellantur. (2) Hi omnes lingua, institutis, legibus inter se differunt. Gallos ab Aquitanis Garunna flumen, a Belgis Matrona et Sequana dividit. (3) Horum omnium fortissimi sunt Belgae, propterea quod a cultu atque humanitate provinciae longissime absunt minimeque ad eos mercatores saepe commeant atque ea, quae ad effeminandos animos pertinent, important proximique sunt Germanis, qui trans Rhenum incolunt, quibuscum continenter bellum gerunt. (4) Qua de causa Helvetii quoque reliquos Gallos virtute praecedunt, quod fere cotidianis proeliis cum Germanis contendunt, cum aut suis finibus eos prohibent aut ipsi in eorum finibus bellum gerunt. (5) Eorum una pars, quam Gallos obtinere dictum est, initium capit a flumine Rhodano, continetur Garunna flumine, Oceano, finibus Belgarum, attingit etiam ab Sequanis et Helvetiis flumen Rhenum, vergit ad septentriones. (6) Belgae ab extremis Galliae finibus oriuntur, pertinent ad inferiorem partem fluminis Rheni, spectant in septentrionem et orientem solem. (7) Aquitania a Garunna flumine ad Pyrenaeos montes et eam partem Oceani, quae est ad Hispaniam, pertinet, spectat inter occasum solis et septentriones. (*BG* 1.1)

(1) All Gaul is divided into three parts, one of which is inhabited by the Belgae, another by the Aquitani, the third by those who are called Celts in their own language, Gauls in ours. (2) All these peoples differ among each other in language, customs, and laws. The river Garumna divides the Gauls from the Aquitani; the Matrona and Sequana separate them from the Belgae. (3) The Belgae are the strongest of these all, since they are furthest from the culture and humanity of our province, and traders very rarely come to them and bring the things that serve to make the minds of men effeminate, and they are nearest to the Germans who live across the Rhine, and with whom they continually wage war. (4) And for

the same reason the Helvetii, too, surpass the other Gauls in *virtus*, because they struggle in battle with the Germans almost daily, when they either hold them off from their own territory or themselves bring the war to German lands. (5) Of these, one part, which they say the Gauls hold, begins from the river Rhone and is bounded by the Garumna, the [Atlantic] Ocean, and the territory of the Belgae, and across from the Sequani and Helvetii it touches the Rhine and turns north. (6) The Belgae begin from the end of the territory of Gaul and run to the lower part of the river Rhine; they look to the northeast. (7) Aquitania reaches from the Garumna to the Pyrenees and the part of the Ocean near Spain. It faces northwest.

The first thing to note is that this passage in fact comprises two complete descriptions.[26] The opening sentence lists the three parts of Gaul: those inhabited by Belgians, Aquitani, and Celts/Gauls. We are told that these groups vary in language and culture. The first description concludes by telling the reader that the three parts are separated by named rivers. Then there is a long digression on the war strength of the Belgae and its source in constant conflict with the Germans. The next sentence but one begins the second description, and its opening words show that the remarks on the Belgae are in fact a digression: "Of these (*eorum*), one part...." The bland pronoun *eorum* would normally pick up some element from the preceding sentence, but there is no plausible referent there. Instead, it must mean the collective Gallic tribes of the first few sentences, as is confirmed by the repetition of the word "part" from the first sentence and the back reference, "which they say the Gauls hold" (1.1.5).[27] In any case, the second description elaborates the description of the same three parts of Gaul; the borders of each are described in a variety of terms (discussed below).

What purpose might be served by this structure of double description plus digression? I suggested above that the position and large scale of this description imply a quasi-cosmographic use; it sets out the limits of the world in which the following narrative will take place. So, for instance, Rome is not on this "map," and the action does not return to Rome the way it might in a standard history. Germany is noted at the beginning of the work, but is swiftly pushed to the margins. The formal subordination of Germany in this structure suggests from the beginning a subordination of its political importance. Throughout *De Bello Gallico*, Caesar engages in a complex negotiation of the relative danger and importance of the Gauls and Germans; that negotiation was played out through changes in narrative (see Chap. 2 below).

Yet, of course, the conclusion cannot have been in doubt when Caesar wrote this passage. Whether that was in 58, 50, or in between, a conquest of Gaul could have been in sight, but conquest of Germany was not. Thus Gaul must ultimately take precedence over Germany.

Another function of this passage, and one noted by previous scholars, is to establish "Gaul" (or rather that part of Gaul in which Caesar was campaigning) as a single entity. This is accomplished first simply by naming. The opening word of the work, *Gallia*, denotes not a people (*Galli*), but a place. "All Gaul" (*Gallia ... omnis*) presupposes the unity of that whole at some level. Even if Caesar's first point is that Gaul is divided into parts, those parts are all components of the same thing. Furthermore, the unification of Gaul here at the opening of the book is particularly pointed given the vast range of individual tribes that will be encountered thereafter. The phrases "all Gaul" and "the whole of (*tota*) Gaul" are repeated throughout the course of the work to remind the reader of the original unity.[28] This unity is important to at least two of the implicit arguments of *De Bello Gallico*. Caesar hints that partial subjugation of the Gauls has led and will lead only to continuing warfare; Cicero says the same explicitly on Caesar's behalf (see Chap. 6). If, as a matter of supposedly objective geographical fact, the entire area north of the province and west of the Rhine is one place, then this strategic argument appears more natural. Gaul either is conquered (as a whole) or is not; partial suppression is no suppression at all. Furthermore, the unity of Gaul allows Caesar to finesse certain questions of responsibility. In his account, the Gauls often bring war upon themselves by violations of *fides*. To the extent that the separate identity of different tribes is submerged in a collective Gallic identity, then it is less important for him to be able to identify which tribes have breached faith in what ways. Collective guilt becomes possible, even if it is not explicitly invoked.

But if this passage takes an expansive view of Gaul in some respects, it takes a restrictive one in others.[29] "All Gaul is divided into three parts...." Upon reading this, what might the reader expect to be included in the rest of the sentence? Caesar's official position at the time of the wars was governor of the provinces of Cisalpine Gaul (northern Italy) and Transalpine Gaul (in southern France) as well as Illyricum. Cisalpine and Transalpine Gaul might well have been construed as two of the parts of greater Gaul, with the remainder of modern France, later the province of Gallia Comata ("long-haired Gaul"), making up the third. But, as Rambaud has pointed out, Transalpine Gaul is always referred to in *De Bello Gallico* simply as "the province."[30] It is also arguable that the whole opening description is focalized from that province, implicitly separating the (Roman) observer from the observed Gaul.

This view of what does and does not constitute Gaul benefits Caesar in at least two ways. It coheres well with the idea that Gaul must be dealt with as a whole; that is, it minimizes the lasting value of previous victories over Gallic tribes by making them, in a sense, not Gallic. It may also have something to do with Caesar's domestic political agenda. As dictator in 49, Caesar arranged for the enfranchisement of the former province of Cisalpine Gaul, and in 45 he granted "Latin" status, sort of a partial Roman citizenship, to many communities in Transalpine Gaul. This may even have been a longer-term interest.[31] It is not unreasonable to see some sort of connection here. This passage may constitute early propagandizing for the Romanization of southern Gaul (especially if it were written after the war), or it might simply reflect a preconception that Caesar held about these areas that generated both his style of description and his legislation.

This passage essentializes Gallic ethnic identity. The ethnographic tradition tended to lump all northern "barbarians" together as nomads; as we will see, Caesar departed sharply from this tradition to give himself a stable target, to allow him to distinguish Gauls (for whom he was responsible) from Germans (for whom he was not), and to describe a particular Gallic character that makes assimilation a potential danger. This geographic description, as noted briefly above, also played a role in localizing Caesar's Gauls, much as geography elsewhere served to enhance the fluidity of other authors' northerners. The first description of Gaul locates the three different kinds of Gauls in three separate areas, clearly demarcated by rivers. (Inconveniently, "Gaul" is the name both of the whole area and of one of its subunits; I will use it in the narrow sense in the rest of this paragraph.) But the geographic distinctions have meaning beyond themselves, for the three populations differ in (at least) culture. "All these peoples differ among each other in language, customs, and laws" (1.1.2). The second description goes beyond this by making distinctions not just at two levels (ethnic/cultural and physical boundaries), but at four (adding absolute orientation and local places). Take, for instance, the second version of the Belgians: "The Belgae begin from the end of the territory of Gaul and run to the lower part of the river Rhine; they look to the northeast" (1.1.6). Here we have a people (the Belgians), a physical boundary (the Rhine), a space (Gaul), and a compass orientation (northeast).

Furthermore, these different frameworks are not simply superimposed; they are treated as interchangeable.[32] The Belgians are said here to be bounded by entities of different sorts: Gaul, not Gauls; the Rhine, not Germans. Similarly, Gallic territory is bounded both by rivers and by the Belgians (1.1.5). Thus it is not just that the various groups happen to be in the particular places they are. Even nomads have to be somewhere at any given moment. Rather,

Gallic identities are linked to particular places (and vice versa). The general Caesar stopped the Helvetians from migrating militarily. The author Caesar stops the rest of the Gauls from migrating textually.

Tactical Space, Surveying, and the Possession of Gaul

Some of the most extensive tactical descriptions in *De Bello Gallico* are of the terrain around Alesia, where the final battle was fought, and of the massive works Caesar's troops built there. Sometimes Caesar divides his position into "interior" and "exterior," but at others, he divides it into "further" and "nearer."[33] The latter division, as Rambaud points out, implies some line that separates here from there. This line, he goes on to speculate, may even have been real insofar as Roman surveyors may have formally established perpendicular axes, the so-called *kardo* and *decumanus*, to orient the construction of the works. More generally, the establishment of such axes, at least conceptually—a move that defines tactical space for Rambaud—might show a connection with the characteristic style of Roman land surveying: the superimposition of coordinate grids on the land.[34]

There are further similarities between tactical space as found in Caesar and the spatial imagination implied in Roman surveying. In particular, there are several surviving surveying manuals, written by the so-called *agrimensores*, that share a characteristic treatment of physical features of the landscape.[35] Both Caesar and the *agrimensores* tend to emphasize physical (especially natural) features around the edge of each area, and both tend to minimize the physical features within each area. The similarities are due partly to borrowing, but partly also to a shared focus on the possession of land.

The evidentiary value of the writings of the *agrimensores* is not without its problems, including the dating of the surviving texts.[36] There are a number of different manuals still extant, though often fragmentary, transmitted together in the manuscript tradition. Attributions of several of the individual texts are uncertain, and even when an author's name is secure, it is rarely clear whether he is to be identified with similarly named figures attested elsewhere (e.g., Hyginus, Frontinus). The earliest texts in the collection are not likely to date before the late first or early second century A.D., whereas the latest texts are considerably later.[37] In other words, most of these texts are probably from 150 years or more after Caesar. Moreover, the dating of some of the texts is so uncertain that it is hard to establish even their relative order, and thus to determine precisely how the tradition evolved.

To what extent, then, may we use these texts as evidence for what was going on in Caesar's time? Three things operate in our favor here. First, like many learned traditions of antiquity (e.g., grammatical literature), this one seems to have been relatively stable over time. Different writers have different views on certain points, or even some differences in their interests, but on the whole they are talking about the same kinds of issues in the same kinds of terms. Thus it is not inherently unsound to extrapolate backward from later texts to a period for which texts are not available. Second, there seems to have been considerable continuity in the actual practices of surveying from Republican to Imperial times.[38] Hence, we might expect that there were few external pressures driving a change in surveying theory in early Imperial times. Third, and most specifically, the writers themselves show an interest in the history of their subject. For some of the questions that will be most important here, we are actually given explicit reference to earlier states of the art.

The central act of Roman surveying is called "centuriation." This is the division of a piece of land into squares (or rectangles) of regular size, called "centuries." Land was assigned to owners and recorded in terms of this grid. In this system, natural features like rivers are a problem. First, they do not follow straight lines, much less the particular grid lines laid down by surveyors. Hence, their effect on particular centuries and particular holdings varies on an individual basis. Second, even in the best cases, the course and shape of a river vary due to seasonal rains and to erosion and sedimentation. Third, more dramatic events (e.g., major floods) can suddenly change the course of a river altogether.

One approach to these problems was to treat rivers as having zero width, that is, essentially to treat them as if they were not there at all.[39] One manual suggests that this was the traditional approach: "Many rivers, and not small ones, disappeared in the assignment by old measure. The records indicate that no breadth was allowed to many rivers" (Agenius Urbicus 43.12–15). The colonists of a town in Spain petitioned the governor to assign a width to the River Ana; since this town was not founded until the 70's A.D., the zero-width approach must still have been in use at least until early Imperial times (44.5–21). When a width was assigned, the preferred value seems to have been that of the river's greatest (normal) extent.[40] This would leave neighboring land-holders in practical (if unofficial and risky) possession of land officially assigned to the river.[41] Like the zero-width solution, this approach allowed officials to make an assessment once (the maximum width), and thereafter to ignore the river.

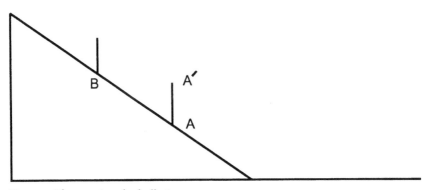

Figure 1. The practice of cultellatio.

The desire to ignore physical features would perhaps be less important if the Romans did not have the technical ability to render them. Treatises on measurement in fact give directions for laying down an entirely regular grid despite difficulties of the terrain. One method, called *cultellatio*, is a device for measuring over slopes (see fig. 1).[42] These are treated in a step-wise fashion. Distance is measured not directly between two points on the ground (say, A and B), but between one point on the ground (B) and another at exactly the same height (A'), and therefore at some distance above or below the other point on the ground (A). Thus lines that might measure 100, 110, or even more yards along the ground (depending on the slope) would all count as 100 yards on the true horizontal. The terrain is flattened out into two dimensions. Another method, apparently lacking its own name, is for measuring across smaller ravines.[43] The trick here is to cross-check enough points on either side of the break to ensure a straight line, even when some intermediate measurements must be skipped. Finally, more geometric techniques were devised to measure across wider obstacles, such as rivers.[44] This combination of techniques allows construction of a regularized grid despite variations in the physical features of the land. They are ways to pretend those features do not exist within the centuriated area.

If some parts of texts talk about ignoring physical features within the surveyed area, we can also see places where they emphasize their importance as boundaries. For instance, Siculus Flaccus (128.9–12) offers a list of typical boundaries between two communities: rivers, mountains, watersheds, and boundary stones. (A pair of colonies may also simply be divided by a line drawn for the purpose [128.12–13].) Hyginus (74.10–18) gives a sample set of boundaries for a territory: "From that hill, to that river, and through that river to that creek, to the bottom of that mountain, and from there along the line of the mountain and through there to the watershed." In both cases, the surveyors rely almost entirely on features of the physical environment that can be readily seen. And although the surveyors do not entirely reject man-made boundaries, natural ones clearly predominate.[45] Moreover, the man-made boundaries (and reference points) they do use are almost never ones built to serve that purpose. We do not see many of the artificially measured lines that are important to the demarcation of, for example, most western American states and Canadian provinces.

The use of physical (and especially natural) features to divide "inside" from "outside" is also written into Frontinus' explanation of the three legal categories (*qualitates*) of land. The first is land measured out, divided, and as-signed to individuals. The second is bounded (measured along the perimeter) and given as a whole to a community. The third is called *ager arcifinius*. Of this, Frontinus says (2.8–12): "Land is called *arcifinius* when it is not enclosed by any measurement. It is defined in accord with ancient practice by rivers, ditches, mountains, roads, trees, and watersheds." He then goes on to derive the name *arcifinius* from "warding off (*arcendis*) enemies," following the first-century B.C. scholar Varro. Note that this use of natural and other physical features is described as "according to ancient practice." That is, the pattern we have observed directly in the Imperial texts is explicitly called "traditional," and so is likely familiar to Caesar.

Illustrations to the manuals demonstrate many of the same features, but they present unique evidentiary problems.[46] (Note that the texts refer to these illustrations; they are not after-the-fact illuminations.) For all ancient texts, there is some danger that generations of copying by hand have introduced errors into the surviving versions. Elaborate techniques for comparison of manuscripts, combined with careful knowledge of the general principles of grammar and usage, are, of course, brought to bear in the editing of verbal texts to remove such errors. For the illustrations, application of both tech-niques is problematic. First, the textual tradition of this particular set of texts consists, for practical purposes, of two manuscripts with no identifiable com-mon source. In some respects, this simplifies matters, but it also means that there are no "descendent" manuscripts that can be mechanically disregarded in favor of their "ancestors." In any case, comparison of illustrations is prob-lematic. In the textual part of a manuscript, a given word (or letter) simply does or does not appear in each manuscript under study; the differences or similarities between two drawings can be harder to articulate.

This leads to the other difficulty compared to editing purely verbal manu-scripts. A knowledge of the Latin can often tell us that, whatever the situation of the manuscripts, a given reading must be wrong; it is simply ungrammatical. We cannot guarantee a correct reading on such grounds, but sometimes we can be certain of error. We lack, at least in a full form, such a grammar for images. Comparisons with other images (often in other media) are possible in principle, but the results may be ambiguous, especially since divergences can always potentially be ascribed to differences in genre. The fullest attempt to treat the problems is Carder's (1978) dissertation on the illustrations in the older of our two manuscripts. His conclusions may be summarized as follows.

There is a basic contrast between two types of illustrations in the manuscripts. One type is diagrammatic (i.e., composed of abstract geometrical features), and the other is pictorial. The former is stylistically similar to that of the *formae* produced by actual surveying, and appears to be a relatively early form of illustration (88aT, fig. 2; succeeding illustrations will be cited here according to Thulin's [1971] edition, where they are collected at the end of the volume, but numbered by the page of the main text on which they are cited).[47] The latter is more reminiscent of traditions of landscape painting, and seems to be a later type. "Early" and "late" refer here both to the widely spread dates of composition of the individual treatises and, to some degree, to the dates of successive generations of copies of all the texts. The tendency over time

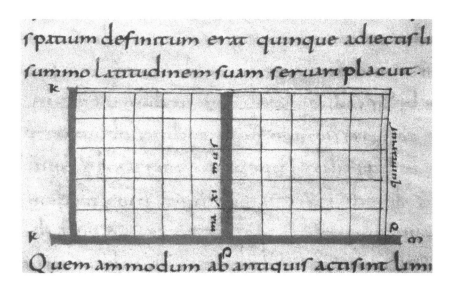

Figure 2. "Diagrammatic" depiction of centuriated land according to the agrimensores. *(88aT, ©Biblioteca Apostolica Vaticana [Vatican])*

Figure 3. "Pictorial" depiction of town surrounded by hills (92T, ©Biblioteca Apostolica Vaticana [Vatican])

toward greater "pictorialization" of the illustrations is also manifested in one of the most common and distinctive types of illustration in the manuscripts: a diagrammatic core decorated with pictorial vignettes of various features, such as towns or hills (92T; fig. 3). In these cases, the composition seems to be largely additive.[48] That is, the newer pictorial features are superimposed on the diagrammatic background, rather than reconfiguring it. In general, a single manuscript can contain illustrations traceable to widely varying times. The relative order of these can be established, at least roughly, on internal grounds. External comparison of certain features suggests that, in absolute terms, the styles of illustration of the particular manuscript Carder studied range from the time of its inscription all the way back to the time of the original composition of the earliest texts in the corpus.[49]

I am interested here in illustrations that are elaborated enough to show (at least) both a man-made centuriation grid and natural features, such as forest, rivers, mountains, such as this (69aT; fig. 4). In most cases, these features (such as the hill on the right and the sea below in fig. 4) appear only outside the centuriated area, often as boundaries to it.[50] Sometimes a natural feature, especially a mountain or river, is placed in the midst of centuriated land, but

Figure 4. Centuriation grid with natural features (69aT, ©Biblioteca Apostolica Vaticana [Vatican])

such cases are treated in a special way. They are set apart in a frame, without a centuriation grid, and usually the frame is not oriented along the axes of the centuriation. In Figure 5, for instance, we see a diamond-shaped lozenge amidst the squares (38T; fig. 5).[51] The mountain is rigorously separated from the surveyed area. Nor is the river (in the lozenge) really "in" the surveyed region. Rather, it separates two areas of centuriation. Most of the time, the natural features are also distinguished by being shown in perspective and in naturalistic detail, such as the trees on the hill and the plants and swans in the water. By contrast, the surveyed area is flat, featureless, and often not even colored. Illustrators, then, were willing and able to draw natural features in their work, but they did not integrate them within centuriated areas. Nor is it the case that all features are simply removed to the edges as ornaments. Cities are regularly placed within grids without being marked in any special way (97T; fig. 6).[52] Here we have some natural features (water below; hills to both sides) around the edges, but the city (schematically represented) is placed in the center of the grid and not marked off by most of the devices used for the river above, except for the city walls themselves, and even so the grid goes right up to them. Conversely, some of the marked features that break up centuriated areas are present, at least in part, to illustrate a particular point. Figure 5 also includes a river to illustrate the difficulties of working around such a feature, yet the separation of natural and man-made features somewhat undercuts its usefulness. The conventions of graphic representation draw a fairly sharp distinction between regular, featureless, human space inside, and irregular, detailed, natural space outside.

Figure 7 (1)–(10) displays all of the extended tactical-level descriptions in the *De Bello Gallico*. In making these drawings I have availed myself of maps of areas in which various events are thought to have taken place. However, I have been rigidly loyal to the text in choosing which features to represent; for instance, the river systems in (3) and (9) were probably in fact more complicated than what Caesar bothers with. The orientation and scale of many features could have been interpreted differently by a Roman reader without access to maps. Nonetheless, I believe that none of these potential variations affect the readings offered below. In seven of the ten descriptions, the core of the space is a town, camp, and/or open plain. The latter is usually mentioned expressly, or is easily inferred, as in (3).[53] In three cases, a water feature (the *palus* in [3] and the rivers in [4] and [10]) breaks up the open space. In the rest, physical features serve as boundaries.[54] Thus mountains and bodies of water can serve the same function on this level that they generally do at the geographical level; they divide one region from the next. The difference is that at the tactical level, we generally do not know what is on the other side of the hill.

Figure 5. Centuriated land divided by river (38T, Herzog August Bibliothek, Wolfenbüttel, Cod. Guelf. Aug. 2° f. [Codex Arcerianus A], 23v)

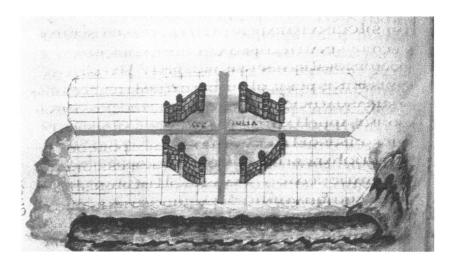

Figure 6. City surrounded by centuriated land (97T, Herzog August Bibliothek, Wolfenbüttel, Cod. Guelf. Aug. 2° f. [Codex Arcerianus A], 49v)

The distinction between interior features and boundary features can be made sharper if we recall the distinction between what Caesar calls mere "hills" (*colles*) and what he labels "mountains" (*montes*). We have already noted the philological reasons to insist on such a distinction. Looking at Figure 7, then, we can see another aspect of the distinction. So-called hills can appear anywhere, but features clearly designated "mountains" always serve to mark the outer limits of a tactical space. That is, only the milder version can appear within such a tactical space. The same is true of the water obstacles. Normally rivers and Ocean serve as boundaries. The river Sabis (4) is specifically described as being only three feet deep where it passes through the battlefield Caesar describes. Marshes (*paludes*) appear twice ([3], [7]). Ordinarily (as we also saw above) *palus* points to an impassable space of indefinitely large size. Only marshes unusual for their insignificance appear in tactical space.

It might be objected that the preceding argument is nearly circular. Naturally, larger features are more able to separate distinct areas on either side of them than smaller features are. If a mountain, for instance, is by definition larger and steeper than a hill, then it follows almost necessarily that putting a mountain in the middle of a tactical space would in fact create two spaces. There is something to this argument, but it begs two important questions, one logical and one contingent: Even if a mountain automatically creates a division between spaces on either side of itself, why can the composite not still be a tactical space in its own right? And why, even if we set aside possible fine distinctions between large and small features, are there parallels between Caesar's practice and that of the *agrimensores*—why do both resist the logical possibility of divided spaces, while using large features only as boundaries? The answers to both questions must, I think, be sought in the same direction. Both have to do ultimately with the connection between spatial models and their use-contexts.

What does it mean to say that large, dividing features can by definition only fall at the edge of tactical spaces? This implies that tactical spaces are by definition unitary. Yet this is clearly not true of, say, geographic space. After all, the express point of the opening description of Gaul is that it has several parts. Indivisibility is, then, a distinctive property of tactical spaces. The phrase "large, dividing features" also conceals another implicit assumption. By what standard do mountains or large rivers *automatically* become dividing lines? Neither stops birds, and at least the latter do not hinder the long-term migration of peoples. Presumably it is the standard of a Roman army on the march. Roman tactical doctrine relied on considerable unit cohesion and structured movement. Fighting on these terms would be impossible across

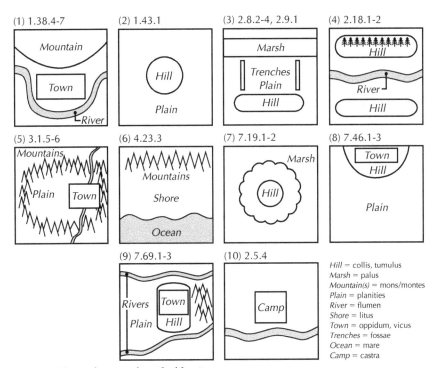

Figure 7. Tactical spaces described by Caesar.

"dividing" features, and even simple movement of large bodies of men would be difficult. A legion on one side of a mountain or river cannot engage an enemy on the other without some effort being devoted to transport, during which the legion is hardly a fighting force. From an offensive point of view, the (indivisible) tactical space occupied by a force is the area within which enemy forces must choose to fight or flee. From a defensive point of view, it is the largest area a single force can be said to occupy at one time. Thus the needs of a large, highly structured army dictate a relatively "clean," featureless tactical space.[55]

If the shape of tactical space is dictated largely by such considerations, then similarities between it and centuriated space will not (or not simply) have been the result of borrowing. Rather, their development will in the main have been parallel. The formalities of centuriation are explicitly driven by the uses to which land will be put, primarily growing grain. Consider the practice of measuring hills and valleys, which "flattens" out the land. A plot on a slope has a greater perimeter and area than a level one with the same "footprint," yet *cultellatio* equates them. Frontinus (18.16–19.4) explicitly justifies this equation by pointing out that grain grows straight up and that a sloped field will not in fact produce a greater yield.[56] The illustrator even draws the hill as a step pyramid to illustrate how the grain will grow (33T; fig. 8). The writers

Figure 8. The effects of cultellatio *(33T, Herzog August Bibliothek, Wolfenbüttel, Cod. Guelf. Aug. 2° f. [Codex Arcerianus A], 71r)*

are not explicit on this point, but the principles behind the overall structure are presumably similar. This kind of farming is easiest on compact, uninterrupted parcels of land. The kind of land that gets settled is the kind of land that gets centuriated. Ease of administration and an ideology of at least proportional equality between settlers reinforce this pattern. Thus large natural features become the boundaries between one community and another.

Caesar's tactical space and the space of centuriation certainly, then, take on similar form because of similar usage. They also, however, share a deeper correspondence. Both are about possession.[57] In a sufficiently broad metaphorical sense, this may be true of virtually any spatial representation. For instance, the regular series of U.S. Geological Survey maps of (largely empty) West Texas might be read, among other things, as a claim on land that is only barely possessed in the physical sense.[58] That is almost certainly the case with most larger-scale Roman maps, such as the now-lost map of Agrippa (in the Porticus Vipsania in Rome) or the figure of the globe used on coins to suggest world domination. However, I have something more specific in mind here. Surveying is about nothing but possession, and in particular possession in an imperial context. Siculus Flaccus begins his work on the statuses of land by noting that those different statuses are embedded in the differing histories of various peoples' relations, mainly in terms of war and peace, with Rome (98.18–99.4). He also points out more explicitly that the land of conquered enemies is the main source of land for distribution to colonists (119.7–10). Finally, the very name of one of the basic categories of land implies this same origin: *ager occupatorius*, "occupied land."

Even outside these passages, though, the exclusive focus on possession structures the surveying manuals in a fundamental way. Take, for instance, Frontinus' basic division of the three classes of land. "Divided and assigned land," the property of colonists, is basically self-explanatory. Then there is land "with measured boundaries," which has drawn boundaries around the outside, but not yet internal divisions. Finally, there is the territory called *arcifinius* (or, by other authors, *occupatorius*); this is "not bounded by any measurement" but by the kinds of pre-existing landmark mentioned above. The three classes are defined formally, but they also amount to three ownership relations: individual land, communal land, and land attached to a political unit but without regular patterns of ownership. Uninhabited land—or, for that matter, any land not subject to a scheme of possession—does not even exist in this classification. Consider, finally, the "controversies" that surveying manuals purport to resolve. They are not arguments between surveyors. They are not, for instance, about the appropriate mathematical approximation for some difficult measurement, or about what kind of information should be collected about parcels of land, or, more generally, about how to standardize methods to make the results of different surveys comparable.[59] They are all arguments between two land-holders. Who owns a given parcel of land?[60]

What does this have to do with Caesar? Again, I should stress that I am not claiming that Caesar has simply taken over centuriation as a model. Although both share two-dimensionality and unitary structure, Caesar's representations do not generally show the mathematical regularity that would prove a connection. Nonetheless, the two modes are similar enough that the interpretation of one could affect the interpretation of the other. The older, more pervasive, and more detailed mode (centuriation) could easily influence the other. In particular, characteristics of centuriation that are absent (but not directly contradicted) in Caesar could "bleed" over.

The connection of measurement to possession is such a characteristic. The style of measurement is, as we have just noted, similar in the aspects that can be compared. The context of imperial expansion is precisely the same. When Caesar gives a fuller description of an area, it is normally just before a battle. There is, so to speak, a controversy over the ownership of a piece of land. Survey is an "objective" means of resolving these disputes. In performing these rough measurements, the narrator takes up the position of the authoritative third party presiding over such a controversy. In this way, the narrative legitimates the dispute over the land (even if it does not actually settle it) before the army wins it.

If the analogy between centuriation and Caesarian description holds, there may be a further implication. As the maps in the *corpus Agrimensorum* suggest, surveying was a localized affair. Territory was measured one colony or municipality at a time. Very rough intervening territories (e.g., high mountains) were not measured.[61] Nor were standard orientations or scales used that would have allowed ready consolidation of individual surveys into a single record of larger scope. Survey imagines islands of ownership against a backdrop of land of indeterminate status. Caesar creates similar islands of distinct spaces that, as we have noted, are similarly unconnected. By contrast with the individual spaces whose ownership is a matter of controversy, the spaces in between are unclaimed altogether. What has not yet been measured does not yet exist; this is perhaps why the specifics of Caesar's original tripartite division of Gaul play such a small role in the body of the work. It would provide the indigenous peoples with a claim to the whole of Gaul. As it is, Caesar generally prefers a style of representation that leaves most of Gaul up for grabs.

My discussion of the relationship between tactical space and centuriation suggested that Caesar's division of Gaul implies that the land is available, that he recalls a context in which ownership is either disputed or nonexistent. Of course, he says nothing of the sort explicitly, nor does he make any overt arguments about ownership. Rather, he exploits the reader's unfamiliarity with the territory. He does not, at the fine scale, illustrate a pattern of (Gallic) ownership, then narrate its seizure by the Romans. Each bit of land is introduced only as it is contested. Slanting the narrative this way is of a piece with the justifications for war interwoven in the narrative, described below in Chapter 6. Many scholars believe that Romans found successful military conquest self-justifying. The fact that Caesar spins his narrative so as to legitimate it perhaps argues to the contrary. Or, more precisely, the self-justification of conquest takes place only in the context of a worldview that presupposes the notions of justice, responsibility, possession, and the like, that would form the basis of an argumentative justification anyway. The role of a propagandistic text like the *De Bello Gallico* (probably not unlike much of Roman historiography in this respect) is, then, not so much to legitimate particular campaigns as to reinforce the worldview in which their legitimacy will be taken for granted.

2. The "Other" and the Other "Other"

The Ethnographic Tradition

We have small traces of Roman (or Roman-directed) views of Gauls (in this case, living in northern Italy) from about a century before Caesar: a few fragments from a historical work by Cato the Elder, and half of a section in the narrative history of the Greek Polybius.[1] Though Williams has been able to trace and explain differences in the perspectives (and so versions) of the authors, the surviving elements seem typical of the later tradition.[2] Because of this overlap with later accounts, and because those later accounts deal with roughly the same territory as Caesar, I concentrate in this chapter on that later tradition. Potential chronological problems that this could raise are addressed below.

We also have three Greek ethnographic accounts of the northern "barbarians" from around Caesar's time, by Posidonius, Diodorus Siculus, and Strabo.[3] The earliest of these, dating to the first half of the first century, comes from the *Historiae* ("Researches") of the polymath Posidonius.[4] Posidonius' work does not survive as a whole, but large sections on the Celts are quoted in the late second century A.D. miscellany of Athenaeus, the *Deipnosophistae* ("Feast of Learning"); due to Athenaeus' interests, the surviving fragments concern mainly dining customs. Posidonius is unique among the three Greek authors in having had direct experience of at least some of the Celtic peoples of whom he wrote (4.45). He also had substantial personal contact with the Roman aristocracy of Caesar's day, including Publius Rutilius Rufus, Cicero, and Pompey.[5] Diodorus Siculus' *Bibliothēkē* ("Library"), a "universal history," contains a substantial section on the people and territory of Gaul (5.25–32). Diodorus refers to Caesar as "the one called a god" (5.25.4), and so must have been writing (or at least revising) after Caesar's death, and a fortiori after the publication of *De Bello Gallico*.[6] In the same passage, Diodorus refers to Caesar's bridging of the Rhine (cf. *BG* 4.17), but he never directly cites

Caesar. Probably the latest of the three is the "geographer" Strabo, who wrote during the reigns of Augustus and Tiberius, in the early first century A.D.[7] Strabo's *Geography* contains a great deal of cultural information in addition to physical geography. He offers separate accounts of the Gauls (4.4), Britons (4.5), and Germans (7.1–2). His sources include both Caesar and Posidonius, as well as the work of the obscure figure Pytheas (especially in the sections to be discussed below), though the latter was perhaps known to Strabo only through the intermediary of Posidonius. He also preserves information from other sources no longer extant (including the histories of Ephorus and the geography of Artemidorus).[8]

The various sources we have—Caesar and the three Greeks just cited— offer mutually consistent descriptions of the Gauls for the most part, and their citations of authors no longer extant make little note of contradictory accounts.[9] Caesar and Posidonius are the only authors likely to have had any direct experience of the Gauls, so it is possible that much of the information in the other texts derives eventually from only a few sources. Even if there is a common ancestor, we do not have enough information to construct a convincing family tree.

In any case, the various accounts share both a general direction and specific details. All might be characterized in modern terms as anthropological rather than sociological. (This is true to a great extent of ancient treatments of any non-Greco-Roman people.) They stress individual behaviors rather than social structure, personal rather than political concerns. They focus especially on what seems to have been picturesque detail for the Greco-Roman audience (long hair, unusual sexual habits, and the like). The nature of their interest can be illustrated by the following passage from Strabo.

> Most of their governments were aristocratic, and they chose one leader annually, and similarly one general was designated by the people for a war. But now they generally follow the orders of the Romans. Their assemblies have a unique characteristic: if someone disturbs and harasses the speaker, an officer, approaching with sword drawn, orders him to be silent with a threat. If he does not stop, the officer does the same thing a second and a third time. Finally, he cuts off enough of the bottom of his cloak to make it useless in the future. (4.4.3)

This is actually one of the most sociological passages we have. Yet we are given only the vaguest idea of the composition or authority of these assemblies and magistrates or of variations from tribe to tribe, despite the fact that this is the only description offered of Gallic government. What interests Strabo here is the honor apparently embodied in the cloaks and the odd method of enforcing order in the assembly. Furthermore, the immediately preceding sections discuss dress and natural resources, including the material used to make the Gallic cloak or *sagus*. Hence, while the entire passage quoted above is something of a digression, it is the second half that makes the main point of the story; the first, more "sociological" part is merely background. This ethnography is like most ancient historiography in that it focuses on individuals, rather than groups or structures. It is unlike historiography (outside of ethnographic digressions), a genre primarily of nobles and high politics, in that the people tend to be generic and the activities day-to-day.

The miscellaneous barbarian characteristics common to the tradition include both physical and behavioral traits.[10] Examples include:

- Northern barbarians are tall and muscular (Diod. Sic. 5.28.1, Strabo 4.4.5).
- They are pale (Diod. Sic. 5.28.1, Strabo 4.5.2), and the men have long, blonde hair (Diod. Sic. 5.28.2, Strabo 4.4.3).
- They wear gold torques (Diod. Sic. 5.27.3, Strabo 4.4.5) and pants (Diod. Sic. 5.30.1, Strabo 4.4.3).
- They characteristically eat large amounts of meat (Diod. Sic. 5.28.4, Strabo 4.4.3, Ath. 4.151e) and drink milk or else wine that has not been mixed with water in the usual Greco-Roman fashion (milk: Strabo 4.4.3, Ath. 4.152c, 153e; wine: Diod. Sic. 5.26.3, Ath. 4.152c, 153e).
- The men are promiscuously homosexual (Diod. Sic. 5.32.7, Strabo 4.4.6, Ath. 13.603a).
- They believe in metempsychosis (Diod. Sic. 5.28.6, Strabo 4.4.4) and practice human sacrifice (Diod. Sic. 5.31.3, 6, Strabo 4.4.5).
- They are highly boastful (Diod. Sic. 5.29.3, 5.31.1, Strabo 4.4.5).

Many of these claims (say, in the case of large gold jewelry), as well as those that will be discussed in more detail below, may have been true of Northerners, or at least of some segment of them. A few of the characteristics—the strange size and coloring of the barbarians—could well have impressed themselves on several different authors independently. Other parallels, however, suggest a literary tradition. The most striking parallel between different sources is the Gallic method of taking trophies in war (Diod. Sic. 5.29.4–5, Strabo 4.4.5). Both Diodorus and Strabo (the latter at least partially following

Posidonius) report that the Gauls cut off the heads of their enemies for display at their homes. Furthermore, the most valuable ones are preserved in cedar oil. The owner of one of these heads will characteristically boast that he has been offered (and refused) its weight in gold as ransom. Appeal to the facts, however, will not explain all the similarities of these accounts; they cover too much of the same ground. That is, even if Strabo, Diodorus, and Posidonius are all reporting only the truth, they still have to select which true statements to include. This suggests substantial use of a common source or sources. On the other hand, there are a variety of points included in only one of the three authors, but not the others. For instance, Strabo (4.4.3) records Celtic names for some garments and weapons, Diodorus (5.26.1) has a great deal to say about the strong winds of Gaul, and Posidonius uniquely records a special type of meat-knife (Ath. 4.152a). Given the highly fragmentary state of the remains of Posidonius' work, it is conceivable that he is the source of many of these shared details (such as the display of heads), but, as noted above, Strabo also cites a number of pre-Posidonian sources directly.[11] Thus we cannot postulate that any of the even partly surviving texts is an archetype for the tradition. In fact, it is probably safest to imagine that there is no single archetype, but merely a loosely connected tradition or "discourse" in the sense of the Introduction.

Within the tradition there are some significant differences, and at least one of them will prove to be thematically important. All three Greek authors (and, as we shall see later, Caesar) offer different versions of the relationship between the Gauls and the Germans. The case of Posidonius, the earliest of the three, is the most difficult. "Germans" as such were late arrivals on the Greco-Roman ethnographic scene; Posidonius provides the first or second known reference.[12] The one thing known for certain is that the preserved reference to his work on "Germans" cites Book 30 of his *Historiae* (Ath. 4.153e), whereas his general discussion of the "Celts" was part of Book 23 (Ath. 4.152f, 4.154a). The distinction has long been recognized, and a number of interpretations for it have been proposed.[13] The distinction raises some questions. First, are "Germans" for Posidonius an entire ethnic group, like the "Celts," or merely a single tribe? The second-century A.D. historian Tacitus suggested the latter, that "Germans" was in origin a tribal name that grew to be imposed more broadly in his day (*Germ.* 2.5).[14] Similarly, many Americans today casually call Welsh, Scots, and even Irish "English," an assimilation that goes on within the United Kingdom with a more pointed political effect and resistance.[15] Second, if Germans are merely a tribe, are they a subset of the Celts? The context of the reference to the Germans in Athenaeus is a discussion of the eating and drinking habits of a number of groups. Most of these are large ethnic/national groups (e.g., Celts, Parthians, Syrians, Indians), which might suggest that the Germans are understood to be on the same level as the Celts, or at least are meant to be opposed to them. On the other hand, Posidonius divides Italy into at least two groups: Romans and Etruscans. If, then, the work is not ordered according to strict principle, we may not be able to infer much from the context. The best guess may be that Posidonius' Germans were a group of the broadest sort, but no certainty is possible.

The situations in Diodorus and Strabo are much clearer. Diodorus uses two terms for Northerners—Galatae and Celtae.[16] He shows a preference for the former term, but in principle they seem to be interchangeable. He never uses the word "German." For Caesar, the Germans are characterized primarily as the peoples living to the east of the Rhine (1.1.3). Diodorus, by contrast, makes reference to "Galatae living across [the Rhine]" (Diod. Sic. 5.25.4), and he does so specifically in the context of Caesar's bridging of that river. Thus Diodorus eliminates the Germans, and perhaps does so polemically. Strabo's picture is also clear, though more complex. He uses the terms "Gauls," "Galatae," and "Celtae" more or less synonymously, preferring the last (Strabo 4.1.1, 4.4.2). He divides his discussion between continental Celts and Britons, and even offers the names of some individual tribes (e.g., Belgae, Bellovaci, Suessiones). The Germans are discussed under that name in a separate book (7.1–2), and Strabo also notes some individual tribes there (e.g., Cimbri, Teutoni). Furthermore, the beginning of the discussion of the Celts draws an explicit contrast with the Germans (4.4.2). Formally, then, Strabo establishes the strong distinction between the two groups that is apparently absent from Posidonius and Diodorus.[17] However, the substance of Strabo's discussion, and even the explicit contrast, immediately undercuts that distinction.

Strabo (4.4.2) says that the Celts and Germans "are similar in nature and government and are kin to each other, and they inhabit neighboring lands, separated by the river Rhine, which have most of their features in common (though Germany is more northerly)."[18] They differ in that the Romans had, by his time, conquered Gaul, and this supposedly moderated their behavior. Nonetheless, Strabo feels that he can infer the Celts' original behavior from what was current among the Germans of his own day. That is, they were similar in Strabo's day and had been even more similar originally. It may be significant that Diodorus draws an analogous distinction among his Gauls. He asserts that it is a true but little-known fact that more southerly Gauls, those from the Pyrenees to the southern slopes of the Alps, were known as Celts, while those to the north were called Galatae (Diod. Sic. 5.32.1). It is the Romans who imposed the latter name (in the Latin form *Galli*) on the whole population. Recall that Strabo defined Germans and Gauls as being divided north and south as well. For us, the Rhine flows generally south to north. Ancient geography tends to exaggerate east-west distances relative to north-south ones, and as a result the Rhine appears to flow from southeast to northwest.[19]

On this geographic understanding, calling the Rhine a dividing line between north and south is more plausible, if not strictly necessary. Strabo may also be influenced here by two long-standing Greek ethnographic traditions. First, the world was divided into climatic zones from north to south.[20] Second, national character was alleged by some to be determined largely by the environment in which a people lived.[21] The combination might have led Strabo to understand the German/Gallic division as a north/south one. In fact, similar thinking might underlie Diodorus' division of Celts and Galatae.[22] Although he says it will be "useful" to draw that distinction, it does not actually play any role in the rest of his discussion. He, or perhaps his source, seems to be trying to rationalize the existence of two terms for what is likely (on the basis of all the rest of the information he has) to be a single group of people. What I want merely to suggest here, and to take up in more detail when we have seen Caesar's approach to the issue, is that in and even after Caesar's time, anthropological knowledge suggested that the northern "barbarians" were relatively homogeneous, and that what distinctions do appear in our texts have more to do with formal compositional features of those individual texts than with the facts.

But it is not simply the case that this particular distinction is weakly attested in our sources. It is broadly true that there are few if any clear divisions among the Northerners. In part, this is because of a refusal to establish a clear geography of their territory. (Keep in mind that accuracy or knowledge would hardly have been required for "clarity.") For instance, Diodorus describes the rivers of "Celtica" as follows:

> Of the many great rivers flowing through Gaul and cutting through the plains with their courses, some flow from bottomless lakes and others have sources in the mountains; some exit into Ocean, and others into the Mediterranean.... There are many other navigable rivers [besides the Rhone, Danube, and Rhine] in the Celtic lands, but it would be long to write of all of them. (Diod. Sic. 5.25.3, 5)

Most of the rivers go unnamed and uncounted. Their locations and directions are not specified. Instead we are told that they flow from everywhere

(various lakes and mountains) to everywhere (both available seas). In between, they wander over the land, flowing ποικίλως "in diverse ways." If
these rivers are everywhere, then they are of no value as geographical reference points. Of the three rivers that are named, we are given the approximate
course of only one (the Rhone); the other two "flow into Ocean," but their
course is otherwise undescribed.[23] Diodorus does not even tell us the relative order of the three named rivers. Mountain ranges are even less useful
as reference points in this account. There are references to the Alps, to unnamed mountains along unnamed rivers that carry gold away from them, to
the "Hercynian Mountain," and to the Pyrenees, which separate the Celts
from the people of Spain.[24] However, nothing in the text gives us the location
of any of these mountains with respect to each other or to other geographical
features. The audience could presumably locate the Alps and Pyrenees, but
these for the most part establish the outer boundaries of Celtic territory, not
divisions within it. With no fixed features, Gaul has no internal divisions.
To this lack of geographical structure corresponds a lack of social structure.
Thus, although Diodorus insists that Gaul was inhabited by "many tribes differing in size," he does not attribute different cultural features to them, not
even individual names (Diod. Sic. 5.25.1).

Strabo's account is more complex in this respect, as one might expect
from a professed geographer. He begins the book that describes Gaul with
a section that summarizes the lands and peoples of that area (4.1.1). Strabo
repeatedly distances himself from the first half of this section with words
that defer authority: "some have divided" and "they say" (the latter three
times). This part seems closely to follow the famous "Gaul is all divided into
three parts ..." passage that opens Caesar's *De Bello Gallico* (discussed below). In fact, at the end he reveals that he has been following Caesar's account.
Then he immediately offers an alternative, quadripartite division based on
Augustus' division of Gaul into four provinces. Then he ends the section
strangely by largely disclaiming both versions as of no specifically geographical interest:

> The geographer must tell how many physical divisions there are and how
> many ethnic (when they are worthy of notice), but it suffices to give in
> summary the arrangements made by the rulers, governing for the mo-
> ment. (Strabo 4.1.1)

The rest of the chapter and the two that follow give what the reader is then
presumably to take as the genuine "physical" and "ethnic" divisions of Gaul

(4.1.2–4.4.1). Here Strabo proceeds region by region (following, incidentally, the Augustan outline), giving a summary of places and peoples. Although these sections perhaps presuppose more knowledge of the relevant geography than some readers had, Strabo nonetheless places the various tribes in fairly specific places.

Who these tribes are is another matter. There are brief notices about this or that group, but the overall impression is a series of indistinct names:

> Beyond the Mediomatici and Tribocchi, the Treviri dwell by the Rhine, downstream from whom is the bridge built by the Romans now in command of the German War. The Ubii, whom Agrippa had transferred to this side of the Rhine, used to dwell opposite. The Nervii border the Treviri, and they are a German tribe. Last are the Menapii, dwelling on either side of the river.... The German Sugambri are situated opposite them. The Germanic Suebi are situated above this whole river zone, surpassing the others in power and number (and those who had been driven away by them recently fled to the territory this side of the Rhine). Others are in power in other areas and pass on the embers of war though their predecessors have been defeated.
>
> The Senones and Remi dwell west of the Treviri and Nervii, as do the Atrebates and Eburones. Adjacent to the Menapii by the sea are the Suessiones and Caleti up to the mouth of the river Sequanna. The territory of the Moini and of the Atrebates and the Eburones is like that of the Menapii. For there is a forest of modest trees of 4,000 stadia (not so large as writers have said), and they call it Arduenna. (Strabo 4.3.4–5)

The material that I have so far been calling "ethnographic" follows the "geographic" section (4.4 vs. 4.1–3).[25] That ethnography makes virtually no reference to the distinctions established in the geography.[26] Thus Strabo gives the Gallic peoples some territorial fixity both in the introduction and in the bulk of the geography. However, he then proceeds to sweep it away in three ways. First, the renunciation of "political" models strongly suggests that such decisions were highly contingent and so could not even in principle be a source of fixity. Second, the mere fact of offering two alternatives (Caesarian and Augustan) without choosing (or at least without appearing to choose) has essentially the same effect as overt renunciation. Finally, the separation of ethnography and geography leaves the Gauls (the distinctive, fully realized culture) figuratively without a home. Without the skeleton of geographical description, the ethnography cannot maintain internal distinctions. What is presented in Diodorus by the content of the work is conveyed in Strabo more by its structure.

The lack of internal differentiation among the Celts is not merely a matter of literary emphasis. That is, Strabo and Diodorus have not simply declined to draw distinctions. Both make positive claims about the mobility and fluidity of the people of the north. Gauls (and Germans) are for them habitual wanderers, and there would hardly be any point in characterizing individual places or peoples. Strabo says that they "betak[e] themselves in herds, army included, or rather households and all, when they are ejected by other, stronger peoples" (Strabo 4.4.2). Later he repeats this for the Germans and remarks on their avoidance of agriculture (7.1.3). He goes on to say that the Romans conquered the Gauls more easily than the Spanish, since the former could be defeated all at once in a mass, whereas the latter remained in separate bands that had to be defeated individually. For Diodorus, this mobility is abetted by the very geography and climate of their land. Not once, but twice, he points out that the many rivers that he said flowed through Gaul are navigable (Diod. Sic. 5.25.5, 5.26.3).[27] In the winter, even the trouble of navigating these rivers is removed, for they are covered in ice and "bridged by their own nature." Diodorus goes on to specify that not only did chance travelers in small groups take advantage of this situation, but also "armies with their tens of thousands, together with their beasts of burden and heavily laden wagons, cross upon it in safety to the other side" (5.25.2). Thus he, too, describes a situation of mass migrations. For both authors, the people and places of Gaul lack distinct identities; they are interchangeable and, in fact, interchanged.

We have already noted that the fluidity attributed to the northern barbarians infects their physical surroundings in both of these accounts. This is admittedly not unique to the Northerners. The Numidians of northern Africa are similarly made to be nomads, and some in antiquity even derived their name and descent from the northern Nomads (Sall. *Iug.* 18.2, 7; cf. Hdt. 4.181). Fortunately, we can leave this fact aside in the present context; what I ask in this chapter is not what is unique to Northerners, but what is expected from them. In any case, fluidity takes on importance even beyond its effect on the environment. As a figure, it is projected not only outward onto the environment, but also inward onto the characters of Celts as individuals. They are described as being, in many ways and on many levels, random, fluid, and unpredictable. In Strabo, the connection between some of these levels is made explicit. He begins his description of the race (φῦλον) as "war-crazed and spirited and quick to battle, but otherwise simple and not ill-behaved" (Strabo 4.4.2).[28] And it is on account of this, he says, that "their migrations easily take place" in the fashion described above. Generally, however, the connections between psychological and social fluidity remain implicit.

Northerners are allegedly faithless in both legal and personal contexts. In a speech delivered at Rome during Caesar's Gallic campaigns (to be discussed at length in Chapter 6), Cicero comes right out and describes them as "faithless," *infidis* (*Prov. cons.* 33). Some years before, in his defense of a former governor of southern Gaul named Fonteius, he had gone on at much greater length about the untrustworthiness of the courtroom testimony of Gauls (some of whom were supporting the prosecution). In the Romans' highly adversarial court system, criticism of opposing witnesses is only to be expected, but Cicero's argument is closely tied to ethnically specific stereotypes.[29] Gauls, he says, have no respect for oaths because they have no fear of the gods (*Font.* 27–29). This claim is supported by reference to the attacks on Delphi (in 279) and Rome's Capitoline (in 386) by Celtic tribes (*Font.* 30). At the beginning of the chapter, we noted homosexual promiscuity as one of the common characteristics of the ethnographic tradition. Diodorus says, "They give over the flower of their bodies to others casually, ... and whenever the ones they approach refuse the proffered favor, they think it dishonorable" (Diod. Sic. 5.32.7). In Strabo, this behavior is attributed to youth—perhaps because it is marginal behavior even among the Gauls, but perhaps simply because they can profit from it most (Strabo 4.4.6). In Diodorus, however, this behavior is not attributed to liminal adolescents, but to married persons who are simply neglecting their wives in favor of sexual adventurism. The emphasis on homosexuality is notable because it creates a field (all the male persons of the society) in which all pairings are possible.[30] Promiscuity means that the sexual field is unstructured in practice; there are a variety of connections. The addition of homosexuality makes it unstructured in theory as well; any potential pairing is theoretically possible.[31]

The most characteristic types of Gallic unpredictability, however, have to do with violence in various forms. Strabo merely asserts that the Gauls are "quarrel-loving" (Strabo 4.4.6).[32] Diodorus gives a specific example. "Even during a meal they are wont to seize upon any trivial matter as an occasion for keen disputation, and then to challenge one another to single combat, without any regard for their lives" (Diod. Sic. 5.28.5). A feast is not the proper time or place for such a fight, but the Gauls do not respect constraint. And the essential randomness of this fighting is signaled by the phrase ἐκ τῶν τυχόντων, "from whatever matter happened to come up." Diodorus claims that they can risk such combat because of their belief in metempsychosis (5.28.6). Here it is their peculiar religious views that underwrite their unpredictable behavior in ordinary life. Posidonius also records these fights as a feature of Celtic ban-queting. He does not, however, attribute them to any metaphysical beliefs, but to a variety of lesser motives: small prizes, the honor of being known as the "strongest," or simply practice fights that got out of hand (Ath. 5.154b–d).

Unsurprisingly, the inclination of individual Gauls to attack each other is matched by our authors with a collective tendency to start wars. Cicero describes the Gauls as "bellicose" (*Prov. cons.* 33), and we have already noted that Strabo calls them "war-mad" and "quick to battle" (Strabo 4.4.2). The latter goes on to say that "if roused, they come together all at once for the struggle.... They easily come together in great numbers, because they always share in the vexation of those of their neighbors whom they think wronged" (4.4.2). This is not a strictly negative portrayal; the Gauls demonstrate a cer-tain level of unity and concern for their fellows. Nonetheless, they can be driven to war by slight and vicarious motivations. The phrase "whom they *think* wronged" suggests that the motivation may even be imaginary. Strabo's description of the Germans is even more negative: he spends an entire sec-tion discussing their habit of surrendering to any enemy, then later revolting faithlessly (7.1.4).

When Diodorus speaks of the Gauls crossing over frozen rivers, his ex-ample is of armies marching (Diod. Sic. 5.25.2). Even their preferred tactics emphasize fluidity. Strabo notes that all the Britons and some of the other Celts use chariots (Strabo 4.5.2), whereas the remainder are strong primarily in cavalry (Strabo 4.4.2). We should remember here that these forces are not equivalent to modern armor or even medieval knights on horseback; in par-ticular, they were not ordinarily capable of attacking organized infantry for-mations without some kind of initial disruption. Their advantage lay in their higher mobility.[33] This aspect of their use is highlighted in Diodorus, who assigns the chariots to all the Celtic peoples (Diod. Sic. 5.29.1). He goes on to describe their use: a charioteer drives a warrior into position to hurl spears, then drops him off for hand-to-hand fighting. The Gauls are also said to rely heavily on combat by individual challenges (Diod. Sic. 5.29.2–3). This style of fighting, with both the chariots and the champions, is strongly opposed to the structured style of the Romans and their organized units, each with its assigned place on the battlefield. By contrast, the Gauls scatter themselves across the battlefield in primitive, almost epic, fashion.

All these representations of Northerners would have been familiar to Caesar's readers, even those who had no particular interest in specialist eth-nography. Such Gauls/Germans fit, both in theme and detail, into the type of the nomad prevalent in earlier Greek literature of many genres. In particular, they resemble the nomads par excellence of the ancient world—Herodotus' Scythians.[34] Both groups of Northerners (Gauls and Scythians) share many ethnic peculiarities: drinking of milk and unmixed wine (Hdt. 4.2, 6.84), head-hunting in battle (4.64–65), human sacrifice (4.62, 72). It is the very fact of their nomadism, however, that constitutes the main similarity of both groups. Herodotus, of course, uses the word "nomad" of the Scythians several times, and makes the practice of wandering the explanation for their other strange customs (4.2). It is also their greatest strategic accomplishment, for when Darius invades their homeland he fails, finding nothing there to conquer (4.46).

Like the Northerners of Gaul, the Scythians are aided in their mobility by the land itself. Scythia, like Gaul, is blessed with many rivers (Hdt. 4.48–57, 82) which are said to be the "allies" of nomadism, especially as they, too, freeze over in winter to allow the passage of wagons (4.47, 28). The role of the rivers in Herodotus is particularly striking because of a contrast with Egypt. Hartog points out that the canals of Egypt, which are expressly compared to the rivers of Scythia (4.47), are given precisely the opposite function. They divide the land into distinct units and prohibit cross-travel by horse or wagon (2.108).[35] There are some differences between northern groups. Herodotus' account gives Scythia considerable internal structure (4.17–22, 48–57), even if that structure is somewhat undercut by his generalizing accounts of Scythian customs and the permeability of the river boundaries. The later, more exaggerated assimilation of land and people is no doubt another example of the "ossification" and simplification of the post-Herodotean nomad tradition already identified by Hartog.[36] Many of the structures of Herodotus' account are reproduced by later authors, who are not necessarily using them to make the same points about Greek, polis-centered identity that Herodotus was.

The parallels with Herodotus are important to the present study for two reasons. First, they confirm an interpretation of Diodorus and Strabo that emphasizes themes of mobility and fluidity. Second, they show that Caesar, even though writing slightly before two of the extant Greek authors, would have had available to him a fairly predictable tradition of depicting northern barbarians, and one that we can reasonably reconstruct from surviving sources. As we shall see, he adopts much of that tradition, but also deviates from it in significant ways. The mutual similarity of the Greek authorities suggests that "deviation" is a meaningful term, and that the innovative features of Caesar's account should have special interpretive significance. That is, a reading of Caesar along with Strabo, Diodorus, or Athenaeus, which is intertextually "backwards" in time, is not thereby ahistorical; broader inter-discursivity means we can (in this case) read in either direction.

Caesar's Ethnography

Caesar begins his account of the peoples and places of Gaul with the very first words of *De Bello Gallico*.[37] Throughout the work he makes further ob-servations, but the most notable passages are the ethnographies of the Gauls (6.11–20), the Germans (6.21–28), and the Suebi, a German tribe (4.1–3). The first section of *De Bello Gallico*, however, sets the stage for the rest and reveals some of the principles of Caesar's ethnography. The first sentence al-ready shows a striking contrast with what we have seen to this point in the Greek sources: "All Gaul is divided into three parts" (1.1.1). That is, he im-mediately insists on internal divisions. The rest of the passage goes on to map out those divisions. For instance:

> The river Garumna divides the Gauls from the Aquitani; the Matrona and Sequana separate them from the Belgae.... One part, which they say the Gauls hold, begins from the river Rhone and is bounded by the Garumna, the [Atlantic] Ocean, and the territory of the Belgae.... The Belgae begin from the end of the territory of Gaul and run to the lower part of the river Rhine. (1.1.2, 5–6)

On what basis does Caesar make these distinctions? He says that the three main groups (Gauls proper, Aquitani, and Belgae) differ from each other in "language, customs, and laws" (1.1.2). He does not give much detail on these differences here, but he does mention that the Belgae were the best fighters and the Helvetii the second (1.1.3–4). It is also clear from the examples just quoted that geography plays a role in establishing the differences. In fact, we can see that to some extent ethnic and geographical boundaries are inter-changeable. Note in the passage above how the limits of Gallic territory are defined both by natural features (Rhone, Garumna, Ocean) and by another people (the Belgae). The Belgae are in turn bounded by both Gallic territory and a river. Furthermore, the one cultural feature Caesar discusses here, mil-itary prowess, has a spatial determinant. The martial virtue of the Belgae and the Helvetii is attributed to their distance from the Roman province in southern France and their proximity to the Germans across the Rhine. In Caesar's Gaul, there are at least three distinct areas, and perhaps more, since the (distinctively brave) Helvetii appear to be a subset of the Gauls. The same

system of equivalences allows Caesar later to make strangely phrased pro-
nouncements like "the Rhine arises from the Lepontii who live in the Alps"
(4.10.3), wherein the river flows from a people, not a place. Unlike in Strabo's
or Diodorus' Gaul, the possibility of regionalization is not contradicted by
various kinds of fluidity. Instead, distinctions remain in name, people, culture,
and physical region; those four characteristics are bound together so that each
implies the other in a pattern of reciprocal stabilization.

In the opening, Caesar also mentions in passing the "Germans who live
across the Rhine" (1.1.3; also 1.2.3, 1.28.4). In itself, this remark need not
make a stronger claim than Strabo's use of the Rhine to distinguish Celts
and Germans in little more than name. It could even be a weaker claim; the
relative clause could be restrictive, and so the wording might not rule out
the possibility of Germans who live on "this" side of the Rhine.[38] Elsewhere,
however, Caesar makes it clear that the Rhine is to be one of the firm dividing lines, like the other rivers mentioned in 1.1, and that the Germans are
by definition the people "across the Rhine." In a speech in the first book,
the Aeduan leader Diviciacus points out that "Gallic land cannot be compared
with that of the Germans, nor this way of life with that" (1.31.11). The narrator later states directly that "the Germans differ from this custom" (6.21.1),
that is, that of the Gauls. Hostilities between Gauls and Germans are marked
by expeditions in both directions across the Rhine (e.g., 1.31.5, 2.4.1–2,
6.24.1). These assertions of difference appear to be borne out by the "facts" of
the later ethnographic descriptions of the Gauls and Germans.

The Suebi of Book 4 and the Germans of Book 6 are essentially indistin-
guishable, as one might expect of an ethnic group and a tribe within that
group. I treat them as a single group—"Germans"—but the citations will
show the reader which specifics are attested for which. Their diet is the traditional meat and milk of nomads (4.1.8, 6.22.1), they are physically imposing
(1.39.1), and they show the territorial and social fluidity one would expect
of the type. They are divided into a hundred districts (*pagi*), though Caesar
gives names to few of them (unlike those of the Gauls). Each of these sends a
portion of its men to war annually, while the rest remain behind to produce
food. In the following year, they alternate roles, the former farmers going
to war and the warriors returning home to provide for all (4.1.4–6, 6.22.3).
"Home," however, is a relative term, for "there are no separate and private
fields among them, nor is it permitted to them to remain in one place, dwelling there for more than one year" (4.1.7; cf. 6.22.2). Furthermore, in recalling
this passage only a little later, Caesar downplays even the modest level of
agriculture he has already admitted (6.29.1).

Among Caesar's Germans, wandering is not a matter of chance, but of science. As befits such a peripatetic people, they have no standing hierarchy or leadership. In peace time they have no collective leadership at all, only local strongmen (6.23.5). Rulers with the power of life and death are chosen only for the duration of war (6.23.4). In their more normal occupation of banditry, the leaders have authority only over those who agree to follow them in the first place (6.23.7–8). The Germans do not have priests, nor do they even accept gods in the normal sense of that term, worshiping only the sun, moon, and fire (6.21.1–2). Ultimately their social structure is so loose that they fall into groups of one: "They are strengthened ... by daily exercise and freedom of life-style because they are accustomed from boyhood to do nothing at all contrary to their will" (4.1.9).

The Germans' personal behavior shows the same lack of structure as their social and geographical organization. When they go to war, they favor using cavalry, like the Celts of Diodorus and Strabo. But they cannot commit themselves firmly even to that: they jump on and off their horses in the course of battle (4.2.3). They also practice banditry (*latrocinium*) even against each other (6.23.6). The choice of wording is important here. Theft, burglary, and the like are designated in Latin by *furtum*, whereas any military mission would be described as something like *bellum, impetus,* or *incursus/incursio* ("war, attack, incursion"). Bandits (*latrones*) are neither criminals subject to the ordinary process of the legal system nor foreign powers against whom wars are declared and fought. They are literally outlaws, who fall between the cracks of human society. The Germans' tendency to banditry is not merely a sign of criminality. It is notionally a sign of their complete divorce from human civilization.[39]

Of course, geography also cooperates in German fluidity. We have already seen how Gaul is given internal structure, primarily by rivers, but also by mountains. We saw other examples of this phenomenon in Chapter 1. By contrast, Germany has no internal boundaries. Caesar does not even give the name of a river or mountain within the area. The two internal features he does describe, both forests, provide an interesting contrast. The first is named Bacenis and is described simply as being of "infinite size" (6.10.5). The other is the more famous Hercynian wood. Allegedly it is nine days' march deep and sixty days in the other direction, although no one, Caesar says, has actually traveled all the way to the far end in the long direction (6.25.1, 4). Bacenis is said to separate two tribes, the Suebi and the Cherusci, but it has no other location or orientation. The beginnings of the Hercynian forest are given clearly enough, and one side of it seems to follow the Danube, but eventually

Caesar or his informants lose track, and all he can say is that "it touches on the territory of many peoples" (6.25.2–3). It, too, becomes effectively infinite. Forests do not naturally lend themselves to dividing up territory beyond a simple inside or outside. By not giving these forests clear boundaries or dimensions, Caesar ensures that they will not be pressed into service structuring Germany.

Caesar's Germans, then, represent a version of the northern nomad type. Geographically, socially, and individually, they are mobile and interchangeable. In Diodorus and Strabo, this was simply a fact, perhaps to be explained by the environment, but not the object of any particular effort. For Herodotus, nomadism was the product of a strategic decision—to avoid having cities or other permanent sites that would provide potential enemies with a target to attack. Thus, for these writers, nomadism is negative (it is framed as a decision to give up certain things) and instrumental (it is a matter of military strategy). Caesar's Germans have a much more active style of nomadism. Paradoxically, it requires organization to achieve complete instability; Caesar even makes the rotation of fields and military service the duty of the leaders who are otherwise seen as quite weak (6.22.2). Furthermore, the results of their labor are an end in themselves. Private property, the Germans feel, is the root of "faction and dissent" (6.22.3). That is, German strategies remove difference for the sake of removing difference. Thus Caesar gives a purer, extreme, and somewhat self-consciously traditional picture of the Germans. This makes it all the more striking that his Gauls are radically different.

Caesar's Gauls have some traditional features. They are rash and volatile, just as they are in the Greek sources (see also Chapter 3). They are tall (2.30.4), as Caesar notes explicitly in the main narrative a number of times (3.8.3, 3.19.6, 7.42.2). One of their particular weaknesses is a susceptibility to rumor (4.5). Interestingly, in the main ethnography, Caesar suggests that the Gauls themselves are aware of this problem and have taken legal steps to contain it by channeling all new information through the magistrates (6.20).[40] Only once is there explicit reference to Gallic treachery (*perfidia*, 7.17.7), but in several instances Caesar's anecdotes probably speak for themselves to an audience expecting an untrustworthy enemy.[41] In particular, we are told repeatedly of the mistreatment of ambassadors (*legati*). One might even see a trace of legendary Gallic impiety in their collective declarations that the Germanic Suebi were greater than the gods (4.7.5). Gauls believe in metempsychosis, which encourages their combativeness (6.14.5). On the whole, these traditional characteristics are depicted outside the formal ethnographic section. Moreover, Caesar has preserved the most negative traditional traits

(whose further exploitation I take up in Chapter 3), while neglecting most of
the merely colorful characteristics that make up so much of the tradition.

Whereas the Germans were marked by the lack of any stable distinctions,
the Gauls are defined primarily by binary division. The first sentence of the
Gallic ethnography establishes this principle: "In Gaul, not only in all states
and in all cantons and parts, but practically in every home, there are factions"
(6.11.2). After discussing the origins of these divisions in a system of patronage, Caesar reiterates the idea: "This same pattern holds in the totality of all
Gaul, for all the states are divided into two parts" (6.11.5). This political division at the highest level had been established as far back as the first book
(1.31.3), and binary division within individual tribes is frequently attested.[42]
The membership and leadership of the factions varies over time (6.12), but the
binary division remains constant. Caesar goes on to say that "in all Gaul there
are two kinds of men who are found in some number and honor" (6.13.1).
It is important to note here not only the recurrence of the number two, but
the lengths to which Caesar goes to arrive at it. In the following sentences he
brings up, only to dismiss immediately, the common people who are considered
"nearly slaves" and depend on the protection of the upper classes (6.13.1–2).[43]
That is, he takes what could have been a simple tripartite division of the whole
society, but immediately builds in a division between mass and elite so that he
can bifurcate the latter. The two groups to whom he alludes are the Druids,
a priestly class, and the Knights, who are warriors (6.13.3). His description
entirely omits the Bards, the singers and possessors of traditional wisdom who
figure prominently in other accounts of the Celtic peoples (Diod. Sic. 5.31.5,
Strabo 4.4.4). It is true that they might overlap uncomfortably with the Druids
as Caesar has defined them, but in the context of his previous description, the
more important point may be to maintain the division into twos.

Thus, unlike German society, that of the Gauls does have structure,
even if it is rudimentary. The idea of structure is reinforced by Caesar's frequent use of terms from the Roman social and political lexicon to describe
the Gallic world: clientage (6.12.2), plebs (6.13.1), various gods given Latin
names (6.17.1–2), and "knights" as an elite group, not just cavalry (6.13.3).[44]
They have had an underlying tendency to banditry (latrocinium), but the
Gauls, in contrast to the Germans, punish bandits by sacrificing them to their
gods (3.17.4, 6.16.5). And when the Gallic leader Litaviccus calls a group
of Romans "bandits" to a Gallic audience, he clearly means it as a reproach
(7.38.8). Sacrifice to the gods is also the punishment for lesser crimes like
theft, and even innocents are burned alive if a supply of criminals is lacking;
the method of sacrifice is burning alive (6.16.4–5).

This brings out another major aspect of Caesar's Gauls. Though they have a society, it is a perverse and even corrupt one. The cruelty implied by this mode of sacrifice is resonant with Caesar's frequent references elsewhere to Gallic torture.[45] This extended to the home. In Rome, slaves (property) could be tortured to investigate the suspicious deaths of their masters; among Caesar's Gauls, even wives are so interrogated in the deaths of their husbands (6.19.3). Beyond the question of cruelty, Gallic family structure is found wanting in *De Bello Gallico*. Caesar asserts that Gauls "differ from nearly all other peoples because they do not permit a man's sons to approach him openly until they have grown up enough to be able to do military service, and believe it is wrong that a son of boyish age take his place in the sight of his father in public" (6.18.3). This is the opposite of Roman tradition, where it is the father's responsibility to see to the education of his young sons after infancy, and senators once even brought their sons to hear the Senate's deliberations.[46] Gallic backwardness even extends to telling time; their days, months, and years begin at sunset rather than at midnight, as in Roman custom.[47]

To return to an earlier point, the formal ethnography backs up the stipulation that the Germans on the far side of the Rhine were a completely different people from the Gauls on the near side. The former were conventional northern nomads, the latter a novel creation with only a few characteristics in common with the Germans. The physical presence of the Rhine, the key to the division, is emphasized by the famous passage in which Caesar describes his engineers' bridging of the river (4.17.1–4.18.1).[48] This takes up almost a page of the Oxford edition of the text; the only other such technical passage of this length in *De Bello Gallico* describes the siege-works used in the climactic battle at Alesia (7.72–73).[49] The beginning of the passage tells us that the engineers were faced with the "greatest difficulties in their construction on account of the breadth, swiftness, and depth of the river." They succeeded by a combination of technique and brute force, such as beams eighteen to twenty-four inches thick. The size of the task described and the lengthy description of it reinforce each other in showing the reader that the Rhine must be understood as a fundamental dividing line.[50]

It comes as something of a surprise, then, that a number of casual remarks in the rest of the work undercut the distinction that Caesar works so hard to develop. Elsewhere he describes physical and cultural migration across the Rhine in both directions. Early on it is pointed out that Ariovistus brought at least 120,000 Germans with him into Gaul with the intent of staying there (1.31.5). Ariovistus was, of course, soon defeated, but in the following book Caesar is still having trouble with the "Germans who dwell on this side of the

Rhine" (2.3.4). Until they were displaced and later slaughtered by Germans, the tribe of the Menapii lived on both sides of the river (4.4.2). Even within the German ethnography, Caesar admits that some of the tribes dwelling across the Rhine were originally Gallic invaders (6.24.1–3). Even when peoples do not move physically, their customs become like those of their neighbors. Ariovistus speaks the Gallic (presumably Celtic) language out of "long habit" (1.47.4). Among the Germans, the Ubii, a tribe whose territory is bordered by the Rhine, are more humane "because they have grown accustomed to Gallic customs on account of their proximity" (4.3.3).[51]

This more confused picture incidentally fits better with our understanding of the archeological and linguistic evidence than does the version in which the Rhine makes a clean break. Rivers, it has often been repeated in this context, are not natural divisions; they unite more than they divide.[52] This seems to have been the case with the Rhine (fig. 9). Central Gaul exhibits a uniform material culture (centered on *oppida*, "hill-towns," of the type recorded by Caesar at, e.g., Alesia), generally called La Tène after such a site in Switzerland.[53] This same culture, however, extends east, far past the Rhine to the areas around Regensburg, Prague, and even beyond. La Tène sites (marked by + in fig. 9) appear from the Alps to the Danube to the Main, slowly fading out for the most part around the Lippe. In areas far north, such as Jutland, we find numerous sites of another culture, poorer and less advanced (marked by • in fig. 9), which could conceivably be made to correspond to Caesar's Germans. In between the two, the finds tend to be intermediate in type. In any case, the main distinctions are north/south, not east/west, and there is no single, sharp dividing line. The "Germans," if that is who they are, are technically east of the Rhine, but only by virtue of being so far north. The linguistic evidence, drawn primarily from proper names, is largely consistent with this picture. In particular, it confirms that the Southerners, east and west, were uniformly Celtic speakers. It is true that in places, La Tène peoples came to be displaced by "Germans," and that this tended to happen east of the Rhine, but these changes date largely after Caesar's time. In fact, it may be that the Roman conquest (and its restriction of migration in northern Europe for several succeeding centuries) helped to constitute precisely the rigid and east/west distinction between Gauls and Germans that Caesar had described earlier.

Whatever the historical facts, the resulting tripartite division of peoples (Romans plus two distinct others) is unusual not just in the narrow tradition of northern ethnography, but in terms of the structure of ancient ethnography in general. "The discourse of barbarian representation in the ancient world is very much a discourse of duality, polarity, of being either one way

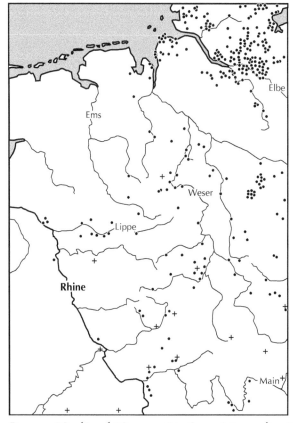

Figure 9. "Gaul" and "Germany" in Caesar's time, after C. Wells 1972, 17.

or the other, although this is often masked by the assignation of otherness to elements of one's own society," says O'Gorman.[54] It is, moreover, also a strongly normative discourse. Hence ethnography is generally deployed in one of only a few ways. It can be didactic and generally positive. Thus Horace, drawing on an already ancient Greek tradition, urges young men to avoid brawling, which he describes as a Thracian vice, not true Roman behavior:[55]

> It is for Thracians to fight amidst drinking-
> cups made for joy. Cast off this barbarian
> habit, and shield modest Bacchus
> from bloody brawls. (Hor. *Carm.* 1.27.1–4)

Or it can be didactic and negative, as when another people are described in terms of their lack of various (implicitly Roman) vices. So the "noble savages" of Tacitus' *Germania* are usually read.[56] Finally, foreign ethnic groups can serve as foils for patriotic celebrations of Roman virtue. For instance, that Greeks hold their assemblies seated allegedly highlights the greater seriousness of Romans' standing assemblies (Cic. *Flac.* 15–16). The discourse could also be some combination of the above in succession. All of these uses assume a simple two-place comparison, or at most a series of such comparisons. Hence, O'Gorman continues, "three-way splitting does not in practice occur. In other words, if two types of barbarianism are represented, one will be assimilated to the Roman."[57] To some extent, one could read *De Bello Gallico* in this way. Germans and Gauls would then be used serially to highlight traditional Roman virtues. And in a very complex way, there is some assimilation of both Germans and (especially) Gauls to the Romans, as we shall see in the next chapter. Nonetheless, Caesar's basic tripartite division remains a striking exception to the general practice of ancient ethnography.[58]

So Caesar went to considerable lengths in the ethnographies of Book 6 to establish a distinction that seems to reflect neither tradition, nor (as far as we can tell) reality,[59] nor even the rest of his own account. Why should this be? Caesar's own campaigns took him through much of Gaul but largely avoided Germany. Given that the German ethnography is the more traditional of the two, it might then be suggested that the difference lies in different sources of information: the Gallic account based largely on autopsy, the German one on second-hand and literary reports.[60] Williams has made powerful arguments in the context especially of Cato and Polybius that factuality is not explanatory in this framework.[61] It cannot be denied that Caesar had different sources of information available, but there are several reasons to think that this does not fully account for the anomalies of his text either. First, if we take the differences between Gauls and Germans as merely symptomatic of Caesar's sources, then the word "merely" begs an important question. However those differences arose compositionally, we should still want to account for their effect on readers. Second, the opposition between autopsy and literary sources is almost certainly drawn too schematically. From time to time Caesar makes reference to information he gained by inquiring of local informants.[62] Yet as both a military commander and governor of three provinces—Illyricum, Cisalpine Gaul, and Transalpine Gaul—Caesar was a very busy man. One might reasonably assume that much of his information, whether German or Gallic, was at best second-hand. Third, one of the most prominent sources in the conventional literary tradition is Posidonius, whom we know also saw Gaul, and who did not have other duties to distract him from known ethnographic interests. Fourth, the autopsy explanation presumes that Caesar's

Gallic account is different by virtue of being more accurate. But if archeological and linguistic evidence arguably supports Strabo's north/south view of the German/Gaul distinction at least as well as Caesar's (as it seems to do), then we should wonder whether this is really the case.[63]

Finally, while Caesar's Gauls do not fit the traditional schema found in the Greek tradition, they are no less schematic for that. Though Gallic society may well have been as contentious as Caesar describes it, the specific principle of binary division is surely just as much a literary construct as the fluidity of the Germans. Furthermore, Caesar's description of those Germans is conventional only in a certain sense. The nomad diet and worship of a restricted pantheon can be found elsewhere in the tradition. The primary theme of fluidity is also traditional, as we have seen. The metaphorical elaboration of this theme, however, is quite different in Caesar than in Diodorus or Strabo (or, for that matter, Herodotus). Caesar touches only lightly on the connection between geography and nomadism, and particularly the freezing rivers. Except for the remarks on the two forests, Caesar's geography supports nomadism only negatively. That is, it provides no natural boundaries, but it does not facilitate mobility either. Consider also his elaborate description, twice repeated, of the way Germans alternate provisioning and war and, within periods of provisioning, switch locations.[64] This is not only not part of the tradition, but is actually incompatible with it. Caesar here provides the kind of sociological information in which the Greek tradition showed little or no interest. The speculations on the social role of private property that he attributes to the Germans are even more out of place in this respect.

It seems best, then, to set aside the question of the source(s) of Caesar's information and to seek alternative, or at least additional, explanations of his ethnographic patterns. I propose explanations at two slightly different levels. In some respects, it is useful to Caesar merely to be able to distinguish two different northern peoples, whatever the specifics of their natures. In other respects, it is important that they have the particular characters that they do. The latter point will also be a topic of the next chapter.

By distinguishing the Gauls and Germans carefully, Caesar limits the task before him.[65] As we see in Chapter 6, one of the contemporary explanations of the need for Caesar's campaigns was that, in contrast to previous leaders against the Gauls, he would subjugate the entire territory once and for all. This would be important to the audience because of previous Roman encounters with the Gauls, but it would be important to Caesar himself for other reasons. Romans understandably awarded the greatest glory to leaders who could argue convincingly that they had not only won battles, but had forced the enemy to submit totally. Thus to claim the right to a triumphal procession, a general would claim that he was able to bring his army back home.[66] Being the general who finished a given campaign was important enough that aristocrats would attempt to "steal" wars from one another by having command transferred after much of the work had been done.[67] In this context, it would be valuable to Caesar to define his military opponents narrowly before his political opponents could do so. Caesar had made tentative thrusts into Germany, and this would have been widely known at Rome (Cic. *Prov. cons.* 33). If, however, he could define the Gauls and Germans as radically distinct, then the conquest of Gaul (still, obviously, an enormous undertaking) would count as a completed task.

The Gauls and Germans are also designed to pose different threats to the Romans. I noted above that Caesar retained some conventional features of the nomad tradition, but partitioned them among the Germans and the Gauls so as to use even tradition to advance the distinction. In the same way, the two northern groups are dangerous for complementary reasons. In the case of the Germans, the problem is their fluidity. A people who do not recognize boundaries, social or geographic, cannot be trusted to stay in their own territory and to not make war on the Romans. With the Gauls, the problem is not randomness, but a more specific tendency to wage war. They are prone to fighting both individually and collectively. Their temerity makes them unable to check violent impulses, even when that would be the prudent course of action. Whatever the source of the danger, the Romans will respond preemptively. As Chapter 6 discusses, this is an important source of justification for military actions. Furthermore, the semi-civilized Gauls provide a special kind of threat. Their similarity to the Romans grows over the course of the work. If they are not conquered now, the threat will only increase. Hence the preemptive strike is required now.

The characterization of both peoples legitimizes their conquest. The specific nature of the Gauls makes them particularly attractive candidates. Chapter 1 showed how Caesar's geographic partition of Gaul breaks it up into easily assimilable chunks. The characterization of the Gauls as a people also makes them more suitable for appropriation. When Herodotus' Darius invaded Scythia, his campaign failed because he found no "there" there. For Herodotus, this was a stroke of strategic genius on the Scythians' part, but we are not bound to accept his understanding. Whether their motivation is external (as in Herodotus) or internal (as in Caesar), nomads offer nothing to potential conquerors by virtue of having nothing in the first place, not even themselves. One might even wonder about the expected value of German captives, if such were ever to be taken, when they are said to have spent their lives training to do "nothing contrary to their own wills" (*BG* 4.1.9).

The unavailability for conquest of the German nomads extends beyond these more or less concrete manifestations. They are stock characters, recognizable as such—the denizens of the northern edge of the world.[68] Romans certainly dreamed from time to time of literal world domination, but in their more sober moments, "world conquest" was in practice more limited.[69] A campaign against the Germans would not be as fantastic as one against, say, the Amazons, but it would be a step in that direction. Caesar's ethnographic narrative, like his whole text, is remarkably sober and matter-of-fact. The radical social engineering (or, rather, de-engineering) of the Germans is nearly as outlandish a feature as he will allow. This is notable because one of the more distinctive features of the Greco-Roman ethnographic tradition is an interest in *thaumata*, "marvelous things."[70] The only examples in *De Bello Gallico* are in the German ethnography, more precisely in the description of the measureless Hercynian forest. There are found unicorn cattle, elk without knees, and bulls the size of elephants (6.26–28). The Gauls, by contrast, live in a space that Caesar makes ordinary, even featureless. They are quarrelsome and hostile, but clearly recognizable as a group of people, not a legend. Hence they are fit and useful objects of appropriation.

Most of this chapter has analyzed the significance of a variety of distinctions on which Caesar insists, especially when he is self-consciously offering ethnographic description (6.11.1). In the work as a whole, however, certain distinctions come and go. Although for Caesar the various Gallic tribes are in principle distinguishable, they are not always in fact carefully distinguished. First, Caesar separates his geography from his ethnography (as Strabo would later do). Thus, even if there are in one sense many different tribes, they are in another sense all more or less the same, since they can be given a uniform description. (One might even say that this difference merely for difference's sake is the essence of Caesar's Gauls.) Second, Caesar invokes the allegedly uniform character of the Gauls not just in one set-piece, but throughout the main narrative. He frequently compares specific acts to what was customary—*mos* or, more often, *consuetudo*—for a given group of people. These groups are normally one of the three major ethnic groups: Romans, Gauls, or Germans.[71] Only three times is the reference to a single tribe (Aedui, Helvetii) or a group of tribes (the Aremoricae of the north coast).[72] We have seen that in other respects, Caesar's formal ethnography and more casual descriptive practice do not always line up. Here, however, they agree in giving the Gauls a uniform character.

Finally, there is Caesar's use of the very names of the various tribes. These he gives in great abundance, 121 names in all.[73] The names are distributed very unevenly, though. They tend to burst out suddenly in long lists or catalogs like the following:

> After word of this battle had gotten around, the greatest part of Aquitania surrendered itself to Crassus [Caesar's legate] and handed over hostages of their own accord; among this group were the Tarbelli, Bigerriones, Pitanii, Vocates, Tarusates, Eluastes, Gates, Ausci, Garumni, Sibuzates, and Cocosates. (*BG* 3.27.1)

As Mannetter has remarked, catalogs serve many functions in Caesar's *commentarii*.[74] Here we are given an impression of attention to detail, eleven confusingly unfamiliar names duly recorded. We also get the expression of an expansive conquest from the eleven separate peoples who had registered their submission. Yet these impressions are not supported by much information. Who are these people? In many cases it is impossible for the reader to tell, because more than half the tribes Caesar mentions appear only in the context of such lists (sixty-two, plus eight questionable cases).[75] The tribes in the passage just quoted are particularly difficult for the reader, since nine of the eleven appear only here. This is not unusual; forty-nine of the 121 tribonyms recorded in *De Bello Gallico* occur exactly once.[76] Caesar's aggressive naming is a gesture of possession (which is, as we saw in the last chapter, echoed by strategies of geographic "mapping"). It can also be paralleled by the written placards (*tituli*) displayed in triumphal processions.[77] It is, however, also a somewhat empty gesture as Caesar uses it. The precise differentiation of Gauls promised (in contradiction to the monolithic accounts just described) is never delivered.[78]

3. Technology, Virtue, Victory

*D*e *Bello Gallico* is above all about war, and this chapter considers the central elements of military success.[1] The Romans start with a marked advantage in the use of siegecraft, which decreases to nearly zero at the end. Yet it may not ultimately matter, because the Romans often use technology just to level the playing field and win in a pitched battle. Success in those battles is typically described as being a matter of *virtus* (conventionally translated "virtue," "courage," or "manliness"). In Caesar's work, as in Latin more generally, this word has a number of different resonances. While exploiting conventional senses of the word, Caesar gradually imposes a new (or at least narrowed) understanding. This sense emphasizes the collective over the individual and acquired skills over natural gifts. This aids our understanding of what would otherwise have been simple ethnographic givens—the relative strengths of Caesar's foes—and makes possible the Gauls' acquisition of *virtus*, not just technology, over the course of the work. The Gauls become greater threats and better trophies. But they are also shown to be in moral decline. In this respect, their conquest is morally legitimized, even required. But at the same time, they offer an equally legitimate model for relationships to authority, allowing Caesar credit for his soldiers' work in a novel, direct way and letting the soldiers retain their masculinity while in a state of submission. This was a conventional situation for soldiers, of course, but Caesar offers a framework that would work equally well in political life.

Siegecraft in De Bello Gallico

The most overtly technological aspect of warfare in *De Bello Gallico* is siegecraft. In this respect, the war can be roughly divided into three phases. In the first (Books 1 and 2), Rome's enemies are overwhelmed by superior technology, to which they have nothing even to compare. When native devices are mentioned, they are strikingly primitive, not well distinguished from nature. In the middle of the work (Books 3 through 6), Roman technology remains superior, but its effects are not nearly so spectacular. Gallic technology becomes dramatically better, largely through piecemeal appropriation of Roman techniques. The final phase is constituted by Book 7 alone. Here we see, in a sense, improvement on both sides, as well as the most direct confrontations of technology in the book. The Romans remain superior, but the position is now vastly more complicated.

The Romans' first technological feat is a virtuoso performance, though it does not by itself have a decisive effect. The migrating Helvetii were slowly crossing the river Arar (now the Saône) by means of linked rafts. When three of their cantons had crossed, Caesar and his army pounced on the fourth (now isolated) and defeated it decisively (1.12.1–3). Caesar then had a bridge built across the river so that he could pursue the rest. The Helvetii are said to have been greatly shaken (*commoti*) by this, "since they understood that [Caesar] had made in one day the river-crossing which they themselves had accomplished only with the greatest difficulty in twenty" (1.13.2). They quickly sent a legate, who offered Caesar concessions, but not complete submission. This he rejected. After several days of intervening activity, the Romans defeated the Helvetii in a pitched battle (1.26). In the abstract, Roman superiority is validated both objectively (by the 20:1 ratio of crossing times) and subjectively (by the Helvetian response). In practice, the bridge allowed not only the pursuit and eventual defeat of the Helvetii, but also the divide-and-conquer strategy that presumably made the final victory easier; Caesar could afford to delay his first attack until most of the Helvetii had crossed since he knew the river was no barrier to his own forces. Nonetheless, technology remains in a secondary role, whereas hand-to-hand combat wins the day.

In Book 1, the enemies are migrating peoples, such as the Helvetii and Ariovistus' Germans. Hence, Caesar's army has little opportunity to bring out its most impressive devices: siege-works and engines. When these are finally employed in Book 2, they have a devastating effect. The first town to fall to the Romans was Noviodunum, a settlement of the Suessiones. When the inhabitants saw the various works (mantlets, a rampart, siege-towers), they were stunned (*permoti*) by the size and speed of construction of works "which Gauls had neither seen nor heard of before" (2.12.5). They surrendered immediately. The results were largely similar when Caesar next besieged an unnamed town of the Aduatuci. At first the inhabitants laughed at the Romans' work, since the various devices were constructed at some distance from the wall. They also remarked on the incongruity of such large devices being built by such small men (2.30.3–4). When, however, they saw the equipment being moved into position next to the walls, "a strange and unaccustomed sight," they had a swift and complete change of heart. They offered to surrender immediately, saying that "they did not think that the Romans were waging war without divine assistance if they could move machines of such height with such speed" (2.31.2).[2] Again, Caesar accepted the offer. Unlike the battle with the Helvetii, these encounters were won directly by the devices.[3]

Caesar did end up having to fight the Aduatuci almost immediately anyway. Caesar removed the troops from the city overnight to protect the surrendered people from his own men. The Gauls seized the opportunity to take up arms again and attack the Romans unawares, but they were defeated. It was not, however, a failure of the technology; Caesar depicts it as a separate engagement. This is precipitated by a combination of traditional Gallic faithlessness and Caesar's tendency (as it is represented) to allow ethical concerns to get the better of his tactical judgment.[4] It should also be noted that in both incidents, the Gauls are made to worry about two things: the combined size and speed of construction of Roman works, and the novelty of the devices themselves. The former will remain a hallmark of Roman technology throughout *De Bello Gallico*. The novelty, as one might expect in reality, starts to wear off quickly, and this alone is enough to reduce the effectiveness of the Roman devices.

Gallic technology in the early part of the war is relatively simple. Noviodunum was fortified by a wall and trench, but we are given no further specifics of arrangement or location (2.12.2). These are fixed-dwelling Gauls, not nomad Germans. Similarly, the town of the Aduatuci was fortified and even had manned stations built into the wall. But their trust lay not primarily in fortifications. They had abandoned most of their towns and forts in favor of "a single town well fortified by nature" (2.29.2). It was surrounded by cliffs on most sides, and could be approached easily only by one narrow route. This naturally defended position was then additionally fortified by walls, rocks, and sharpened beams (2.29.2–4). This combination of natural and man-made fortifications is the norm for the Gauls throughout *De Bello Gallico*, as it seems to have been in real life.[5] It is also worth noting the relative lack of detail of construction in both places. Wood is sharpened, but otherwise things are vague: a wall or ditch is built. The Aduatuci use "rocks of great weight." This construction takes them a step beyond their naturally existing defenses, but only a step, as we see by contrast with some Roman devices and even later Gallic ones.

Since the Gauls relied heavily on these hill-forts, and since they had long fought each other, naturally they had developed some technology for siege warfare themselves. This we see in the Belgian assault on Bibrax, a town of the then-Roman allies, the Remi. The method, said to be common to the Belgae and other Gauls, was as follows:

> A multitude of men surrounds all the walls of a place, and, when they have started to throw rocks at the walls from all sides and the defenders have taken cover, a "tortise-shell" of shields is formed, and they move up to the gates and undermine the wall. (2.6.2)

This is a technique of a sort, but it could hardly be more low-tech. In the following sentence the narrator notes that weapons (*tela*) were hurled in addition to rocks in this particular case, but the closeness to nature is still clear. This whole passage is unusual this early in *De Bello Gallico* in that it reports an event at which Caesar (and, in fact, Romans in general) was not present.[6] This points to a strong need to introduce this material now, to make more sense of the Gallic reaction to Roman siege warfare later in the book.

In the middle phase of *De Bello Gallico*, Roman siege warfare was still effective, but much less dramatically so. In part, this is simply because the general tide of the war changed, and the Romans were more often back on their heels. However, even when they did have an opportunity to bring out their devices, the effects were different. This becomes clear in the middle of Book 3, when the Romans (here under the legate Crassus) assault the town of the Sontiates:

> When [the Sontiates] resisted, he brought in screens and towers. They first tried sallies in some places and elsewhere dug mines up to the ramp and mantlets (the Aquitani are far the most skilled in this thing because there are mines and quarries in many places in their territory). When they realized that the diligence of our men prevented them from accomplishing anything by these means, they sent legates to Crassus and asked him to accept their surrender. (3.21.2–3)

Obviously, the Romans won again. Here, however, the opposition was not so stunned that they could offer no resistance. Nor was their resistance predicated on an ignorance of Roman abilities, as in the case of the Aduatuci; they had appropriate, if ultimately unsuccessful, technological counter-measures to hand.[7] We should also consider the implication of the narrator's parenthesis. The Aquitani, among whom are numbered the Sontiates, are said to be "the most skilled" in mining. The Aquitani are of course one of the three grand divisions of Caesar's Gaul (1.1.1). The superlative suggests that, despite the impression that the earlier passages might have given, even the other Gauls were not all unfamiliar with assault techniques more sophisticated than throwing rocks.[8] Though the Gauls' increasing ability to deal with Roman technology may well reflect a "real" historical trend, that trend is nonetheless accentuated by the narrative.

The subsequent Gallic reaction to the capture of the Sontiatate town reflects increasing Gallic ease with Roman technology.[9] Furthermore, it introduces an important new theme to the discussion of technology. The narrator begins to describe the Gallic reaction with words strongly reminiscent of those that introduced the surrenders of the Suessiones and Aduatuci in the previous book: "Then the barbarians, shocked when they heard that the town had been taken within a few days of [Crassus'] arrival even though it was fortified both by the nature of the place and by hand...." Again the Gauls' defense was based on a hybrid of nature and skill; again they were disturbed (commoti) by the failure of these defenses. The result, however, was completely different. "They began to send legates back and forth, to plot, to give hostages to each other, and to ready troops" (3.23.2). Most important, they sent to Spain (to unnamed related tribes) for experts on fighting the Romans. Some of their Spanish allies had fought more than a decade previously in support of the insurrection of the Roman Quintus Sertorius (3.23.5).[10] Sertorius had had some success against the Roman government for several years until he was assassinated by his own comrades in 73. From this source, the Aquitani then learned to fight in more Roman ways. "These peoples started to establish their positions according to the habits of the Roman people, fortify their camps, and cut off our troops from lines of supply" (3.23.6). Even in the short run, these Roman tactics did not save the Aquitani. Still, they did at least force Crassus to change his tactics; he was compelled to risk an immediate pitched battle (whose outcome remained uncertain until the end) lest the enemy eventually gain too great an advantage by weakening the Romans while adding to their own numbers (3.23.7–8). Nor would this be the last time the Gauls appropriated Roman ways of fighting.

By Book 5, the Gauls have turned the tables on the Romans almost completely. The Nervii demand that the Roman legate Quintus Cicero (the brother of the orator) remove his troops from their winter quarters in Nervian territory. He refuses to treat with enemies under arms, and they proceed to lay siege to the legionary camp:

> The Nervii surrounded the camp with a nine-foot wall and a fifteen-foot trench. They had learned these things from us by way both of their

experience in prior years and of Roman captives whom they were holding secretly. But there was no supply of hardware that would be fit for
this use.... And they began to make and ready towers to the height of
the palisade, hooks, and sheds, which the same captives had taught them
about. (5.42.1–3, 5)

After the fact, Caesar himself (the character) "wondered at" the large and
sophisticated works the Gauls had left behind (5.52.2). This episode does not
show either side at its best. On the one hand, the Romans were not in a permanent fortress or town; winter quarters (*hiberna*) were bases of offensive
action, defense more against harassment than serious attack.[11] On the other
hand, the Gauls lacked some of the materials required to build their own
works. Nonetheless, Roman technology no longer clearly trumps Gallic. In
any case, the result was largely the same as in the assault on the Sontiates:
the Romans won a hard-fought victory, but only by changing the terms of the
fight. After the Nervii succeeded in setting part of the Roman encampment on
fire, Cicero sent for reinforcements. The Gauls recognized the approach of this
relief force and fell back with the battle at the camp still undecided.

The last book constitutes a third phase unto itself. It is particularly notable
for direct technological confrontations between the two sides. Two incidents
merit special attention. This first is the Roman siege of Avaricum (modern
Bourges), seat of the Bituriges. The Gauls, under their new (and overall) leader
Vercingetorix, were pursuing a scorched-earth policy to deny the Romans
access to supply. Against Vercingetorix's better judgment, this city was left
standing on the theory that the inhabitants "would easily defend themselves
by means of the nature of the place" (7.15.4). We learn later that the town was
not only elevated, but surrounded by a marsh (7.19.1).[12] If the Gauls could
have finally held this town, they would have regarded it as a great victory
(7.21.3). As expected, the Romans arrived and laid siege to Avaricum. At least
at this point in the narrative, the Gallic devices (nooses, towers, boiling pitch,
and sharpened sticks) appeared to be effective. Earlier, the effectiveness of
similar Nervian responses had been limited by their lack of resources. Now,
however, the Bituriges countered the Roman attempts "all the more skillfully
because among them there are great ironworks and every type of tunnel is
known and frequently used" (7.22.2). This need not contradict anything in
the earlier narrative; after all, this is a different tribe, and in any case, several
years have passed since the earlier assault. Still, whether from coincidence or
selective reporting, the narrative presents rather matter-of-factly a large and
apparently sudden leap in Gallic technology.

How did they manage it? The account of the siege proper begins with a direct appeal to the Gauls' ability to imitate, here described as an ethnic characteristic: "[They are] a race of the highest cunning and most ready to imitate anything and do whatever they have learned from others" (7.22.1).[13] This phrasing conceals something new. Since "imitation" of the Romans is already an established theme, and since it is expressly referred to here, the phrase "do[ing] whatever they have learned from others" is easily read as a redundant gloss. But what is the ultimate source of these techniques the Gauls pass from hand to hand? The narrator does not say, but it may be important that the Romans are not named as the source. Certainly at least some of the tactics described in what follows must be understood as entirely native (as they are appropriate only to the defense of *oppida*, not of Roman camps). Here, then, the door has been opened to the possibility of genuine technological innovation on the part of the Gauls.

This possibility is strongly reinforced by the following section, which is devoted entirely to the construction of the walls of Avaricum (in a form usually referred to today as *opus Gallicum* or *murus Gallicus*):

> All Gallic walls are of roughly this form. Long straight beams are set on the ground facing outward at equal intervals of two feet apart. They are bound on the inside and "clothed" in much earth. The intervals we have noted are filled in with big rocks. Once these have been placed and fixed together, another course is added on top, so that the same interval is preserved and the beams do not touch but, each separated by an equal space, they are artfully held in place by the insertion of the corresponding rocks. Thus the whole work is interwoven until the full height of the wall is reached. (7.23.1–4)

The narrator goes on at greater length to discuss the aesthetic appeal and practical utility of this type of construction. Up to this point, Avaricum had been described in much the same terms as other Gallic *oppida*. The manmade defenses were merely an extension of those provided by nature. The very existence of a wall, though hardly surprising, is not actually mentioned until three sections after the description of the natural defenses (7.19.1–2, 22.3). Yet the regular intervals and angles of *opus Gallicum* emphasize the constructedness of the wall. Here the sheer length of the passage is significant, suggesting both the size and the importance of the works. Here, at last, the Gauls have separated themselves firmly from nature. That this separation occurs only near the end of *De Bello Gallico* is all the more striking when one notes that it is surely an artifact of the narrative. *Opus Gallicum* and similar structures are easily identifiable in the archeological record throughout the region; it is virtually certain that the Romans would have encountered them before this battle.[14] The narrator almost says as much in the opening sentence of the description: "All Gallic walls are of roughly this form." Earlier we saw a few cases where the narrator seems to withhold information temporarily to emphasize a narrative progression in Gallic technical abilities; here is a dramatic example.

How did the Romans respond to this display? They brought in devices that neutralized the enemy's technological advantage, then won by actual fighting.

> The soldiers were impeded in their siege-work by all those things and were slowed by constant cold and rain. Nonetheless, by constant labor they overcame all obstacles and in 25 days built a ramp 330 feet wide and 80 feet high. (7.24.1)

After Gallic attempts to destroy the new works were repulsed by the diligent response of the Roman soldiers, the Romans stormed the walls at an opportune moment and took the town, killing most of the inhabitants. The ramp itself was clearly huge, and the narrator says it took nearly a month to build, yet that construction takes only a sentence in the text; contrast the much longer description of the Rhine bridge built in a much shorter time. The Romans' decisive technological edge is presented casually and quite simply.[15] The narrative emphasis for the next two pages is then on actual fighting, first in defense of the new ramp, then inside Avaricum. When there is a direct technological confrontation, the narrator seems to want, on the one hand, to show decisive Roman superiority (even in the face of vast improvements on the part of the Gauls), but on the other hand, to change the subject altogether. Nor are the Romans captives of a single technology; they know what is needed in particular circumstances, even if what is needed is relative simplicity.

Even the final battle at Alesia shows a broadly similar pattern. Caesar had invested the Gallic leader in the stronghold of Alesia and was in turn besieged by a Gallic relief force, fenced off by a series of walls, trenches, and man-traps. After a second failed assault, the Gauls planned one final (as it happened) attempt, based on an assessment, made only now according to the narrative, of the weakest point of the Roman lines (7.83.1–4). The plan was apparently to have crack troops attack this point in particular, while the rest of the Gallic forces put pressure on the entire remaining length of the Roman fortifications simultaneously. The narrator again remarks that the Roman troops were really too few to hold the whole line at one time (7.84.3). In addition to the assault by troops, the Gauls from Alesia brought more devices to bear (the above plus poles and portable sheds: 7.84.1), and it was a Gallic ramp that eventually allowed the Roman defenses to be breached at one point, both covering buried sharpened sticks and bringing the Gauls up to the height of the Roman wall (7.85.6). This, the narrator says, was the crucial moment of the war, and he defines the crisis in terms of the Roman fortifications:

> Both sides realized that that was the time for them to strive their hardest. The Gauls, if they could not break through the fortifications, had no hope of salvation. The Romans, if they could hold on, could hope for an end to all of their labors. (7.85.2−3)

That is not, however, quite how the battle goes in the subsequent narrative. Eventually, the Gauls breached the Roman lines; Labienus sent to Caesar for aid "after the ramparts and trenches were unable to withstand the force of the enemy attack" (7.87.3, cf. 7.86.6). Caesar then appeared with reserve troops, and the battle, set up and fought over many pages, was won in a few sentences:[16] "Our men got rid of their spears and went at it with their swords. Suddenly they noted the [allied] cavalry behind them; other cohorts approached. The enemy turned tail. The cavalry fell on them in flight, and there was a great slaughter" (7.88.2−3).

In some respects, this battle followed the pattern of that at Avaricum. The competing technologies more or less canceled each other out, and the Romans easily won in the subsequent hand-to-hand combat.[17] Caesar takes pains to point out that his troops were not even using something as simple as a thrown spear. This very fact seems to be one of the main factors that turned the battle. What is different in this passage is that, in a sense, the Gauls overcame a Roman technological advantage, rather than the other way around. It was they who forced Caesar's hand. In another sense, however, such a reading misses one of the main emphases of the passages setting up the eventual battle. The Roman fortifications were essentially defensive. They were not designed to overcome opposing technology (e.g., the walls of Alesia). Rather, they were meant, according to Caesar's repeated claims, to neutralize the enemies' overwhelming numerical superiority and prevent the Romans from being surrounded and defeated by sheer numbers. From this point of view, the works were a complete success. Scattered soldiers held the length of both rings against the bulk of the Gallic forces, while the crack troops of both armies met in fairly straightforward combat at a single point.

There is a pattern underlying this technological back-and-forth. The Gauls are never completely without man-made devices, but, especially at the beginning, these are only partially distinct from natural features. This is in line with Caesar's general ethnographic distinction between Gauls and Germans, examined in the preceding chapter. The Germans are symbolically denied civilization altogether; the Gauls have an ordinary (if supposedly inferior) human civilization.[18] Over time, the Gauls acquire more technological sophistication. This takes the form both of devices of their own and of dealing better with what the Romans bring to bear. The improvement has two sources, as Caesar depicts it. In the first instance, the Gauls are said to be naturally skilled imitators (7.22.1).[19] Toward the end of *De Bello Gallico*, we also see developments that are implicitly or explicitly indigenous. This begins to go a little beyond the traditions. As Gallic technology becomes more formally sophisticated (in the sense of being more distinct from nature), it also becomes more effective. The Romans are never clearly defeated by Gallic technology, but they are from time to time forced to change their plans in response to it. The final confrontation at Alesia complicates the issue because there it is not entirely clear who wins the technological battle. Finally, as shown below, direct technological confrontations are rare. When they do occur, they are not made decisive (except, arguably, in the Romans' initial successes in taking Gallic *oppida*). Instead, resolution of the battle is deferred to other grounds.

One effect of all of this is to reinforce a theme already noted. The general thrust of Caesar's ethnography depicts the Gauls in concrete terms (relative to the Germans) and so makes them viable objects of appropriation. The increasing technological "normalization" of the Gauls (from a point of view from which, of course, only the Romans themselves count as fully "normal") has a similar effect. Gauls, unlike Germans, are people in the full sense, and so can be conquered and ruled in the same sense as the Romans' other subjects. More important, though, the technological progression introduces another point. The Gauls become an increasingly formidable enemy over the course of the war, and the change is due directly and indirectly to contact with the Romans. In Chapter 6, I consider how this danger-value contributes to the legitimization of the war; what I am interested in here is how it magnifies its significance. First, the mere "fact" that the Gauls are relatively similar to Romans tells against generic Roman prejudice against "barbarian" tribes. It makes the Gauls a more worthy opponent, and so increases the credit due to a commander who defeats them. Second, the increase in the Gauls' technical skills makes them not just an opponent, but a threat. On Caesar's account, they go from being barely out of the forests to near-equals (and arguably equals) in some respects. From this point of view, it was important to defeat them immediately. Otherwise, they might become not merely a worthy opponent to fight in their own homeland, but a positive threat to the Romans themselves. Thus Caesar's conquest contributes not only to Rome's majesty (and his own *dignitas*), but to its safety (and so, all the more, to Caesar's *dignitas*).

Virtus *in* De Bello Gallico

When Roman forces do finally get beyond technology and join battle, it is typically *virtus* that wins the day. The history of this term is discussed in more detail below, but it is necessary to establish a few points immediately. The etymological meaning of the word, which should have been transparent to any native Latin speaker, is "manliness."[20] In actual usage, the main sense of the word seems to have been "excellence shown in serving the state, especially the courage and endurance of an ideal soldier. . . . A soldier's *virtus* is, in short, all that leads to success in battle, with the notable exceptions of skill and wisdom."[21] There are a variety of extensions to other areas, such as politics or struggles against nature, but the military sense is the prototype.[22] *Virtus* is an unambiguously positive quality. Different persons might disagree on whether this or that act is an example of *virtus*, but the claim that something is *virtus* necessarily implies approval. The possibility of "excessive" *virtus* is almost unheard of (see note 46 below). There are two problems to be noted in the *De Bello Gallico*, both revolving around the question of what makes for *virtus*.

The first problem arises from the narrator's descriptions of Gallic softness. He establishes a hierarchy of strength in war ranging from the Germans (the toughest), to the Gauls near Germany (e.g., the Belgae), to the remaining Gauls. This hierarchy is established virtually at the beginning of the work, and is repeated throughout:

> Of all these [tribal groups,] the strongest are the Belgae, because they are very far away from the culture and humanity of our province,[23] and merchants rarely reach them and bring those things which contribute to the weakening of men's spirits (*effeminandos animos*), and they are next door to the Germans, who live across the Rhine, with whom they wage continual war. (1.1.3)

The phrasing varies, but, not surprisingly, the issue is usually put in terms of *virtus*;[24] even when it is not explicitly so phrased, toughness in battle remains the central theme of these rankings, as it was in the charges and counter-charges about *virtus* just discussed.[25] The narrator has a consistent explanation for the gradient of *virtus*, and it, too, is spelled out in the passage just cited about the Belgae. Proximity to and intercourse with "civilization" has harmed the pristine virtue of the tribes nearer to Rome. To the extent that different tribes have had more or less contact with Roman traders and the Roman province, they retain more or less *virtus*. By contrast, contact with the fierce Germans promotes *virtus*.[26] One could infer from this progression that the Romans would represent the bottom of the ladder. Yet, of course, the Romans consistently defeat not only Gauls but Germans in pitched battles (and not only in those contexts which arguably involve some trickery). Certainly neither the narrator nor Caesar ever explicitly denigrates Roman *virtus*. The problem, then, is this. How is it that exposure to one strong people (the Germans) strengthens, whereas exposure to another (the Romans) weakens?

The second question has to do with the importance of *virtus* to victory. Battles in which there was some direct technological confrontation were usually settled (according to the narrative) on some other grounds. Consider the successful Roman assault on Avaricum. After the fact, Vercingetorix tried to reassure his remaining forces by telling them that "neither by *virtus* nor in the line of battle had the Romans won victory, but by a certain artifice and skill in taking towns, a thing in which they themselves [the Gauls] were unskilled" (7.29.2).[27] Earlier parts of the narrative, to say nothing of the eventual battle at Alesia, undercut the claim of the last clause (5.42, 7.22.1), but the substance of the main assertion is harder to dismiss. The reader has already heard nearly the same thing, when the Helvetian leader Divico deprecated Caesar's victory over the single canton attempting to cross the Arar. He remarked that "[the Helvetii] had learned from their fathers and all their ancestors to fight more by *virtus* than by trickery (*dolo*) or relying on traps (*insidiis*)" (1.13.6). If one accepts the simple opposition of *virtus* to "trickery," then both of these hostile descriptions of the Romans are at least plausible. In the siege of Avaricum, it might have been argued that superior technology merely gave the Romans an opportunity actually to fight the Gauls, rather than watching them on their walls. However, the narrative as we have it goes out of its way to emphasize the confrontation of the devices on both sides. Insofar as the incident itself is ambiguous, it is striking that the narrator allows Vercingetorix to bring out the more negative (for the Romans) interpretation. One might then wonder whether the underlying opposition between *virtus* and trickery is suspect.

Against this possibility is the fact that each of the above criticisms of the Romans is mirrored later in its book by Caesar's disparagement of his enemies in very similar terms. Caesar reassures his troops that Ariovistus' history of victories is insignificant on the grounds that "he won more by planning and calculation than by *virtus*" (1.40.8). Later again, he consoles his soldiers for their defeat at Gergovia, warning them "not to attribute to the enemy's *virtus* what their advantage of place had accomplished" (7.53.1). Thus one cannot say in any straightforward way that the "barbarians" have simply gotten their values confused; their values look a lot like Caesar's.[28] Indeed, since these judgments address four different incidents, they could simply all be true (or at least their truth values could be mutually independent). This is a fair point, but it does not explain why Caesar allows the issue to come to the fore. The similarity of phrasing of all four passages (as well as the standing importance of *virtus* in Roman culture) suggests that we should wonder why the issue is raised so insistently.

To take the first question first, let us consider the sources of *virtus* in *De Bello Gallico*, beginning with the Germans. In the first book, Ariovistus warns Caesar that if he were to join battle, he would come to "understand what the unconquered Germans, who (having passed the last fourteen years outdoors) were very experienced in arms, could accomplish by *virtus*" (1.36.7). That is, the Germans are made to credit their own *virtus* to exercise both in the actual use of arms and in exposure to natural elements. This is not unlike the explanation of Germanic war strength expounded by the narrator elsewhere.[29] Later, moreover, we are given considerably more detail on the training the Germans undergo to reach this state. They are said to survive primarily by hunting and herding, not by farming in settled fashion. They expose themselves to cold and other elements. Even when not fighting actual wars, they "from earliest youth dedicate themselves to labor and toughness" (6.21.4). This style of life makes men who "from boyhood … are accustomed to do nothing contrary to their own wills," and it "nourishes their strength and gives them their huge bodies" (4.1.9).

It is easy for a modern reader to mistake these Germans for "noble savages," and the two types undoubtedly have shared features and a genealogical relationship. This should not, however, blind us to important differences. German *virtus* is nowhere claimed to be a "natural" characteristic in the sense of being inborn. Rather, it is a hard-won discipline arising from *confrontation*, with nature and with other tribes.[30] It is resistance to (external) nature that makes the Germans who they are. The Gauls can shield themselves from confrontations both with nature and with outsiders. They can avoid nature by the devices of civilization, and they are not subject to constant warfare, since the Romans are far more peaceable neighbors (to the south) than are the Germans (to the east).[31]

Whence, then, comes Roman *virtus*? From essentially the same sources as the German version: experience and exercise. For instance, the narrator at one point lists three factors that made for Roman success in a battle: "A favorable location, the lack of skill and tiredness of the enemy, and the *virtus* of [our] soldiers and their experience in prior battles" (3.19.3). More than such brief descriptions, though, the narrative itself shows experience to be the main source of martial virtue.

On the one hand, we can see this negatively in the actions of Caesar's staff officers. These "tribunes of the soldiers" were not men who had risen from the ranks, but young aristocrats who needed to accumulate some military experience before setting out on a political career.[32] Caesar reminds his audience of this fact early in his account of the abortive mutiny at Vesontio. The troops, mostly new recruits with little combat experience, grew fearful on hearing rumors of the German forces they were about to meet for the first time. "This [fear] arose first from the military tribunes, *praefecti*, and the others who, though having followed Caesar from Rome out of friendship, had no great experience in military matters" (1.39.2). It spread from them to the main force, and only then to the centurions (experienced officers in charge of company-sized units), who would have known better on their own. The result of this fear was a refusal, clothed in various pretexts, to engage the Germans. In a long (and successful) speech responding to this threat, Caesar asks why they have despaired of their own *virtus* (1.40.4). Indeed, soldiers being exhorted before battle throughout *De Bello Gallico* are almost formulaically urged to "remember their *virtus* of old."[33] The staff officers lack this *virtus* because they lack experience. A combination of exhortation and concession is required to persuade them to go on.

On the other hand, and fortunately for Caesar and the Romans, there is a way out. This kind of *virtus* can be acquired artificially. As the Vesontio episode showed, most of his troops were originally suspect for the same reason as the staff officers—inexperience. Early in the second book, Caesar was still uncertain of them, despite their success against Ariovistus' Germans. As both sides maneuvered in the vicinity of the Gallic town of Bibrax, "At first and because of the number of the enemy and their outstanding reputation for *virtus*, Caesar decided to hold off battle; instead each day he made trial in cavalry engagements of what the enemy could accomplish by *virtus* and what our side would dare" (2.8.1). Here he was uncertain of the *virtus* of his troops both in absolute terms and relative to the immediate enemy. Only after the results of these exploratory measures were favorable (and, not incidentally, gave the Roman troops further, controlled experience of their foes) did he join battle. Finally, by the middle of the book, accumulated experience has made the Roman troops completely reliable. Because of a sudden attack by the Nervii, most of the army lost touch with Caesar. Nonetheless, "two things helped out in the face of these difficulties—the knowledge and experience of the soldiers—because, having had the exercise of previous battles, they were just as well able to tell themselves what should be done as to be taught by others" (2.20.3). Part of the issue here is merely technical—how should the troops be disposed? Clearly, however, this was not an occasion to display that knowledge in the abstract. The Romans also needed the will to execute these designs. After this point, we hear of no further doubts about the *virtus* of Caesar's troops. The Romans, then, derive their strength and determination in battle from a source similar to the Germans'—the discipline imposed by experience—but it is achieved collectively rather than individually. This will be crucial to the issue of the *virtus*-gradient.

To expand on what has already been said about ordinary Latin usage, Büchner has defined *virtus,* as the term is used in pre-Caesarian Latin, as "not heroic-bold aggression, not vigorous action, which we connect with the form of the Greek hero. *Virtus* is rather steadfast holding-out, stubbornly pulling oneself up by the bootstraps, rigid unwaveringness." Eisenhut produces a few examples to show that this view is not entirely accurate; even as early as Plautus and Terence, *virtus* could have a more "aggressive" sense. Hence he prefers to make general "effectiveness" (*Tüchtigkeit*) the core meaning of the word.[34] Nonetheless, the strong tendency is for *virtus* to have the reactive sense of determination to continue a course of action in the face of resistance. When Caesar uses the term, one of the main components we have seen so far is determination to stand and fight. We have also already noted the formulaic instruction to the soldiers to "remember their *virtus* of old" as a form of encouragement, and *virtus* is elsewhere explicitly opposed to the fear of death (6.14.5). More specifically, the most common context for the display of *virtus* is tough, hand-to-hand combat.[35] Sometimes, it even seems to be used by synecdoche in place of a more literal word for such fighting.[36]

The will to fight these battles is not, however, sufficient either for success or for *virtus* specifically. The Gauls, supposedly the weakest of the three peoples, are usually eager for a fight (often seemingly more so than the Romans); this is in fact one of the features that Caesar chose to carry over from the ethnographic tradition. The problem, of course, is that this initial eagerness almost always leads the Gauls into defeat.[37] So, for instance, Labienus is able to lure the Treveri into attacking him before their German allies arrive to support them (6.7.6–9). It must be noted that Caesar never attributes such overeagerness to *virtus;* Gallic courage may not, then, despite first appearances, embody that virtue. After his own troops were repulsed in their (overly aggressive) assault on Gergovia, Caesar called a meeting to criticize them and tell them what they must do in the future. His summary instructions were that "he desires no less restraint (*modestiam*)[38] and self-control (*temperantiam*) from a soldier than *virtus* and greatness of soul (*animi magnitudinem*)" (7.52.4). Here *virtus* has a very aggressive sense, as shown both by the term with which it is paired[39] and by the restraint and self-control to which it is contrasted. What is problematic here is that *virtus,* which had heretofore been an unambiguously positive quality (as is normal in Latin), is shown now to be (at best) incomplete. Moreover, while *virtus* certainly entails determination and mental toughness, we may wish to add that it is not in itself an aggressive tendency. In fact, Caesar can use it in a situation of positive restraint:

> But so great was the *virtus* of the soldiers and their presence of mind was such that, although they were being scorched by flame on all sides and pressed by the greatest mass of missiles and they recognized that all their baggage and all their fortunes were going up in flames, not only did no one leave the palisade to flee, but scarcely did anyone even look backward. They all fought hard and most bravely. (5.43.4)

The Roman soldiers are manning the walls of their camp while their supplies burn behind them. Now these soldiers are certainly engaged in close combat, but their *virtus* is not required to counteract fear of the Gauls in front of them. Rather, it keeps them from turning to face a different but still daunting challenge. Though neither redefines the term, the passages do set up a tension within the value system of *De Bello Gallico*—between the meaning of *virtus* and its valorization—that will shortly result in explicit redefinition in more abstract terms.

Having said that *virtus* is not necessarily a spur to aggression, let me offer a more positive and more thoroughgoing redefinition. *Virtus, De Bello Gallico* implies, is the mental toughness to do what is required of one. Germans acquire it by individual exercise in confrontation, as we have noted, with nature and with enemies in battle. Though obviously effective to a certain extent, this approach is fatally self-limiting. Its products are individually strong warriors who, "accustomed from boyhood to no duty or discipline, do nothing at all that they do not wish to do" (4.1.9). Collectively, then, their *virtus* breaks down because the individual's will may not correspond to what duty or necessity require. Romans to some extent acquire *virtus* in the same way, as we have also noted. But more important, they acquire it as well by submission to authority. Roman soldiers do what they must because they are told to do so, whether that is by fighting or not fighting. For instance, in the passage quoted above in which Caesar's formerly raw recruits have at last become completely trustworthy, the visible sign of this is that they fight as if they were being given orders (2.20.3). The act of fighting, though, is not the touchstone, as in a more traditional view. Rather, it is obedience under difficult circumstances.

This modification of the sense of *virtus* is made explicit by a Gallic leader named Critognatus. While the Gallic army at Alesia awaited the as yet uncertain arrival of the relief force and supplies ran low, there was some debate about what they should do. An Arvernian named Critognatus, in by far the longest piece of direct discourse in *De Bello Gallico*, argued against those who proposed to break out of the town and through the Roman lines. This proposal, he admitted, seemed to reflect the "memory of [our] virtue of old" (7.77.4). The formulaic phrase is used in its conventional context of battle lust. Critognatus, however, immediately turned their logic on its head. "That is softness of spirit (*animi ... mollitia*), not *virtus*, not to be able to bear want for a little while" (7.77.5). He then argued that, although loss of life should not itself count for anything, this plan would in fact be counterproductive in terms of winning the war for Gaul as a whole. They must therefore wait out the siege inside the town.

Implicit in Critognatus' phrasing is an argument about the nature of *virtus*. As noted above, the transparent etymological sense of the word is "manliness." Softness, especially as expressed by the *moll-* root, is one of the most important stereotypical characteristics of the feminine in Roman culture.[40] The narrator himself previously opposed *virtus* to softness and effeminacy (2.15.4).[41] Thus Critognatus offers not only an alternative description of the opposing plan, but one that suggests that the justification for that plan by appeal to *virtus* is incoherent. Anything that is "soft" in its particular circumstance could not possibly count as *virtus*, whatever the usual value placed on physical courage. Sometimes not fighting is more manly.

Critognatus also remarks that "those who willingly offer themselves to death are more easily found than those who can bear suffering patiently (*patienter*)" (7.77.5). The patient man does not give in to his suffering; this is the kind of internal strength we have discussed. But there is a problem with "patience." It, too, can suggest effeminacy.[42] Men, according to the stereotype, are supposed to act, whereas women are acted on (*pati*). Sometimes "passivity" is a code word for sexual receptivity, but even the broader sense of the word takes on gendered implications. If you control yourself (internally), you are arguably giving in to external forces. Depending on how the control metaphor is applied, its force in precisely the same circumstance can be radically different. The man who can "take it" is either particularly strong or particularly weak. This is an ambiguity that a skilled rhetorician like Caesar can exploit.

Caesar, then, essentially preserves the structure of the meaning of *virtus*, but changes its content significantly by setting it in a somewhat unusual metaphorical context. He can support this move by implicit appeal to yet another traditional feature of *virtus*, its highly positive associations. If everyone grants that *virtus* is a good thing, then it is easy to argue that supposed "*virtus*" that leads to failure is not *virtus* after all.[43] And of course, it is Caesar's version of *virtus* that brings success. Moreover, our original definition included "excellence shown in serving the state," and the element of benefit to the community has been noted by most authorities on the subject.[44] This is part of a larger pattern. Republican Romans rarely speak of any "virtue" as being exercised for its own sake; traditionally all virtues directly benefit the community.[45] Caesar's narrative presents situations in which a more aggressive style of *virtus* would harm not just individual heroes, but the Roman cause more generally.[46] Such stories, then, constitute an implicit argument for Caesar's perspective on *virtus*.

Before proceeding, I should address two alternative readings of the above facts that have been suggested to me. I contend here that Caesar locates a tension within the nature of *virtus:* resisting outside forces (like the enemy) versus resisting internal ones (like the urge to rush into battle too soon). Might this not be better described as the more conventional opposition between aggressive *virtus* and restraining *disciplina* ("discipline")?[47] Even I will refer to the Caesarian version of *virtus* as "disciplinary." Nonetheless, Caesar has merged the two ideas, somewhat contrary to tradition. First, this way of framing the issue would have been so natural that it must count against this view that Caesar does not explicitly address it. In fact, he uses *disciplina* of Roman forces only twice, and both uses are in contexts where the word drives combat forward (1.40.6, 6.1.4). If anything, he leads the reader away from the "conventional" usage. Moreover, to make sense, the *virtus-disciplina* opposition requires the presence of an actual general giving orders. As we shall see shortly, Caesar's version allows for "virtual" leaders. Finally, the reconfiguration of *virtus* does appear explicitly in Critognatus' speech. One could question his reliability (see below), but he does frame the issue as I have suggested. Lendon has argued that the main tension is between an essentially Greek view that character, of which *virtus* would be a component, was not important to victory, and a more Roman and "atavistic" emphasis on that character.[48] As a matter of principle, I would prefer not to see Caesar at the mercy of his sources (especially in the case of a notion so thematized in a given work), but in this case there are specific reasons to favor the internal-conflict explanation. To the extent that *virtus* is subordinated to "stratagem" (preferred by the Greeks to all else) in some passages, it is a fairly impoverished notion of strategy at stake (that is, waiting for the right moment). The real opposition in *De Bello Gallico* is simply whether to fight or not. That *virtus* can be deliberately acquired in itself suggests a modification of earlier views of character. In the light of all this, the explicit redefinition or revision of *virtus* in Critognatus' speech should be taken seriously. The resulting, inner-directed *virtus* is comprehensible, if not self-evident, in Roman terms, and it gives *virtus* back its certain centrality to success in battle.

Logically, one could hold a more disciplinary view of *virtus*, yet keep it at an individual level. In Caesar's version, however, hierarchy does have an important role in creating *virtus*. We see this in a recurrent motif of the combat scenes in *De Bello Gallico*—visual connection with an audience. Before the battle with Ariovistus' army in the first book, Caesar carefully assigns officers to each of the legions, "so that each one might have them as witnesses of their *virtus*" (1.52.1). The sea battle with the Veneti was won easily, "and all the more so because it took place in the sight of Caesar and the whole army, so that no deed of special valor could remain hidden" (3.14.8). The final battle at Alesia is described as a similar spectacle: "Because it took place in the sight of all, neither things rightly nor foully done could be hidden, and both desire for praise and fear of ignominy excited both sides to *virtus*" (7.80.5). To some extent, these passages merely reflect the spectacular character of Roman culture in general. A common Roman view conceived of value as a function of community judgment, rather than of absolute standards. This in turn encouraged the view that human activity took place as if onstage, with the community as a (judging) audience.[49] So, Livy and his characters, for instance, tend to stage battles as well as other events as spectacles.[50] The cases in *De Bello Gallico*, however, have special characteristics of their own. In all three instances noted above, the audience is not merely an inevitable fact, but a spur to success and, explicitly in two of those cases, to greater *virtus*. Furthermore, in the first two instances, the audience is not simply anonymous or composed solely of peers; it pointedly includes superior officers (legates in one case, Caesar in the other). Given these precedents, the reader is then aware that the "all" who look on at Alesia include Caesar and his officers. The gaze that brings out *virtus* (and so success) is especially one from above. It works because in locating external judgment particularly in the commander, it aligns success with discipline and failure with disobedience.

The role of hierarchy in creating *virtus* is even clearer in several passages where the audience looking on is virtual, not real. The first of these is one we have already noted twice: the dutiful soldiers who, when attacked suddenly by the Gauls, "were able to give themselves orders no less comfortably than to be instructed by others" (2.20.3). This is a matter of a surprise attack, but a similar situation also arises in two set-piece battles. Both involve Caesar's chief lieutenant Labienus. In the first case, seeing that his detachment was about to be attacked by a group of Gauls, he encouraged his soldiers to fight bravely: "Show the same *virtus* under my leadership that you often showed the General, and imagine that he is present and watches these doings face-to-face" (6.8.4). Part of the hierarchy was missing, so Labienus supplied it rhetorically, and the Romans went on to victory. A similar situation occurs in the following book. After the Roman repulse at Gergovia, Labienus' force was attacked by a Gallic contingent at Lutetia (now Paris). Again he encouraged his troops to imagine Caesar's presence: "Labienus urged the soldiers … to imagine Caesar himself, under whose leadership they had often overcome the enemy, was actually present there" (7.62.2). Again, the Romans won. In both cases, nearly the entire normal chain of command is physically present, but Caesar himself is engaged elsewhere. Both times, Labienus nonetheless manages to fill that slot at the top virtually.

These incidents all involve Roman successes. There are, however, occasions when the Romans fail to establish the appropriate hierarchy, whether in reality or virtually. When this happens, they lose. Take the assault on Gergovia, the one clear defeat for Roman troops under Caesar's command. The problems there were foreshadowed when Caesar gave his instructions to the individual legates before the Roman assault on an undermanned hilltop nearby:

> First of all, he warns them to contain the soldiers lest they go too far out of eagerness to fight or hope of booty; he explains the problems posed by the unfavorable terrain, how this could be changed by speed alone, and that the point is to seize an opportunity, not to fight a battle. (7.45.9–10)

The soldiers quickly achieved their limited objective, and Caesar ordered the recall to be sounded. At this point, two problems supervened. First, topography prevented most of the soldiers from hearing the horns used to transmit the order. Second, the soldiers, buoyed up by their success so far, ignored their officers' attempts to hold them back, and instead decided to pursue the Gauls up to the walls of the town (7.47.2–3). The narrator says, "They judged nothing so difficult that they could not achieve it by their *virtus*" (7.47.3; cf. 7.50.1), whereas the Gauls trusted in numbers and superior position (7.50.1). This sets up a somewhat unusual tension between Caesar's authority and tactical judgment (which would predict trouble for the Romans) and the invocation of the *virtus* of the soldiers (which otherwise signals Roman victory). The Romans, attacked from all sides, were eventually forced to withdraw with heavy losses. Caesar's orders turned out to be more important than his troops' individual willingness to fight. It is important to note that the author wants to have it both ways in these battles. The troops depend on Caesar's more or less direct command for their success. Yet, on the one hand, losing contact with him is represented as exceptional, when in fact it must have been the norm on the ancient battlefield;[51] on the other hand, even in circumstances when Caesar was clearly not exercising real control (the sea battle with the Veneti, Labienus' campaigns), his symbolic presence was made to suffice. The narrative goes to some lengths to construct the soldiers' dependence on their commander, and in particular the strain it puts on a conventional notion of *virtus*.

We can also see the mechanism clearly in a set of incidents involving lower levels of the chain of command. While Caesar was fighting his second, more ambitious campaign in Britain in 54, there was a large-scale uprising of Gallic tribes on the continent. Caesar hurried back to quash this, but many units of his army had previously been ordered into their winter quarters, and most of them had to decide essentially on their own how best to fight. Among these were the legion and a half jointly commanded by Caesar's legates Quintus Titurius Sabinus and Lucius Aurunculeius Cotta. Ambiorix, leader of the Eburones, told the legates that he had been forced to join this uprising against his will (and despite his personal ties to Caesar) by the common council of the Gauls. Though he could not allow the Romans to remain where they were, he would give them safe passage to rejoin the rest of the army. The Roman commanders were uncertain whether to trust the Gauls and leave their secure base without Caesar's orders. As a result, they brought the matter "before a meeting and there [was] a great controversy" among the legates, along with officers on both sides (5.28.2).[52] After considerable discussion of the merits of accepting safe passage versus staying at the base, the debate concluded with anonymous complaints about the very fact that there was disagreement.

The meeting broke up. They [apparently the officers] took each legate and begged that they not lead everything into the gravest danger by their disagreement and stubbornness. There was no problem, whether they stayed or left, so long as all shared and approved of one plan. Otherwise they could see no hope of salvation in disagreement. (5.31.1–2)

Eventually Cotta gave in, and they decided to leave the camp. Shortly thereafter the Romans were ambushed by Ambiorix's forces, and, after hard fighting on both sides, were largely wiped out. On one level, the disaster was obviously caused by Titurius' misjudgment of the Gauls. More generally, however, it is an example of the kind of authority problem at which we have been looking. Titurius gave in to the pressure to take action when staying in place would have been more beneficial—hence Cotta's argument that the Romans should not do anything "rashly" (*temere*, 5.28.3). Caesar later ratified this judgment when he told the troops that they suffered their losses "due to the fault and *temeritas* of the legate" (5.52.6).[53] Moreover, this failure of nerve was part of a failure of command. First of all, as Cotta and his supporters pointed out, they should have waited for aid from Caesar (5.28.6). Second, in the absence of Caesar both in person and in spirit, the legates did not provide even a semblance of authority: contrast the way Labienus evoked Caesar's presence to inspire his troops in the commander's physical absence. Finally, the legates themselves did not provide a model of authoritative leadership. They held a debate instead of giving orders. The passage quoted above (5.31.1–2) shows that not only did the characters themselves recognize the lack, but they also connected that lack to their imminent failure.

Ambiorix then moved quickly to attack Quintus Cicero and his legion in its camp, before they could get news of what had happened to Titurius and Cotta. He used precisely the same ploy, offering safe passage if only the Romans would leave this particular site. Cicero offered the conventional Roman reply that he would not negotiate with an enemy under arms (5.41.7). Then followed the siege of the Roman camp discussed above. The text goes to some lengths to point out the difficulties Cicero faced in communicating with Caesar. His initial round of messengers was captured (5.40.1), as was the second (5.45.1). When finally a Gallic turncoat succeeded in getting the news through to Caesar, the return message promising aid remained unnoticed for two days, tied to a spear stuck in a Roman tower (5.48.8). As soon as Cicero read the letter to his troops, signs of the relief force appeared over the horizon anyway, and the Gauls gave up their siege. Unlike Titurius, Cicero did not give in to the urge to take action; instead, he stood pat until he received orders to the contrary.

The difficulties of communication (which are mentioned only in this episode, though we may suspect they were common throughout the course of the war) emphasize his steadfastness. Nor did Cicero call for discussion on the issues; he simply gave the appropriate orders. The soldiers responded to this with the "*virtus* and presence of mind" to hold their stations, even as parts of the camp burned behind them (5.43.4). The Gallic stratagem was essentially the same in both cases, and their forces were, if anything, larger the second time around. Cicero's force was smaller than Titurius' and Cotta's. The different result under these circumstances was due precisely to Cicero's (and his soldiers') strategic restraint based on obedience to authority.[54] In the end, they engaged in as much fighting as Titurius and Cotta and their troops did, if not more, but because of their steadfastness they did so on their own terms.

The point of the double paradigm as I have framed it is fairly clear. Unfortunately, without the benefit of that particular version to read, Cicero did not learn the lesson of his own story. In the next book, we again find him in charge of an isolated encampment, here at Aduatuca. A German plundering expedition had come across the Rhine, and their initial Gallic victims sought to redirect them to Cicero's allegedly undermanned garrison. Cicero had strict orders from Caesar to keep his soldiers inside the camp in case some trouble should arise while the latter was attempting to intercept Ambiorix (6.33.3). After about a week of diligent obedience, however,

> doubting that Caesar would keep his promise about the date of his return (since he heard that [Caesar] had gone further than planned, and no report had been received about his return), and also moved by voices that described his patience as virtually a siege ... he sends five cohorts to gather grain in the nearby fields. (6.36.2–3)

A number of camp-followers also took the opportunity to leave the walls. The Germans, of course, arrived at precisely this moment. There was fierce fighting, and most of the Roman soldiers were able to return safely to the camp only because of the self-sacrifice of a number of recently promoted centurions who fell fighting to prove themselves worthy of their new positions (6.40.7–8). Once the Romans returned to their camp, the Germans gave up their attempt and left. Though the raw number of casualties is not given, it seems to have been substantial. Furthermore, in Roman casualty reports, "quality" (i.e., a conflation of rank and social standing) can be as important as quantity.[55] The loss of a large number of centurions is thus particularly serious. Unlike Titurius and Cotta's force, Cicero's did not meet annihilation, but, according to Caesar's assessment shortly thereafter, this was largely a matter of good fortune (6.42.2). Cicero's problems began when he started to disobey Caesar's orders. Worse still, he was not merely substituting his own judgment for that of the commander, but obeying his own subordinates; it was at their prompting that he released them from the camp. Naturally, the double violation of hierarchy was punished by subsequent events, though not as harshly as it might have been.

The Gallic Assimilation of Virtus

In the face of the near-mutiny at Vesontio, Caesar delivered a long exhortation (in indirect discourse) to his troops. After saying a few words about the enemy, he addressed the subject of the Romans themselves and asked what possible basis there could be for their fear. "Why did they [the soldiers] despair over either their own *virtus* or his [Caesar's] diligence?" (1.40.4). It was to the former issue he turned first, listing similar forces of northern barbarians previously defeated—the Cimbri and Teutons beaten by the Roman general Marius (in 102–101), the Northerners who fought in Spartacus' slave revolt defeated by Crassus and Pompey (73–71), and these Germans, often defeated by the very Helvetii that Caesar's men had just crushed.

   In part, these remarks are intended to downplay the strength of the enemy forces and so to calm the troops. However, as James has argued, they also serve performatively to increase the *virtus* of Caesar's army. It does so by providing these relatively raw troops with the experience and discipline, albeit vicariously, that are the source of martial virtue.[56] Caesar's attempt to educate his soldiers into *virtus* is intracultural, but his speech itself claims that the same process could work interculturally. The slave war had been won, he says, despite the fact that "the experience and discipline that they had acquired from us" brought extra strength to the other side (1.40.5). The Romans had not, of course, been trying to create a fighting force out of their own slaves.[57] Mere exposure to superior Roman discipline in carrying out their various tasks brought about this improvement. If this were the case, then it should have been possible in principle for the Gauls to acquire Roman-style fighting skill *and* discipline, just as they acquired Roman technological sophistication over time.

   This is precisely what happens in the narrative of *De Bello Gallico*. The Gauls do learn to fight in a more "Roman" way. Unlike the assimilation of engineering technologies, however, this phenomenon is largely restricted to the last book. There it is closely tied to the rise of the Arvernian noble

Vercingetorix to leadership of the entire Gallic war effort. On the narrator's account, Caesar was distracted in the early part of 52 by political chaos back in Rome, which had brought the government there nearly to a standstill.[58] (There is likely some truth to this story, though the fact that Caesar was also levying new troops might equally suggest foreign or domestic adventures.) In any case, the Gauls apparently took the commotion as an occasion for large-scale, concerted resistance to the presence the Romans had established in their country. The first overt act of this resistance, according to the narration, was the massacre of all Roman citizens, mostly civilian businessmen, at the town of Cenabum (7.3.1).[59] The young Vercingetorix supposedly saw in this act an incipient opportunity both to free his people from the Romans and to recover the personal preeminence once held by his father, but currently denied to him (7.4.1–2).

As the revolt spread, so did Vercingetorix's authority; more and more tribes threw their support behind him. This, it should be noted, runs counter to the type carefully established in the Gallic ethnography, and indeed, throughout the entire earlier narrative. The Gauls were, as noted in the previous chapter, written as a people defined by division. The present chapter has noted how that division leads to disaster; success comes from obedience to a single authority. The Gauls, as a nation of Titurii, had not been able to compete with Rome. Vercingetorix realized this and did something about it. For instance, during the battle for Avaricum, he was attacked by the others for going on a mission with the cavalry to harass Caesar's foragers, without leaving anyone behind with the authority to engage the Romans (7.20.1). He said in response:

> He had intentionally failed to hand over command to anyone when he left, lest this person be impelled to start a fight because of the eagerness of the masses. He saw that all were spoiling for such a turn of events because of their softness of mind, since they were not able to bear labor any longer. (7.20.5)

Then he went on to produce the fake Roman soldiers to support his claim that his strategy is working.

Whereas Caesar could reasonably hope that his subordinates would maintain discipline in his physical absence, Vercingetorix's grip is less sure. He cannot afford to create a subordinate authority lest it become an alternate authority and the Gallic pattern of division reappear. He also takes it as self-evident that the result of such a division would be (in structural terms) a complete breakdown of order in which the soldiers tell the commanders what to do, and (in practical terms) a quick attack on the Romans. Again, failure of discipline is not tied to simple cowardice, but to ultimately unproductive aggression. This is characterized as weakness; his own people, he says, suffer from "softness of mind" and are "unable to bear labors." Caesar's Vercingetorix has read the war itself in much the same way as I have read Caesar's narrative.[60] When Avaricum fell shortly thereafter, Vercingetorix rightly pointed out that he had not wanted to defend it in the first place, and that the decision to do so was due to "the imprudence of the Bituriges and the excessive appeasement by the rest" (7.29.4). In the light of what had gone before, this was not only an argument for the superiority in practice of Vercingetorix's individual wisdom, but for the superiority in principle of deferring to the wisdom of a single individual.

Despite the Gauls' eventual defeat at Avaricum, the battle does include one of the clearest signs of their "Romanization" by Vercingetorix, as noted already by Mannetter.[61] The relevant episode takes place shortly after the description of the *opus Gallicum* defensive works and of the Roman countermeasures. The narrator even calls attention to it as something "that seemed worthy of memory and [that] we thought not to be passed over in silence" (7.25.1). The story he then tells is of a series of Gauls who approached the Roman works with various incendiary devices and tried to set fire to them. The first was killed by Roman artillery fire and was immediately replaced by another. This action was then repeated a second and a third time, until all the Gauls in the area were gone. We may build on Mannetter's observation by characterizing more precisely what is Roman about this particular episode. It is a motif of *De Bello Gallico* that, whereas outnumbered Roman soldiers often have to fight without a break, Gauls come in successive waves to relieve each other.[62] In fact, precisely this happens earlier in the very sentence announcing the event "worthy of memory." The motif is in line with the traditional view of northern barbarians as virtually uncountable. Here, the size of the action shows that sheer Gallic numbers are not at stake; what is on display is their determination.[63] Moreover, though perhaps suicidal, the Gallic assault was certainly controlled. Exactly one person was setting fires at a time. If the Gauls had succeeded, much would have been gained for their side; when they failed, little was lost. In this respect, the episode resembles the sally of Pullo and Vorenus two books earlier. Vercingetorix's direction is not invoked directly here, but the Gauls are now acting with the discipline and submission to authority characteristic of Roman soldiers. This keeps them focused on the common good, rather than individual glory.

Of course, the Gallic troops were new to this. So Vercingetorix tested and exercised them, just as Caesar had done with his new recruits at the beginning of the work (2.8.1). "He did not let a day pass without trial (by equestrian combat) of what courage and *virtus* there were in each of his men" (7.36.4). Their courage was apparently increased by this exercise, which took the form of small, controlled bouts of aggression. They were being Romanized. That is, not only did they take on new skills, but the ensemble of exercises inculcated submission to hierarchy, and so to a more robust type of *virtus* than is available from confrontation with nature. Roman technique per se was less important than its *virtus* consequences. And although Vercingetorix may originally have accused his followers of being unable to bear labor, that soon changed under his leadership. Once his position had been secured by the fall of Avaricum, "the Gauls first at this time resolved to fortify their camps, and these folk, unaccustomed as they were to labor, were so alarmed that they judged that they must suffer whatever was commanded of them" (7.30.4). The importance of the point is further emphasized by the fact that this remark is not strictly true. It ignores the real first time in *De Bello Gallico* that the Gauls learned to fortify their camps (3.23.6).

As noted above, Vercingetorix proposed a "scorched-earth" policy to deny the Romans access to supplies. Villages and fields would be burned wherever the Romans might go. The Romans would be harassed by cavalry whenever they left their camps, but apparently the Gauls would not offer open battle or assault Roman strongholds. First and foremost, the Gauls would not attempt to defend their own large towns; these would be burned, too. In a way, this is reminiscent of Caesar's Germans or of Herodotus' Scythians. The Gauls were to turn themselves virtually into placeless nomads. There are, however, several important differences. First, for the Germans and Scythians, nomadism was said to be a strategic matter; it was the way they had always lived. For the Gauls, it was a tactical response to a specific situation. Vercingetorix began by asserting that "every effort had to be made to this end: that the Romans be prohibited from forage and other supply" (7.14.2). This is not defensive nomadism (where there is "no 'there,' there"), but part of a larger strategy that will (eventually) harm the enemy. Second, as the Gauls were not nomads before, so they would not be in the future. Vercingetorix has a clear end-point in sight. Third, this nomadism is spatially limited. Supposedly impregnable places are spared, as are places in which the Romans appear by surprise (7.56.5). Finally, this nomadism is a tactic of an identifiable individual, not of the culture as a whole. Though the Gauls temporarily give up some localization in space, they gain a social center.[64] This action is more like

Quintus Fabius Maximus "the delayer," hero of the Second Punic War, than like the Scythians or Ariovistus. The superficial reversion to a more primitive condition should not, then, distract attention from Vercingetorix's appropriation of the Romans' civilized style of *virtus*.

Despite all this, the Gauls did lose. Their failure on the field was mirrored by a last-minute failure of discipline. Once Vercingetorix had taken shelter at Alesia, but before the Romans had completed their fortifications, he sent messengers to all the Gallic tribes asking that they send all men of an age to bear arms (7.71.2). Instead, the Gauls held a council where explicit, smaller levies were exacted from the various tribes (7.75.1). Not only did they fail to follow the specifics of Vercingetorix's orders, but the very mechanism of calling a meeting undercut his authority (as with Roman legates' *consilia*).[65] Even the plan they did work out was itself compromised by disobedience. "The Bellovaci did not fill out the required number because, they said, they would wage war with the Romans in their own name and according to their own judgment, nor would they obey the command of anyone" (7.75.5).[66] This was essentially the problem Vercingetorix had foreseen when he left no commander in charge of the troops at Avaricum; an alternative authority would start making its own decisions.[67] Even worse here, in the lack of a clear authority, the Gauls reverted to their usual bickering and made the decision by committee. And the breakdown in authority was more fundamental even than that. Within Alesia, where Vercingetorix was present, a council was still called to discuss strategy. This is the context of Critognatus' speech urging the Gauls to hold their position absolutely as long as possible. The great irony here is that whereas the content of the speech urges a Romanized view of *virtus* and the conduct of war, the very fact that the speech could be given (and given by a character who makes no other appearance in the work) suggests that that message is in vain. Strategic questions are not, in this text, matters for debate; they are the subject of a commander's orders. Unlike some earlier councils, neither the one inside Alesia nor the one outside produced any obviously "wrong" result. It is not clear that their decisions led directly to the eventual defeat, or that one of the other plans proposed would have had a better outcome. Instead, it is left to the reader to draw the conclusion that an army that argues like this one ultimately fights like this one—inadequately. The author has not, after all, replaced traditional *virtus* with an entirely new virtue; rather, he has made that tough fighting spirit dependent on discipline. Vercingetorix tried to teach his people that lesson, but at the crucial moment they rejected it.[68] They had not internalized his lessons well enough to fight for a "virtual" Vercingetorix.[69]

Conclusion

Undoubtedly there was real borrowing of Roman technology (and perhaps of tactics as well) by the Gauls. Burns has argued that there is archeological evidence for considerable "transculturation" at this period, that is, mutual influence of all three cultures (Roman, Gallic, German) on each other.[70] This, however, does not account for what Caesar narrates. First, the borrowing he depicts is almost entirely one-way: the Gauls take on various Roman customs, but not the reverse.[71] Second, the Germans do not participate in the technology transfer at all. Third, Caesar only gradually reveals indigenous technologies (Aquitanian siegecraft, *opus Gallicum*) in order of increasing sophistication. This crescendo resonates with the Gauls' growing skill in borrowed technologies and so exaggerates the importance of the latter. Fourth, Caesar's knowledge of the details of the Gallic command structure is dubious, and he certainly could not have known the text of the Gallic speeches he reproduces (if they were in fact ever given). Finally, Caesar suppresses the greenness of his own recruits after early in Book 2. Despite the fact that Caesar holds at least three further levies totaling more than five legions (5.24.4, 6.1.4, 7.1.1), there is only one mention of trouble with new soldiers (6.39.2), and none of further training. Hence, the appropriation of *virtus* in Book 7 is also largely fictional (even if it happens to coincide with the truth, though we will never know). The constructed events emphasize unidirectional borrowing to the advantage of the Gauls, coloring the reading even of descriptions that are arguably relatively accurate.

The situation on the whole is like what we have seen already in the previous chapter with respect to the distinction between Gauls and Germans. Caesarian descriptions are likely inspired by certain real features of the immediate circumstances, but may freely exaggerate or depart from those circumstances. Even if this were not the case, we would be entitled to inquire as to the effects of Caesar's emphasis of certain facts over others. As it is, we can see even more elaborate textual constructions that actually demand explanation in terms of both those effects and the intentions behind them.

Caesar's version of *virtus* in *De Bello Gallico* has several effects. First, we can now resolve the contradictory applications of the *virtus*/trickery opposition. As a learned skill, *virtus* is not radically different from other, more technical skills, such as siege warfare. The former is certainly held (by all parties) to be more important, but different skills are better described as levels in a hierarchy than as opposites (as the characters at first appear to describe them). And insofar as the substance of this learned skill is fighting at the appropriate times—both in starting a battle and in not giving up prematurely—then the opposition to trickery is more complicated than it first appears. The Romans never simply lie to the opposition, as Ambiorix does to Titurius and Cotta and later to Cicero. Nor do they seize or attack ambassadors, as it was claimed the opposition habitually did.[72] Instead, the Romans encourage the Gauls' tendency to join battle even on unfavorable terms by not communicating at all. Even when Caesar tells the Helvetii that he will consider their request to go through Roman territory (to allow his own troops to gather), nothing he says is strictly false. Here, then, a principled distinction might be drawn in the work's terms between legitimate strategy and illegitimate trickery (though Caesar never in fact makes such an argument explicitly). Were that done, moreover, the Gauls would come out on the wrong side of the line and the Romans on the right one. The opposition adduced by the Gauls between trickery and *virtus* would have been comprehensible, even plausible, in isolation, but in the context of this work, it shows their misunderstanding of the terms. Caesar's "trickery" is simply an exploitation of the fact that the Gauls lack the skills and discipline of his own troops.

To the extent that *virtus* is technological, its assimilation by the Gauls has consequences like those of their acquisition of siegecraft. The Gauls become a more formidable foe as the war goes on, making Caesar's victory more dramatic. They also become a greater threat as the war goes on, making Caesar's victory more valuable as well. Not only do these arguments carry over from the discussion of sieges and logistics, but they are even stronger here. *Virtus* is more central than engineering, both morally and practically, both to the work and to Roman thought in general. Here we find the most important consequence of the contrast between Gauls and Germans. Because of their individual discipline, the Germans were better fighters than the Gauls when Caesar first found the two groups; they were the greater short-term opposition and short-term conquest. However, because the Gauls were (in the *De Bello Gallico* and in the tradition more generally) good imitators, and because the crucial war-making skills are imitable, they became the long-term prize. Both sides are made to say that this war will be the last in Gaul; whoever wins will control Gaul ever after.[73] Some of the resonances of this claim will be explored in Chapter 6, but one point can be made here. Caesar not only wins this war, but, according to his own description, he wins it just in time. The Gauls under Vercingetorix were never completely able to put the Romans' lessons to work, but one can imagine the great foe they might have become had a "lesser" general been unable to break them while they were still learning.

Vercingetorix even threatened that a united Gaul could not be stopped by the entire world (*orbis terrarum*, 7.29.6).

We also noted in the discussion of siegeworks that, although the Gauls approached Roman levels of skill, they never clearly caught up. Caesar, whether out of respect for national pride or because he wants to minimize any failings in his personal army, keeps a fine tension between Gallic progress and Roman superiority. The same is the case with *virtus*. Even when it looks like the Gauls have mastered it (early in Book 7), they break down at the last moment.

There is another element that is also used to counter-balance the Gauls' progress in practical matters. Two moral themes remain consistently anti-Gallic throughout. First is the notion of Gallic cruelty. This was one of the features attributed to the Gauls both by the ethnography and by the main narrative; Caesar refers at least eight times to Gallic torture (never to Roman). Nor is this merely an expedient of war. Other Gauls are more often the victims of Gallic cruelty than Romans. There is a pattern to these references: they become denser over the course of the work.[74] None of this is paralleled by Roman behavior. It is of course true that Caesar admits to a number of (from a modern point of view) atrocities in the course of the war.[75] Several times he has entire towns or tribes killed or, more often, sold into slavery. Yet, as Collins has pointed out, these events are noted frankly, even casually. This is not, to Caesar, cruelty, nor did he himself have anyone tortured. Acco, the leader of an abortive revolt, is executed by the *more maiorum supplicium* (6.44.2), that is, scourging followed by decapitation. He, however, was tried in a formal judicial proceeding (*quaestio*). Collins implies that the punishment was unjust because the conspirators had already been pardoned (6.4.3), but it is strongly suggested there that Caesar was merely putting off a reckoning for tactical reasons.[76] Even the narrator picks up the theme of cruelty by the last book. Normally, as we shall see in Chapter 5, the narrator avoids strongly evaluative language. Critognatus' speech is marked in advance for his "singular and nefarious cruelty" (7.77.3). Here, the cruelty at issue is cannibalism of the elderly and useless. Of course, the Romans do not do this either.[77] Thus, over the course of the work, although the Gauls become more like the Romans in skill, they become less like them in humanity. The second moral theme, which we have already discussed, is Gallic treachery. Thus, whereas the Gauls gain ground in practical matters, Caesar continues to invoke, in increasingly emphatic fashion, their stereotypical moral failings.

Above, I argued that Critognatus serves as Caesar's most explicit mouthpiece on the understanding of *virtus*. Yet one might wonder whether a Roman reader would find a Gaul to be a reliable guide. Moreover, we just noted that the narrator specifically and unusually tags this speech for its cruelty. This speech needs to be taken together with the episode of the Gauls setting fires at Avaricum (7.25). The introductory phrases are strikingly similar: *visum praetereundum non existimavimus* (7.25.1) and *non praetereunda oratio…videtur* (7.77.2). The former passage, as noted above, marked the height of Gallic assimilation to the Romans in acquiring true *virtus*. The latter caps the Gallic descent into cruelty just mentioned. This is where Vercingetorix has brought the Gauls. He is not, as he is sometimes casually described, a "noble savage." In *De Bello Gallico*, he is precisely the opposite of both "noble" and "savage," and to the extent that he has remade his followers into his own image, they, too, are neither. Caesar has radically separated the two issues. Cruelty, then, is not counter-evidence to Critognatus' credibility. Critognatus is just another Gaul who has only learned half of what it is to be Roman. Fortunately, his speech regards the point on which he can speak authoritatively.

De Bello Gallico's notion of *virtus* is also important for what it claims about Caesar himself. Caesar takes credit for his army's technical feats directly. In a few cases he reports that he "saw to it" that something be built (*faciendum curat*, 1.13.1) or simply "decided to" build something (6.9.1). More often, however, he simply does the construction himself, at least according to the strict grammar of the text. Most notably in the descriptions of the construction of the Rhine bridge and Alesia fortifications, Caesar is the subject of all of the active verbs of making.[78] In a less direct way, Caesar seems to have been taking credit for his troops' actual fighting. The *virtus* of the soldiery was traditionally distinct from the qualities of the commander. Aristocratic commanders formulaically justified defeats under their commands by claiming failure of the *virtus militum*.[79] In one recorded case, we even see the reverse: a victorious general's opponents argued that he should not be awarded a triumph because he had failed, but was saved by the *virtus* of his troops.[80] In any case, the merits of the troops and the command are widely regarded as distinct. Caesar's version preempts the possibility of that distinction. The *virtus* of troops in *De Bello Gallico* depends on their preparation by the commander, on his ability to impose his will on them, and in many cases on his presence, real or virtual. If Caesar's troops fight well, it is because Caesar has made them truly his own.

A version of this lesson may even be applicable outside the realm of war, though this argument must remain speculative. Given the etymology, it would have been impossible for discussion of *virtus* not to have been entangled in gendered rhetoric, and we have seen examples of just this, such as Critognatus' opposition of *virtus* to *mollitia animi*. But the particular version of this rhetoric that Caesar develops would not have been the only one feasible. It has often been noted that for the Romans, manliness was closely tied to control.[81] In different circumstances, however, the emphasis falls sometimes on self-control and sometimes on control over others. Caesar's emphasis on the role of self-control in *virtus* conceals the fact that he has also built submission to hierarchy (and, in particular, to himself) into the idea. Although his ideal of discipline could be redescribed as feminine, he can ignore that possibility because his preferred, masculine description is at least equally plausible owing to the inherent ambiguity of the idea of control and long-standing institutional support for military discipline. So much, I think, is fairly clear within the text itself. It is possible, however, that Caesar was also looking forward while writing this, whether to a dictatorship such as he eventually established or, probably more likely, to some more conventional but still exalted position at Rome. As part of the "first triumvirate," he had already seen the difficulty other aristocrats had accepting the long-term superiority of one of their fellows.[82] The reconfigured notion of *virtus* gives these aristocrats a moral excuse to fall in line and support Caesar. If submission to Caesar could be manly in war, why not in peace? This also gives us an explanation of Caesar's choice of a complicated reconfiguration of *virtus* over the more traditional confrontation between it and *disciplina*. Soldiers were naturally expected to follow their commanders' orders. That logic could not be projected into the civilian world. The logic of the new *virtus* would apply everywhere.

4. Alien Nation

In examining the general question of ethnic identity in *De Bello Gallico*, I concentrate not on the representation of otherness (and its instrumental value for Caesar), but on how Roman identity comes to be defined in the presence of its various others and how that identity is entangled in other political questions. The speech of Critognatus during the siege of Alesia is important to this examination. The character of Critognatus draws a sharp line between Roman and Gaul, whereas Caesar's composition and incorporation of the speech complicates the opposition and indeed suggests that there is no fundamental opposition at all. A comparison of *De Bello Gallico*'s rhetoric throughout the work with that of a variety of modern colonial texts shows a Caesar surprisingly hesitant to define Romanness by simple opposition to the various others readily available. This rhetorical tendency can be located in two historical contexts: the peculiar relationship between center and periphery in Roman imperialism, and Caesar's personal position in Roman society. The latter context allowed Caesar to see and exploit certain inclusive (albeit not democratic) tendencies inherent in the practice of Roman imperial expansion.

Playing the Cannibal

Quintilian famously remarked that "had Caesar only had time for the Forum, no other among our [orators] could be put up against Cicero" (10.1.114). Though Caesar did in fact devote a certain amount of time to oratory, we now have only the most fragmentary remains of his speeches. One of his two longest and only complete surviving pieces of oratory is the speech of Critognatus at *De Bello Gallico* 7.77.[1]

> (3) "nihil" inquit "de eorum sententia dicturus sum, qui turpissimam servitutem deditionis nomine appellant, neque hos habendos civium loco

neque ad concilium adhibendos censeo. (4) cum his mihi res sit, qui erup-
tionem probant.

quorum in consilio omnium vestrum consensu pristinae residere virtutis memoria videtur, (5) animi est ista mollitia, non *virtus,* paulisper
inopiam ferre non posse. qui se ultro morti offerant facilius reperiuntur
quam qui dolorem patienter ferant. (6) atque ego hanc sententiam pro-
barem—tantum apud me dignitas potest—si nullam praeterquam vi-
tae nostrae iacturam fieri viderem; (7) sed in consilio capiendo omnem
Galliam respiciamus, quam ad nostrum auxilium concitavimus: (8) quid
hominum milibus lxxx uno loco interfectis propinquis consanguineisque
nostris animi fore existimatis, si paene in ipsis cadaveribus proelio decer-
tare cogentur? (9) nolite hos vestro auxilio exspoliare qui vestrae salutis
causa suum periculum neglexerunt, nec stultitia ac temeritate vestra aut
animi imbecillitate omnem Galliam prosternere et perpetuae servituti ad-
dicere. (10) an quod ad diem non venerunt, de eorum fide constantiaque
dubitatis? quid ergo? Romanos in illis ulterioribus munitionibus animine
causa cotidie exerceri putatis? (11) si illorum nuntiis confirmari non po-
testis omni aditu praesaepto, his utimini testibus adpropinquare eorum
adventum, cuius rei timore exterriti diem noctemque in opere versantur.

(12) quid ergo mei consilii est? facere quod nostri maiores nequaquam
pari bello Cimbrorum Teutonumque fecerunt: qui in oppida compulsi ac
simili inopia subacti eorum corporibus, qui aetate ad bellum inutiles vide-
bantur, vitam toleraverunt neque se hostibus tradiderunt. (13) cuius rei
si exemplum non haberemus, tamen libertatis causa institui et posteris
prodi pulcherrimum iudicarem. (14) nam quid illi simile bello fuit? de-
populata Gallia Cimbri magnaque inlata calamitate finibus quidem nostris aliquando excesserunt atque alias terras petierunt; iura, leges, agros,
libertatem nobis reliquerunt. (15) Romani vero quid petunt aliud aut quid
volunt nisi invidia adducti quos fama nobiles potentesque bello cognove-
runt, horum in agris civitatibusque considere atque his aeternam iniun-
gere servitutem? neque enim ulla alia condicione bella gesserunt. (16)
quodsi ea quae in longinquis nationibus geruntur ignoratis, respicite
finitimam Galliam, quae in provinciam redacta, iure et legibus commuta-
tis, securibus subiecta perpetua premitur servitute."

(3) "I will say nothing about the opinion of those who give the name of
'surrender' to slavery most foul, nor do I think they ought to be considered citizens and given a place in public council. (4) My quarrel is with
those who approve of a breakout.

"You all seem to agree that in their plan lies the memory of our former (*pristinae*) *virtus*. (5) But that is softness (*mollitia*) of spirit, not *virtus:* not to be able to bear want for a little while. Men who give themselves freely up to death are easier to find than those who bear suffering patiently. (6) Now, insofar as my own dignity is a consideration, I would accept that plan, if I saw that nothing but our lives would be lost; (7) but we should look to all Gaul when taking council, having summoned them to our aid. (8) What kind of courage do you think it would give to allies and relatives, when 80,000 men had been killed in one place, if they were forced to fight virtually on top of the very corpses? (9) Don't rob them of your aid, when they have discounted their own danger for the sake of your well-being, nor overthrow all Gaul and subject it to perpetual slavery out of your own foolishness and rashness or weakness of mind. (10) Do you doubt their trustworthiness and constancy, just because they have not arrived precisely on the appointed day? What then? Do you imagine that the Romans busy themselves daily on the outer works as an exercise? (11) If you cannot be comforted by messengers (since all approaches have been cut off), then use these [Romans] as evidence of their advance. It is out of fear of this thing that the Romans involve themselves in this work day and night.

(12) "What then is my plan? To do what our ancestors did in the war (in no way equal to this one) with the Cimbri and Teutoni: those who were pushed back into their hill-towns and pressed by similar hunger did not surrender, but held on to life by means of the bodies of those who, from age, seemed useless for war. (13) And if we had no example of this, nevertheless I would judge it a very fair thing to be established for the sake of liberty and handed down to our descendents. (14) What in this war is similar to that earlier one? When Gaul had been ravaged and a great calamity had come about, the Cimbri eventually left our territory and sought other lands. They left us our rights, laws, fields, and liberty. (15) But what else do the Romans seek or wish, unless (led on by jealousy) it is to establish themselves in the fields of those whom they know to be noble in reputation and strong in war and to put them in eternal slavery? They wage wars in no other way. (16) But if you do not know what they have done in far-off nations, look at the neighboring part of Gaul, which has been rendered into a province, its rights and laws changed, and is pressed by perpetual slavery under the axe."

This particular speech has received some previous attention. Fabia and Holtz have noted a number of Gorgianic figures (e.g., antitheses, tricola, alliteration) and other features of classical handbook rhetoric (e.g., rhetorical questions, certain vivid images, exempla). In his monograph on direct speech in the *commentarii,* Rasmussen remarks on the pathetic quality of the whole, and especially on the development of the theme of freedom vs. slavery. Schieffer builds on these readings to analyze the role of this speech in Caesar's ongoing (in his view, negative) portrayal of the barbarian other. Canali sees a way to think out Roman imperialism.[2] I return to a more rhetorical reading, though in a somewhat different mode than has been used before. Previous analyses have concentrated primarily on aspects of rhetoric described in the ancient handbooks, and in terms that are not very genre-specific. That is, the speech is considered in terms that would be appropriate to nonoratorical sections of the *commentarii* or, for that matter, to virtually any other ancient text. After all, antithesis, alliteration, exempla, and the like are features of all formal Roman literature. I here look at the speech specifically as oratory and apply knowledge gained from recent study of the preeminent orator of the day, Cicero. For the most part, this involves departing from the language of classical rhetoric, though I do not want to deny the value of previous analyses in that language. They illustrate, for instance, the extent to which Caesar was treating this speech as the *oratio* he calls it (7.77.2), not simply as another part of the text.

STRUCTURE

Critognatus' speech is as carefully and traditionally structured as my paragraphing above indicates. It begins with a proem consisting of little more than the first sentence (3–4).[3] Though the proem itself is somewhat unconventional in form, it does serve a conventional function. By playing one opposing position against the other, Caesar can have Critognatus completely reject one alternative, but still appear reasonable by admitting that the other is worthy of debate. By rejecting surrender as "slavery most foul," Critognatus also seizes the moral high ground. Important as this is in modern speaking, it was an even more critical source of authority for the Romans. Thus this brief introduction establishes the credibility of the speaker by creating a firm but fair persona.

The proem is followed by a rebuttal (4–11) and a proof (12–16) of approximately equal length. The former rejects the idea of breaking out through Roman lines; the latter presents Critognatus' own plan of holding out indefinitely, even by resorting to cannibalism. The division is clearly marked, as has been widely recognized, by the rhetorical question, "What then is my plan?" (12).[4] What has not been noted is that the two sections have similar shapes. Each begins with logical argument, then moves to an appeal to visible "proof" (see below). Moreover, there are patterns of repetition with variation (see below) that take place largely within rather than across the sections as I have demarcated them. Only a real peroration is lacking to make this a complete speech according to ancient canons. However, given the peroration's conventional functions of summary and emotional appeal, it is the least necessary in this context. The speech is so short that no summary is needed, and the pathos of the whole obviates a special section to produce that effect. Hence, this speech not only makes use of the rhetorical figures common to all ancient genres, but is structured very much as an oration.

APPEAL TO THE VISIBLE

The rebuttal opens with a logical argument about the nature of *virtus*. This shades into a hypothetical discussion of what will happen, both to the Arverni and to the other Gauls, if they attempt a breakout. It closes, however, with an appeal to the concrete and visible. If we see the Romans working so hard, it must be because they believe the relief force will arrive soon. Vasaly has demonstrated the importance of the visible in Ciceronian oratory.[5] Cicero often draws on features of the visible (especially the built) environment to reinforce his arguments. This was particularly useful in a Roman context, where purely syllogistic reasoning was viewed with some suspicion; appeal to the obvious then took its place beside appeal to personal authority as a source of reliable information.[6] To the modern eye, the use of these objects often seems symbolic rather than evidentiary. Yet, Cicero's example seems to show that the tactic was successful, so it should not be surprising to see Caesar use it as well.

The proof is structured similarly to the rebuttal. Critognatus starts with an exemplum of the Cimbrian invasion, over a half-century earlier, then shifts into discussing Roman imperialism generally. Again, though, he stops himself as if this is all too distant to be sure, and offers something closer to home: the Roman province of Transalpine Gaul. Though not literally visible at the moment, this is at least something of which his audience would have had more direct experience. Caesar establishes a point of view from which Critognatus' position is obviously the correct one. If the choice is really best described as one between freedom and slavery, then Critognatus is certainly right to pick freedom. Then Critognatus pulls one specific, concrete feature out of the environment to show that that point of view is "true" or "natural" and so demands adherence to his views. The situation of the Gauls in the Roman province makes it plausible to describe the question as freedom vs. slavery.[7]

REPETITION WITH VARIATION

Repetition is used extensively within this relatively short passage. The key thematic term "slavery" (*servitus*) appears four times, but there are also a number of other doublets, as well as a more complicated pattern of repetition near the end.[8] Consider the following parallels:

softness of spirit (5) ~ weakness of spirit (9)
(*animi est ista mollitia ~ animi imbecillitate*)

all Gaul (7) ~ all Gaul (9)
(*omnem Galliam ~ omnem Galliam*)

Daily they are working on those exterior fortifications (10) ~ day and night they are busy on the works (11)
(*in illis ulterioribus munitionibus ... cotidie exerceri ~ diem noctemque in opere versantur*)

in a war in no way equal (12) ~ what was similar in that war? (14)
(*nequaquam pari bello ~ quid illi simile bello*)

rights, laws, fields, liberty (14) ~ fields and cities ... eternal slavery (15) ~ right and laws ... perpetual slavery (16) [~ perpetual slavery (9)]
(*iura, leges, agros, libertatem ~ agris civitatibusque ... aeternam ... servitutem ~ iure et legibus ... perpetua ... servitute [~ perpetuae servituti]*).

This kind of repetition (usually with the same slight variation) is common in Cicero's speeches and serves at least two purposes there. It is useful when giving a long speech to a live audience whose attention may fade in and out, who may not remember every detail without a text to which to refer, or who simply may not hear every word.[9] None of those dangers exists in this case, but preservation of the stylistic features of oral discourse again shows Caesar writing as if he were not merely continuing the text of *De Bello Gallico*, but actually composing a speech.

When, however, an orator is being this redundant, he will want to guard against boring any members of the audience who *are* following everything. Hence the need for artful variation. (The antitheses often noted throughout this speech would also serve in the same way for actual oral delivery.)

The other value of repetition (whether exact or not) lies in a phenomenon described by Craig as "resonance."

> Resonance arises when a theme sounded in the course of an argument recurs in another argument. When the stronger argument precedes the weaker, the dual result of this thematic echoing is that the audience is reminded of the stronger argument, and the apparent probability of the weaker argument is buttressed by association. When the weaker argument precedes, it may gain plausibility retroactively. If both arguments sharing a theme are of equal cogency they are mutually reinforced.[10]

The repetitions in Critognatus' speech highlight some of its important themes, even beyond freedom and slavery: the notion of a single Gallic nation (*omnem Galliam*), sources of distinct (i.e., Roman-free) Gallic identity (e.g., rights, laws, fields, liberty), the argument from lesser to greater (e.g., "a war in no way equal"), the visible labor of the Roman troops (e.g., "daily they are working on those exterior fortifications"), and the redefinition of *virtus* (e.g., "that is softness of spirit"). Verbatim repetition could serve the purpose of creating resonance, but it runs the risk (especially in the short compass of this speech) of creating a refrain and so making the audience aware of the repetition as a device. Instead, Caesar (like Cicero) varies the pattern. So, for instance, sections 14–16 give three different versions of what is at stake in the war: laws, land, and freedom/slavery. Each element is used twice, but no two of the versions are precisely the same; there is even alternation between *aeterna* and *perpetua*, "eternal."

PATTERNS OF EMPHASIS

One of the most important strategies, or rather families of strategies, in Roman oratory is to emphasize one's strongest arguments (not necessarily the most salient ones), while making the less attractive ones more obliquely. Many scholars have noted this feature in passing in Cicero's orations, without studying it as such. By a "strong" argument I mean here one whose terms retain the value, positive or negative, they would have had in a more neutral context. Consider, for instance, Critognatus' repeated insistence that his plan is the only one that would permit the Gauls to avoid slavery. *Libertas* ("freedom") and *servitus* ("slavery") are among the least ambivalent terms in the Latin language; though political propagandists may have had trouble agreeing on what counted as freedom or slavery, the effort on all sides was premised on an unquestionable assumption that the former was good and the latter bad.[11] In this particular case, if the terms of freedom and slavery are to be applied at all, they tend to fall out in Critognatus' favor. Hence he repeats those words over and over in an attempt to impose that description of the choices on his audience as the salient standard of judgment.

There are, however, at least three elements of Critognatus' argument that do not fall so neatly in his favor. In these instances, Caesar must expend more effort locating and establishing a description of affairs that will be plausible, but still favorable to the position being defended. The first of these involves the redefinition of *virtus*. The other side claimed that a breakout would constitute a display of *virtus* (4). *Virtus* is as unequivocally positive as *libertas*, so Critognatus must argue that the opposition has misapplied the term. This is especially difficult here, since *virtus* is closely associated throughout *De Bello Gallico* with hand-to-hand combat (see Chap. 3). As a result, Critognatus has to take a step back into the assumptions behind the opposing claim. We saw in Chapter 3 that Critognatus' response is to make an implicitly etymological argument. The transparent sense of the word is "manliness." Softness, especially as expressed by the *moll-* root in *animi ... mollitia* (5) (echoed later by the somewhat less evocative *animi imbecillitate* [9]), is one of the most important stereotypical characteristics of the feminine in Roman culture. The narrator had previously opposed *virtus* to softness and effeminacy within the main text of *De Bello Gallico* (2.15.4, cf. 4.2.6). Thus Critognatus offers not only an alternative description of the opposing plan, but one that suggests that the justification for that plan is incoherent. An action that was "soft" in context could not possibly count as *virtus*, whatever the usual valorization of physical courage. Critognatus does not have to spell this out step-by-step; he just lets the loaded words do their work. Furthermore, the groundwork for this argument had already been laid in the proem. The very first sentence questions the proper use of the terms "surrender" and "citizen" (3). By the time the audience reaches the important argument, it has been prepared for another term to shift meaning. (This might be construed as another instance of resonance, though here without any specific verbal repetition.)

The next step of Critognatus' argument is to pull back and try to establish a "big picture." Restraint, however much toughness it might demonstrate, only makes sense if it has some further goal in mind. That goal, according to Critognatus, is freedom for Gaul as a whole (*omnem Galliam* 7, 9). The rhetorical problem here is that Gallic unity, unlike *libertas* or *virtus*, has been nonexistent in reality and marginal as an ideal up to this point in *De Bello Gallico*. Critognatus therefore takes an active role in creating an "imagined community."[12] One way of doing this, of course, is simply to use the phrase *omnem Galliam*, which presupposes a unity, instead of the more fragmented *omnes Gallos*, "all Gallic persons," or individual tribal names.[13] Then Critognatus hints that his fellow Arverni have already implicitly accepted the idea of Gallic unity: "We should look to all Gaul ... having summoned them to our aid" (7). If Gaul has an obligation to the Arverni, then perhaps the reverse should also hold; no explanation for the obligation is offered beyond common Gallic identity. The symmetry of obligation is shortly reinforced by the parallelism of "of your aid" and "for the sake of your well-being" (9). Again the trick is to hint at the connections and to presuppose them without arguing explicitly for the more controversial points.

The last and most difficult problem is in Critognatus' central proposal— that they eat the old (and perhaps also the very young) so as to be able to hold out longer. Cannibalism is, of course, a hard sell (as shown by the fact that it is the part of his plan that was rejected). But, as this is the very thing of which he is trying to persuade his fellows, he cannot simply avoid the issue as he did in the cases above. One approach to the problem is to phrase the actual proposal as euphemistically as possible.[14] First he suggests that they should "do what our ancestors did," then says of *them* that they "held on to life by means of the bodies" *corporibus ... vitam toleraverunt* (12). Eating is not expressly mentioned. Then he adds that the ancestors did this rather than surrender themselves to the Cimbri. This creates in effect a false dilemma; it omits both the option against which Critognatus had just been arguing (breakout) and the compromise that was eventually adopted (resistance without cannibalism).[15] In comparison to the already discredited idea of surrender, cannibalism does not look quite so bad. One remark in the rebuttal might also be seen as having some resonance on this point. Critognatus had made the argument that the morale of the main force would be harmed if they arrived at Alesia after an attempted breakout and had to fight "on top of the very corpses" (8). Although it is clearly not the main point of the phrase, this may nonetheless carry the suggestion that Gallic corpses are going to be violated one way or the other. Again, a background is implied against which cannibalism becomes a preferable alternative.

CONTEXT SENSITIVITY

More than any other prose genres, forensic and deliberative oratory are closely tied to their immediate context of production. A specific audience must be persuaded to reach specific conclusions. Cicero himself remarked that a successful orator must know the prejudices of his particular audience to be persuasive (*Clu.* 17, *Tusc.* 2.3). Scholars have noted how he could take diametrically opposed positions on various issues as the local need arose.[16] Furthermore, as shown above, this particular speech is very context-sensitive at a tactical level. Arguments are made more or less obliquely based on an evaluation of the audience's tolerance for their direct form. It is this calculation of persuasiveness to a specific audience in a specific context that I take to be characteristically "oratorical." The same is true on a higher level as well. On the one hand, Critognatus' speech is merely part of the larger scheme of *De Bello Gallico*. It picks up themes of the larger work, it increases the drama of the final showdown, it gives a final illustration of Gallic character in the work, and so on. On the other hand, it is still written as a piece of oratory. That is, it sets out to be as persuasive as possible to a particular audience, albeit an imaginary one, in a particular context, again admittedly imaginary. Take, for instance, the argument about *virtus*. Critognatus introduces it by suggesting that the consensus up to that point was that the plan of breakout represented the *pristinae ... virtutis memoria* (4). This "(memory of) former *virtus*" is a formula in *De Bello Gallico*, and its use here recreates a specific situation.[17] The phrase is spoken to hearten the troops for a difficult battle. In particular, it is used in situations where the army can save itself only by fighting its way out of trouble. Critognatus' opponents have invoked a common frame of reference in which there are only two options (fight or surrender), and in which the former is clearly to be preferred. His rhetoric, then, needs both to make clear the existence of a third possibility in this case and to overcome the presumption in favor of battle that derives from the usual context of the decision. These are precisely the problems that Critognatus' speech addresses.

Another example of Caesar's sensitivity to the imagined context is his presentation of a remarkably Gallic point of view. To some extent, this is conventional; even hostile figures are allowed to speak well in ancient history.[18] But consider Critognatus' evaluation of Roman motivation for the conquest of Gaul (15). It would hardly occur to most Romans that they might be thought jealous of the Gauls, or of any other people. And although barbarians traditionally boast of their strength, courage, or incorruptibility, it is striking to hear one of them claim that they rival the Romans in "nobility" (15). The exemplum of the Cimbric War that Caesar puts in Critognatus' mouth is also revealing. Both the practice of Roman oratory (as represented by Cicero) and its theory (as represented indirectly by Valerius Maximus' collection) suggest that the most valuable exempla were overwhelmingly Roman (most of the rest being Greek). Here, however, the hypothetical audience is Gallic, so an exemplum from the Gallic past is chosen. Even more striking is the event chosen. The Cimbric invasion had a great impact on Roman historical consciousness (visible, for instance, in the rest of *De Bello Gallico;* see Chap. 6), yet Caesar is here able to see it as an event in Gallic history as well. Furthermore, to do so he must disentangle these Gauls from the tradition that tends to see all northern barbarians as essentially the same. Even the Romans end up aligned with the (conventionally barbaric) Cimbri in opposition to the Gauls, who are in both cases defending their own homes against the invaders who have wandered into their territories.[19] In that context, note also that the Gauls are defending towns (12) and their own rights and laws (14, 16). They are made stable and civilized. In these respects, Caesar has constructed a counterintuitive argument for a Roman audience.

Some scholars have suggested that one function of the speech is to characterize Critognatus negatively, presenting him not merely as un-Roman, but as sub-Roman, an out-of-control barbarian.[20] The proposal of cannibalism certainly supports this view. The narrator recognizes this in advance when he asserts the exceptional "cruelty" of the speech or of the man himself (7.77.2). But as noted in Chapter 3, except in the suggestion of cannibalism, barbarism was hardly evident in the rest of the proposal.

Scholars, then, have tried to move their argument to Critognatus' rhetoric instead. The main line of this case is that the rhetoric is overwrought (especially by comparison with the spare prose of the narrator). The high frequency of rhetorical questions is particularly noted in this context. There is unquestionably a difference in the rhetorical levels of this speech and of the surrounding text, but that is a difference of genre. The difference is explicitly flagged by the narrator's use of the word *oratio* in introducing the speech. An audience accustomed to different standards of decorum for different genres will not have been surprised by contrast.[21] But is the speech perhaps too extreme, even as a speech? This is an uncomfortably subjective question, but a few observations will suggest that the speech is not as problematic as it has been made out to be. Two of the most dramatic devices, exclamations and apostrophes, are absent from the speech.[22] There are few superlatives (and Latin is ordinarily much freer with those than English is). The redundancy already discussed has the effect of slowing down the movement of the speech. Finally, Critognatus is arguably correct; the fate (if not precisely the freedom) of the entire Gallic people rides on this battle. If we use for comparison, say, Cicero's *Catilinarians* rather than the rest of Caesar's *commentarii,* the charge that Critognatus' speech is overheated proves to be mere prejudice.[23] It seems to be driven by an insistence on the "anti-Roman outburst of Critognatus' concluding appeal," which Schieffer finds in conflict with the "thorough-goingly apologetic stance of Caesar's depiction of the war."[24] If we accept that the relationship between these two admitted features of the text may be more complicated, then our reading of the speech will not be entirely determined in advance.

In other respects, moreover, this speech is highly Roman. The overall structure of the speech is that recommended by the Greco-Roman handbooks, as are the ornaments and figures. The speech also assumes that for its audience, terms such as *virtus, servitus,* and *dignitas* are resonant, and further, that they are resonant in the same ways as they would be for a more obviously Roman audience. That is, not only does Critognatus' speech assume that *virtus* is good and *mollitia* is bad, and that both are evocative, but also that they are opposed to each other, something the raw etymology of the words would not reveal. The speech also assumes certain Roman values that are not so tightly bound up with individual words. As already seen, both this speech and much of Cicero's oratory seem to share the prejudice in favor of the visible against the logical. Also relevant are the specific claims about the exemplarity of the action Critognatus proposed. Not only is there precedent for cannibalism in this situation, he argues, but even if there had not been, the forces at Alesia would still be doing their descendants the favor of leaving them their own example. Argument from precedent is hardly unique to the Romans, but the moral force attached to it and the projection forward (i.e., asking how you will be used as an example in the future) show a particularly Roman emphasis.[25] Compare the words of Caesar's adoptive son Augustus: "By new laws passed on my proposal I brought back into use many exemplary practices of our ancestors that were disappearing in our time, and in many ways I myself transmitted exemplary practices to posterity for their imitation."[26] The audience for this speech, then, is a group of mirror-Romans. They occupy a different place from the Romans and view the world from that different position. The nature of their gaze, however, is Roman. They see things largely in Roman categories; only the concrete referents of the terms "we" and "they" have been reversed.

SPEAKING FOR THE OTHER

The classicists cited above were suspicious of Caesar's move to speak for the other because, not without reason, they questioned his more or less conscious motives. Students of later European imperialism have gone so far as to suggest that such speaking-for is inherently problematic, that attempts to capture another culture in one's own language inevitably do violence to that other. On this account, claiming to speak for the other can only conceal (whether out of ignorance or malice) the assault.

The burden of this book is, of course, that translation was, and still is, the central act of European colonization and imperialism in the Americas. (Cheyfitz 1997, 104)

The first [interpretation] is that in order to make the alien familiar, it has to be translated into the categories of one's own culture. The second is that by doing so, the risk of suppressing alternative organizations of knowledge is difficult to avoid. (Mignolo 1995, 199)

In its broader sense, it [viz. Derrida's "anthropological war"] includes the entire system by which one culture comes to interpret, to represent, and finally to dominate another. It includes, in other words, the discourses of colonialism as produced in such forms as imaginative literature, journalism, travel writing, ethnographic description, historiography, political speeches, administrative documents, and statutes of law. (Spurr 1993, 4)

Before we apply this reasoning to Caesar, however, we must ask at least two questions. Is the "violence" of the acts of translation documented by these authors a necessary aspect of the process, or a peculiar feature of modern European colonialism? And even if such violence is indeed inherent in translation between cultures, does it play the same role in Roman imperialism as in its successors?

Is translation between cultures necessarily mistranslation? It has been shown that, if language is grounded in reference to a commonly available real world, then the translation problem need not exist.[27] Translation between cultures differs from translation within them (and, indeed, from the initial acquisition of language) in degree rather than in kind. Mistranslation, of course, remains a practical likelihood, but not a necessity. Largely the same argument can be made if language stands in a causal rather than a representational relationship to the world. However, I am more persuaded by arguments of George Lakoff that combine features of both.[28] Language is referential within the broader mind (pointing to patterns of meaning rooted eventually in nonlinguistic experience), whereas it is the system as a whole that has the causal (nonrepresentational) relationship with the outside world. In this case, differently situated individuals will have incommensurable languages as a result of different lived experiences. In colonial situations (at the least), those differences will be ineradicable, not least because the leveling process would have to go both ways; in practice, the same gaps would remain unbridged, even within a given language and culture. In some respects, Caesar's putting the Gauls in Roman terms is clearly contrary to their interests. If the Gauls are simply barbarian others, then they are contemptible. But if they are in some sense other Romans, then they implicitly have an obligation to operate by Roman rules. Much the way that the legitimate competition for offices within the Republic justifies some kinds of behavior (invective) but not others (open and random bribery), interstate relations allow for some conflicts but not all. The Gauls are criticized for the seizure of Roman legates "which name [legate] had always been sacred and inviolate for all nations" (3.9.3). Mannetter, noting that Caesar here perhaps protests too much, wonders if "perhaps the universality of the sanctity of legates is overstated."[29] Historically, this may well be right, though we will probably never know. But the universality (or not) of the Roman rule is not particularly important if the Gauls, the specific people being charged here, are sufficiently assimilated to the Romans. More fundamental to Caesar's project is the concept of *fides*, the obligation, on the one hand, of states that have once surrendered to Rome to toe the line thereafter, and on the other, of Rome to "protect" its allies and dependents (often by further conquest). This concept is central to the justification of Caesar's various campaigns, even if it is not discussed explicitly. Here again the universality of Roman standards is unimportant as long as the opponents are Romanized enough that they can be assumed in some implicit way to have accepted them. What is at stake here, then, is the legitimization of Caesar's conquests by the legitimization of several particular strategies of justification. When Caesar "grants" his opponents (Roman) common sense, when he de-barbarizes them, he does so only to gain their tacit approval to their own subjection.

Yet at the same time, many of the specific injuries done by mistranslation, both those just described and those in the accounts of Mignolo, Cheyfitz, and Spurr quoted above, hinge more specifically on a radical binary opposition of self and other. This developed easily in the encounters of Europeans with non-Europeans in the early modern period. The novelty of the encounter for the participants at the time, and the radical asymmetry of results, encourage generalization into dyads of national subjects: European and non-European, English and Hawaiian, etc. In any case, to the extent that these readings are politicized, they are the politics of the encounter of pairs of peoples. Thus they require essentially unified national subjects for their coherence, and focus falls on questions of identity. But Caesar's circumstances were quite different, and we have already seen in Critognatus' speech at least some reason to believe the consequences were also different. Caesar's (mis)translation is both less and more aggressive than those of his imperial successors. It is "less aggressive" in that the blurring of Roman and other is a running feature of the text. It is "more aggressive" in that it allows the same kind of authority being asserted over Gaul to be projected back inward. If aliens can become Romans, why can't Romans become imperial subjects?

Rhetorics of Empire

David Spurr's fascinating study, *The Rhetoric of Empire: Colonial Discourse in Journalism, Travel Writing, and Imperial Administration* (1993), provides a framework to advance a comparison of *De Bello Gallico* with some much more recent imperial writing. As the subtitle suggests, Spurr studies three genres of writing with close ties to the imperial and colonial projects of the modern West. (He limits himself by and large to texts from the nineteenth and twentieth centuries and from England, France, and the United States.) His book catalogs a number of "tropes" common to these diverse genres exemplifying a common discourse on colonial subjects and their Euro-American masters.[30] Without positing a single *mentalité* in which all these writers are enmeshed, he can show that these tropes are common not only to different genres and periods, but even to writers whose intentions toward the subject peoples are sympathetic as well as those who are openly hostile. So, for instance, Thomas Carlyle and John Stuart Mill could argue about why (creation or contingency) there existed a hierarchy of races in the world of their time, but both assumed that the races were discrete and rankable entities. Similarly, the nostalgia-tinged "noble savage" and the fearsome headhunter are only slight variations on the same theme of the atavistic alien.[31] Finally, and whether or not one feels that moral judgment is helpful or necessary, Spurr notes that all of the tropes he has found tend to draw sharp lines between European and Other, which can be (mis-?)used to justify imperialism and colonialism. Here I take four examples from Spurr's list of tropes and show how Caesar avoids and or undercuts them in *De Bello Gallico*.

The "noble savage," Spurr notes, could serve as a specific example of the broader patterns he has identified as "idealization" or "aestheticization."[32] The prime candidate here would seem to be Caesar's Vercingetorix, whose identification as a noble savage is affirmed in a recent study, though qualified in a footnote by two examples of less-than-noble behavior: using torture and deception to ensure support for himself.[33] As we have already seen, however, Vercingetorix is anything but a noble savage. The claim is based on the fact that that category is almost the only positive image of the Other we recognize today. Vercingetorix (here I mean the character, not the historical individual) is arguably not noble, and his whole reason for being is that he is *not* a savage. His contribution, as argued in Chapter 3, is to make the Gauls more civilized in at least some respects, to bring to them the discipline of (idealized) Roman society. The word *barbarus* is not even used in the last book of *De Bello Gallico*. Nor should we forget that this progress goes hand-in-hand with an acceleration of Gallic technological progress in the final book. As noted in Chapter 2, Caesar goes to some length to construct a distinction, perhaps not one entirely "natural" to the original audience, between bad civilization (the Gauls) and no civilization at all (the Germans). Thus the people Vercingetorix came from and led were not savages in the first place. Yet, they have been referred to as "leaderless hordes." Their problem, as I hope is now clear, is not that they lack leaders, but that they have a surplus of them. The immediate distinction is perhaps slight, but the long-term consequences are quite different. German hostility to leadership will keep them permanently in their savage state. Gauls, having already taken a large step in the direction of (Roman) civilization, can move further in that direction with relative ease.

A second trope is "negation," whereby "natives" are described in terms of lacks and absences: lack of history, of language, of presence in the landscape.[34] Spurr quotes an extreme example from a traveler's report of the Belgian Congo in 1907:

> To tell what the place is like, you must tell what it lacks. One must write of the Congo always in the negative. It is as though you asked "what sort of house is this one Jones built?" and were answered "Well, it hasn't any roof, and it hasn't any cellar, and it has no windows, floors, or chimneys. It's that kind of house."[35]

There are certainly signs of this strategy in Caesar's description of the Germans. They lack leaders, priests, and (most) gods (6.21.1–2), as well as private property (6.22.2). They judge themselves successful in war if the territory surrounding their own is empty (6.23.2). As Chapter 2 showed, however, the Gauls are not presented this way. Though divided, they are concrete peoples. This is largely what distinguishes them from the fluid Germans. Chapter 1 suggested that Caesar's tactical descriptions neutralized features of terrain to create empty spaces into which the Romans could move. Yet the Gauls themselves were not entirely eliminated by the strategy; in fact, the tactical spaces were always either centered on or bounded by the opposing army and/or Gallic town. Clearing the space heightens the confrontation with the Gauls (even if it biases the moral terms of that confrontation) rather than negates it.

Another of Spurr's tropes is called "surveillance."[36] The colonizers watch the colonized and their land. This gaze is asymmetric; the conquerors watch without being watched. Surveillance can be performed on many scales. Landscape descriptions are the clearest cases, since the landscape by nature cannot look back (this is easily combined with negation). The view, however, can also penetrate walls, revealing what (the author imagines) is going on inside. In either case, the colonizer's gaze takes on a superhuman extent. Even when there is no physical barrier to reciprocal viewing, the gaze remains one-way:

> They [a group of black workers singing for a white audience] are obligated to show themselves *to view* for the white men, but they themselves lack the privilege of the gaze.... When the song is ended, Agee handed some money to one of the men: "He thanked me for them in a dead voice, not looking me in the eye, and they went away."[37]

It is easy enough to find examples of this trope in *De Bello Gallico*. The opening panorama is a classic landscape description, and in fact, all of the geographic (in the sense of Chap. 1) descriptions serve the same function. And not only do the ethnographic passages penetrate within the homes and personal relationships of the Gauls and Germans, but, because of their generalization, no return gaze is possible.

Outside of these set-piece descriptions, however, Caesar repeatedly undercuts the scheme. First, Roman vision is not entirely reliable. For instance, in the first book, the Helvetians temporarily escaped Caesar's grasp when his scout failed to recognize that a hill was held by Labienus (as planned), whose forces he took for Helvetians (1.22.2). Caesar's troops at Gergovia were terrified by the sight of approaching allied Gallic troops on their flank, mistaking them for enemies (7.50.2). More generally, Romans could not see into marshes and forests, whereas their enemies apparently could (see Chap. 1). Even when the Romans are seeing correctly, the Gauls can occasionally take advantage of that fact to reverse the power relationship usually inherent in the gaze.[38] "Some of [the soldiers trying to get a message from Quintus Cicero to Caesar] were captured and tortured to death in sight of our soldiers" (5.45.1). Moreover, it is quite clear that the Gauls are often able to look back. It is true that in several of the examples that demonstrate this, the Romans deceive Gauls by deliberately giving false impressions. Labienus had his men make noise and motions to simulate fear (6.7.8). Caesar disposed cohorts in an open formation to make their numbers appear greater and so to conceal the fact that he had moved a large part of his force elsewhere (7.35.4).[39] Nonetheless, the Gauls are watching back. Romans on the whole manage this better than Gauls do, but both are playing the same game. There are even cases where Gallic and Roman vision are explicitly put on equal footing. During the final conflict at Alesia, both sides are driven to *virtus* "because the battle was waged in the sight of all, and neither fine deeds nor foul could be concealed" (7.80.5). Romans and Gauls view and are viewed simultaneously. This dual objectification of Romans and barbarians is paralleled as early as the first book: "[Ariovistus said that] this Gaul was his own province, just as that was ours" (1.44.8). Here Ariovistus takes the same broad view that the narrator did in the open geographical passage and the ethnographies, but he looks down upon Gauls, Germans, and Romans alike. The equality of position is emphasized by the antithetical language of the passage ("his own ... ours," "this ... that") and by the substance of the argument (that Romans and Germans have the same rights over Gaul). Less visual, but similar in effect, are passages where Gallic or German leaders analyze Caesar's position within Roman politics, performing a kind of reverse ethnography (1.44.12, 4.16.6, 7.1.2).

The last of Spurr's tropes I want to consider is "classification." By this he means not just any system of division or classification, but a more specific form previously singled out by Foucault—a

> classification [that] moved beyond the mere nomination of the visible to the establishment, for each natural being, of a *character* based on the internal principle of organic structure. This principle gave rise to a system of ordering that allowed for a hierarchy of characters depending on their relative complexity of organic structure.[40]

The clearest examples are attempts by nineteenth-century scientists to rank the "races" of the world, placing them on the ladder then used to model the evolution of species.[41] The underlying evolutionary narrative makes such a classification not just descriptive but explanatory. Purported racial characteristics indicate a particular place in the order of things, which in turn explains those characteristics and makes them virtually inevitable. If other races have a lower place in the "natural" order, then European political domination is also inevitable. Ancient authors, of course, did not have access to this kind of evolutionary theory, but they did nonetheless employ classification in Spurr's sense. This is clearest at the individual level, where behavior was thought to be evidence of an underlying character that in turn explained that behavior.[42] At the group level it could be established, for instance, by mythological genealogy.

Caesar obviously "classifies" in the nontechnical sense of that word. The ethnographic passages in Book 6 emphatically divide Gauls and Germans, and even in the opening description of Gaul, he is already establishing a hierarchy of strength: Germans > Belgae > other Gauls. Yet Caesar's classifications turn out not to have the ontological force of those of his colonialist successors. First, as described in Chapter 3, there are at least two distinct and conflicting hierarchies of peoples in *De Bello Gallico:*

> *Virtus:* Romans > Germans > Gauls
> Civilization: Romans > Gauls > Germans

Hence, placement in the order of things is not so clearly defined. Second, the existing hierarchies are dependent on contingent historical circumstance. Strong groups are so by virtue of living in places where they are forced to fight for survival. They also reject the temptations of civilization, whereas weaker groups are explained by their proximity to that civilization. Third, as Jervis rightly emphasizes, the Suebi owe their position on the *virtus*-axis to deliberate avoidance of Roman commerce so as to avoid contamination. Their virtue is contingent not only on history, but also on choice.[43] Finally, and reinforcing the previous point, groups can in fact move along the axes of hierarchy. Once, Caesar says, the Gauls were stronger than the Germans. And if the argument of Chapter 3 is correct, the movement of the Gauls with respect to both *virtus* and civilization is one of the most important implicit themes of the work. Caesar's classifications are of how particular things happen to be, not how the world is in a deeper sense.

The tropes described here, as well as several others Spurr discusses, were all ways for European writers to set themselves apart from their colonial subjects, to make them an entirely different order of being. If these devices simply did not appear in *De Bello Gallico*, it would not be particularly interesting; after all, Caesar predates the authors Spurr surveys by many centuries. This appears in fact to be the case for several of Spurr's other tropes. I think, however, that a stronger claim than mere absence can be made for at least these four. Caesar's stratagems and the (literally) spectacular character of the battle at Alesia point out that the Gauls look back at the Romans rather than simply failing to raise the issue of vision. Caesar does not omit classification; he classifies, then rearranges. Varying uses of "barbarian" by different voices in the text put the meaning of that category into question, preempting both the rejection of and acquiescence in the "noble savage" type (see Chap. 5 at fig. 10).

The point of this is not, of course, to try to find an anti-imperialist read-ing of *De Bello Gallico*. Nor am I suggesting that Caesar is offering the Gauls any more sympathy in practical terms than Critognatus offers the Romans in his speech. Rather, what can be suggested is that Caesar refuses numer-ous self-created opportunities to draw a sharp distinction between Roman self and alien other. The manifest hostility of both sides is not made to rest on essential difference. In this respect, then, the complication of identity in Cri-tognatus' speech is not aberrant; it is typical of *De Bello Gallico*. Why should this be? What is Caesar up to? Or, less intentionally, from what point of view would he have written such things? To address these questions, we will need to pull back once more from the text of the work and consider some further features of the context of its composition and reception.

What Is a Roman?

Roman identity had been under increasing pressure over the decades before Caesar wrote *De Bello Gallico*. Even before historical times, Rome had ceased to be a face-to-face community, but it did remain primarily a city-state based on a single urban center. The people were relatively homogeneous linguisti-cally and ethnically. After centuries of relatively slow (but cumulatively ex-tensive) growth of Roman territory, there was a sudden leap around 90 B.C. The roughly half of Italy made up of Rome's subject "allies" staged a revolt that was resolved, after massive bloodshed on both sides, by grants of Roman citizenship to all the communities of peninsular Italy over a short period of time. The link between Romanness and Rome, already problematic, became almost impossible to account for. In what sense were all Italians now Romans? Were Romans now equally Italian? Could one have both a local and a higher level (national?) identity?[44]

Simultaneously, another transformation of the Roman population had been occurring. When Romans freed slaves, the ex-slaves became Roman citi-zens. These slaves were generally prisoners of war or their descendants. Thus over time the ethnic make-up of the citizen body came increasingly to reflect that of the empire as a whole.[45] In 131, the general Scipio Aemilianus is said to have complained that the populace that was criticizing him over the murder of Tiberius Gracchus was made up of his former captives.[46] Nearly contemporary with *De Bello Gallico*, Cicero's brother Quintus wrote (in an electoral context) that "Rome is a state constituted by the assemblage of nations" (*Comment. pet.* 54). Neither of these passages gives real quantitative information, and the first is presumably exaggerated for rhetorical reasons, but they point directly to a trend that the legal situation already strongly implies.[47] "Romans" had ceased to have a common appearance or common history.

Even beyond the question of legal citizenship, the question of who was "inside" or "outside" the Roman world had become a more complicated one in other respects. Recall the discussion in Chapter 1 of the shape of empire. Following Rose, we noted the conceptual importance of a sharp distinction between a harmonious world "inside" and a hostile one "outside."[48] But, the "inside" here clearly includes not just Rome or Italy, but all Roman-controlled territory, and the binary division tends to homogenize everything within that territory. Another trace of this assimilation of formerly alien peoples can be found in Oniga's reading of Sallust:

> Sallust notes that the foreigners no longer act solely as outsiders, from time to time enemies or allies of Rome, they have now become protagonists of the political struggle within Rome: the Allobroges betray the conspiracy of Catiline, the Numidians are the occasion for the adventure of Marius, Lusitanians and Mauri are the muscle of Sertorius' army, Spartacus' rebel slaves are a sampler of all the peoples. Rome herself had become a cosmopolitan city, a pole of attraction for those who came together from every part of the world, especially Hellenistic intellectuals, who furnished the Romans with the very instruments needed to think other peoples. The problem of alterity is thus posed in a particularly pointed way by Sallust.[49]

Rome never explicitly conquered to assimilate, and rarely valued itself as a "melting pot" in any of the senses of that term,[50] but by the end of the Republic it was apparently growing increasingly difficult to deny that assimilation as a matter of fact.

That Caesar was aware of this assimilation is also reflected outside *De Bello Gallico*. I already noted in Chapter 1 that Caesar would later bring about the enfranchisement of Cisalpine Gaul and the Latinization of Transalpine Gaul, moves perhaps foreshadowed in *De Bello Gallico* by his refusal to name either of those areas "Gaul." He also established Roman colonies in North Africa, Illyricum, Greece, and Spain.[51] Colonization had long been a device to pension off soldiers (with land grants) and thereby to expand Roman territory. As long as Italian land was available, it was used nearly exclusively.[52] But it was Caesar's decision that finally established that Roman colonies need not be an Italian institution. In these cases, Caesar moves across formal geographical and legal boundaries.

He also glosses over more abstract cultural divisions. Sinclair has pointed out that this seems to be the major work done by Caesar's grammatical treatise *On Analogy*, written during his time as provincial governor.[53] Though now largely lost, the work argued for the doctrine of "analogy"—the idea that usage should be governed by regular principles rather than the usage of a specific group:

> In the five times Caesar held these *conventus* ["assizes"] of Roman citizens throughout his province in the tenure of his proconsulship he had plenty of opportunity to witness the struggles of provincials who were eager to accommodate their public-speaking abilities to the restrictive *consuetudo* ["custom"] of Cicero and the urban Roman elite—and whose shortcomings that elite delighted in mocking so mercilessly....If every one can learn a set of logical rules for proper speech, it is much easier for the ambitious provincial to steer clear of at least some of the treacherous rocks placed in his way by the arcane dictates of urbane *consuetudo*.[54]

At a time when the line between Roman and non-Roman was hard to draw, Caesar did little to reinforce or clarify it. In fact, the moves described here appear to exploit or even exaggerate the blurring of that line.

Why, the question remains, does Caesar take such a position? His consistency suggests that we need an answer or answers of some generality. Let me propose three: practical politics, Caesar's intellectual resources, and his social positioning. Some of the political advantage lies in the self-presentation made possible by assimilating Gauls and Romans. As already noted, Caesar magnified both his conquest and its rewards by taking the Gauls more seriously. But Caesar also stood to gain more directly from this attitude. Sinclair posits a political motivation for his regularized grammar:

> In this way one barrier to social advancement is made at least understandable and the path to fame and fortune is opened a little bit wider. Who would not be grateful to Caesar for such a manifestly populist, "democratizing" grammatical agenda?—who, other than Cicero, that is?[55]

Grants of land and extensions of the franchise were traditionally means to amass political support. Taking a broader view of who can count as Roman opens up a potentially much broader scope for patronage. Furthermore, the textual and administrative projects can be connected. Descriptions like those in *De Bello Gallico* help make the legal changes understandable and palatable.

Caesar's intellectual position includes a recognition of what would today be described as the "constructedness" of community.[56] He alternates between different versions of what constitutes Gaul. At one extreme, there is the unified people, the "all Gaul" of the opening sentence, the ethnographies, and brief, isolated generalizations elsewhere.[57] This also seems to be the idea behind Caesar's argument that all of Gaul needed to be conquered at once, and the purportedly Gallic argument that Gauls should rightly prefer other Gauls as masters to Romans (1.17.3). At the other extreme, there are the dozens of individual tribes cataloged throughout the work. It is by these tribes that Gallic characters are normally identified on their first appearance (compare the use of praenomen and, often, rank to introduce Roman characters). Even when these tribes try to get together, they want to exchange hostages to ensure loyalty, and have (for practical reasons) to resort to a religious oath (1.2.2). These two views appear to be contradictory. In both cases, the identifications are of the same type, what might plausibly be called political, governed by the principle of faction, yet at two different levels. The division at the lower level specifically contradicts the characterization at the higher level, which is notable for its self-identity. The significance of the contradiction might be questioned, since the differing representations seem to have been independently motivated. They might suggest that Caesar just did not have (or at least rely on) any particular view of Gallic identity. But the same cannot be said of another crucial passage we have already analyzed. One of the major aims of Critognatus' speech was to reinforce Gallic identity (mostly by presupposing it in his more explicit arguments) at a time when it was clearly threatened in practice. Critognatus is treating Gallic identity as a goal, not a fact. The effort in this speech to take on Critognatus' position shows that Caesar was writing with a high degree of self-awareness. Caesar, then, is presumably capable of generalizing the principle. Roman identity is a matter, if not of individual volition, then at least of social convention, and is therefore subject to change and manipulation.

On the approach adopted here, Caesar's view of Romanness is distinctive in at least two related respects. First, it is fairly broad. Some of his contemporaries—like Cicero—concentrate on Roman control of Italy. Caesar takes all of Italy for granted as a unit, including Cisalpine Gaul, which was still juridically distinct. Second, and more unusual, it is conceptually expandable. "The Province" in southern France is already not "Gaul" for him, and, as argued above, there is no firm line between any Gauls and Romans. Most other contemporary discourse around Romanness can be construed as a variety of attempts to "solve the Italian problem."[58] Tatum has pointed to Catullus, a municipal aristocrat boosting his fellow Italian Cornelius Nepos and worried whether he will receive his due from "friends" who were also Romans.[59] When the provinces appear in his poems, they are merely another locale for powerful Romans to display their good (or more often bad) faith toward Italian comrades.[60] Cicero famously tried to keep both Roman and Italian in play (but also in harmony), arguing in *On the Laws* (2.5) that, coming from a municipality, he had two *patriae*, "homelands."[61] Other writers (including Cicero at other times) were more aggressive about subordinating the Italian to the Roman.[62] Toll sees the *Aeneid* offering a least-common-denominator version of Roman values easily assimilated by the new Italian Romans.[63] Caesar simply leaps over these issues. By invoking more exotic foreign peoples, he can presuppose some kind of Romano-Italic fusion without really giving an account of its form. The question his text raises is how much further unification can go.

It has been argued that a central effect of the civil wars of the late Republic was a victory of the Italians over the old Romans.[64] Yet more recently we have been warned—rightly—that that claim requires more nuance:

> Syme's vision of a cultural revolution consisting in the displacement of a Roman aristocratic ideology by an Italian municipal one seems to me in several crucial respects flawed. We may leave aside the misleading use of the term "bourgeoisie," which smuggles in assumptions of a class with a different socio-economic base from that of the Roman landowning nobility which Syme surely never intended in earnest. The assumption that "Italy," the national unity of which even today is undercut by a fierce sense of regional diversity, had already by Augustus' day achieved a cultural and ideological coherence in contrast to that of Rome, is premature.[65]

How much the more this must have been true for the empire as a whole! Yet this actual diversity was perhaps a greater obstacle to actual coherence than to more proscriptive conceptions of unity. This brings me to the third reason for Caesar's unusual view of Gaul and Roman—his social position within the Roman world. By the time of the completion of *De Bello Gallico,* he had almost every individual advantage one could want at Rome: ancient, patrician, even divine lineage; immense wealth; the highest civic and religious offices; military fame; high-culture skills like grammar and oratory; loyal soldiers (and perhaps also beneficiaries of his civil career, like land grantees). If he had not yet surpassed Pompey in sheer military reputation, he nonetheless had extremely broad claims to distinction. From this point of view, in an openly

hierarchical world, it would not have been hard for Caesar to see Roman society extending out from a center (himself) in a range of concentric circles.
The addition of a few more circles or the introduction of new individuals to
the old ones would not affect his own position. Caesar, recall, is generous
with praise for socially inferior centurions so long as they do as they are told;
"superior" legates who show initiative are criticized. This, I suggest, is essentially Caesar's attitude toward ethnic groups. He is concerned that members
of subordinate peoples or classes maintain a proper relationship with *him*; if
this or that Italian municipality or Gallic tribe did not feel a common identity
with another of its sort, that was hardly of interest to him.

This aristocratic inclusiveness is not without parallel in Roman history.
Hallet has pointed out that persons on the edge of the ruling class were always
more concerned to maintain gender hierarchy than those at its core.[66] Closer
to the questions of citizenship and national identity, we may note both Gaius
Gracchus and the emperor Claudius. The former, the most famous "populist"
of the late Republic (along with his brother), was situated much as Caesar was
to be later; they shared impeccable birth, connections, and cultural skills. And
though Gracchus' programs were various, the important point here is that his
populism extended to proposing enfranchisement of the Latins, potentially
to the disadvantage not only of his elite competitors, but also of the current
lower stratum of the citizen population.[67] Claudius carried through the introduction of Gauls into the Roman Senate. In addition to exalted Julio-Claudian
birth, he of course held imperial power. In fact, expansion of Roman citizenship beyond Italy was an Imperial project, despite centuries of Republican
rule over some provinces. As long as the overall structure of the society did
not change much, the person at the center benefited from expansion in an
absolute size, rather than being threatened by it.

Over the centuries, power in the Roman Empire ceased to be vested in
Italy and Rome—as opposed to, say, the British Empire, whose power never
left England or London. This shifting of power had multiple causes, some of
them brutely material: The original Roman center never had much of a technological advantage over the periphery, and the army provided a means of
advancement and even imperial succession for "outsiders." At the same time,
we may suspect that other causes are better described as ideological. Habinek has recently discussed the rise of Roman "literature" (in something like
the modern sense, especially the divorce of written texts from any particular
performance context) as a tool of empire. It became a way of creating and
reinforcing a transnational aristocracy. Imber has suggested a similar use for
much educational practice. Geographical and ethnic distinctions are flattened

in favor of status.[68] Caesar, I suggest, foreshadows another contribution to this shift. He never makes the argument Claudius would: that the history of the Roman people was precisely the history of the expansion of the Roman people. He does, however, adopt a similarly casual attitude to breaching the line between Roman and non-Roman. From the elevated vantage of Caesar, all men start to look alike, and if empire is marching into Gaul at one point, there is no reason it cannot march inward to Rome soon after.

5. Formal Questions

The genre of *De Bello Gallico*—called in antiquity the *commentarius*—has been the object of considerable scholarly scrutiny, albeit with unsatisfactory results.[1] The foremost problem is that precious few classical *commentarii* (at least explicitly so described) have survived, and only one is roughly contemporaneous with *De Bello Gallico*. These are the *Commentariolum petitionis* ("little *commentarius* on electioneering"), apparently written by Cicero's brother Quintus in 64;[2] a large fragment of Asconius' commentary on Cicero's speeches dating to perhaps a hundred years after Caesar was writing; and four late first- and second-century A.D. works: Frontinus' catalog of military stratagems and his work on the aqueducts of Rome; Aulus Gellius' chrestomathy, the *Attic Nights;* and Gaius' textbook of Roman law, the *Institutes.* Other examples are either much later or survive in only small fragments. One peculiar result of this is the tendency, pointed out by Görler, not only to be guided overmuch by *De Bello Gallico* in characterizing the genre, but also to guess what is generically *atypical* about *De Bello Gallico* by looking at its own text.[3] More positively, we do have extensive testimonia about the genre. Much of the present chapter is based on a database search for the term throughout classical literature, but in fact, most of the important data have been readily available since the publication of von Premerstein's (1900) article in Pauly's *Real-encyclopädie der klassischen Altertumswissenschaft.*

The discussion of *commentarii* here addresses three questions. Who wrote *commentarii,* and on what topics? To what ends were they written? What points of view were adopted in writing them? The discussion touches on most of the open controversies surrounding the genre (and some novel issues as well), but I do not intend a complete account of everything that might be said about the *commentarius.* I include discussion of the genre only as a way of examining questions I find important for *De Bello Gallico.*[4]

Who and What?

One of the most striking things about the *commentarius,* in contrast to most literary genres of antiquity, is its wide range of authorship. Known writers are spread broadly in time, space, and social status; they include:

- Magistrates (consuls, kings, provincial governors, the emperor, colonial founders, prefects, and municipal officials); also senatorial and "public" *commentarii;*[5]
- Priestly colleges (pontiffs, augurs, and fetiales); also on "sacra" in general;[6]
- Jurists (e.g., Gaius, Celsus, Labeo, Hyginus, Tutidianus, Capito, Sabinus, Brutus);[7]
- Grammarians (e.g., Nigidius Figulus, Tiro, Caesellius, Probus, Lucius Aelius, Servius Claudius, Sextus Aelius, Iulianus, Velius Longus, Marcus Iunius, Cornutus);[8]
- Philosophers (e.g., Democritus, Aristotle, Zeno, Cratippus, Posidonius, Taurus);[9]
- Builders;[10]
- Private individuals;[11]
- Schoolchildren.[12]

Commentarii, then, were not restricted to the usual run of literary producers in ancient Rome. In addition to aristocrats and learned specialists, this list also includes mere architects; even among the normal literati, there is an unusual emphasis on lower-status (often foreign) specialists. Children are not attested as authors of literary texts, but would have composed *commentarii* routinely, at least at a certain socioeconomic level. Women are also rarely literary authors, but we do have reference to at least one woman's *commentarius* (Agrippina, mother of Nero; Tac. *Ann.* 4.53). There is also a great chronological range. Some of the texts date well before the so-called invention of Latin literature in the mid-third century, back into the regal period.[13] Another peculiarity of the *commentarius* is, apparently, its frequent collective authorship—colleges of magistrates or priests. There are also family records, perhaps collectively authored over time, called *commentarii.*[14] Moreover, *commentarii* are spread widely in place of origin. Many are Roman, but some are also known among the other towns of Italy. They are even attributed to foreigners, who could not have used the word themselves: Hanno of Carthage, Greeks of various sorts, Macedonian and Pontic kings, and Egyptian Pharaohs and priests.[15]

The range of topics covered by *commentarii* is equally great. Many, though far from all, can be grouped under two main headings. The first of these approximates "official records." These include records of colonial land grants, construction projects (e.g., individual aqueducts and temples), portents, in at least one case a legal prosecution, and of course the general records of public officials already mentioned.[16] The second general grouping consists of various tools of scholarly inquiry. The topics may be literary or philological, legal, or philosophical. The forms include not only what would today be described in English as a commentary, but also lecture notes and perhaps also treatises (on the last, see further below). There are, however, a number of known *commentarii* that do not fit comfortably under either of these headings. For instance, Cicero's notes and outlines for his speeches were called *commentarii*.[17] The same holds for his brother Quintus' notes on how to run an election campaign, Varro's on senatorial procedure, Frontinus' catalog of military stratagems, farm commentaries referred to by Columella, and Agatharchus' commentary on the stage-painting for a production of a tragedy of Aeschylus.[18] Lastly, the term is applied to chrestomathies, such as Gellius' *Attic Nights*, culled from the reading of wildly varying texts.[19]

Nearly all of these *commentarii*, whatever their specific topics, share the function of recording some specific, human project or projects—whether those projects be texts, official acts, aqueducts, or battles. We do not have records of a *commentarius* on, say, a town or region, a specific year (or other unit of time), a class of animals, or the phases of the moon. Many *commentarii* are known only from a single reference, so it is admittedly difficult to prove this generalization in every case. Thus we cannot really identify, for instance, the topic of an attested commentary by one Caecilius other than to say that it mentioned certain insects (Plin. *HN* 29.85). But a slightly fuller record of another natural-historical commentary (Plin. *HN* 37.197) shows that one that might otherwise have been described as "about gems" was in fact about "what to do with gems."[20] There are some marginal cases, which for the most part are works that in English would be described as "treatises" rather than "commentaries."[21] So, for instance, "the ancient grammarians also taught rhetoric and the *commentarii* of many of them—on both subjects—are extant."[22] Some of these "treatises," however, will have been lecture summaries (i.e., notes on a particular performance), like those of Gaius.[23] Some, like Caesellius', may have fallen somewhere between the modern "commentary" and chrestomathy rather than giving a systematic overview of a field; this is the implication of Gellius' remark that Caesellius' title (*Ancient Readings*) marked a work of the same type as his own. Finally, others may have been understood as "what I

I[the author] have to say about topic X" (as opposed, again, to a claim to cover the field systematically). When Cicero mentions rhetoricians' commentaries, the context implies that they are lists (and incomplete at that) of common-places rather than systematic treatises of the sort he composed himself.[24] So, for instance, Lucius Aelius' work on axioms is described as an aid to his own memory (Gell. *NA* 16.8.3). The same seems to be true of Nigidius Figulus' *Grammatical Commentaries*.[25] Even Quintus Cicero describes the composition of his electioneering commentary as "the things which *came into my mind* as I pondered your candidacy days and nights."[26] This is almost certainly not true, but it suggests what the appropriate stance for the author of a *commentarius* was. In any case, these topics are all defined by human intentionality rather than being pre-existing categories in the world, even if a few of them become fairly general.

It is often assumed that the *commentarii* of magistrates were autobiographical in at least a limited sense. Yet these would have been restricted to the brief terms of the magistrates in question and, to judge from the admittedly sparse surviving references, mentioned only official acts. Furthermore, the tendency of our sources to refer to these records by name of office suggests that they were kept corporately. At the least, the records of individual office-holders (or priests) would have been intermingled; they might even have been rendered anonymous by use of titles instead of individual names.

Memoirs are attested for several late-second- and early-first-century political figures: Marcus Aemilius Scaurus, Publius Rutilius Rufus, Quintus Lutatius Catulus, and the dictator Lucius Cornelius Sulla.[27] Scholars have described some or all of these as *commentarii,* but there is no direct ancient evidence for any of those claims. Catulus, according to Cicero (*Brut.* 123), wrote "on his own consulate and deeds," so it is not clear that he went much beyond the usual consular *commentarius* anyway. Rufus' and Scaurus' works are both uniformly entitled (or at least described) by the phrase "on his own life" (*de vita sua*).[28] Bömer argues that these writings were nonetheless "polished and published magistrate's diaries, i.e., *commentarii* [according to his own earlier definition]."[29] Leaving aside until later the definition of *commentarius* assumed by Bömer, we should still question the accuracy of his description of the individual works. "On his own life" indicates a much more inclusive text, as does the fact that Rufus, at least, wrote five entire books (Charisius 1.120, 139K).

These cases all rest on highly fragmentary evidence, but for Sulla we are somewhat better informed. He wrote twenty-two books, and in the second he was still telling the story of ancestors.[30] Plutarch frequently refers to these memoirs as a ὑπόμνημα, a word that is the standard Greek translation for *commentarius* (in part, no doubt, to the shared appeal to memory, on which see below). The reverse inference, however, need not hold. Precisely the kind of work in question here, the autobiography of relatively broad scope, not well attested in Latin as a *commentarius,* is ordinarily identified as a ὑπόμνημα when written by Greek authors such as Aratus of Sicyon.[31] When Latin authors refer to Sulla's work, they use other terms, such as *historia, res gestae,* or *res suae* (the latter two both "deeds").[32]

In any particular instance, it would not be hard to imagine the casual use of one of these terms (or of "on his own life") to describe a work that could also legitimately be called a *commentarius.* But the fact that most of these more inclusive works are never so described should make us hesitant to label them *commentarii.* The only examples I know of are the "*commentarius* on his own life" of the emperor Tiberius (Suet. *Tib.* 61.1) and the commentary in which "the mother of the emperor Nero [viz. Agrippina] recalled for posterity her own life and what befell her family" (Tac. *Ann.* 4.53.3; cf. Plin. *HN* 7.46). These are more than fifty years after our period, and perhaps show the influence of Greek ὑπόμνημα finally rebounding on Latin *commentarius.* In any case, the former work is expressly described as a "brief and summary" account of the emperor's life, and the extent of the latter is not clear. For reasons to be discussed below, I would not exclude entirely the possibility that an autobiographical work could be described (even in Republican times) as a *commentarius,* but the evidence as a whole suggests that the two were not a usual or natural combination. This is in line with the general observation above that *commentarii* tended to focus on a specific, human project.

The structure of the *commentarius* was more distinctive than its content, albeit in a negative way. Vitruvius says of the project of writing his treatise on architecture:

> When, Emperor, I noticed that many men had left behind precepts on architecture and volumes of *commentarii* not in good order, but merely inchoate (like little bits), I first thought it a worthy and most useful thing to reduce the body (*corpus*) of the discipline to a sequence and then lay out the qualities of the various *genera,* written up in individual volumes. (4.pr.1)

Later he draws the same contrast between *commentarii* and his own corpus, that is, between earlier miscellaneous records on which he is drawing and a more inclusive, organized work (7.pr.1, 10). It appears, then, that lack of order and perhaps incompleteness are not just characteristic of the specific works on which Vitruvius happens to be drawing, but are the very features that make those works *commentarii*. This conclusion can be supported by considering terms with which other authors associate the *commentarius*. The word is paired or even equated with "chapters," "annals," and *satura* in its general Latin sense of "medley."[33] This suggests a simple, paratactic structure for the *commentarius*, with items arranged like beads on a string.

To the extent that individual *commentarii* do have some structure, it will normally have derived accidentally from the subject matter in one way or another. This might be physical, as when commentaries on a colony's land distribution or an aqueduct followed the order of the thing itself. Alternatively, it might be temporal. The *commentarius* of the magistrates must have at least observed the sequence of the years and could also have been organized chronologically within years. Finally, *commentarii* on texts followed the order of those texts, whether retrospectively (as with commentaries in the narrow modern sense) or prospectively (as with outlines for speeches to be given). In all of these cases, however, reference to the object does not create a particularly complex organization; it merely provides an interpretation for the underlying linear structure.

It has been claimed, admittedly, that there is a set of counter-examples to the relative formlessness of the *commentarius*. Rüpke has noted that for several *commentarii*, either extant or with salient surviving fragments, there is evidence for a tripartite structure:

> Keep in mind three questions: what state this is, what you seek, and who you are. Virtually every day, as you descend from your house to the forum, you must keep in mind "I am a *novus homo*, I seek the consulate, this is Rome." (Q. Cicero *Comment. pet.* 2)

> The world is divided under three names: Europe, Asia, and Libya or Africa. (Agrippa, fr. 1 Klotz)

> We have divided these into three books. In the first will be examples that are relevant before battle is joined; in the second those which pertain to battle and the aftermath; the third will contain stratagems for laying and lifting sieges.[34] (Frontin. *Str.* pr.2)

> All Gaul is divided into three parts.... (Caes. *BG* 1.1.1)

> But all the law that we use pertains either to questions of persons or of things or of actions. (Gaius 1.8)

Rüpke suggests, in fact, that such a division is a standard feature of the genre. The coincidence is striking, but it is just that—a coincidence. Caesar's sentence gives the structure only of his opening description of Gaul, not of the whole work.[35] Agrippa's commentary is on a map; the tripartite division, to the extent that it exists, is a feature of the underlying representation. Gaius' work, entitled "Institutes" (*Institutiones*), is likely to have derived from a course of lectures (see note 23 above). There, too, then, the three-part division may be secondary. Only in two of the cases (Frontinus and Quintus Cicero) does the author appear to introduce the division *de novo*. And Cicero gives two different orders in his question and answer, so even if he does have a tripartite structure, it is not clearly signaled by the introduction. The mass of pseudo-parallels is primarily a result of the ancient tendency to divide almost any topic into three parts.

We come finally to the question of definition. Given the above examples, can we generalize, at least provisionally, about what a *commentarius* is? Previous attempts have been plentiful, but they have generally suffered from at least one of a family of problems. Here are some examples:

Commentarius means any record serving to aid the memory.[36]

It seems evident that *commentarius* used by Cicero as a characterizing term would be referred to an assemblage of material lacking in literary quality.[37]

[Caesar appeals to the sense of *commentarius* as] the records of a Roman office-holder for private use.[38]

Commentarii are the predominantly official records from which the magistrates' office-books developed, which then took on this name.... In Caesar's case *commentarius* is synonymous with the records of an official personage on matters of state.[39]

The Greek word [ὑπόμνημα] and its Latin equivalent [*commentarius*] are used of written matter that serves the purpose of an *aide-mémoire*.... [There is another type of *commentarius* that] may be the material which the writer of *historia* can take and transmute by the alchemy of his literary art.[40]

The *commentarius* is therefore—as also the Greek ὑπόμνημα—both a rough aid to memory, lacking all art, and a collection of material to serve a future historian as the basis of his narrative.[41]

> Under the rubric of *commentarius* the Romans could understand differ-
> ent things. In the pure sense it is a matter of *aides-mémoire*.... In addi-
> tion to this, there is a second type of *commentarius* ... [that] over time
> becomes concentrated in three particular areas of specialist literature:
> 1. philological commentaries; 2. autobiographical records; 3. collections
> of mixed content.[42]

> Normally a *commentarius* or ὑπόμνημα provided just the bare material
> for historical narrative, without any stylistic elaboration.[43]

> [The *commentarius* is] that genre in which an (ex-) magistrate lays down
> his experiences with an eye to his colleagues and successors.[44]

In all of these attempts, the evidence is distorted by wrongly privileging some
subset of it in one of three ways. First, those *commentarii* which seem to have
been most similar to Caesar's are often, if only implicitly, taken as a norm for
the whole genre. Second, too much weight tends to be given to *commentarii*
connected to other notable figures (especially Cicero). Third, some subset of
the testimonia is picked out on the basis of (perceived) historical or numerical priority or simply greater seriousness and treated as the truest or most
typical *commentarii*. But if we wish to define *commentarius* in a way that
genuinely includes most or all of the attested examples, *commentarii* must
be simply "notes" on some topic or other. This is admittedly a very broad
category, and I suspect that one impetus for privileging various subsets of
the *commentarius* is that high literary genres tend to be defined much more
narrowly in terms of subject matter.[45] But the breadth of the *commentarius*
is not unparalleled. The English speech genre of "conversation" has if anything wider limits on subject matter and is defined primarily by its (also quite
loose) formal structure. Such a nonliterary genre is a better candidate as a
comparandum for the *commentarius* anyway.

Given this very broad definition and the fact that the genre was not subject to elaborate theorization in antiquity, we need to be especially careful
about two points. The first is a distinction between "types" of *commentarius* and "uses" for it. When, for instance, Kaster says in his commentary on
Suetonius' *De grammaticis et rhetoribus* that "the word *commentarius* could
denote what we should call a 'notebook,' or a 'commentary,' or a 'treatise,' "
he is correctly pointing out that the Latin *commentarius* has a broader range
of application than its English derivative.[46] But to retroject these modern categories into antiquity, or even to postulate any division of the *commentarius*

into "types" (or *Arten*), would be a move unsupported by ancient evidence. The second point has to do with titles and descriptions of works. The examples of Frontinus, Gellius, and Cicero show that a work describable as a *commentarius* need not have the word in its title (any more, one might add, than Seneca's *Phaedra* would be expected to have the word "tragedy" in its title). So Bömer probably worries too much about the relative dates of attestation of certain priestly records as *commentarii*, or as the even vaguer *libri*. Nor does the fact that certain legal works are first attested as *commentarii* only in the late Republic, later than their actual composition, necessarily indicate that there had been any evolution in the conception of the genre.[47]

I have been assuming so far that *De Bello Gallico* is itself a *commentarius* and so that description of the genre is relevant to its study. This is the conventional assumption and rests firmly on the basis of early identifications of Caesar's works as *commentarii* by Cicero (*Brut.* 262) and by Caesar's own lieutenant Aulus Hirtius, who wrote the continuation of *De Bello Gallico*.[48] On the other hand, it is also common to question whether *De Bello Gallico* is a typical example of the type. In particular, some have argued that over the course of the work, Caesar drifts toward a style more like that of "history" proper.[49] There are certainly stylistic changes, though the issue of genre is more problematic. Moreover, Görler has rightly called into question some of the specific arguments used to support the view of *De Bello Gallico* as *historia*,[50] and I here add two further considerations in favor of *De Bello Gallico's* normalcy. The first has to do with those first early testimonia. Cicero and Hirtius do not merely refer to Caesar's works as *commentarii*; they both raise explicitly the issue of history. For instance,

> [Brutus:] "I have read many of his speeches and also the *commentarii* on his deeds which he himself wrote." [Cicero:] "[They are] deserving of great admiration. For they are clear, direct, and charming, with all decorative language removed like an article of clothing. But while he was hoping to provide material that others could draw from to write history, he may have done fools a favor, men who would scorch them with curling-irons, but he put wiser heads off of writing. You see, nothing is sweeter in history than pure and shining brevity. (Cic. *Brut.* 262)

There is no mention of a progression here. Moreover, the style is described as a simple one; if this is useful for history (and Cicero is perhaps polemical on that point), it is hardly a distinctive feature of the genre, especially in comparison to the *commentarius*.[51] (The same argument can be made for Hirtius' closely similar remarks.) The second point has to do with a single feature that clearly does change over the course of the work and has been associated by some with history: direct speech. The first instance of direct speech in *De Bello Gallico* does not occur until the middle of Book 4. Thereafter the number and length of speeches increase, culminating in the long speech of the Gaul Critognatus near the end of the last book. Imaginary speeches are one of the most distinctive features—at least for modern readers—of ancient historical writing; in the *commentarius* they might be thought to provide unwonted ornament. Hence, it has been easy to read increasing use of speeches as a symptom of increasingly "historical" writing. Detailed examination, however, shows that Caesar uses his speeches in a fashion hardly specific to the historians.

"Historical" speeches are usually delivered by significant characters, such as generals exhorting the troops before battle. They are often tied less to the needs of the character vis-à-vis the internal audience than to the historian's desire to provide analysis of the situation or depiction of the speaker's character.[52] Labienus and Vercingetorix each are awarded one brief direct address, but speeches in *De Bello Gallico* are generally delivered by minor characters, otherwise unknown to history or even to the rest of the text: the anonymous standard-bearer of the Tenth Legion (4.25.3), or Marcus Petronius, centurion of the Eighth Legion (7.50.4–6). Their content usually serves no analytic function. Rather, these speeches are epigrams that cap anecdotes of isolated acts of heroism or the like. Though not alien to literary history, a closer parallel would be Valerius Maximus' collection of improving anecdotes, *Memorable Deeds and Sayings*.[53] Even the unusually long speech of Critognatus is introduced in a way that suggests such a context: "It seems that Critognatus' speech cannot be passed over because of its singular and nefarious cruelty" (7.77.2).[54] Gellius records that Xenophon wrote "*commentarii* on the words and deeds of Socrates" (14.3.5), so this kind of material may be typical of the genre—the secular equivalent of the portents collected by priests (Plin. *HN* 17.243). Though almost certainly composed by Caesar (all are set outside his presence), these little speeches may make a peculiar claim to being more real than their counterparts in history. Their "noteworthiness" requires a break in the narrative; they appear to impose themselves on the author. If they neither explain nor advance the story, then their value lies in their having (supposedly) actually happened. Whatever their precise function, however, the direct speeches of *De Bello Gallico* are plausibly a characteristic of the *commentarius*, not a departure from it.

If, then, *De Bello Gallico* is a fairly typical *commentarius*, we might ask on what it is supposed to be a *commentarius*. This is particularly significant since, as argued above, a *commentarius* typically derives what structure it has from its subject matter. One approach to this question has been to examine the title. This, as it happens, is easier said than done.[55] Kelsey long ago demonstrated that "the manuscript transmission of the title is hopelessly corrupt."[56] We are left, then, with the wording of the same testimonia that established *De Bello Gallico's* identity as a *commentarius:*

- Cicero (*Brut.* 262): commentarios quosdam … rerum suarum.
- Hirtius (*BG* 8.pr.2): Caesaris nostri commentarios rerum gestarum Galliae.
- Suetonius (*Iul.* 56.1): rerum suarum commentarios Gallici civilisque belli Pompeiani.

Sheer numbers might suggest *res suae* (or perhaps *res gestae;* either "deeds") with or without some further qualification for the individual wars. On the other hand, these authors, who were all writing after both *De Bello Gallico* and *Bellum Civile,* may simply have arrived at such standard phrases to cover both works at the same time. The observed variation between *res suae* and *res gestae* might support this.[57]

Kelsey offers some more circumstantial arguments for a vague title (like *res gestae*) without specification of Gaul; these seem to have convinced those subsequent writers who have confronted the question directly.[58] The main argument has to do with the purported goal of Caesar's propaganda:

His appointment in Gaul, as in the case of other proconsuls, included civil as well as military functions; and, though in his administration deeds of war overshadowed and obscured deeds of peace, it must be remembered that his career of conquest had been sharply criticized and even viewed with alarm at Rome.[59] He was not so lacking in tact as to characterize the work in which he gave to the Roman people an account of his stewardship by a term exclusively, to some offensively, military.[60]

This might possibly have been sage political advice had it been offered to Caesar at the time, but it bears little relationship to what Caesar actually wrote. For instance, his entire report of activities not related to the war for 58/7 is (the last sentence of Book 1): "He himself [Caesar] set out into Nearer Gaul to call *conventus* ('assizes')" (1.54.3). For 55/4, the report extends over two sentences: "Caesar, departing from the winter camps into Italy (as was his yearly custom)…. The *conventus* of Nearer Gaul having been completed …" (5.1.1, 5).

In some years this visit to conduct the annual assizes is not even recorded, and it is never given more than a few lines of the greatest generality. Even some war-related activities—establishing winter quarters, ensuring supplies, recruiting new legions—are dispatched in a few brief sentences. Virtually the whole work deals with battles, maneuvers, and direct conversation with the enemy. Caesar arguably shows leadership in many dimensions, but civil administration is not one of them. Conversely, Caesar is himself not present for much of what goes on in *De Bello Gallico*. War remains the subject even when Caesar does not.

Kelsey also questions whether the several operations against many peoples would at the time have appeared as a unitary "Gallic War." Cicero refers to the entire enterprise in this way many times.[61] It is certainly true that there was not "in fact" a single war, nor is there clear evidence that it was uniformly so perceived. *Bellum* is a flexible word that could refer to a single campaign or a series thereof.[62] But this argument, too, ignores what Caesar actually wrote. We have already seen how Caesar goes out of his way to construct a unitary Gaul out of what may "in fact" have been a set of loose and variable assemblages of tribes. We have also seen how he stresses the all-or-nothing character of his campaigns; if some Gauls remain outside Rome's jurisdiction, more war will result. Moreover, Kelsey's purported individual wars cut against the basic structure of the work, the year-by-year book divisions.[63] So although Caesar could have distinguished Gallic, Belgian, and Aquitanian wars if he had wanted to, his text (like his single triumphal celebration for all Gaul in 46) does not actually do so.[64] The campaigns in Germany and Britain could surely also have been played up as separate wars had Caesar so desired, but, as we have seen, he claims to fight in those places only to the extent needed to secure his position back in Gaul.[65] Nor does he celebrate a triumph over either of these other peoples. Rüpke has noted the significance of the opening word *Gallia* for establishing the reader's horizon of expectations.[66] By contrast, the character of Caesar does not appear until 1.7.1—more than three pages into the text of the Oxford edition. Whatever the original title of *De Bello Gallico* may have been, Gaul and the Gallic War are its subject.

Kelsey was right to claim that drawing the war in such narrowly military and narrowly Gallic terms would have been loaded choices, but the fact is that Caesar made those choices. The decision to write up the entire episode as one war has already been explained as part of Caesar's implicit justification of his project, but that still leaves the question of his narrow focus on war-fighting. Part of this has simply to do with maintaining the reader's interest. No one in the ancient world ever wrote an epic poem about the administration of the civil law, nor do we see much mention of judicial work in Roman epitaphs. But there may also be a more specific motive at work here.

In discussing the so-called third-person narration of *De Bello Gallico*, Rüpke asserts that Caesar could borrow this feature from history (of which it was allegedly a distinctive characteristic) because his own work appeared apolitical, operating at an "un- or better supra-partisan level."[67] He then goes on to suggest that Caesar abandoned his later commentary on the civil wars because the same apolitical style clashed with their overtly political content. We shall consider the function of the "third-person" narration later, but here I want to examine the designation of *De Bello Gallico* as "supra-partisan," and particularly to complicate the relationship between style and political content.

Rüpke's theory (including the implied contrast with the more partisan *Bellum Civili*) had already been put forward at length by Collins, and at some level it is indisputable.[68] I argue, however, that the apolitical character of *De Bello Gallico* is not something that just happened, or even that derived automatically from the subject matter. Rather, Caesar's topic was chosen to naturalize his "apolitical" narrative choices. So long as Caesar is talking about war—especially in the narrow sense noted above—the conflicts will be us (Romans) vs. them (non-Romans). This is made explicit by the idiomatic use of first-person pronouns to designate Roman troops.[69] Were he to detail, for instance, his judicial activities, or even his levies, other Roman protagonists might be introduced, and with them would come the potential for conflict, partisanship, and politics. The only other Roman actors allowed are Caesar's staff, and their position is strictly subordinated to his, both by Roman tradition and by Caesar's (the author's) reconstructed ethic of *virtus*.[70] In fact, when politics comes up, it is slightly more likely to be in the mouths of the enemy, who twice suggest that internal Roman dissent could aid their military efforts (1.44.2, 7.1.2). If, as I have argued, *De Bello Gallico* was meant and received as a commentary on the Gallic War, then the exclusion of a purely political event like the Luca conference of 56 would have been not only plausible but obligatory. It is perhaps not surprising that Caesar should have wanted as depoliticized a Gallic War as possible. What should be noted is that the narrow, matter-of-fact focus of the *commentarius* means that he need make no excuses for that choice.

To What End?

Returning to the *commentarius* in general, there remain questions about the function and social context of the genre. The easiest way to start this discussion is by reference to their different potential audiences. The first is the author himself; *commentarii* were frequently used as *aides-mémoire*: "It often happens that the memory of things we have learned fails us and we have to refresh them from a *commentarius*" (Collumela *Rust.* 11.3.65).[71] These might include notes for a speech, whether forensic or declamatory; student notes; or family records of achievements, finances, or planting (though this last category would presumably have been available to later generations as well). *Commentarii* were also produced for the benefit of a single individual other than the author. Examples are the selection of political gossip Caelius sent to Cicero during the latter's governorship of Cilicia (Cic. *Fam.* 8.2.2, 8.11.4), the dossiers prepared for the emperor L. Verus (Fronto 2.3.1), the case files mentioned by Suetonius (*Calig.* 15.4), and, taken at face value, Quintus Cicero's electioneering guide and Varro's *commentarius* on senatorial procedure for Pompey. A third category, and one we have already noted several times, consists of public records of various sorts.[72] Finally, there are numerous *commentarii* directed at a more or less generalized posterity: "Our ancestors wisely and usefully taught the habit of handing down what one has learned to posterity by the device of *commentarii*" (Vitr. 7.pr.1). The best attested of these are scholarly works, such as Nigidius Figulus' philological commentaries and other legal, literary, and philosophical works that we have already noted. Not to be sharply distinguished from these works of scholarship are didactic works, such as Asconius' *commentarii* on the speeches of Cicero and Gaius' *Institutiones*. A few of these *commentarii*, however, were directed less at preserving some important information than at enhancing the reputation of the author. The most famous case, outside of Caesar's works, is probably Cicero's Greek-language commentary on his own consulship.[73] Tiberius' brief *commentarius de vita sua* is another, though the line between the princeps' own *commentarius* and state records must have been hard to find. If the known memoirs of Republican figures such as Sulla were ever called *commentarii*, then they would belong in this category. Diversity, then, is the hallmark of the *commentarius* in audience and object, as in other things. Note, however, that most of these purposes are quite utilitarian. The use of the *commentarius* as a vehicle for immediate self-promotion seems to have been a late and marginal development (perhaps all the better for *De Bello Gallico*'s use thus).

It will by now come as no surprise that there is no single standard relationship between the *commentarius* and publication. The question is somewhat clouded by two considerations. First, many (if not most) were internal records of a sort that could have been of interest only to the most limited audience.

This fact aggravates the second, more general problem that in antiquity (and certainly in Republican Roman times) there was no hard and fast line between private circulation and "publication."[74] Nonetheless, we can pick out at least three categories. Most *commentarii* were probably never published in any sense. This would be true not only of items of narrow interest (speech outlines, family records, student notes), but also of the elder Pliny's chrestomathy, which his nephew and heir refused to sell even at great price (*Ep.* 3.5.17). Others, such as the scholarly and didactic ones noted above, were presumably composed specifically for circulation. A third group, however, seem to have been written for an internal audience but later leaked to the general public, such as Cicero's *commentarii* for his speeches (cited by the younger Seneca, Asconius, and Quintilian), or the notes of the rhetorician Iulianus, which were later "taken widely public" (*pervulgatis*, Gell. *NA* 18.5.12). It is also possible that the pirated notes of his own lectures, of which Quintilian complains, would have qualified as *commentarii* (1.pr.7). Though such leaked texts are not unique to the *commentarius*—Cicero's speech *In Clodium et Curionem* was so distributed (Cic. *Att.* 3.12.2)—it may be a fate to which they were particularly subject.[75]

Although *commentarii* themselves were often not published, it is sometimes suggested that they were conventionally meant as source material to be written up (perhaps by someone else) in more polished style, as history proper, which would then be published.[76] The recent literature has tended, rightly, to move away from this view. Cicero's *commentarius* on his consulship was intended not exactly for publication but as the basis for hoped-for histories never actually written by Posidonius and perhaps by Lucceius.[77] Catullus may have intended his memoirs for use by the poet Furius (Cic. *Brut.* 132), but neither the *commentarius* nor history is implicated, and his literary ("Xenophontian") style seems to mark it as a free-standing work in any case. Lucian's monograph on "How to Write History" briefly identifies the ὑπόμνημα as a desirable preliminary to full history (§48). But Lucian seems to envision the same author for both the outline and the final history, in contrast to the scenario (often proposed) in which one person writes a *commentarius*, then offers it up either to specific persons or to the world to be transformed into history. This is just like the notes (*commentarii*) orators used for their speeches. Cicero and Hirtius both claim (in the passages cited above) that Caesar's *commentarii* discouraged their use by others as a basis for someone else's history, but only because of Caesar's masterly style. These are prominent examples, but they turn out to be fairly isolated. In fact, known instances of digesting material into *commentarii* are more common than those of transforming *commentarii* into something else.[78] And even the case of

De Bello Gallico itself is somewhat equivocal. Although Hirtius and Cicero use quite different language, it should perhaps still be surprising that both make the same, unusual claim. Kelsey saw in Hirtius' unusually pithy *praerepta, non praebita facultas scriptoribus* ("an opportunity stolen from, not offered to, writers") an "echo of a *bon mot* of some friend of Caesar's who epigrammatically expressed the contrast between the modest purpose and surpassing merit of that work."[79] One might go a step further. The "modest purpose" (of serving history) is not expressed in the work itself, nor, as we have just seen, could it have been inferred automatically from the genre. Perhaps the suggestion that *De Bello Gallico* was so intended was itself part of a private conversation, and Cicero and Hirtius represent the purpose (whether real or purported) only of the individual work without speaking to expectations for the *commentarius* more generally. In any case, there is little reason to think that *De Bello Gallico* would have been broadly received as mere raw material for someone else's history.

Some scholars, on the other hand, have suggested nearly the reverse as the origin of *De Bello Gallico*. That is, we know that Caesar (like any commander in the field) wrote periodic dispatches to the Senate describing his activities.[80] *De Bello Gallico* might consist, at least in part, of a compilation of these dispatches, whatever the degree of revision.[81] Though this claim is not historically implausible, the alleged stylistic traces of these original reports have proven elusive, even in passages that must have had textual sources (e.g., for events where Caesar was not present).[82] Even when a distinctive style can perhaps be detected, other explanations are possible (and sometimes seem the more plausible). For instance, Fraenkel points to the telegraphic character of the account of the end of the battle of Alesia:[83]

> Our men, spears cast aside, work with their swords. Suddenly the cavalry is seen behind; other cohorts approach. The enemy turns tail; the cavalry fall upon the men in flight; there is a great slaughter. Sedulius, leader and prince of the Lemovices, is killed. Vercassivellanus the Avernan is taken alive in flight. Seventy-four standards are brought before Caesar. Few out of the great number managed to return alive to their camp. (*BG* 7.88.2–4)

Citing letters of Cicero (and some inscriptions), Fraenkel argues plausibly, though not definitively, that letters to the Senate would have taken this kind of style. Yet the Alesia episode is otherwise the most expansively narrated of the entire work, and this is its most crucial moment. It would be strange to think that Caesar would stop, only at this point, to quote himself for a few words. And even if he had been cribbing from himself here, it could be only because the earlier account happened to be in the style Caesar wanted to employ anyway. Here the short, choppy sentences express the swift and decisive character of the final engagement.[84] Similar purposes would explain the form of similar passages elsewhere. Thus there is little value in tracking official dispatches supposedly lurking behind the text of *De Bello Gallico.*

Bömer has advanced compelling arguments for a more distant relationship between the two. A commander such as Caesar, he reasons, would have kept a running record of his activities. (Whether this was solely an official record or a more general personal journal need not concern us at present.) Both the formal reports home and the eventual *De Bello Gallico* would have derived (separately) from this source. If Bömer is right to posit the existence of this third, more expansive document (as he must be on purely administrative grounds), then it becomes the most logical candidate for the source of the other two. Not only does this solve the technical source problem, but it also has, I think, important consequences for the reception of *De Bello Gallico* that Bömer missed. He follows the argument just sketched by claiming that Caesar did not choose the *commentarius* to produce a sense of objectivity; rather, the readers would have recognized it as a conventional vehicle for self-promotion.[85] On the one hand, this claim seems to rely on the questionable identification of earlier political memoirs as *commentarii.* On the other, "objectivity" is perhaps a more complicated issue than is sometimes thought. For one fraction of the audience—those who tend to read the "third-person narration" literally—Caesar's text should produce an objectivity effect. But if this had been his sole strategy, Caesar might, for instance, have commissioned a third-party work (much as Cicero tried to recruit sympathetic historians). *De Bello Gallico* can also work for an audience that reads *through* the third person to the historical Caesar. As a conventionally internal document, the *commentarius* makes an implicit claim rather to authentic subjectivity. (On whose "subjectivity" might be at issue, see below.) This strategy is more like the release of an originally private letter. As the younger Pliny's letters show us, the mere choice of genre can give readers the impression of a behind-the-scenes look, even when they know that the texts were (at least) scrutinized by the author before publication.[86] Given the semi-private nature of most *commentarii,* it would not be surprising if they could have an effect similar to that of letters. Caesar may have been aided in this by the particular compositional history sketched by Bömer. Not only is *De Bello Gallico* a *commentarius,* but we might well expect that the same word would describe the original notes on which they were based.[87] The potential confusion of these two levels (especially since the compositional history is never spelled out in the text) increases the reader's sense that *De Bello Gallico* represents the authentic documents that were relied on in the conduct of the war. Their warrant of truth, then, is not so much objectivity or even unusual honesty, but practical necessity.[88]

Whose Voice?

The most famous distinctive feature of *De Bello Gallico*, alluded to above, is its consistent reference to the "Caesar" character by name or by the title "imperator" rather than by "I."[89] This has led most contemporary writers to refer to *De Bello Gallico* as a "third-person" narrative, and some recent translations have even gone so far as to "correct" this peculiarity by turning the "Caesars" into "I's."[90] This view is misguided. At the most basic grammatical level, there is already a narrator who refers to himself repeatedly in the first person.[91] In eight of those instances, both the first-person narrator and Caesar appear in the same sentence, for example, "Convictolitanus the Aeduan, to whom we have shown that the magistracy had been adjudged by Caesar" (7.37.1). There are two places where the narrator might be taken to merge somewhat with Caesar:[92]

> We learned nothing about this [long northern winter night] from questioning except that we saw by precise water-measurement that the nights [in the summer] are shorter than on the continent. (5.13.4)

> As we watched, something happened that ... we thought should not be passed over. (7.25.1)

In both cases there is an ambiguity between two more or less idiomatic uses of "we" in Latin. On the one hand, it can stand in for the first-person singular (under circumstances that are not well understood,)[93] and in fact the narrator does identify himself as "we" several times. If that is the case in either of these passages, then the narrator locates himself firmly as one of the Romans, Caesar being a prime candidate.[94] On the other hand, Latin writing is ethnocentric enough that "we" can mean simply "the Romans" (see note 69 above). If that is its use here, then neither passage tells us anything about the narrator. Furthermore, in another passage, the narrator distances himself not just from Caesar but from the Romans altogether: "There was a narrow approach, as we said above, to the camp that was cut off by the river and the marshes" (7.17.1). The passage he refers to here is a bit of indirect discourse in which the Gallic Bituriges argue to their fellows that their town of Avaricum should be defended rather than abandoned and burned (7.15.5).

There are also substantive differences that, inter alia, separate Caesar and the narrator. Take, for instance, the use of the word *barbarus*, "barbarian." Nearly all instances can be put into one of two categories. One of these I call "negative"; in negative contexts, the logic of the individual passages relies on the specific and pejorative force of the term, for example, "[Diviciacus said that] he [Ariovistus] was a barbarous, wrathful, and rash man" (1.31.12). The other type is "neutral"; in neutral contexts, *barbarus* could be replaced by a more neutral term (such as *hostis*, "enemy") without damage to the sense. "If tree-trunks or ships were to be sent [downstream] by the barbarians to knock down the work, the force of these would be diminished by these defenses so they would not harm the bridge [over the Rhine]" (4.17.10).[95] If we compare the narrator's use of *barbarus* to that of the individual characters (including indirect discourse), a sharp difference appears (fig. 10). The characters (including Caesar) always rely on the negative connotations of *barbarus.* The narrator nearly always uses it simply to mean "the other side."[96] The narrator and Caesar also seem to show differing religious attitudes. The narrator views the gods at a distance; in the ethnography, he matter-of-factly matches Celtic gods with Roman on the basis of portfolio (6.17.1–2). Nor does he object explicitly to tortures that the Gauls carry out in the name of religion (6.16.3–5, 6.17.3–5). A little later, when the Germans nearly overwhelm Quintus Cicero's camp, he notes somewhat cynically that "most fashion new religions for themselves on the spot" (6.37.8). And he is indifferent about the reason ("chance" or "the immortal gods") for which Caesar was able to annihilate a particular Helvetian canton that had earlier defeated a Roman army: *sive casu sive consilio deorum immortalium* (1.12.5). The character Caesar is, only a few sections later, much clearer on this point. He warns the Helvetii that the delay in their punishment (for wrongs done the Romans) means merely that the gods have greater vengeance in store for them (1.14.5). He later credits the defeat of Titurius and Cotta to the former's rashness, but subsequent Roman success to the men's *virtus* and "the gift of the immortal gods" (5.52.6; see also 4.7.5). References to the gods from any point of view are rare in *De Bello Gallico,* but the differences between the few examples may not be coincidental. In respect both of theodicy and of barbarism, Caesar takes a more morally engaged stand than the narrator.

The separation of the narrator from the character "Caesar" (and by implication from the author Caesar) has certain advantages. Although the *commentarius* form may not have produced in and of itself an objectivity effect,

	Character	Narrator
Neutral		2.35.1, 3.6.2, 3.14.4, 3.15.2, 3.23.2, 4.17.10, 4.21.9 (cf?), 2.24.1 4.32.2, 4.34.5, 5.34.1, 6.29.2 (cf), 6.34.6, 6.37.7 (cf), 6.37.9, 6.39.3, 6.40.8, 6.42.2
Negative	1.31.5, 1.31.13, 1.33.4, 1.40.9, 1.44.9, 4.22.1	4.10.4, 6.10.2 (cf)
"cf" indicates a passage of narrator-text that seems to show character focalization.		

Figure 10. Uses of barbarus in De Bello Gallico.

this separation does so in at least a limited, local fashion. For instance, James shows that in the story of the near-mutiny at Vesontio, it acts this way: first (in the midst of an episode deeply concerned with the problem of the valid-ity of speech), the "independent" voice of the narrator confirms the essential truth of Caesar's words of reassurance to his troops. To the extent that the character and narrator are separate, the former is shown to be a wise leader. Second, in revealing Caesar's "role-playing" during the incident, which al-lowed the troops to save face in backing down from their demands, the nar-rative offers itself as an "act of self-exposure and unveiling." To the extent that the narrator is allowed to "unmask" the character "Caesar," the author Caesar adds "the quality of openness ... to his public persona."[97] But such quasi-epistemological effects are not all that is at stake here. Caesar, we noted above, has a more moralizing persona than the narrator. We also saw in Chap-ter 3 that, although the entire narrative is structured to justify Caesar's actions, in the rare cases when explicit argument is called for it is put directly in the general's mouth (as in the debate with Ariovistus).[98] Though there is frankly very little direct evidence on the point, one might still plausibly speculate that the distanced, matter-of-fact stance of the narrator is a genre feature.[99] This moral distance contributes to the sense of epistemic objectivity Caesar is ap-parently trying to exploit. Such a stance, however, would be less appropriate for Caesar's own self-presentation. The ideal Roman political leader was not an "objective" technocrat, but a moral and even moralizing figure.[100] Moral judgment (existimatio) was one of his ongoing responsibilities.[101] Caesar (the author) wants to have it both ways, and he can do so as long as he keeps his narrator and "himself" separate in the text.

  If the so-called third-person style is useful to Caesar, we may still ask whether he found it ready for use as a genre feature or whether it represents an innovation on his part. The direct evidence here is weak. Asconius (like any textual commentator) did not participate in the subject of his commentary and so had little choice but to let the third person predominate. Quintus Cicero's electioneering commentary is framed as a letter, and its frequent second persons derive from epistolary custom. Rüpke cites a brief fragment of a *commentarius* of the emperor Trajan to suggest that a first-person form was customary: "Thence we went to Berzobis, then to Aizis" (Priscian 2.205.6K).[102] We should ask, however, if this is not perhaps an imperial phenomenon. This fragment is presumably from the *commentarius* of the *princeps*, the subject of which was the acts of the emperor. These are likely to have been similar to Augustus' first-person *Res gestae*, though not nearly so compressed.[103] I would speculate that this is an imperial development, not only chronologically but conceptually. Only under such a government can the records of an individual be so confused with those of state.[104] In Trajan's case, we happen to have several letters to Pliny that illustrate the conflation: "Your question as to freeborn children who are exposed ... is often asked, but nothing is found in the *commentarii* of the emperors before me that applies to all the provinces."[105] In the Republic, the annual and collegial character of the magistracies would have made the first-person records not only impolitic but hardly comprehensible (amidst a sea of different "I's").

Of course, Caesar need not have been writing here an official record of his term as proconsul, and that takes us back to the question of the title (or at any rate the topic) of *De Bello Gallico*. If it is, as I argued above, a commentary on the war instead of on Caesar, then Trajan's commentary is not a parallel and the third person is unsurprising. Or, more precisely, the dominant third person of the narrative is one of the features that tells the reader what *De Bello Gallico* is supposed to be about. The same is true for the ever-widening range of spatial points of view of the narrator. That *De Bello Gallico* opens with a "digression" followed by an "alternative" narrative strand (Orgetorix) is a particular argument against the close identification of the narrator with Caesar and of the narrative with Caesar's story. These forms of narration, then, are small, seemingly neutral formal devices that Caesar uses to naturalize omissions (and inclusions) that in turn have political consequences.

Even if the narrator is not to be identified too closely with "Caesar" (and so with Caesar), one might still ask whether he can nonetheless be located in the story-world with some specificity. Here I want to consider his place in space and in time.[106] For most of the first two books, the narrator seems to follow Caesar around, and the same is true for substantial parts of the rest of *De Bello Gallico*. This basic pattern is, however, disrupted in at least three ways. First, in many scenes, especially when opposing forces have engaged, the narrative skips back and forth between the two sides, following chains of action and counter-action rather than watching from a fixed point.[107] Second, starting with Publius Crassus' expedition against the maritime tribes (2.34), missions led by legates create entirely new "narrative strands" that have little or nothing to do with Caesar.[108] In a few cases, these narrative strands do not even depend on a Roman legate; the most notable of these is the story of Orgetorix and his plans, which precedes the eventual conflict between the Romans and Helvetians (1.2–5). One striking feature of this episode is that, until his death, it follows Orgetorix as closely as most of the rest of the book follows Caesar. Finally, there are the long "digressions," such as the opening description of Gaul (1.1) and the major ethnographic passages (4.1.3–4.3.4; 5.12–14; 6.11–28). One might also consider as digressions the little anecdotes Caesar tells of acts of bravery by individual soldiers. These are stipulated to have taken place within the main narrative strand, but neither narrative logic nor the overall style of De Bello Gallico requires the presence of any of these stories. Nor, on the other hand, would they appear out of place if they were inserted into a history of the Punic Wars (or any other). In these passages, too, the narrator occupies a location very "close to the ground," if not necessarily corresponding to a named character. De Bello Gallico's narrator, then, takes up a flexible set of positions spatially according to the needs of the moment, ranging from identification with a single character to the broad view of a battle to an "Olympian" view on a geographic scale.

In time, however, the narrator seems to be more constrained. Time progresses fairly steadily throughout the narrative. The narrator never looks forward and rarely looks far back from the time of the main narrative. There are a few references to the invasion of the Cimbri and Teutoni in the late second century and to the Helvetian defeat of the Roman general Lucius Cassius in 107, and to two other defeats in southwest France later (3.20.1); about half of these are put in the minds or mouths of various characters.[109] The digressions have no very specific time (though they do share a distant past with the time of the main narrative).[110] In general, though, the narrative stays within the time of the war itself. Even within that time, the narrative moves forward almost without interruption. There are several back-references to earlier segments of the text as well; all are brief and of forms like "as was said before" and "as we showed above."[111] There are no forward references of parallel form. There is one form of prolepsis that occurs several times, and it shows an interesting conflict between the narrator's spatial and temporal point of view. Five times the narrator justifies a particular claim with a phrase like "as [Caesar] later learned from prisoners."[112] Four of these occur in the first two books, in passages where the narrator generally stays close to Caesar. That spatial feature of the narrative requires some informant for things like the enemy's state of mind; since Caesar cannot yet know it, the similarly placed narrator explains how the information eventually came to him. But this move conflicts with the temporal imperative not to refer forward in time. When the narrator's spatial continuity starts to break down after Book 2, the temporal imperative asserts itself completely.

It is hard to tell whether the anonymous narration and the flexible point of view are features of the *commentarius* or merely features the *commentarius* permits, but the situation is a little clearer for the lack of prolepsis in *De Bello Gallico*. Asconius' commentary on Cicero's speeches uses only back-references.[113] This is particularly noteworthy because Asconius certainly had access to the entire corpus at once and could, before publication, have inserted forward references as well. This is best explained as a genre feature. The *commentarius*, it was argued above, generally derived its structure from its subject matter. In the case of linear objects like texts or simple historical events, the *commentarius* then becomes a running record. The magisterial *commentarii*, we may suspect, were written "on the fly," so that forward references would have been difficult or even impossible. This property is useful for Caesar's project. If he can create the illusion that *De Bello Gallico* was composed on a write-as-you-go basis without redaction, it strengthens the impression of "authentic subjectivity." Again, if these are "real" records, then practical considerations make them more trustworthy; they pose as a look behind the scenes. Although the supposition must remain at least partially hypothetical, it is nonetheless plausible that the *commentarius* form benefited Caesar by promoting precisely this illusion because of its conventional associations.

6. Empire and the "Just War"

One of the most famous passages in the *Aeneid* is Anchises' speech to Aeneas prophesying the destiny of their descendants. After a long description of notable individuals from Roman history comes a brief prescription in explicitly national terms. Other peoples will sculpt or give speeches or measure the stars, but "You, Roman, remember to govern the peoples under your empire (these will be your arts), and impose the habit of peace, spare the conquered, and beat down the proud" (*Aen.* 6.851–853).[1] On the one hand, it goes without saying that the Romans will be defined by war. Anchises assumes that and simply gives advice on style. On the other hand, the substance of that advice should perhaps be a little surprising for such a warrior people. In the context of their imperial destiny, the Romans are not told to fight fiercely, bravely, or even wisely, but with restraint. Vergil's speech exemplifies complications that existed in Roman attitudes toward the moral value of war.

It has been argued that *De Bello Gallico* contains only the slightest and most incidental justification of Caesar's initiation and conduct of the war in Gaul, and furthermore that this is because no such justification would have been necessary for the Roman audience.[2] On this theory, a successful war against barbarian tribes, as the Gallic wars would surely have been viewed at the time of the publication of *De Bello Gallico*, would never have needed explanation or justification; Caesar had merely to stress the scale of the victory and the extent of his responsibility for it. Although this account certainly catches the emphasis of *De Bello Gallico*, it neglects the serious efforts Caesar makes in places to justify his campaigns, as we shall see in this chapter. This fact naturally calls into question the notion that the war needed no explanation. There are a number of good general treatments of Roman imperialism,[3] but here I concentrate on treatments of the narrower topic of the "just war." Consideration of the narrower issues, however, will lead to certain insights into the general tenor and history of Roman imperialism.

The Theory of the Just War

In seeking to establish a Roman "theory of the just war," it is important first to explain what I mean by several of those terms. I do not restrict "theory" to fully articulated theories of the sort one expects from philosophers; rather, it will include folk theories more easily seen in the form of unexpressed presuppositions.[4] Such theories need not match precisely with each other or with Cicero's version, though there must be substantial overlap to justify the use of the term "theory." Moreover, I do not claim the theory must be autonomous and developed specifically around the idea of war. In fact, one of my conclusions will be that Roman just war thinking was not developed specially to license the otherwise unacceptable (as, in a sense, Catholic just war theory does), but rather amounts primarily to the application of "ordinary" moral principles to interstate interactions. Finally, although I use the terms *iustum bellum* and "just war" (more or less interchangeably), very little is claimed to hinge on those particular words.[5] A technical theory might (but might not) reify such an entity by using it as a technical term, but there is no reason to expect this in a folk theory. So, for instance, it is more telling that Cato the Elder does claim it would be wrong to make war on Rhodes (see below) than that he does not appeal to the verbal category of "just war" (or to the various subcategories postulated in formal theory).

A pair of Ciceronian texts gives a sense of Roman thinking on when (potentially "always") going to war was justified. The first is in the third book of Cicero's *Republic* (3.34–35), first circulated in 51 B.C.[6] The salient portion of the work is not preserved in our fragmentary manuscripts of the dialogue, and so we must rely on quotations and paraphrases preserved by Augustine (in *City of God*), the grammarian Nonius, and Isidore, the collector of etymologies. The individual fragments are all reasonably clear, and they are mutually consistent and even overlapping enough that we can be fairly sure of the sense of the discussion (or at least the single section of it that these fragments seem to represent). The second treatment is in Cicero's *On Duties* published in 44 B.C. (*Off.* 1.34–36).[7] Because of its better preservation, I begin with the later-written text; its view is clearer and, unlike the earlier work, its argumentative justification is generally clear. Although Cicero speaks mainly in theoretical terms, he does occasionally touch on the historical question of the justice of Rome's past wars according to those standards. There are probably internal contradictions in the historical account, but the problems are in the "facts" (*Off.* 1.35, 3.46);[8] this does not indicate a gap in the theory.

Cicero's main surviving discussion of the rules of war makes up the longest, and really the only, topic treated under the general heading "there are certain duties that must be observed even toward those by whom you have been injured" (*Off.* 1.34); this is in turn part of Cicero's discussion of the virtue of justice. This is relevant to war, Cicero says,

> for there is a limit to vengeance and punishment, and perhaps it is enough that he who did the harm repent of his injurious act (*iniuria*), so that he himself will not do any such thing afterward and others will be slower to do injury (*iniuria*) as well.

A fragment from the *Republic* makes a very similar point: "Those wars are unjust which are undertaken without cause. For outside of taking revenge or of repulsing enemies, no just war can be waged" (Isid. *Etym.* 17.1.3). Such a theory, then, is crucially different from its modern counterparts. The latter are, broadly speaking, theories of self-defense at the interstate level. States are compelled at some point to protect their own right to exist. In Cicero's version, the issue is more global. The books of justice must be balanced. (Varro, too, took war as a response to "injury," according to Nonius [850L].) So we must be careful when we read another remark from the *Republic:* "No war is undertaken by the best kind of state unless for the sake of its obligations to other states (*pro fide*) or for the sake of its well-being (*pro salute*)" (August. *De civ. D.* 22.6). "Well-being" does not set a very high threshold for going to war. A state need not be in danger of its existence to respond with military force, it need only have been wronged, or merely expect an injury. In particular, states already defeated must respect the Roman domination that is "peace" (*pax*). Thus self-defense in the modern sense (as *pro salute* is sometimes understood) is only incidentally a legitimate reason for war.

Moreover, we should note the allowance above not only for avenging, but for preventing injury. Even in claiming that reason is to be preferred to force where possible, and that "therefore wars should be undertaken only for this cause: so that it be possible to live in peace without injury," Cicero opens a space for preemptive and preventative warfare.[9] Then he goes even further, stating, "In my opinion at least, it is always necessary to aim at a peace that holds no *insidiae*" (*Off.* 1.35). Literally, *insidiae* are snares or ambushes. In the metaphorical usage here, the word cannot refer to ongoing hostility, for that would hardly be a surprise attack. Rather, it means an attack by a professed friendly state, such as allied Italian communities Cicero had mentioned a few sentences earlier. If, on the other hand, a state remained dangerous, it was to be destroyed completely, like his contrary examples—Carthage and Spanish Numantia. Rome need not wait for injury.

All of the above rules have addressed when it is appropriate to begin a war, roughly what is called post-classically *ius ad bellum.* Cicero has essentially nothing to say about *ius in bello,* rules that treat conduct in war. The only partial exception proves the rule. Cicero says, "It is necessary both to take account of those whom you have beaten down by force and to accept those who, putting down their arms, have taken refuge in the trustworthiness of generals *(imperatorum fidem),* even if the ram is striking the wall" *(Off.* 1.35). However, this merely extends the logic governing the initiation of wars. Once the opposition has submitted (and the Romans rarely recognized a conditional surrender),[10] there was no reason for further war; the Romans had prevented future injuries and could extract appropriate penalties for past ones.

The two works also specify both formal and substantive requirements for going to war. In the *Republic,* Cicero claims: "No war is considered just unless it has been declared, unless it is announced, unless reparations have first been sought *(repetitis rebus)"* (Isid. *Etym.* 17.1.3). In *On Duties* it is: "No war is just unless it is waged after reparations have been sought or it is announced beforehand or declared" (1.36). The latter remark, however, gives us a crucial context for both comments; the principles are prefaced by an acknowledgment that Cicero is reproducing the rules of a specific Roman ritual for the declaration of war. Some have argued that this so-called fetial procedure was purely formalistic, and in any case anachronistic, and so undercuts the higher-minded aspects of Cicero's philosophical project. I address in the next section whether the historical claims there can be sustained. But in terms of the present text, we should note two things. First, the form of the ritual was precisely an appeal to the gods not for an ad hoc favor, but for judgment of substantive claims. Cicero could have adduced any number of unilateral rites, which might have had an undercutting effect, but instead he picked precisely the one that would not. Second, historical evidence suggests that the form and extent of these "things" were in fact set unilaterally, and that they did not represent items that had been lost or the valuation thereof. Examples include large cash payments, surrender of enemy political leaders, and territorial concessions.[11] Hence, both theory and practice share content: a sense of penalty rather than recompense.

One other important aspect of Cicero's theory can be revealed by consideration of its complicated relationship to the professed source for *On Duties—On Appropriate Action,* by the Greek philosopher Panaetius. Dyck has pointed out the important contradiction.[12] Cicero's first comments in *On Duties*—that wars should be fought only for proper cause (1.35, 56)—seem to represent Panaetius' views fairly faithfully. Later remarks on wars fought "for the sake of empire" (1.38) are apparently not only a Ciceronian innovation, but almost certainly one that was in contradiction to Panaetius' views.[13] Yet Cicero himself saw no contradiction, for he explicitly states that wars for empire must meet the earlier requirements (1.38). Cicero can make this move, I think, because he has changed the meaning of the original (superficially Panaetian) injunctions by setting them in a different meta-ethical context. Traditional Stoic ethics had a strong internal component; truly correct action depended on intention. Such action had, by definition, to be taken for the right reason.[14] Overt Ciceronian additions to the Panaetian model elsewhere in *On Duties* are often Romanizing in that they tend to take a more external view.[15] Cicero tacitly makes the same shift in meta-ethics in his discussion of the just war. For him, a "just cause" (*Off.* 1.35) is not a motivational requirement, but solely a circumstantial one. Hence, it made sense to fight a "just" war for the sake of empire, so long as justification happened to exist independently.[16]

Just War Theory in the Real World

The Ciceronian passages discussed above are well known, but many scholars have felt that the ideas expressed there (and ideas of that sort generally) were not of any real significance. They were allegedly parts of a philosophical game or, at most, of a post hoc rationalization of Roman foreign policy.[17] Some scholars have tried to minimize the importance of Cicero's theoretical discussions on precisely the grounds that they are too theoretical, too idealized.[18] Some have gone so far as to claim that this discussion is so internally inconsistent that the issues could not have been much considered by the Romans, even on a theoretical plane.[19] Hence, it is argued, they cannot tell us anything about the real process of empire-building. This view follows from two general methodological errors—an excessive objectivism and an excessive binarism. The former consists in identifying our own "objective" judgments too freely with the Romans' subjective awareness.[20] So, for instance, historians observing the (to us) appalling cruelty with which Romans frequently treated recently conquered peoples or the rapacity with which they exploited them thereafter sometimes regard Roman claims to "just" treatment as a mere show of words (though for whose benefit it is usually hard to imagine). That is, the Romans must in their own minds have understood the world only in terms of realpolitik. Similarly, the apparently pragmatic character of elite *amicitia* "friendship" was once used to argue against an affective aspect of that relationship despite direct ancient assertions to the contrary.[21] But the former inference is clearly as unacceptable as the latter.[22] The second, related error assumes that legal and moral principles are imperatives that are simply obeyed or not.[23] Consider the fetial procedure by which the Romans declared war; Cicero claimed that it had historically ensured the justice of the Romans' cause in their wars (*Off.* 1.36). Since we know of few if any cases in which Romans put off a war because they could not legitimately carry out this procedure, it has been suggested that it could not have had any real effect. This view ignores the possibility that the existence of norms for declaration of war may have had more subtle effects. If, for instance, the Romans were compelled to frame their wars in certain ways, it could have affected their choice of which states to attack and which to subordinate diplomatically. Looking again outside the military sphere, we might compare the "rule" that Roman women were not to take part in politics. In a literal sense, this rule was constantly violated in the late Republic, but even in the breach, it still had an effect. Women doing political favors apparently needed to work through relatives, so that they could claim to be conducting family rather than public business.[24] Conversely (as we shall see later), some military targets seem to have been selected because they offered especially easy justifications for war.

The most basic specific objection to the significance of just war theory is that it is essentially an anachronistic notion. The later appropriation of the idea of the just war in a very different (Christian) context has perhaps been retrojected into a world to whose ethics it would have been quite foreign.[25] After all, the Romans lacked many of the bases of modern pacifism. Neither common creation nor common descent nor common faculties are broadly invoked as the bases for the moral equality of human beings, which might in turn ground ethical responsibilities toward foreigners.[26] Nor did they enjoin each other to "turn the other cheek." Part of the problem here, I think, is that the substance of the ancient theory has to some extent been misconstrued anachronistically, especially in the matter of what constitutes "self-defense." If the theory has been unduly modernized, it would hardly be surprising that it has lost touch with its roots in Roman ethics more generally. Properly construed, however, just war theory is not only compatible with more general ethical thinking, but can even be seen to flow from it in certain respects.

This theme will be developed in more detail below, but let me give one concrete example here. Roman attitudes toward violence even among themselves were complex and grew more negative over time, but it is fair to say that they were permissive by modern standards.[27] Particularly striking today is the extent to which self-help was (throughout the Republican period) a tolerated means of achieving one's otherwise legitimate ends. Kaser has noted that the notion of the just war parallels the broad civil law notion of self-defense on the plane of interstate relations.[28]

A second line of argument suggests that, although Cicero may in fact have said certain things about war in his more philosophical moments, they meant nothing in real life. Before getting into the specifics of these claims, let me suggest that they presume a questionable view of the role of Cicero's philosophical writings. Whatever the academic sources of those works, they are calculated to have had a broad impact on elite culture. In his *Tusculan Disputations* (1.1) and *On Divination* (2.6–7), Cicero describes his philosophical and rhetorical writings as substitutes or equivalents for the speeches he could no longer give under the domination of the first triumvirate and later of Caesar. The first *Tusculan Disputation* is modeled closely on Plato's *Phaedo*, but Cicero's claim to distinction is that he has brought his rhetorical skills to bear to make Plato's logically correct conclusions palatable to a real-world audience.[29] (Note that it is the form, not the topic, that is novel; there is no suggestion here that just war is an esoteric theme.) We can even see Cicero's engagement in the dramatic settings of his many dialogues. In them, philosophy and rhetoric are not discussed by Greek professionals like Posidonius or Molon of Rhodes (the latter his one-time teacher), but by Roman statesmen like Scipio, Cato, Laelius, or the elder Crassus and Antonius. The positions Cicero and his various spokesmen take are presumably polemical. They may or may not even represent Cicero's own views. They are, however, surely engaged with the real world of Roman politics.

In any case, there are two slightly different versions of the argument that Cicero's theory is merely that—a theory. One claims that in practice, the theoretically available grounds of justification could be extended to fit any actual case and so the theory never comes into play (except perhaps after the fact, and always as a matter of rationalization). The other claims that, though theory might actually have had something to say about which wars should be fought, real Romans simply did not listen to such philosophical niceties. The former version is almost certainly false. Livy has the Senate of 195 B.C. debate whether there was sufficient cause to go to war with the Spartans (eventually referring the decision back to the proconsul on the scene; 33.45.4).[30] In this case, "cause" may be something more general like "reason" (rather than "pretext" or "justification"), but there is no such ambiguity in the next case. In 187 the bellicose proconsul Gnaeus Manlius was alleged to have considered several peoples near his command before attacking the Galatians, because only they offered a *belli causam* (38.45.4).[31] A little later, Cato the Elder argued against an attack on Rhodes on ethical grounds (see below), and Sallust's "Caesar" says that was why the war was not in fact fought (*Cat.* 51.5). Even the Third Punic War seems to have been delayed because of Roman doubts as to the existence of a legitimate reason to fight (Livy *Per.* 48; Polyb. 36.2). These examples are admittedly few, but we should note how they entered the historical record. We know about one of them only because the war was eventually fought, and another because the same general went on immediately to fight other people. That is, the annalistic tradition shows little interest in wars that were not fought.[32] Hence, there may in fact have been many more cases than these. Furthermore, even a general who hypothetically put no personal stock in the idea of the just war still exposed himself to potential criticism back home if he failed to follow the forms (e.g., Cic. *Pis.* 85, *Fin.* 3.75).[33] The earlier historian Sempronius Asellio had even claimed that one of the virtues of narrative history was precisely to make men reluctant to do wrong.[34]

Moreover, even if we could not point to a single war that might have been stopped, delayed, or otherwise affected by theories of the just war, we could still not call those theories merely philosophical. As we will see, it is not only in Cicero and not only in philosophy that we see an insistence on the correct conduct of wars. Cicero followed his own prescriptions in narrating his own campaigns in Asia and advertising Caesar's in Gaul. Caesar himself goes to some lengths to set up justifications both in the narrative proper and in the indirect speech that allow for commentary and analysis. The purely discursive importance, at least, of the just war is clear. Nor was this solely a late Republican fad. Polybius and Diodorus both noted a peculiarly Roman insistence on having a justification for their wars.[35] Harris points to a number of specific cases in the second century.[36] Livy even has the Samnites make the same point in 320 (9.11.7). And, of course, the fetial ritual is much older than that. Admittedly, several of the foreigners who noted this Roman characteristic also questioned its good faith. This does not bear on the present question of the discursive importance of justification (and it is not clear to me why conquered Greeks, for instance, should be considered more objective on this point than conquering Romans). Nonetheless, it does bear on the next point (the third objection)—the significance of the idea of the just war relative to competing forces.

Various authors have rightly pointed out that, at the very least, there were competing discourses about war, whose values had little or nothing to do with justice, however defined. In the religious sphere, for instance, a number of texts clearly value and seek expansion of the empire.[37] At the end of the quinquennial census-taking, the procedure once ended with an official prayer "by which the immortal gods were asked to make the possessions of the Roman people better and larger" (Val. Max. 4.1.10).[38] Similar notions appear in a prayer offered at the *ludi saeculares* (theoretically held at one-hundred-year intervals) and in an oath sworn to the quasi-revolutionary Livius Drusus in 91. Gruen notes some occasional remarks of Cicero to similar effect.[39] Territorial expansion also plays a prominent role in the self-promotion of Republican nobles.[40] Cicero did not list gain as an appropriate cause of war, nor is it a significant feature of narratives of justification.[41] Do these prayers contradict the views expressed in his philosophical writings? Perhaps not. The religious texts are all vague and presumably refer primarily, if not exclusively, to domestic prosperity rather than to victory in war.[42] But even if we focus on the military aspects, there is no necessary incompatibility with the philosophical texts. To see a conflict is, I think, mistaken; to see hypocrisy is anachronistic.

Let me draw two parallels—one modern, one ancient—to suggest that the discourses of expansion and of justification could have coexisted without much conflict. The contemporary analogy is a hypothetical one. Consider someone setting off on a career as a police officer or fire-fighter. This person might well dream of catching dangerous criminals or rescuing families from burning buildings. These dreams presuppose the ongoing existence of criminals and fires, but one would not normally say that the hypothetical police officer or fire-fighter harbored a hypocritical *desire* for these things. Rather, we share with him or her the "commonsense" assumption that neither of these problems will go away in the foreseeable future. A young Roman aristocrat looking forward to his political career might well have simply assumed that war would come and, presumably, hope for success. Indeed, given that Rome was almost constantly at war throughout the middle and late Republic, this assumption does look commonsensical.[43]

Next, consider the ethics of individual wealth in the Roman world. Wealth was, at least in some respects, positively valued by the Romans. After all, the richer one was, the more powerful one's vote in the centuriate assembly; there was also apparently a minimum wealth qualification for holding political office.[44] Even the strictest Roman moralizing is at worst ambivalent about wealth. Seneca the Younger suggests that a man may honorably possess "ample wealth, but taken from no one nor stained with another's blood, and acquired without injury to anyone or sordid practices.... Wealth is honorable, however much a man may claim as his own, if it contains nothing that another can call his own" (*Vita beata* 23.1). Seneca here is using the Greek Stoic notion of wealth as an ἀδιάφορον, or an "indifferent," that is, something that has no intrinsic moral worth, good or bad. Some such "indifferents," like wealth, are still to be preferred over their opposites, other ethical issues being equal. But the idea that wealth, properly gained (and to some extent, properly used), is to be positively valued goes back to non-Stoic sources in Roman tradition.[45] In a famous funeral oration delivered in 221, Quintus Caecilius Metellus recounted the goals that his father Lucius had set for himself and achieved, among them "to come into a great fortune in a good way" (Plin. *HN* 7.140).[46] In this view, wealth is at least such a preferred indifferent; more likely, in the context, it is simply a good thing. Nonetheless, this positive value is only realized if the wealth is acquired in accordance with general moral principles. Essentially the same could hold for empire-building. A larger, more powerful state is, in itself, a desirable thing. That need not, however, justify all means to that end, even in Roman eyes. Neither this analogy nor the other proves, of course, that desire for wealth, glory, and power did not overwhelm interest in morally correct wars. They do show, however, that no mere quantity of evidence for the former desire can be taken as evidence against the latter interest.

In fact, both tendencies did coexist. There are at least three reasons to believe this. First, charges of Roman hypocrisy presume an anachronistic relationship between motivation and justification. Second, the theory of the just war is well grounded. That is, its connections to the ethics of individual life are close enough to give it real moral force. Thus Republican Roman claims to have fought "just" wars are not, in their own terms, special pleading. Third, there were religious reasons for the Romans to think that their wars both were and should be just.

Turning to the first point, contemporary Western ethical theories tend to stress motivation. This may take the form of overtly Christian good conscience, Kantian ends-orientation, or even a folk theory like, "It's the thought that counts." This, however, is not the predominant viewpoint of Republican Rome.[47] Stoicism and other formal schools of philosophical thought were certainly interested in motive, but there is little trace of that in ordinary moral and political traditions. One occasionally sees anxiety expressed about a person who "conceals" his bad character (e.g., Cicero's Gabinius or Tactius' Tiberius).[48] But the problem there is not the moral value of their past (good) actions, but the presumption that the bad character will ultimately display itself in practice. Similarly, although there are extensive ancient criticisms of flattery, they are premised on the presumed falsity of the flattery, not on its insincerity as such.[49] I argued above that Cicero re-read Panaetius by making "justice" a circumstantial consideration rather than a motivational one.

That, I now suggest, was not an ad hoc move on Cicero's part, but a natural Romanization of just war doctrine. So long as a Cicero or a Caesar waged his wars under the proper ("just") circumstances, his motives were simply not at issue. Hence, Cicero's obvious enthusiasm for crushing small Cilician tribes, or Caesar's apparent interest in taking all Gaul before he had any pretext for attacking many of the individual tribes, are not careless admissions.[50] Ethically, they are just not to the point.

The second reason to doubt that claims of fighting just wars were simply special pleading is that the rules were not that different from those for individual behavior.[51] Earlier in this chapter I noted that, although violence between citizens was not glorified like war between states, there was a certain resignation toward its use to secure legitimate ends. We will also see below that an expanded notion of injury, which includes damage to the *maiestas* ("majesty," "superiority") of the state, was parallel to *iniuria* law's protection of a very broadly conceived legal personality. A third parallel lies in the notion of justice in its most general sense.[52] In *On Duties*, Cicero defines justice as *tribuere suum cuique*, "to each his own" (*Off.* 1.15): in fact, he uses similar formulations in five other treatises.[53] Similar language is picked up by Sallust to describe a golden-age style of justice (*Cat.* 2.1), and by later legal writers in their definitions of justice (Ulp. *D.* 1.1.10.pr.; Just. *Inst.* 1.1.pr.). Wenger also notes it in scattered literary and documentary texts.[54] What is this *suum*? The Roman political system openly favored certain citizens, and elites like Cicero and Pliny explicitly idealized this.[55] Equity was valued over strict equality. Justice then lies in the precise calibration of inequality. Hence there is no a priori objection to a system whose outcome is Roman world domination; that state of affairs merely reflected their greater "worthiness." The notion of moral inequality might also encourage individual parties (i.e., Rome) to pass judgment on others while ignoring judgment in the reverse direction.

Finally, as has been noted by many writers, religion verified the justice of Rome's wars. For much of Rome's early history, wars were initiated by the specialized rites of the fetials. This been described, plausibly enough, as a formal requirement. Nonetheless, Hausmaninger has noted that the formal ritual implies a substantive component. Not only does Cicero make explicit that the fetials are the connection between war and justice, but Varro does as well.[56] Fetial procedure did not ipso facto justify Roman wars; rather, it stated their case to or before the gods.[57] The gods showed their approval by granting victory to the Romans. Since the Romans won most of the time, they must have been in the right most of the time. Much has been made of the decline of the fetial rites through the third and early second centuries, but in fact the Romans continued to seek divine approval for military action through less specialized means, such as auspice-taking. Domestic political pressures reinforced the connection between victory and divine favor. The aristocracy found it convenient to be able to blame military defeats on divine disfavor instead of command failure.[58] Generally this disfavor was traced to purely ritual defects, but occasionally substantive questions of justification were raised as well.[59] If the gods could and did punish wars unjustly waged, it was quite easy to take victory as after-the-fact proof of the justice of the cause.[60] Such a theology would encourage the beliefs both that wars needed to be "just" and that Roman wars in fact were.

I alluded above to Cato's argument against a war with Rhodes; in that incident, he appeals not just to moral considerations, but to the same kinds of moral consideration found in Cicero's theoretical works. In the wake of the Third Macedonian War (171–168), the Romans considered going to war with the island of Rhodes.[61] The Rhodians had long been allies of the Romans, but they also had ties with Perseus, the just-defeated king of Macedon. Although they apparently had not actually taken the side of the Macedonians during the war by material support, or even by official declaration, their sympathies were very much suspect. The considerable wealth of the island was allegedly also an attraction to war for some would-be conquerors. Some Romans, particularly those who had been actively involved in the war with Macedon, wanted to go to war to punish the Rhodians for their alleged duplicity. Debate on the question in the Senate featured a speech in defense of Rhodes by Cato the Elder, better known for severity such as was demonstrated in his later demand for the destruction of Carthage.[62] Cato's view prevailed, and his published speech survived at least down to the time of the second-century A.D. collector of anecdotes Aulus Gellius (6.3.7). Substantial fragments of the speech are preserved by Gellius, along with rhetorical criticism of them by Cicero's freedman Tiro and Gellius' own defense against these criticisms. This debate is valuable for two reasons. It shows us explicit Roman objections to war, and not merely from a pragmatic point of view.[63] This is proof that such objections on principle could be made. Furthermore, the principles underlying these objections are largely the same as those which later justify support for the Gallic Wars. Hence the rhetoric of our late Republican sources is not ad hoc, but governed by long-standing convention.

Several of Cato's arguments, like those Caesar attributes to Convictolitavis and Ariovistus, propose a moral equivalence between the Romans and their (potential) opponents. For instance, in fragment 3 Cato asks whether it makes sense for the Romans to abandon long-time friends (the Rhodians) on the grounds that the Rhodians were contemplating precisely the same action.

There then follows a series of arguments that stress the inappropriateness of punishing the Rhodians for, at worst, bad intentions. "Who among you, for his own part, thinks it right to pay a penalty because he is said to have wished to do wrong?" (fr. 4). By way of *reductio ad absurdum*, he offers some hypothetical laws that would penalize individuals who wished to increase their estates or flocks (fr. 5).[64] The form of this argument, its direct appeal to the sensibilities of the audience ("Who among you, for his own part"), presupposes the same kind of moral symmetry. The quasi-legal argument makes a similar appeal ("We all wish to have more and we are not punished for it," fr. 5). The very fact that the argument is put into legal terms has a similar effect, since Roman law (as much ancient law) was conceived of as the law of a people, not of a territory. Yet here Cato insists that what holds in the domestic context should be valid internationally as well.

The comparison with domestic ethics is made most explicit in fragment 2. After arguing at some length that Rhodian disloyalty, if such there was, was caused by enlightened self-interest rather than hostility to Rome per se, Cato makes the following comparison:

> Consider how much more carefully we act on our own behalf among ourselves. For each of us, if anyone thinks something has been done contrary to his own interests, works against it with the greatest effort (*vi*), lest anything negative come about. And those [the Rhodians] have nevertheless put up with that.

When used literally, *vi* means "force" or "violence," and the final sentence claims that the Rhodians have shown considerable restraint in not pressing for their own interests. Thus this passage comes near to suggesting that another people might rightly take up arms against the Romans rather than vice versa, though as always it does not quite reach that conclusion. All of these arguments equate the Rhodians not just with the Romans as a people, but with them as individuals. Relations between Roman citizens are offered as the model for relations between Rome and other states. At the beginning of this chapter I suggested that the centrality of "justice" to Roman ethics would require the Romans to take steps to justify their wars. Cato's arguments show that the generalization of justice to international affairs could be used to force just that. That Cato could assume rather than argue for that generalization may imply that it was always lurking in the background.

The form of Cato's arguments suggests that we have been right to look for justification of war, at least in passing, from authors such as Cicero and Caesar. Their content confirms that the substance of that justification must be like that

which our analysis of those writers suggested. For instance, his long argument
that the Rhodians should not be punished for mere intentions implies that disagreement alone is not sufficient reason for war. There must be some (threat
of) actual injury. Sallust's (*Cat.* 51.5) summary of the debate states simply
that the Romans decided against war "lest anyone say that the war was begun
for the sake of riches more than of injury (*iniuriae*)." And what was the nature
of the Rhodian self-interest that Cato claims was natural to a Roman as well?
"They feared that, if we feared no one, … they would be under our rule only
and in our service (*servitute*). I think it was for the sake of their own freedom
(*libertatis*) that they held their views" (fr. 2). Here Cato offers precisely the
same metaphor that Caesar's Gauls had used to justify themselves.

One of the specifics of which the Rhodians had been accused was *superbia*, "pride." In response to this charge, Cato pointed out that he would not
want the same said of himself or his sons, and asked, "Should we be angry if
anyone is haughtier than we [Romans] are?" (fr. 7). I have here translated the
Latin *superbior* with the somewhat archaic "haughtier" to reflect the fact that
it, unlike English "proud," is (as has long been recognized) invariably pejorative. The cleverness of the remark conceals the weakness of the argument, as
is perhaps clearer if for "haughty" is substituted something like "aggressive."
That is, Cato has intentionally distorted the basis of his opponents' claim so
as to deflect it more easily. The charge against the Rhodians was virtually
the same as the *arrogantia* of which Caesar accused Ariovistus (1.33.5). The
salient point here is that Cato does not subsume the charge of *superbia* under
his argument that there can be legitimate differences of interest. Perhaps he
could have simply denied the characterization, but he found it easier to make
a joke. At some point, difference becomes (as we have suggested) an injury to
Roman dignity, and Cato is apparently unable to deny that.

Recall finally Cato's claim that the Romans were abandoning the Rhodians just as they accused the Rhodians of abandoning them. Tiro's response
was that if they did not, they would "be caught and of necessity fall into their
ambush (*insidiae*)," because they had not taken proper action earlier (Gell.
6.3.27). Once again a war is justified not by a past harm, but by a potential
future one. It is unfortunate that we do not know what response, if any, Cato
would have had for this. Nonetheless, it offers further confirmation of the
legitimacy of preemptive strikes.

Cicero's Textual Practice

The importance of just war theories, whether of the folk or the academic
variety, arises from their role in the evaluation and justification of individual

wars, as in Cicero's accounts of his own campaigns in Asia Minor and of Caesar's in Gaul. "Justification" should be taken here in a broad sense. In neither case does Cicero indicate that he is addressing an audience that objects to the legitimacy of either war, nor does he overtly discuss that legitimacy. Nonetheless, Cicero's arguments concerning *how* the Gallic War should be conducted incidentally support the very prosecution of the war. Similarly, his narrative of his own campaign is structured so as to illustrate the same points. His accounts illustrate how a few standard subsidiary patterns help make just war stories more plausible to the Roman audience.

In 51–50 Cicero was dispatched as governor of Cilicia (in southeast Asia Minor), in part to get him out of Rome. The situation with the nearby Parthian Empire was still tense in the aftermath of Crassus' failed invasion of 53. Against this backdrop (and perhaps more closely connected to it than that), there appear to have been some uprisings among the tribes of Cilicia. Our knowledge of these derives solely from Cicero's three letters back to Rome describing his apparently successful campaigns against the tribes. The letters were all written at about the same time and give consistent (if not precisely identical) accounts, so I make little effort to distinguish them here.[65] There were two main engagements, one at Mt. Amanus, another at an otherwise unknown location called Pindenissum (apparently nearby). Cicero was no doubt motivated to add military laurels to the civic accomplishments of his political career. Though he gives no formal account at all of the reasons for fighting, his narrative opens up three lines of justification. First, the Cilicians started it: "Then we went to Pindenissum, a town that ... was in arms" (*Att.* 5.20.3). He describes it as the "most hostile (*infestissimam*)" part of Cilicia (*Fam.* 2.10.3).[66] Second, the Cilicians are Roman dependents. Parts of the area had been a Roman province since the late second/early first century, and Pompey added more territory to the province in 64.[67] Hence, any resistance was treachery subject to fierce Roman reprisals. Cicero refers to this situation when he describes the opposition as "long-standing" enemies in all three letters (*perpetuum hostem, Fam.* 15.4.8; *hostes sempiternos, Fam.* 2.10.3; *hostium ... sempiternorum, Att.* 5.20.3). His description of the neighboring Tebarani as "equal in crime (*scelere*)" to the Pindenisstae also implies that their hostility was not merely dangerous, but a violation of faith (*Fam.* 15.4.10). Finally, making a lesson of the people of Pindenissum would preempt trouble from other nearby tribes: "I thought it relevant to the reputation of our empire to crush their audacity so that the spirits of persons disaffected with our rule might be crushed" (*Fam.* 15.4.10). This program, Cicero goes on to claim, succeeded when the nearby Tebarani subsequently offered up hostages without a fight (*Fam.* 15.4.10). All three lines of argument presuppose an underlying hostility of the natives toward the Romans, which is plausible, though we need not assume it. The present point, however, is not that Cicero's campaigns were "really" just, but that he has narrated them in a way that makes their justification transparent. Given knowledge of the doctrines of self-defense, *fides*, and preemptive action, the reader notes in passing that Cicero (at least as a writer) has respected the rules of war. This is not entirely surprising coming from the most articulate exponent of those rules. Still, Cicero is exquisitely sensitive to audience, so his taking the same attitude in different contexts should count as a different kind of evidence. Moreover, his letters provide a good illustration of the construction of argument by having a (superficially nonargumentative) text read against suitable intertexts.

Cicero's speech *On the Consular Provinces* was delivered in 56. It discusses which provinces should be given to the consuls of 55 to govern after their term in office. It is generally agreed that the central issue under debate was which sitting governor or governors were to be displaced from their current positions of power and profit. Cicero argues that his long-time personal enemies Piso and Gabinius should be removed from Macedonia and Syria respectively, whereas Caesar should be allowed to continue in Gaul.[68] In Caesar's favor, there is a brief legal argument having to do with the terms under which part of his command was originally given (§§36–37), but most of the Caesarian part of the speech is devoted to praising his conduct of the war to that point. In the course of that praise, Cicero claims that the Gauls constitute a danger to the Romans on three grounds: historical (their past wars with the Romans), "cultural" (their ethnic disposition to rash and violent action), and geographical (their proximity to Italy). Words denoting fear and danger occur throughout this part of the speech: "danger" (*periculo*, §30), "funereal grief" and "fear" (*luctibus funeribus, metus*, §32), "Gaul greatly to be feared" (*Galliam maxime timendam*, §33), and "a great cause of fear for Italy" (*Italiae pertimescendum*, §34). Cicero also argues that this danger can be averted only by subjugation of all Gaul (for which task Caesar is uniquely suited).

Cicero begins with a brief account of other wars against the Gauls. These have served (he says) merely to repulse them, rather than to conquer or even hurt them (*Prov. cons.* 32). Even the great Marius fought his battles against the invading Cimbri and Teutoni on Roman soil (104–101 B.C.).[69] More recently, Gaius Pomptinus had checked in battle a Gallic tribe, the Allobroges, who had rebelled against the Romans in a war that arose "suddenly" in response to Roman domestic political problems (61 B.C.). Caesar's plan was different. "He understood that he had not only to wage war against those whom he saw presently in arms against the Roman people, but that he had to reduce all Gaul into our power" (*Prov. cons.* 32). The vague reference at the beginning to the purpose of previous Roman conflicts with the Gauls is disingenuous, but it does make one true and relevant point—that the Romans had already had considerable military history with various northern "barbarian" peoples. Cicero's two explicit examples are chosen to put the Gauls at fault. In the first, Roman territory was in fact invaded. The story of the second is vague, but Cicero hints at a connection with the Catilinarian conspiracy, here described as "this criminal conspiracy." The former certainly made Roman response justified according to the rules discussed above; the latter is less clearly connected, but did put the Romans on the side of right in a more general way.

This part of Cicero's speech can be related to his "rules of war" in two other ways. First, we saw above that "defensive" wars were not limited to protecting the existence or even the well-being of a state. They also extended to vengeance and punishment for wrongs that were long past. Though the Gauls had "done injury" to the Romans (*lacessierant*), Roman policy to this point had been to "repulse (*refutandas*) rather than injure (*lacessendas*)" the opposing peoples (*Prov. cons.* 32). A little later, Cicero reiterates that "we have always offered resistance when injured (*lacessiti*)," (*Prov. cons.* 33). Thus although the Romans had defended themselves in previous encounters, they had not yet exacted the revenge to which they were entitled on the basis of those incidents. Nor were they yet in a secure state of "peace." Whether or not there was some equivalent of a statute of limitations (and there is no evidence for that), the second fact about just war theory is relevant (as well as the fact that the last war cited was fought only six years previously). The official justification for exacting vengeance was to deter future wrongdoing. That the Romans "had" to keep fighting wars with the Gauls proved ipso facto that the latter had not yet been sufficiently punished. Thus both the specifics of the past wars and their general trend could be used to justify the current war.

Cicero also begins to establish here an ethnic characterization of the Gauls on which he will build in the following sections of his speech. In the whole speech, only three northern groups are specifically named: the Allobroges (§32), and the Germans and Helvetii (§33). Caesar's narrative suggests that the various peoples of Gaul, far from being a single entity, were frequently at war with each other. Cicero's preference for the generic terms "Gaul" (the place), "Gauls" (the people), and "Gallic War" enables him to finesse the issue of just who was responsible for which injury and thus who was subject to Roman vengeance. The reference to broad national groups also allows him to bring traditional ethnic stereotypes into play. This characterization is hinted at by the narrative we have already discussed, and then explicitly described in the following section. The Helvetii and Germans whom Caesar had recently fought are the "fiercest and largest nations" (§33). The Gauls in general are "hostile to [our] empire or faithless or ... certainly savage and barbarous and war-like." The power and sheer numbers of the Gauls (§33) combine with this rash and hostile ethnic character to create a threat to the Romans. These characteristics—unpredictability, hostility, and raw numbers—were all traditional themes in the discussion of the Gauls, as we saw in Chapter 2. Their invocation is what justifies the expressions of fear cited above.

The danger posed by the Gauls is increased by their immediate proximity.[70] Northerners of course had sacked Rome around 390, an event still commemorated on the Roman calendar in Cicero's day and beyond. The Roman province of Transalpine Gaul had been invaded as recently as 101, and there were internal uprisings there as late as 90 by the Salluvii and 61 by the Gallic Allobroges.[71] A letter of Cicero from 60 expresses a supposedly general fear at Rome of Gallic war in connection with the movements of the Helvetii (*Att.* 1.19.2). Cicero's discussions of history and of Gallic national character both allude to this proximity. He mentions the "huge masses of Gauls flowing into Italy" (§32) that Marius had checked. And one of the passages in which he notes the Romans' previous strategy of minimum retaliation is phrased strangely: "We have always resisted when injured; now at last it has come to the point at which the limit of our empire is also the edge of the world" (§33). Simply pushing the Gauls back into their own territory did not help; it left them next door, where they could attack again. The solution, according to Cicero, is to absorb them.

Cicero goes on in the next section to address the geographical issue more directly. The gods put the Alps where they did for the protection of Italy. They serve to protect Rome from the "fierceness and vast numbers of the Gauls" (§34). This protection has allowed the Romans to develop an empire stretching to Ocean in which they are unchallenged, but it is obviously imperfect. Time and again a Gallic incursion has had to be checked "by fear or hope or punishment or reward or arms or laws." "But if matters are left rough and unfinished, however cut back now, they nonetheless gather themselves again and recoup strength to renew the war." These features are not formally part of the just war theory, but they help Cicero put it in play.

Another of Cicero's major lines of argument is to contrast the behavior of "bad" governors to Caesar's. When he speaks of uprisings in the province of Macedonia caused by Piso's exactions and by his failure to protect the province from "barbarian" incursions, he says of the subjects that "to enjoy peace, they had handed their silver over to our noble commander; to be able to refill their drained homes, they waged a nearly just (*prope iustum*) war against us in lieu of the peace they had bought" (*Prov. cons.* 4).[72] Shortly thereafter he catalogs briefer accusations against Piso, including the following: "I pass over his lusts, whose most bitter instance both as regards the infamy of his personal turpitude and as regards the nearly just (*paene … iustum*) hatred of our empire is [several attempted rapes]." The repetition of "nearly" is particularly significant because of the immediate rhetorical context. The whole point is to blacken Piso's reputation as much as possible, and especially to question his administration so as to justify his replacement. Furthermore, Piso had been an enemy of Cicero's for some time (Cicero held him partly responsible for his exile in 58), so there would be no personal reason to pull punches. Even so, Cicero could not quite bring himself to say that Piso's actions justified the provincials' war against Rome. Cicero's inability to describe non-Roman aggression as "just" shows the deep ideological significance attached to that notion, as does his hesitancy to question past Roman military decisions.

Caesar's Textual Practice

Caesar's descriptions of his own campaigns follow a pattern broadly similar to that of Cicero's speech. Moreover, he explicitly ascribes motives to himself, which makes the justification even clearer. Caesar's account also includes some elements that were not present in Cicero's theoretical or practical discussions of war. These new justifications were, however, implicit in the old ones. That is, they amount to a combination of the specific views of war we have already seen with some more general ideas about justice and injury that were already current in Roman thinking. This extension of the idea of the just war aggravates the "problem" (or perhaps virtue) of that notion noted above; it is sufficiently flexible to cover almost any eventuality. Three passages in Caesar's *Gallic War* demonstrate this.[73] The first is the narrative near the beginning of the first book of the initial contact with the Helvetii, which led to the hostilities (1.6–11). The second and third are explicit explanations of why Caesar went to war with the Germans (1.33) and with the Venetii of Brittany (3.10).[74]

   The Helvetii were attempting a migration of their whole people from their long-time home in modern-day Switzerland to the territory of the Santones on the west coast of France.[75] They had originally intended to take the physically easier route through the Roman province in southern France, but when Caesar learned of this, he cut the bridge across the Rhone and summoned troops to block their way. After trying unsuccessfully to negotiate a crossing (negotiations Caesar admits to having entered to stall for time) and then to cross the river against Roman opposition, the Helvetii resolved to try a different route through the territory of neighboring Sequani, and after them the Aedui. Despite their previous alliance, the Helvetii began to despoil the territory of the Aedui and their dependents, the Ambarri, and to threaten the neighboring Allobroges. Meanwhile, Caesar had begun to move his troops into the territory of the Allobroges and the Segusiavi (to the north of the Roman province) to intercept the Helvetii. This move, Caesar emphatically points out (1.10.5), took him outside the boundaries of his province, even before Rome's allies asked for help and without any clear attack on the Romans themselves. Collins feels that this is the smoking gun that shows that Caesar was interested only in demonstrating his initiative and skill, not in justifying himself: "His mere statement that he crossed the frontier with his army before he received any request from the [Aedui], and before he had any knowledge of the plundering by the Helvetii, would suffice to hang him in a modern war-crimes trial."[76] Yet Caesar's failure to meet or, for that matter, address himself to modern standards does not really tell us much about whether he had to deal with some other set of standards.[77] Closer examination of this part of his narrative shows that, like Cicero's, it complies with the requirements later expressed in *On Duties* and *Republic.*

When Caesar first denied the Helvetii passage through Roman territory, he offered the reader two motivations for his actions (1.7.4). The first was his memory of the defeat the Helvetii had inflicted on the consul Lucius Cassius in 107, forcing him into a formal surrender. The second was to deny them the opportunity to inflict "injury and harm" (*iniuria et maleficio*) on the Roman people; they would not restrain themselves since they were essentially hostile (*inimico animo*) to the Romans. Cassius' defeat is brought up again in more detail a few sections later. Caesar was able to cut off and destroy the canton of the Helvetii that had been primarily responsible, a success he suggests may have been the work of the gods (1.12.6).

Caesar goes on to claim that "in this matter Caesar avenged not only public, but personal injuries, since the Tigurini [the canton in question] had in the same battle killed a legate named Lucius Piso, the grandfather of his [Caesar's] father-in-law Lucius Piso" (1.12.7). Cicero had used this kind of historical reference to suggest that war with Gaul was in a sense ongoing and had been so for some time, that the Romans had not avenged, or at least had not adequately avenged, previous injuries (*iniuriae*). Here Caesar implies the same. The Helvetii had not yet paid for the harm done to Rome in the previous war. That war was itself presumptively just, being the work of the ancestors, and Caesar emphasizes the ancestral aspect of the chronology by use of the formula "in the memory of our fathers" (1.12.5) to describe when the defeat occurred. And even if someone considered the books to be balanced, the previous conflicts could still be used as evidence of a basic hostility that would make the Helvetii a plausible potential threat. Similarly, their abortive attempt to cross the Rhone against both Caesar's orders and Roman military forces showed actual aggression against the Romans. Hence the second of Caesar's worries, that the Helvetii would use passage as an opportunity for plunder, was shortly to be supported by their behavior.

The main conflict, however, began over a somewhat different issue: the defense of allies. Caesar spends most of *De Bello Gallico* 1.11 describing the legates of the Aedui who begged for help as their territory was laid waste (§§2–3); the similar requests of the Ambarii, who also suggested that they might soon be forced to go over to the enemy (§4); and the fears of the Allobroges, who were concerned that they would be next (§5). Cicero does not offer these claims in *On the Consular Provinces*, but it does accord with the best-attested theoretical justification of war (*Rep.* 3.35).

Caesar's two more overt explanations of his actions, as in the case of the Helvetii, occur in the context of specific campaigns against specific peoples. Nonetheless, they are phrased in sufficiently general terms that they could apply to all of his wars. They are also similar enough that it will be easiest to consider them thematically, rather than serially. Like Cicero, Caesar describes the physical danger to the Romans due to the barbarians' great numbers, their violent and unpredictable character, their proximity to Rome, and their history of war against Rome. He worries that a "great multitude" of Germans was entering Gaul (1.33.3) and later suspects a "conspiracy of many peoples" (*tot civitatum coniuratio*, 3.10.2). The Germans are also "wild and barbaric" (1.33.4), and their leader Ariovistus is characterized by his "great arrogance" (1.33.5). Nearly all Gauls, on the other hand, "eagerly desire revolution (*novis rebus*) and are quickly and easily moved to war" (3.10.3). We have already noted Caesar's two early references to the defeat of Cassius by the Helvetii. He also brings up the Cimbri and Teutoni, using them to suggest that, if the Germans move into Gaul, they will proceed into Italy as their predecessors had (1.33.4). There are four other mentions of these invaders in *De Bello Gallico*, all but one in the first two books.[78] These references are all the more striking since Caesar is normally sparing of historical background information, especially when (as in 1.33.4) it is not relevant to understanding the narrative. The Cimbri and Teutoni typically come up in contexts like "after the Cimbri and Teutoni were beaten by Gaius Marius … " (1.40.5).

The concentration of references to both military encounters (the invasion of Italy and the war with the Helvetii) in the early part of the work may suggest that Caesar is using them to suggest the notion of ongoing hostilities described above. Had he merely been trying to stir up indignation against his foes, a more even distribution would have made sense. Nor can he be trying to establish more specific historical context, since the events of these campaigns are fairly distant in time, are described redundantly, and are given only in detail that would have been well known.[79]

Caesar offers two additional arguments that Cicero did not make in *On the Consular Provinces*. The first has to do with the treachery of the Gauls. He begins the justification of the campaign against the Veneti with the following list: "The injurious act (*iniuriae*) of detaining Roman knights, the rebellion made after surrender, defection after hostages had been given" (3.10.2). The first item refers to four junior officers who were taken hostage by the Veneti and their neighbors when they had come on a diplomatic mission (3.7.3–8.3).[80] These same tribes had already given hostages to the Romans to guarantee their good behavior and now saw an opportunity to force the Romans to return them (3.8.2). The original hostages had been given to the Romans after a brief campaign by Caesar's legate Crassus the previous year (2.34). Thus the hostage-taking and subsequent conspiracy (3.8.3–4) are apparently the whole of the "rebellion," together with the defection.

Caesar's tricolon is thus more rhetorical than informative; it emphasizes the bad faith of the Gauls. Although there was no universally recognized international law in antiquity, Greeks and Romans seem to have felt that heralds, envoys, and the like were normally sacrosanct.[81] Hence the taking of the knights can be portrayed as a violation of a general obligation. It was also a violation of specific obligations imposed by the previous settlement between the Romans and the various tribes. Like the other historical references we have seen, these portray Roman military aggression as part of a larger, ongoing military action, not as the initiation of a struggle. The resonances of the theme of *fides*, however, have a new significance. We saw above that *On Duties* (1.35) recommended that surrender be accepted as far as possible, but if there was danger of surprise attacks (*insidiae*), any measures, including total destruction of the opponent, were acceptable. Here Caesar lays the groundwork not only for aggressive prosecution of the war, but also for the extreme measures (verging on the genocidal) that he will take in the course of the book.[82]

The other novel theme, which appears in *De Bello Gallico* 1.33 and 3.10, concerns the habituation of the Gauls. In the first passage, Caesar worries that it will be dangerous if "little by little the Germans grow accustomed to cross the Rhine and a great multitude of them come into Gaul" (1.33.3). If they are allowed to do so, then (as we have seen above) they will not keep themselves from crossing over into the province and thence into Italy as the Cimbri and Teutoni had done before them (1.33.4). In the second passage, Caesar argues that the "conspiracy" must be crushed immediately "lest, if this area be neglected, the other peoples think they could do the same" (3.10.2). The Germans engaged, literally, in geographically transgressive behavior by crossing the boundary of the Rhine. If not stopped, they would continue to cross boundaries. In the case of the Gauls, the transgression is metaphorical; obligations rather than physical boundaries were being crossed. The Romans must train the barbarian peoples to respect boundaries of both kinds. Thus on the one hand, Caesar establishes the need for a preemptive strike, whose theoretical justification was discussed above. It is particularly important given the characterization of northern peoples as fierce, unpredictable, and essentially in flux. Both descriptions contain key phrases ("fierce and barbaric," "revolution ... quickly and easily moved") that would remind the reader of the general characterization. Such peoples would be predisposed to transgression and would need to be disciplined by the Romans.

To this point, threats to Rome have taken the fairly concrete form of potential military actions—uprisings and invasions. The idea of potential harms, however, needs to be elaborated somewhat. Most of Caesar's long argument at 1.33 is divided into two main sections marked off by parallel constructions. He describes German attacks on the allied Aedui, concluding that "he thought that it [Roman allies being under attack] was most disgraceful (*turpissimum*)" (§2). Then he begins the next section with "he saw that it was dangerous (*periculosum*) that little by little the Germans grow accustomed to cross the Rhine ... " (§3) and goes on to discuss the direct danger to the Romans. In some sense he is creating an opposition between reasons of duty and reasons of practicality, which could call to mind the opposition of wars *pro fide* and *pro salute* (August. *De civ. D.* 22.6). But are they really so opposed?

In the immediate context they represent not opposites, but two aspects of the same phenomenon. The argument for this starts a little further afield, in Roman civil law. Roman law allowed an action to recover damages from *iniuria*, "injury."[83] This was not limited to physical injury, but included attacks on personal dignity such as slandering a man, breaking into his house, or assaulting one of his dependents. Thus this body of law tended to equate injury to body and to dignity. "*Iniuria*, however, is committed not only when someone is struck or beaten by, e.g., a fist or club, but even if a clamor is raised against him" (Gai. *Inst.* 3.220). *Iniuria*, of course, is a word that we have seen repeatedly in the passages cited above. It is the governing category of Cicero's entire discussion in *On Duties,* and it appears a number of times in the sections of Caesar we have seen. Now, the contemporary form of the law in this area had been developing for over a century by the time Caesar wrote. It is possible that over that time its meaning as a legal term of art had drifted considerably from its ordinary usage. The "not only ... but also" phrasing in Gaius (second century A.D.) might be taken to suggest more specifically that the nonphysical aspect was a late or otherwise technical addition to the category of *iniuria.*[84] On the other hand, the etymology of the word suggests a very general sense: *in-* ("not") + *iur-* (< *ius,* "right, law") = "contrary to right."[85] The story, preserved by Gellius, explaining the origin of "modern" (i.e., second century B.C.) *iniuria* law revolves around a case in which a man wandered around the forum slapping people with an open palm (20.1.13). As far as we can tell, physical injury was not the central issue there.

If we accept the equation between injuries to body and to dignity, then wars fought to avoid "danger" and those waged to prevent "disgrace" are justified on essentially the same grounds. Both are matters of self-defense (in the broad sense, which we have seen gives a great deal of room for preemptive action). *De Bello Gallico* 1.11.3 emphasizes the fact that the Aedui are being attacked "practically in the sight of the Roman army," as if this act were an insult to the Romans themselves. Such a unified theory helps explain an anomaly observed at the end of justification of the war against the Germans. Caesar concludes the main part of his argument with the words, "And he thought that he must attend to these matters as quickly as possible" (1.33.4). But he adds one last remark before he goes on to describe his consequent action: "Moreover, Ariovistus himself had manifested such audacity and such arrogance that it no longer seemed possible to bear him" (1.33.5). This motivation is defense neither of allies nor of self (narrowly defined). If we take that as an admission of a baser motive, it is in a surprisingly marked position, separated from the rest of the argument. But we need not read it that way. The German's attitude itself is a blow to the majesty of the Roman people. That is why it is a signal disgrace (*turpissimum*) for Rome's allies to suffer at the hands of the Germans when Rome herself is "so great an empire" (1.33.2).

If, however, this argument is formally correct, we might want to ask on the one hand whether it is possible to imagine a Roman war that was not just, and on the other whether even-handed application of the same definition might not show that some or all wars against the Romans were also just. We have already seen that Cicero seems to resist the latter conclusion, though he does so by assertion rather than by argument. The former question does

not really arise in the passages we have considered. However, Cicero's failure
to spell out the apparent assumption that a neighboring state is inherently
dangerous could be seen as a way of avoiding that question, just as his casual
labeling of the insurrection against Piso as "almost just" avoids the other.
Caesar's work also evades answering either question in a direct fashion, but
he does come closer than Cicero does to raising them. His treatment of the
inside/outside scheme and of the motif of slavery and freedom in *De Bello
Gallico* sheds light on the issue of the (im)possibility of an unjust Roman
war; Ariovistus' debate with Caesar (*De Bello Gallico* 1.43–45) is, moreover,
a long, overt justification for war against the Romans.

I have already raised the question of boundaries and danger as it relates
to the idea that the Germans needed to be "trained" to take or avoid certain
actions. Specifically, if allowed to cross one boundary, they would be more
inclined to attempt the next one, and so on. Thus these boundaries—at least
insofar as they are thought of *qua* lines of demarcation, not *qua* physical
barriers—will serve as enticements to aggression, not deterrents. The most
striking expression of this fear occurs in the last clause of Caesar's explication
of the danger: "He did not think fierce and barbaric men would hold off, ...
especially since the Rhone divides the Sequani [German dependents] from
our province" (1.33.4). The reader may have recognized by this point that the
Romans and Sequani have adjacent territories (1.8.1), but it is not clear until
now that the Rhone constituted the border. To this extent, Caesar is clarifying
the geography, but what are we to make of "especially" (*praesertim*)? Most
of the boundaries discussed to this point in the work (except the Iura range)
are rivers. And Caesar made a point earlier of mentioning that the Rhone
could not be forded at any point (1.6.2; cf. 1.8.4). As a physical entity, the
river should serve as a line of defense, but as a boundary, it, too, is apparently
an invitation to invasion. The Romans are obliged to cross that line in force
before the Germans and Sequani do. Nonetheless, Caesar does not make this
argument explicitly.

The other question Caesar dances around is whether resistance to or attack on the Romans could itself be justified. Although he does not give a direct
answer, he does offer an extended metaphor, connecting slavery with imperial
subjection, and that at least raises the issue. In the first book, Caesar demands
that the Aedui supply his army with grain that they had already promised.
Their representative Liscus responds with a speech explaining why they have
had to defect to the side of the Helvetii. Among other things, "if they were
unable to hold the first place in Gaul, they preferred Gallic commands (*im-
peria*) to Roman ones. Nor did they doubt that, if the Romans should defeat

the Helvetii, they would take the freedom of the Aedui along with the rest of Gaul" (1.17.3–4). "Freedom" (*libertas*) was an even more politically charged term for the Romans than it is generally today, for it is deeply rooted in the pervasive social institution of slavery.[86] Despite the many and varied situations to which it was applied, *libertas* remained a powerful slogan because of its unambiguously positive primary sense. Conversely, "slavery" (*servitus*) recalled the degradation of slaves seen daily in a society in which, as we have already noted, personal dignity was a fighting matter. The first sentence of the passage just quoted uses a relatively neutral word for Roman domination. *Imperium* was, among other things, the power of a Roman general over his own troops. The second sentence, then, does not simply redescribe the situation, but puts it in much more affective terms. At this point, the reader might reject Liscus' entire analysis as inaccurate (after all, it is put into the mouth of an enemy); perhaps the Helvetii would have oppressed individuals more.[87] However, to accept it at all is to accept that the Aedui face a terrible fate, one much to be avoided.

Later Caesar puts a similar claim in the mouths of the Veneti as they try to stir up a revolt against the Romans. "They pressure the other states to prefer to remain in the state of liberty that they inherited from their ancestors rather than endure being slaves to the Romans" (3.8.4). Here a purely political interpretation is never offered, the negative term ("slavery") is expressed, and an appeal to tradition (another Roman favorite) is added. This might be considered a more pointed and rhetorically powerful appeal than the previous one; it almost certainly would be if it were uttered in a purely Roman context. One of the passages that we have been considering in detail follows this section almost immediately, and it picks up the theme of freedom and slavery: "[Caesar] understood … that all men by nature are eager for freedom and hate the condition of slavery" (3.10.3). Unlike the two previous examples, this passage introduces the metaphor in Caesar's voice, so it is not so readily dismissed.[88] Furthermore, the references to "all men" and "nature" assert the universal validity of the desire for freedom that had only been implied by the rhetoric of the Aedui and the Veneti. This comes very close to suggesting that war against the Romans could be made to appear, whether or not "just," at least justified.

The interpretation of these passages is further complicated by the general problem of the status of political "freedom" and "slavery" in *De Bello Gallico*. In the later books, and particularly in the climactic seventh, freedom and especially "the common freedom" are found frequently in the mouths of Gauls as they encourage each other to resistance against the Romans. In the early books, however, the issue is not so simple. The first occurrence of the idea is in the appeal of the Aedui to Caesar for protection from the Helvetii (1.11.3). They complain that their children are being led away into (literal) slavery. A little later, Caesar "sees" that those same Aedui have fallen into the "servitude and control" of the Germans (1.33.2). Thus the rhetoric of freedom and slavery can cut both ways; Gauls and Germans can and do enslave each other even without the Romans present. It is also interesting that the word used here for "control" (*dicio*) is standard for peoples in a state of formal legal dependency on the Romans and is the word Cicero used for the state of affairs Caesar hopes to establish in Gaul (*Prov. cons.* 32).[89] Caesar here accepts the equation of this state of political dependency with that of "servitude"; otherwise the order of the phrase is oddly anticlimactic. Elsewhere, however, this equation is questioned. On the one hand, as early as Book 2, the Bellovaci are made to claim that the Aedui, inferior allies of the Romans, had been "led into slavery" by them (2.14.2; cf. 1.11.3). Yet on the other, the narrator had earlier reported that the Aedui had used their influence on the Romans to bring them to spare another defeated tribe (the Boii), granted them part of their own territory, and "thereafter received them in an equal position of rights and freedom to what they themselves held" (1.28.5). Literal freedom and slavery are not matters of degree. Hence the metaphor does not here lend itself to a relative interpretation, namely that the Aedui shared with the Boii the (limited) degree of freedom they themselves had, even though this is likely to be close to the truth. Rather, the narrator's phrasing suggests that the Aedui were free not only despite their alliance with Rome, but even (given the circumstances) because of it.

The ambiguity of the danger of slavery appears in the very first passage in which the Romans are blamed for trying to bring it about. As we have seen already, it reads: "[The Aedui] preferred Gallic commands to Roman ones. Nor did they doubt that ... [the Romans] would take the freedom of the Aedui along with the rest of Gaul" (1.17.3–4). It is possible to read this to suggest that only foreign (i.e., Roman) control would constitute servitude, but such a reading is strained. The point is that the Aedui are merely changing masters. Elsewhere in the early books, the danger to the Gauls comes, as we have seen, from both sides. Once the war is well under way, the metaphor of freedom is used by a single group (Gallic leaders) addressing a homogeneous (Gallic) audience and, not surprisingly, has a fairly simple import: Roman conquest equals the enslavement of all Gaul. But earlier, when Caesar is actively justifying his actions and explaining why the wars were begun, the waters are muddied, perhaps intentionally. Different voices offer different interpretations of just what counts as slavery, and there are strong hints that it is in any case an inevitable fate for the Gauls, the only question being who the master will be. Although fear of being reduced to Rome's slaves remains perhaps an understandable motivation for the Gauls at a historical level, its value as philosophical justification is reduced. Conversely, Caesar suggests that enslavement was not a primary goal of the wars, even if it were arguably the primary instrument.

This leaves us to consider more broadly the question of a just war against the Romans, and particularly Caesar's exchange with Ariovistus in Book 1. The crucial issue, however, can be seen in a single sentence from Book 7. The Aeduan leader Convictolitavis, who owed his position to Caesar's intervention, explained to the seditious youth of his people why they should defect and join Vercingetorix's revolt. "For why," he asks, "should the Aedui come to Caesar to settle their legal disputes, rather than the Romans coming to the Aedui?" (7.37.5). Caesar never has to ask such a thing, and the fact that such questions are only asked in one direction implies that the Aedui (and the others) have conceded superiority to the Romans. This is inherently degrading, and it also means that the Roman perspective will always be the one that decides which war is just. In this light, it is worth noting that all of Caesar's (and Cicero's) "arguments" consist of lists of Roman motivations for war. They do not allow for the possibility of contradictory accounts or countervailing factors. But Convictolitavis is allowed to question not merely the specific facts that are intended to back up Caesar's claims, but also the whole logic behind them. Why, indeed, should Caesar's and Rome's perspective prevail? This same problem is raised much earlier and more urgently by Caesar's debate with Ariovistus.

The two meet on a hill between the two armies at Ariovistus' request before battle is to take place. Caesar makes the first speech, Ariovistus gives a longer one, and then Caesar offers a brief reply until he is cut off by an attempted German sneak attack. Caesar's initial arguments are fairly simple. First, Ariovistus is personally indebted to the Romans for their freely given political support, "friendship," and other unspecified *munera* ("gifts, considerations," 1.43.4 – 5). Caesar also argues that the Romans cannot allow their other, long-standing "friends," the Aedui, to suffer any harm while they bear that title (1.43.6 – 8). He then demands that Ariovistus give up his military adventures in Gaul, return hostages he has already taken, and (if he does not send his people home entirely) prevent more Germans from crossing the Rhine (1.43.9). The first argument, that Ariovistus is indebted to the Romans, is relatively novel, but hardly surprising. If Ariovistus fails to show the Romans the respect that he allegedly owes them, then naturally the Romans will claim to have been injured and will respond militarily. The second argument, Roman friendship with the Aedui, however, is one we have seen before: "Who could permit that what the Roman people had brought to this friendship would be taken away from [their allies and friends]?" (1.43.8). The particular phrasing here makes clearer what I have already asserted: that the basis of this obligation to defend friends is in no way altruistic, but is a matter of defending one's own reputation and honor. Caesar's demands resolve both the injury to Roman dignity (i.e., the harm to their Gallic allies) and the potential physical threat (i.e., that the Germans may grow accustomed to crossing boundaries).

Ariovistus' reply is much longer and more complicated, and breaks far more new ground. To give a schematic account, he argues that:

- The Germans were invited and even paid by Gauls to enter Gaul (1.44.2, 6);
- Whatever they had taken was theirs by ordinary right of conquest (§§2, 3–4);
- The Gauls attacked him first (§3);
- If Roman friendship is supposed to be of value, then why should the Germans have to give up their gains in its name (§5)?
- The Germans had gotten there first, and therefore were entitled to the conquest just as the Romans were entitled to southern Gaul (§§7–8);
- The Romans were not really friends of the Aedui (§§9–11);
- It would be to Caesar's personal advantage to drop the conflict, but to his disadvantage if he were to continue (§§12–13).

Even if we take into account the fact that some points are made more than once, Ariovistus offers a wider array of arguments than Caesar did. The appeals to Caesar's self-interest are presumably represented to make Caesar look good when he ignores them. Appealing to right of conquest begs the question of the legitimacy of the Germans' original acts. Most of Ariovistus' claims seem plausible, at least in relative terms, but they vary subtly from the accepted rhetoric displayed in Cicero and Caesar. Most notably, Ariovistus never describes his own local ties (to the tribes that invited German incursion) as *amicitia*, "friendship." Rather, this was a commercial venture; the Germans came "not without great expectations and great rewards" (1.44.2). In practice, social and commercial ties often went hand in hand in the Roman world (as still today), but conceptually they were strongly opposed.[90] The salient point here is that a social relationship is in theory an ongoing affair with a past and a future.[91] That is why the honor of one party can become caught up in the fortunes of the other in the way Caesar had just described. The Germans, here depicted as mere mercenaries, have no such ties, no moral investment, and therefore have not been wronged by harm to their "allies." The self-centered nature of the obligation (*fides*) to defend allies contrasts here in a new way with (official) explanations of the superficially similar obligation expressed by statesmen today. Merely being invited does not act to justify intervention in the scheme we have been describing here.

Ariovistus' claim that Roman friendship should not restrict German activities comes close to unmasking the self-interested character of Roman *fides*. "The friendship of the Roman people should be a decoration and bul-wark for [us], not a detriment, and it was in that spirit that [we] had sought it" (1.43.5). Here he echoes a remark Caesar had just made: "The custom of the Roman people was to wish their allies not to suffer any loss, but to be increased in influence, worth, and honor" (1.43.8). But if a state gains various goods at the expense of Rome itself, then Rome's vicarious prestige-interest in the well-being of its allies is balanced by the loss of territory, income, other dependents, etc. Further, its own prestige is directly harmed by allowing this other state to be the arbiter of its foreign policy (which possibility, as we have already seen, will be raised openly near the end of the work). This argument of Ariovistus' might then be seen as an attempt to reveal what lies behind Roman claims of *fides*, but if so, it does it only indirectly. Ariovistus certainly does not speak, here or elsewhere in the speech, at the level of abstraction at which opposition to the Roman view could be clearly understood. Perhaps, then, it is better to point out that this passage could be read in much the same way as the claims that the Germans had been invited into Gaul. It, too, offers an argument that, while not overtly irrational, nevertheless will have seemed to much of the (Roman) audience to have missed the point.

Finally, Ariovistus makes explicit a claim at which Caesar's narrative had already hinted. He asserts that Germans and Romans had the same kind of right to Gallic territory. Furthermore, he claims, the Germans got there first and so had just title to most of Gaul, even as the Romans deserved to hold their southern province undisturbed (1.44.7–8). "This Gaul is his province as that one is ours." This claim assumes that Gaul will be overrun and sub-jugated; the question is who will do it. Recall that Caesar had already heard Liscus, an Aeduan magistrate, speculate that his people might have to choose between a Gallic and a Roman overlord (1.17.3). If it is inevitable that the Gauls will be enslaved, then the Romans do them no special harm by claiming them. If that inevitability is proclaimed by an opponent, it becomes yet more plausible.

Caesar's answer to this speech is brief and strikingly unresponsive.[92] He does not address the question-begging argument about rights of conquest. He says nothing about the arguments that, I have suggested, are not clearly relevant by Roman standards: that the Germans should suffer for being friends of the Romans and that the Germans had been invited in by Gauls. Nor is there any clear reference to Ariovistus' threats or bribes directed toward Caesar personally. Caesar does briefly respond to the claim that the Romans and Aedui are not really friends. Though he does not argue the point, he does reiterate the connection (1.45.1). (The phrasing here—"Neither his custom nor the Roman people's allowed him to desert worthy allies"—is the only reference to a personal motive on Caesar's part.) The one point he does make at length and with logic and evidence is that Ariovistus was wrong to argue that the Germans had first claim on Gaul. He asserts that Quintus Fabius Maximus had defeated the Arverni and Ruteni in 121 (1.45.2). That Gaul was neither a province nor even tributary to Rome was, according to Caesar, because of a decision by the Roman people to spare them. "If priority was to be considered, the rule of the Roman people in Gaul was most just (*iustissimum*); if the judgment of the Senate, then Gaul should be free, since it had preferred that they, defeated in war, should use their own laws" (1.45.3). We have already seen the suggestion in both Cicero and Caesar that the Romans retained a dormant right to vengeance against the Gauls. Here Caesar goes even further by claiming that the Romans had, in a sense, already done so by defeating them before. Any semblance of freedom the Gauls might have was therefore at the sufferance of the Romans, an example of generous, laissez-faire administration.[93] Naturally, any attack on these Roman subjects would be an attack on the Romans themselves. But the situation Caesar describes would also serve to justify aggression against these Gallic tribes, should they ever prove uncooperative.

Caesar responds only to those of Ariovistus' points which could be construed as matters of fact: Were the Romans and Aedui allies? Who had first beaten the Gauls? He ignores those points which suggest, however indirectly, the possibility of different standards of evaluation. Is Caesar here trying to hide the weak points of his position? Is he economically avoiding the irrelevant ramblings of a barbarian? Even to address these various possibilities, we need to think about the broader questions they raise about the audience for this work and the effects they might have had (and might have been hoped to have) on them.

In two respects, Germans and Gauls are treated differently from Romans. First, the equation of inside/outside with safe/dangerous is interpreted only from a Roman point of view. For instance, if Gaul is absorbed, it becomes "inside" and is therefore assumed to be safe. If the Germans invade Gaul, the threat actually increases, as the potential danger remains "outside." Second, the notion of individual responsibility is allowed to work only in Rome's favor. There is never any suggestion that Caesar would settle for the surrender of German or Gallic leaders instead of waging war. Vercingetorix, in fact, offered himself up in this way, to no effect (7.89.2), admittedly after his army's defeat. We saw earlier how these two devices (the inside/outside schema and individualization), when applied to Roman narratives, justify Rome's actions. When they are removed or are working in the opposite direction, they make it harder for the opposition to appeal to the same "just war."

The emphasis of this chapter, as of ancient theory, has been on the legitimate grounds for starting (and ending) a war. There are, however, a few indications of rules for conduct of a war once it has begun. Two principles are at stake here. First is the idea that some wars should be prosecuted more vigorously than others. Battles for existence allowed for any means; those for glory of empire should show more restraint (1.38). Second, even opponents in war had claims on Roman *fides*, unless they renewed hostilities after surrender (1.34). Caesar shows sensitivity to both issues, though he perhaps allows himself more flexibility than Cicero, as a philosopher, would have. This is seen most easily by considering Collins' list of "atrocities" in *De Bello Gallico*. In an attempt to demonstrate that *De Bello Gallico* was not propaganda for the legitimacy of the war, Collins has gone to some lengths to collect any even questionable moves on Caesar's part: [94]

- Execution or sale of 6,000 Helvetii who fled for the Rhine after their surrender (1.28.2);
- Sale of all the Aduatuci (2.33.6);
- Execution of the Venetian elders and sale of the people (3.16.4);
- Annihilation of the Usipetes and Tencteri after the arrest of their leaders, who had come to negotiate (4.13–14);
- Near-annihilation of the Eburones (6.34.5);
- The "indiscriminate sack" of Avaricum (7.28.4; cf. 7.47.5).

The Helvetii and Aduatuci had both surrendered before they took the actions (flight and attack respectively) for which Caesar took his revenge. Their violations of *fides* exposed them to his fierce retaliation. The Veneti and the Usipetes and Tencteri had violated Roman legates and a truce respectively. The Eburones had broken their promise of safe passage to Sabinus and Cotta.

In these cases, Caesar again depicts himself as responding to the enemy's bad faith. There is also a more subtle justification for the execution of the Venetian senate. Three sentences after Caesar's orders, the Aulerci, Eburovices, and Lexovii execute their own senates for failing to take a stand against the Romans (3.17.3). Of course, one massacre does not directly justify the others, but if the Gauls can do such things to themselves, it is hard to say that Caesar's actions were inherently excessive. The massacre at Avaricum, on the other hand, is explicitly described as revenge for the Gallic slaughter of Roman civilians at Cenabum (7.28.5). Although Caesar does not usually justify his tactics explicitly, he is aware of incidents that might be problematic on precisely the grounds we would have predicted. In these situations, the narrative provides an implicit justification on one or both of two grounds: either the Gauls broke faith (and so forfeit all rights), or they had already done the same thing he was about to do. Thus Caesar can explain—as Cicero the philosopher might not have been able to—his decision to take the Usipetan and Tencteran leaders captive.[95] He does so not by appeal to special exigencies of war, but by the common moral logic of tit-for-tat.

This chapter has spoken at length of "justification" of the war, an idea already touched on briefly in earlier chapters. If that goal affected the texture of *De Bello Gallico,* as it seems to have done, we are led back to a question raised in the Introduction. How far did Caesar need to move his audience's dispositions toward himself? This is best answered in the broader context of Caesar's whole self-presentation and his domestic political needs. That is the topic of my next and final chapter.

7.   New and Improved, Sort Of

Although Caesar fought far from Rome, we know that foreign wars can have a dramatic impact on domestic politics, all the more so for the dissemination of *De Bello Gallico* "back home." Previous chapters have made topical suggestions about the political content of *De Bello Gallico*; this chapter continues that inquiry, but also considers the question of how documents like this were used in and were an influence on the broader political scene.

In an excellent article on battle narratives in Caesar's *commentarii*, J. E. Lendon notes Caesar's inclusion of a variety of material that might be considered tangential, such as praise of his soldiers' courage in a battle seemingly won by superior tactics. Some, he suggests, would attribute these inclusions to propagandistic tendentiousness. After sketching some local (though still compelling) objections to this reading, however, he poses a deeper challenge to the explanatory power of the theory in general:

> Why, given the infinity of possible ways of deforming or falsifying the narrative of a battle, does Caesar choose to emphasize morale and courage in addition to tactics? Perhaps Caesar's battle descriptions are tendentious, but to tell lies Caesar must have a grammar of battle description from which to build the lies, a grammar which exists before the lies. How does that grammar work and where does it come from?[1]

Later I return to the specific issues of battle descriptions and the nature of propaganda. My general purpose here, however, is to consider a broader version of the question Lendon poses. Nearly all scholars, whatever their view of the trustworthiness of *De Bello Gallico*, would agree that the work was designed to make its author look good to his audience. Thus Ramage has offered a valuable survey of the virtues explicitly attributed to Caesar and his troops.[2]

But what can we glean from other features of the text? What can we tell about what counts as "looking good"? What did Caesar think his late Republican readers wanted to see in a leader?

Facing the Alternatives

In a 1990 study, "*Etsi:* A Tendentious Hypotaxis in Caesar's Plain Style," W. Batstone examines all instances of *etsi* and *tametsi* ("although") in the Gallic and Civil War commentaries, and shows that these clauses tend to cluster around Caesar and his subordinates. By expressing deliberation over contrasting factors, they tend to convey the ideas of Caesar's good political and military judgment. Moreover, this particular marker of concession (as opposed to, say, *tamen*, "nevertheless") is particularly suited to this purpose because

> with *(tam)etsi* the reader is notified that the content which is to come will eventually be overlooked. Consequently, the content of the *(tam)etsi* clause is itself suspended, held in abeyance, until the terms under which it is conceded are made clear. The author may linger over what he claims is to be overlooked. Thus, *etsi*, like the formal, hypotactic sentence in general, has an affinity for leisurely and complex consideration....*(Tam)etsi*, then, offers a complex event as a whole, and, inasmuch as the concessive thought is ascribed to the actor, it presents the conceder as a man of complex thought. Simple *tamen*, on the other hand,...narrates a simple event and then takes away or denies the normal expectations that one would have had based upon the simple event.[3]

The study I propose to undertake here is both broader and narrower than Batstone's. It is narrower in that it covers only the *De Bello Gallico*. It is broader in that it takes into consideration all expressions containing an explicitly contrastive particle (i.e., *tametsi, etsi, tamen, melius, potius, malle*). Batstone is right about the special properties of the hypotactic expressions he considers, but other contrasts can express similar ideas, even if they do not enact them in the same way. Moreover, the narrator of *De Bello Gallico* uses very little overtly evaluative language, so explicit contrasts (which are somewhat more common in Caesar's style) bring often implicit ideologies into the open.

As was pointed out in Chapter 5, *De Bello Gallico* is constructed as if on a write-as-you-go basis. The narrator refers rarely to past events, and even more rarely to events in the "future." The future can be touched on only indirectly, by the speculative words and thoughts of characters. One of the common uses of explicitly contrastive expressions is to indicate Caesar's deliberations over a proposed course of actions. This is most common when things did not go entirely well, and we are given the justification (honor or longer-term strategy) in advance.[4] So, for instance, despite the imminent end of the campaigning season of 55, Caesar decided to proceed with his first invasion of Britain because it might impede support flowing to Gaul and would at least provide a source of intelligence (4.20.1–2). As it happened, information was about all he gained. The reader, however, has been prepared in advance for the potential problem and the outcome; hence, from the point of view of these lowered expectations, Caesar's invasion can be construed as a success.

In addition to directing reader response, this device also contributes to characterization. Caesar is the only character allowed to defeat the rigid chronological sequence of the text in this way, giving him special powers of foresight.[5] Moreover, the narrator several times notes the limits of foresight (2.22.1, 6.34.7, 7.16.3). Thus the reader is directed to admire Caesar's unusual facility in general, as well as his "successes" in particular cases.

Although the "third-person" narration of De Bello Gallico has a number of functions (see Chap. 5), it also produces the potentially undesirable side-effect of distancing the reader. The reader's knowledge of the character is, at best, hostage to the narrator's willingness to share information, and perhaps to his ability as well. (Of course, even a narrator speaking of himself can be unreliable, but conflation of narratological functions—narrator and character—in one "person" makes it easy to ignore one or the other of those functions.) Increased distance tends to lessen sympathy (see below). Yet presumably Caesar the author wants audience sympathy for Caesar the character. His use of contrastive expressions helps to alleviate this problem. The same distributional facts are as important to this question as they were to the issue of foresight; the contrasts tend to cluster around Caesar and (to a lesser extent) his subordinates and their deliberations. Not only do these contrasts express content that is significant in various ways, but they also show something about process. As Batstone pointed out, they illustrate a weighing of options.[6]

Moore has shown how this process might affect the reader's relationship to Caesar. Among characters in comedy, at least, there is a "hierarchy of rapport" with the audience. Characters succeed in creating this rapport by several means, among them "shar[ing] knowledge with the spectators not shared by others."[7] Information about Caesar's thoughts conveyed via the narrator is available to the audience, but not to the other characters. Moreover, it is most commonly Caesar who has this special relationship of knowledge shared with the audience. Bal has observed that this principle of rapport operates beyond the genre of comedy, and indeed, beyond Rome entirely. In general, characters who can focalize "nonperceptible" objects (such as their own thoughts) have a great advantage over those who cannot. Bal also finds the effect more manipulative outside of "first-person" narratives, since the source of the inequality is not so obvious.[8] Caesar the author, then, puts Caesar the character in a position to generate exceptional rapport with the audience by reporting his conundra.

A third function of these contrastive expressions is to sharpen or emphasize various substantive themes of the work as a whole. To take a minor example, Caesar several times expresses a prudent skepticism in this way, as when he suspected that the Ubii asked for a truce only to retrieve their cavalry, but "nonetheless said that he would go no further than four miles that day to draw water" (4.11.4; cf. 5.28.1, 7.54.2). The thought shows caution, even when the action does not. As we have seen, one of the hallmarks of Gallic recklessness in De Bello Gallico is susceptibility to any rumor or rash decision (6.20; cf. ch. 2.3). Caesar never expressly says that Romans are different in this respect, but he certainly shows it in specific cases (as, say, when he avoids battle in unfavorable circumstances). And even when he does not obviously have the facts on his side, he introduces ambivalence by the expression of contrasting motives.

Caesar also uses the display of contrasting motives to make more sustained arguments. A cluster of passages shows, in various parallel ways, that Caesar looks always to the "big picture." First, as in the case of the invasion of Britain mentioned above, he prefers to go after a target of (purported) strategic importance rather than tactically easy ones (4.20.1, cf. 5.21.2). Second, he is happy to accept a safe but boring enemy surrender instead of a potentially more glorious victory in battle (1.14.6, 3.22.4).[9] Third, he will nonetheless take on a campaign of considerable *military* risk for a sufficiently good *political* or *ethical* reason, such as the defense of Rome's "friendship" with its allies (7.10.2, cf. 7.33.1).

In the background to all of these choices is the contention that this could, or even would, be the last Gallic war. Vercingetorix tells his supporters that they can hope for "eternal power and freedom" (7.64.3) if they win, whereas Critognatus warns that they face "eternal servitude" (7.77.15, 16) if they lose. Nor is this just a Gallic conceit. As we saw above, Cicero expressed similar sentiments in his speech on the consular provinces in 55. Caesar is willing to defer or give up small victories for the sake of the greater, lasting conquest. He is not, of course, self-sacrificing or self-effacing in these choices. What he shows here is rather *continentia,* "self-control," a central elite value and one at the core of the justification of aristocratic rule.[10]

Caesar characterizes not only himself, but also the Gallic tribes through contrastive expressions. If the supposed finality of the war is made to bring out the best in Caesar, it highlights ethical problems for the Gauls. Convictolitavis admits owing his personal advancement to Caesar's favor, but he will take the other side in the war for the sake of "common liberty" (7.37.4). Caesar's "trusted" ally Commius is swayed to oppose his benefactor by similar considerations (7.76.2). Collectively, and despite their own privileging of manly combat as the way to settle disputes, the Gauls are willing to work by cutting off Roman lines of supply when it seems safer (3.24.2, 7.14). I suggested in Chapter 3 that the "problem" with the Gauls in *De Bello Gallico* is not that they are "noble savages," but that they were moving in the opposite direction—culturally sophisticated but morally corrupt. The passages just cited are not unambiguous. It could be argued that some sacrifice of individual integrity was justified on the Gallic side for the sake of the greater good.[11] But Caesar never requires himself to make such a choice. In the rare instance in which he assigns himself a personal motive, it is closely parallel to a public one. Furthermore, the rest of the text calls into question the supposed higher goal of Gallic "liberty." Early and often the reader is told of Gauls who would be enslaved by other Gauls (or Germans) were it not for the intervention of Caesar (1.11.3, 1.17.3, 1.33.2, 5.27.2), and in all but one of these cases (1.33.2), the analysis was put in the mouths of Gauls, concealing the potential tendentiousness of the description. Moreover, in the Gallic ethnography we are informed that in all of Gaul, the ordinary people are in states of de facto or de iure servitude (6.13.1, 2 respectively). Gaul as a whole could conceivably be free from Rome, but Gauls will never be free in the way that Romans are. Thus the global justification for Gallic betrayal is illusory. Only the trickery itself remains.

Comparanda

Caesar was hardly the first Roman general to have his own accomplishments advertised, or even to advertise them himself. Romulus was alleged to have celebrated the first formal triumph, and such processions were fairly regular by the late third century B.C.[12] Second-century generals had "in-house" literary figures to immortalize their exploits, and it was not long thereafter that some sorts of autobiographical accounts started to appear (see Chap. 5). The whole topic of Roman aristocratic self-presentation is, of course, an enormous one, and the subject of much ongoing research, which I cannot hope even to summarize here.[13] In evaluating Caesar's commentaries in the light of other self-representations, therefore, I restrict myself to contexts that are primarily and overtly military: "general's inscriptions" (of various genres), "triumphal paintings," battle narratives, and triumph claims. It must be admitted immediately that, with the partial exception of the inscriptions, these share a common evidentiary problem. Very little actually survives from before Caesar. What postdates him is arguably either derivative (as some have suggested for, e.g., Livian battle narrative) or anachronistic (as, perhaps, Livian concerns for justice.)[14] These objections cannot be conclusively refuted, but there are reasons for hope. A number of inscriptions predate Caesar. Pre-Caesarian triumphal painting is now entirely lost, but in at least some cases it survived long enough to be available to the authors of surviving, post-Caesarian written sources. The evidence of surviving descriptions tends to line up well with that of the inscriptions. As for battle narrative and triumph debates, it may be possible to be too suspicious of our later sources. After all, we know that these were both established traditions long before Caesar wrote. To discount a slightly later source like Livy, then, is to suggest that Caesar's *commentarii* (or some other literary phenomenon) suddenly swept all that away. It is not impossible, but not likely either. This does not, of course, mean that evidentiary concerns can be ignored entirely. Nonetheless, it seems to me that we should set the question of anachronism aside until specific evidence raises it in specific cases.

The category of "general's inscriptions"—by which I mean any inscriptional text that makes overt reference to military action or its aftermath—is a somewhat artificial one, but it is composed of inscriptions from just a few types that would have been readily recognizable to a Roman reader: epitaphs, dedications, honorifics, and so-called *tabulae triumphales*.[15] About thirty of these survive from the Republic, primarily on stone, but some are known only from reports in literary texts. A minimal case is of the form "so-and-so took such-and-such a place" or "so-and-so took [an object] from such-and-such a place," such as "M. Fulvius Nobilior, son of Marcus, grandson of Servius, consul, took [this] from Ambracia" (no. 11). In fact, forms of *capere*, "take," appear in nearly all surviving Republican inscriptions with a clear military content; those that do not are either incomplete or contain a more specific word for booty (*praeda, manubiae*).[16] It might be objected that this prominence is an artifact of the sample; after all, many of these inscriptions are dedicatory. Dedications are indeed our largest source, but the inference does not hold. First, the predominance of dedications is not a neutral fact.

In itself, it emphasizes the importance of plunder in war. Second, nonmilitary dedications conventionally say the donor "gave" something to the god; deviation from this form, which would have been equally intelligible in the military dedications, again emphasizes plunder. Third, "taking" is almost equally prominent in nondedicatory inscriptions of generals: epitaphs, honorifics, and the one *devotio* surviving from our period.[17] "Plunder," it should be noted, is not an entirely accurate description. The thing "taken" can just as well be a territory as movable property from that territory. This could be taken to suggest the interchangeability of the two, and we see clearer evidence for this view shortly.

In addition to their focus on plunder (in the broad sense), these inscriptions also share a sharp focus on the person of the general himself. The verbs in these texts are nearly all active and singular, and the general is always the subject.[18] The troops, by contrast, appear only three times in our sample (nos. 3, 13, 15), and in the last of these cases it is first emphasized that the general prepared and equipped the men (*ornavet paravetque*). In fact, the enemy troops are slightly more likely to come in to view than the Romans (nos. 3, 10, 13, 15).[19] In a slightly different context, Cicero as often as not uses the same self-focus in his Cilician letters, as when he "single-handedly" lays siege to the obscure hill-town of Pindenissum:

> I invested it with a ditch and rampart. I reinforced these with a large camp and six smaller outposts. I made an assault with a ramp, sheds, and towers, and having used many artillery pieces, many archers, and much of my own labor, I finished the business on the fifty-seventh day without any trouble or expense to our allies. (*Fam.* 5.4.10)

Even when he does use the morphologically plural form, it seems to be in the peculiar Latin usage where this means simply "I," as in (literally), "We were acclaimed victorious generals" (*imperatores appellati sumus, Att.* 5.20.3).[20] The army typically makes no appearance, nor does the general even "see to" (*curare*) waging war (as is not uncommon for civilian building projects.)[21] It is as if he fought the wars himself.

Beyond these two nearly universal features, there are a number of others that recur among the military inscriptions at lesser frequencies. Some of these are specific to one or another of the ancient genres that I have taken together. So, naturally, the triumphal inscriptions often mention the triumph itself (nos. 3, 15, 21, 23, 28), but three also share similar formulae expressing the triumphator's command authority, *auspicium* and/or *imperium* and/or

ductus (nos. 13, 15, 21). This appears to address one of the informal requirements to be eligible for the celebration.[22] Dedications by definition mention
one or more divinities. If we ignore these cases, however, we can reconstruct
a rough hierarchy of values. I do not mean to suggest that such a hierarchy
was ever thought of per se by a Roman. Rather, we have inscriptions of considerably varying length, and generals of very similar political and cultural
upbringing. The shorter inscriptions tend to show only the crucial features;
the longer ones add material that is not as important. The most common of
these, though still less frequent than the capture motif, is some direct indi-
cation of the actual military victory (nos. 3, 10, 13, 15, 17, 23, 25, 27, 29).
The importance of victory itself is also emphasized by the existence of a common formula here (*fundere et fugare*; nos. 10, 13, 23, 27). Still, it is interesting that the looting and capture after the fact are allowed to stand for all the
actual fighting by metonymy. This suggests that the ends of war may have
been more important than the means.

Several categories of information appear occasionally: the fact that a king
was defeated, some strategic objective achieved (e.g., stopping the pirates),
"firsts" accomplished by the general (also common in nonmilitary contexts),
or some kind of numerical measurement of success. Typically, this means
numbers of casualties or captives, but in one case it is the value of prizes taken.
A column was erected in the forum honoring the victory of C. Duilius over
the Carthaginians at Mylae in 260 (no. 3).[23] It concludes with an accounting
of the booty from the battle: "He took a septireme and thirty quinqueremes
and triremes, along with their crews....Of gold he took 3,600 coins. Of silver:
100,000 coins. Total: HS 2,100,000."[24] Given the attention to plunder as a
category, one might have expected such a detailed accounting more often. On
the other hand, very similar lists (of cash values) are common in Livy's accounts of triumphs, and, more summarily, in one of Cicero's accounts of his
war in Cilicia.[25] Hence, the rarity of this approach in surviving texts may be a
quirk of our sample. Such a final accounting may have been too far after the
fact for most of these texts. What we see in the Duilius inscription seems to
imply the sale of items that would still have been in the commander's hands
for the triumph and so perhaps the inscriptions. If such counting was in fact
the norm, it would be further evidence of the interchangeability of plunder.
Whatever was taken could be reduced to cash value.

One rarity in military inscriptions is an account of the commander's personal conduct in battle. We are told the outcome of his actions, but of the
details we are as ignorant as in the case of his troops. It will be suggested later
that a failed commander could redeem his personal reputation by brave action.

It seems from these inscriptions that a successful one may not have needed even to answer that question. Another thing largely lacking, at least from this sample, is the extended list such as we have seen Caesar use (see the end of Chap. 2 above). This could be accidental. One partial inscription (no. 23) might have had such a list, and the "nine towns" in Livy's version of a very early *tabula triumphalis* (no. 1) could well conceal a list in the original. Still, the late appearance of the list might reflect a change in the underlying historical circumstances. The example that survives is Pompey's (no. 28), nearly contemporary with *De Bello Gallico*. The expanded extraordinary commands of the late Republic gave much greater scope for such display, and starting with Augustus they become a familiar feature of imperial rhetoric.

A second category of self-representation comprises what are generally called triumphal paintings (and sculpture).[26] These can be divided, at least roughly, into two categories based on context.[27] On the one hand, there were paintings that were part of the triumphal procession itself.[28] These tended to represent the places taken, as in the triumph of Scipio Asiaticus: "He carried in triumph 220 military standards and 134 images of towns [and much wealth]" (Liv. 37.59.3). Such a restricted subject matter and well-defined context would have made these paintings quite legible; whatever was shown was something that had been taken. Such representations were carried in the procession mixed in with the actual booty and prisoners. Once works of art became typical elements of at least eastern triumphs,[29] the boundaries between categories (if they had ever been significant) must have collapsed. Here, as in the inscriptional texts, the emphasis is on the consequences of the war (what was taken) rather than the war itself (how it was waged).

On the other hand, there were also paintings that may conceivably have originated in triumphal processions, but are in fact attested as later, static installations in temples and other venues. For one of these, for instance, Ti. Sempronius Gracchus dedicated a "map of the island of Sardinia with images of battles painted on it" in the temple of Mater Matuta (174 B.C.; Livy 41.28.9). Holliday plausibly speculates that we may have here a "topographic" painting of the sort best known from the famous Nile mosaic of the Palazzo Barberini in Palestrina (fig. 11).[30] That is, we may imagine Gracchus' artists creating a rough image of the island and decorating it with small vignettes of battles in more or less appropriate locations. (It should be kept in mind that neither the island nor locations thereon are likely to have been located very precisely; see Chap. 1.) If Holliday is even roughly correct, then the images of individual battles cannot have contained much specific information, even beyond the possibility that they were entirely conventional in composition. Moreover,

Figure 11. Nile mosaic, Palazzo Barberini, Palestrina. (Alinari/Art Resource, New York)

the geographical organization of the image would mean that it conveyed little information about the course of the campaign as a whole; chronology would be collapsed.

Others of these stand-alone images, however, must have focused on particular events. So, for instance, the elder Pliny claims:

> But the esteem [of painting] grew sharply, as I understand it, from the time of Manius Valerius Maximus Mesalla, who first set up on the flank of the Curia Hostilia a painting (*tabulam*) of the battle in which he had conquered the Carthaginians and Hiero in Sicily. (*HN* 35.22)

For this type of work, Holliday adduces as parallels the Alexander mosaic (of the Casa del Fauno in Pompeii) or a tomb painting (of somewhat problematic interpretation) from the Esquiline in Rome (fig. 12).[31] If this generic identification is correct, then we have at least the potential for more individualized information about the conduct of battles and campaigns (though the possibility of highly conventionalized representations exists here as well). Even a single large scene might give some impression of, say, the nature of the enemy or the thoroughness of the Roman victory. A painting with multiple registers could even develop an extended narrative. It seems clear, however, that there were problems with the legibility of such paintings. At least some triumphal processions (as well as the Esquiline painting) relied on written labels to explain what was going on to a large and diverse audience. Others went unlabeled, and Ovid suggests that they could be difficult for casual observers to follow, except in the most general terms (*Ars am.* 1.219–228).[32] L. Hostilius Mancinus avoided the problem by standing in the forum next to images of himself involved in the assault on Carthage at the end of the Third Punic War and explaining them (Pliny *HN* 35.23). The point, apparently, was

Figure 12. Esquiline tomb painting, Rome. (DAI)

that Mancinus had gone over the wall personally and had been the first to do so. To make this clear, he chose to rely neither on images nor on written language. These pictures, too, then, may have concentrated more on the "what" of war and battle than the "how," though with more variation than in the strictly triumphal paintings or in the inscriptions. Also, the triumphal procession and triumphal paintings, in both the broad and narrow senses, did not eliminate the army entirely (as in the inscriptions). Nonetheless, our limited evidence would suggest that the focus was still on the individual leader. Certainly the formal triumph was an award to and focused on the general. Paintings of the booty type were interchangeable ornaments in his honor. Narrative paintings of the sorts adduced above emphasize the leader by scale, central place in the composition, labeling, representation of special dress, or some combination of these. The painted general may not have won the war alone, like the written general, but *he* did win it.

A third form of self-representation is battle description. Here the evidentiary problems alluded to above are particularly acute. We have virtually no general's *self*-representations before or after Caesar, though a considerable amount can be gleaned or confirmed from Cicero's contemporary letters describing his own campaigns in Cilicia (cf. Chap. 6). Fortunately, however, we have a considerable body of both theory and practice in the description of other people's battles. By "theory and practice" I mean, respectively, military handbooks and battle descriptions in the writings of historians, conceived of here as guides to rhetoric rather than to actual warfare.[33]

Although nearly all surviving military manuals, indeed most known ones, are in Greek, we know that late Republican aristocrats were nonetheless reading such things and perhaps deriving an important part of their military education from them.[34] Much of the content of these manuals involves cataloging stratagems for use in various situations, and I will skip over that material. What is perhaps more interesting in the present context is a pair of observations of Campbell on Frontinus, the only Latin military writer at all near Caesar's time (late first century A.D.).[35] First, whereas the first three books of his *Strategmata* are composed of the conventional lists of stratagems, the last turns to maxims on generalship, focusing primarily on the "character and moral qualities" of the commander. Second, whereas the first three books are illustrated primarily by Greek examples, the fourth book uses mostly Roman. The deviation from tradition in subject matter and the nationality of the exempla suggest that in this last book, Frontinus was trying to introduce a particularly Roman perspective on his subject. This would not be surprising given the emphasis we have already seen on the person of the commander rather than on the army as a system. It does, however, introduce a new element. That individual focus is based on character rather than, say, technical expertise.

More important than the rules of the military manuals are the various folk rules[36] and assumptions about battle that can be reconstructed from a variety of narrative sources. In the article cited at the beginning of this chapter, Lendon offers a sophisticated comparison of the rhetoric of battle descriptions in Caesar with those in his (Greek) predecessors. In the absence of earlier Latin comparanda, it is difficult to tell when Caesarian differences are his own innovations and when they are markers of deeper cultural difference. However, since at least part of Caesar's audience would have been familiar with these Greek accounts, the comparison is worth making, even if only the latter is true. Two important parameters noted by Lendon are the importance attributed to morale and bravery by various authors.[37] In some Greek authors, morale is almost entirely ignored in favor of a physics-like version of tactics. In others, it can be important, but is logically subordinated as an effect brought about by some (but not all) stratagems. Finally, a minority tradition took morale to be one of the primary elements of military success. As for bravery, the Greek tradition was much less conflicted. (Bravery here is meant to indicate a relatively long-lasting feature of character, as opposed to morale, which fluctuates from minute to minute.) Bravery could be a source of interesting anecdotes, but was hardly ever decisive in an entire battle.

Although our direct evidence for narrative patterns comes largely from Greek sources, we do have useful indirect indications in Latin. Our historical sources frequently tell us of reactions in Rome to outcomes of battles. The historicity of individual battles and reactions can be problematic, but all we really need to know about here are general norms. What is likely to look like a military success or otherwise? Or, more specifically, "What was held to be usual and acceptable, or daring and innovative, in the conduct of army commanders?"[38] On the basis of various accounts of Republican wars, we can identify at least three desirable traits. First, as Goldsworthy has demonstrated, Romans expected an aggressive, offense-oriented approach from their generals.[39] One could go too far and be accused of recklessness (especially in defeat), but only in extreme cases. Even Cicero, who is clearly distrustful of his own troops in Cilicia (*Fam.* 2.10.2, *Att.* 5.20.1), is careful only about whom he attacks, not whether to go on the offensive, despite seemingly imminent invasion by a superior force. Second, generals were expected to be personally active and engaged in battle. They should lead by example.[40] They should remain near and move along the front lines, both to be visible to their troops and to make adjustments during battle. And, most important, a general should stand his ground in battle, even in the face of personal danger and sometimes even to death.[41] This leads to the third point. To some extent, although there was certainly ambivalence here, the commander's willingness to "go down with the ship" could shade over into a more soldierly physical courage.[42] Although too rare to be of much practical importance, the general's highest honor derived from defeating his opposing number in hand-to-hand combat.[43] Aristocrats displayed their scars (at least those on their chests) in judicial and deliberative assemblies to demonstrate their virtue.[44]

Conversely, we can identify certain things that seem not to have been expected of generals. Most striking among these is victory. Rosenstein's study of the political fortunes of defeated generals shows that they cannot, as a group, be distinguished from their competitors. To explain this, Rosenstein looked at recorded explanations for victory and defeat. Technical skill is rarely a consideration either way; to a large extent, aristocrats conspired to paint their various tasks (including commanding armies, dispensing justice, governing provinces) as a matter of general character and ability rather than specific skills.[45] When defeat did occur, it was often referred to divine displeasure over (usually inadvertent) religious errors.[46] Another common explanation was a failure of courage on the soldiers' part. If Roman soldiers left the field (as must normally have occurred in defeat), no matter what the circumstances, it left the door open for this explanation. As one might expect, this failure could be laid at the feet of the commander, but what is striking is how rarely blame was so spread, even when the commander's own behavior in battle was subject to reproach.[47] Similarly, although some successful commanders were praised for working to instill morale and discipline in the ranks, failed ones seem not to have been criticized for failing to do so.[48] As long as the commander showed the requisite personal courage, his position remained fairly secure. These standards are somewhat different from what we saw in other contexts, but that is not surprising, since they represent a different level of accomplishment. Inscriptions and paintings make a claim to greatness by recounting victory and plunder. The defeated commander is simply trying to prove he is not personally a failure. Moreover, at both levels of success, the evaluative importance of the army is subordinated. For the victorious general, it is an extension of himself (if not ignored altogether); for the loser, it can be represented as a burden that could not be overcome.

To the extent that the army is in view, we have confirmation of the suggestion that evaluations of general and soldier were carried out on similar, particularly Roman, grounds. Both were expected in the first instance to show *virtus*, to demonstrate that they brought the right character to the field of battle. We might summarize by pointing to some conclusions of Steel's study of Cicero's public, oratorical praise of generals (Pompey and Murena in particular).[49] An ordinary general like Murena needed only a few soldierly virtues to be respectable: show up for work, endure physical hardship, maintain proper hierarchy. Pompey, on the other hand, had more positive virtues, most notably military knowledge and actual success. Caesar is clearly putting himself in Pompey's league.

How Does Caesar Compare?

There is, at first glance, surprisingly little in *De Bello Gallico* about the profits of war.[50] There is little mention of precious metals, or even slaves. Not only was this a conventional theme, but contemporary sources suggest that there was a lot to show off. One might contrast Catullus 29.1–4, but Powell and Jervis have already shown the same by comparing Caesar to his continuator Hirtius and to Cicero, respectively, on the wealth from these campaigns.[51] This surprise should be qualified in two ways. First, the accounting of plunder might be said to belong to a "triumphal" tradition as opposed to a "battle narrative" tradition. That is, you only count your winnings after the war is over. The singular "war" is important here. As we saw in Chapter 5, it is convenient for Caesar that there be only one extended war here, lest he be recalled before he is finished. Caesar's pose (which, of course, may be genuine) of writing as he goes essentially requires he take the battle-narrative approach. Conversely, writing battles reinforces the impression that he is composing as he goes.[52] Second, Caesar is not entirely without his prizes. We noted at the end of Chapter 2 the lists of somewhat cryptic tribal names that Caesar favors. Places, I suggested above, are more or less interchangeable with movables as objects of plunder, and given Caesar's stabilized version of Gallic society, tribes stand for places, even if the reader does not know precisely where they are located. Such lists of names, then, are similar to the conventionalized images of cities or, even better, their guardian deities carried in triumphal processions. Thus, although the war is not at an end, the audience gets some hint of the triumph to come.

Caesar's reported generalship is typical in kind, if not in quality.[53] He fights campaigns that are aggressive and offensively oriented. Tactically, he shows a little more restraint, avoiding battle on unequal ground or in other unfavorable situations, but even then he is generally putting pressure on the enemy. Once battle has been joined, he is among his troops, giving encouragement and making adjustments. If he is never recorded fighting himself, he does put himself in imminent danger on a few key occasions (2.25, 7.88). And he never leaves the field of battle. He also shows concern for other matters, such as intelligence-gathering and supply. This may be meager by modern standards, but in terms of narrative, he does more than is required by contemporary tradition. His concern for intelligence-gathering and supply might also be taken as special cases of the foresight hinted in the descriptions of his deliberations discussed above.

Even when the substantive detail of the above is slightly unconventional, it shares the focus on the person of the general with the other traditions we have considered. He is brave, he is aggressive, he is wise. Sometimes (though certainly not always) the army disappears entirely, after the manner of an epitaph or dedicatory inscription. Thus, for instance, "Caesar" puts the enemy to flight (5.51.4), secures provisions for the army (7.32.1), and builds the works at Alesia (7.72). In one famous passage, he seems to stand in for the entire officer corps:

> Everything had to be done by Caesar at the same time: the standard (which was the sign that it was necessary to rush to arms) had to be shown, the horn-signal had to be given, the troops had to be recalled from the works and those who had gone a little further afield to collect earth had to be summoned, the battle-line had to be drawn up, the soldiers had to be encouraged, and the sign had to be given. (2.20.1)

There is one respect, however, in which Caesar puts a very novel spin on this traditional focus on the general. I noted above Rosenstein's observation that the quality of the general and the *virtus* of the soldiery could conventionally be thought of as independent. In fact, since the quality of troops was generally treated to excuse a loss, the two were really opposed. Caesar, as argued in Chapter 3, takes a remarkable degree of responsibility for the *virtus* of his troops. It is not just a matter of the drilling he gives green troops to get them battle-worthy; this is attested, if rarely, for earlier generals. What is really novel here is the way the soldiers' *virtus* is made to depend conceptually on the commander. Full (i.e., Roman) virtue, recall, depends on fitting in to a hierarchical structure, and in particular on looking always to the top of that structure.

Finally, the Caesar of this narrative demonstrates, even if he does not much discuss, a concern for justice. It was argued in Chapter 6 that the narrative works hard to establish that the war against the Gauls was just in terms of traditional categories and in a way that could have been reduced to a formal argument. Chapter 1 suggested that Caesar's style of spatial representation legitimized the conquest in a more imagistic way—Romans and Gauls squaring off over empty space. And in the first section of this chapter, I argued that Caesar goes to some lengths to undercut the ideal of *libertas* as a potentially sympathetic rationale for the Gallic resistance. That discussion of contrastive expressions also pointed to other motives (in addition to justice) made to drive Caesar: he takes risks for the sake of Rome's honor or long-term victory, but not self-aggrandizement; he weighs alternatives carefully; he displays *continentia;* he (unlike the Gauls) holds to *fides.*[54] In short, *De Bello Gallico* has a lot to say about Caesar's values as well as his skills. He is morally, and therefore politically, correct. In this respect, Caesar does not contradict other traditions of Roman generals' self-fashionings, but goes well beyond most of them.[55] Given the scale of the work in contrast to, say, a dedicatory inscription, this expansiveness is hardly surprising, though some might have denied it. At the least, it is worth noting the quite conventional stance Caesar takes with respect to these themes. Even before the truly revolutionary part of his career, Caesar had a maverick reputation.[56] In *De Bello Gallico*, he offers a version of himself that would have been acceptable to those who wanted him to be a normal (if highly successful) Roman politician. This is a Caesar that Cicero could sell in *On the Consular Provinces* as the option of traditional virtue. He is perhaps also a Caesar that a Cicero could convince himself should be negotiated with until the last possible moment.

Propaganda

The Caesar of *De Bello Gallico*, then, largely succeeds in ways typical of Roman aristocrats, at least as they would wish it—by being uniquely outstanding in terms of extremely conventional categories.[57] But that might have been true even if the story had been written by a less partial observer. He did, after all, take Gaul. One occasionally sees the claim that a reasonable telling of the facts is all that Caesar relied on for his favorable impression.[58] In the Introduction, I disclaimed the opposite argument, that Caesar has clearly falsified his narrative to make himself look better. That still leaves open the possibility that Caesar "spins" his text in ways that have little to do with truth or falsity. This third possibility is an increasingly popular one, with some further support developed over the course of this book. The following features are not required by anything in the facts, even as Caesar represents them:

- Using image schemata, like the inside/outside version of the empire or empty, surrounded spaces (see Chap. 1);
- Juggling multiple representations as needed (for instance, one of unified Gaul versus one of discretely partitioned Gaul; see Chap. 2);[59]
- Not "showing" Gallic wall construction until Book 7 (see Chap. 3);
- Setting ethical dilemmas for the Gauls, but not for himself (see above).

Another way to reach a similar conclusion is to return to a claim I made in the Introduction. *De Bello Gallico* (perhaps unlike *Bellum Civile*) is merely descriptive on its surface. Taken along with various, readily available intertexts, however, it becomes argumentative:

- The limitation of the war to Gaul (as opposed to Germany) depends on Caesar's playing off the ethnographic tradition (see Chap. 2);
- The need to redefine *virtus* is driven by a "problem" that is much more apparent intertextually (see Chap. 3);
- The narrative of the war answers the questions of justification that would be raised in more explicit discourse (see Chap. 6);
- Caesar's traditional presentation answers known objections to his radical persona (see above);
- Intertextuality with the genre of the *commentarius* supports the authenticity of the whole text (see Chap. 5).

In other words, *De Bello Gallico* is apparently designed to sell a particular point of view.

In its elaborate construction of a very positive image of Caesar, *De Bello Gallico* might be described as propagandizing for its author. There are those, however, who would object to this term, and especially to its application to the self-justificatory aspects (as I have described them) of the work. In fact, the whole idea of "propaganda" has fallen into disfavor with most classicists who have discussed it in recent years, and not without reason. In some cases, this is because specific alleged examples have been found wanting.[60] It has further been suggested that, in a broad historical context, propaganda's effects are simply not that important, even when the thing itself can be convincingly identified.[61] Although the historical paradigms of these authors vary (World War I Europe for Collins, apparently Cold War Soviet Union for Galinsky), the models they derive from these examples are essentially the same. "Propaganda" is regarded as being imperative; it tells its audience directly and precisely what to do and think. It is also stipulated to be highly tendentious. The propagandist purportedly will not admit of any failings on his side and will freely omit or fabricate to make his work conform to the desired worldview. Galinsky is surely right to question the long-term viability of such propaganda in convincing its audience, though one might argue that it can still have other desirable (for the author) effects.[62] It is also clear that he, Collins, Wallace-Hadrill, and others are right to claim that propaganda in this sense was very rare in ancient Rome. More specifically, it is incontrovertible, as Collins claims, that *De Bello Gallico* is not propaganda justifying a war in the same way that *Bellum Civile* is.

Nonetheless, this model of propaganda, even though it conforms well to the ordinary-language understanding of that word, is unnecessarily narrow. The problem is the same as with a closely related and equally contested term—"ideology." Ideology carries with it, both in popular thought and in some formal theorizing, the idea of falsity, or at least willful neglect of the truth.[63] It also sometimes is understood to imply an explicit program, much like propaganda; on this interpretation, an ideology is essentially the content conveyed by some act of propaganda. In any case, problems surface in defining ideology in terms of "false consciousness" and the like. First, what are we to make of the bits of truth that inevitably appear in the most obvious organs of propaganda? Is an account of atrocities in the African slave trade "propaganda" if it is in *Pravda* circa 1980, but not if it is in a Western academic journal? Or do we go through *Pravda* sentence by sentence marking this line as propaganda, but not that? Neither approach seems profitable. Second, there is the difficult question of deciding what is tendentious enough to qualify as propaganda. We need not descend to a total (and therefore useless) relativism to see that this question will frequently require highly subjective decisions. For instance, if bias is claimed to lie in selection rather than outright fabrication of material (as is often the case), how are we to arrive at an "objective" standard of relevance to distinguish the ideological from the nonideological?

The best solution, it seems to me, is to accept the approach of Louis Althusser, at least in its broad outlines. On this understanding, ideology is "a representation of the imaginary relationship of individuals to their real conditions of existence."[64] "Imaginary" is meant here not in the sense of random fantasy, but as it relates to a self-image. Thus, Althusser goes on to say, "Ideology hails or interpellates concrete individuals as concrete subjects." Subjectivity implies a self-image, which is constituted by the acceptance of one or more ideological positions.[65] We need not accept all of Althusser's propositions

about ideology, nor in particular his rather narrowly deterministic view of
how a totalizing ideology determines the individual.[66] The important point for
present purposes is that ideology in this sense is necessary for making us who
we are, and so it is something everyone, not just the other guy, "has."[67] Propaganda in the narrow sense described above attempts to impose specific beliefs
and even whole ideologies in the most crude and direct way possible; that it
ignores other and especially pre-existing sources of identity makes its relatively low efficacy unsurprising. But if we take a broader view of propaganda,
the picture is different. Suppose we define propaganda as any communication,
regardless of truth value, that tends to shape the beliefs and values of its audience.[68] Then the most effective propaganda will be that which is best calibrated
to the ideology of that audience, and so looks the least like "propaganda" in
the narrow sense.

Even better, we should not regard propaganda as a particular type of
discourse at all, since that runs the risk of "mak[ing] propaganda less distinguishable from other kinds of discourse especially in semiotic terms."[69]
Rather, propaganda is a function of discourse. A book, for instance, is not to
be thought of as an instance of propaganda (or, for that matter, an instance
of not being propaganda). It is instead *propagandistic* insofar as it tries to
reshape readers or reinforce their identities, but it may at the same time be
entertaining, informative, devotional, or whatever else. Here again the questions surrounding propaganda reflect broader intellectual problems. Lynne
Cheney, responding to modern notions of the "political," writes:

> What was clearly happening is [sic] that something that was trivially true
> (we can never get totally outside ourselves and divorce ourselves of all
> our interests) was being inflated. Politics writ small had become politics
> written so large that it drove out the possibility of human beings doing
> anything nonpolitical—such as encouraging the search for truth.[70]

The presumption is that a political action is exclusively that. Hence, if other
motivations can be attached to an action (e.g., desire for the truth), that action must for Cheney be apolitical. This way of looking at "politics" conceals
the exercise of an enormous amount of power by ruling out any activity that
can be construed in any other way. It conceals inequality. Suppose that we
see the political again as an aspect of action—that is, the use or distribution of power—not as a type of action. We can then analyze the political *in*
any activity without contradicting the quite plausible intuition that there are
things that are not *simply* politics. The insistence on defining propaganda as

a specific type of discourse similarly conceals the exercise of power, both in antiquity and today. The definition I have offered makes it reasonable to look for propaganda effects even in innocent-seeming texts, but also reminds us that even the most obvious propaganda can also serve other functions.

Those who have viewed just war discourse as mere show have not always paid sufficient attention to the audience for which that display might have been intended. The usual suggestion is that it was meant for an external, presumably Greek audience. Though Romans would certainly prefer a broadly favorable reputation abroad, the idea that their entire concern for "justice" was public relations seems to stem from a single (and ethnocentric) remark in Polybius (36.2).[71] The Roman plebs have also been suggested as an audience. This view is sometimes connected with the now-abandoned idea that religion was in serious decline among the late Republican elite, but continued to be used to manipulate the masses. Neither the Greek nor the plebeian theory takes much account of the likely audiences of the individual documents that are informed by the idea of the just war. All the texts examined in this chapter were written for a Latin-reading audience. The potential literate audience would have been a small fraction of the population, and the actual audience for literary texts such as *De Bello Gallico* and *On Duties* would presumably have been vastly smaller and very much elite.[72] Cicero's *On the Consular Provinces* was delivered to the Senate. His letters about his campaigns were written to individual senators and an equestrian. The audience of these texts, then, is roughly the same group of persons who produced them, or perhaps a slightly larger circle. Contrast the larger and more diverse audience for a public triumphal procession or monument, celebrating the expansionist side of Roman war-making. If anything, concerns about justification seem to have been intra-elite issues. To what end, then, are Cicero and Caesar (and quite likely others) talking to themselves about just wars?

These texts in general, and *De Bello Gallico* in particular, can be described, at least in respect to their treatment of war and empire, as examples of what Ellul has described as "propaganda of integration." That is, it is "a propaganda of the *longue durée*, which looks to achieve stable dispositions and reproduce itself *indéfiniment*, which adapts the individual to his daily life, which seeks to recreate thoughts and behavior in accord with a permanent social milieu."[73] It is not simply imperative, but takes advantage of the more subtle effects to which we have already been directed by Althusser. Caesar's task was not to argue against a presumption that war was wrong in most circumstances, or even to enter into an evenly balanced debate on the topic, as an American president's task might be. A closer contemporary parallel might be the announcement of trade sanctions against Japan or China. The domestic and particularly the popular resistance to these measures are usually negligible. Still, their description must be phrased in a highly constrained manner. The announced goal must not be national or ethnic advantages. Nor can it even be simply the enrichment of certain domestic industries or their workers, despite the fact that such a claim might suffice to justify domestic economic policies. Rather, the stated goal must be "free" or "fair" trade, of which economic advantage will be claimed as the inevitable but incidental consequence. There are of course a few laissez-faire capitalist extremists who may or may not want to be persuaded, but the main effects of this discussion lie elsewhere.[74] It is intended to *reassure* its audience that the president's (and thus the nation's) actions have been, as they always are, just. In precisely this way, Caesar is telling his audience something they already know—that Rome has been fighting another *bellum iustum*. When Caesar, and Cicero arguing on his behalf, do this, it may be a deliberate rhetorical strategy designed to please their audience, or it may well be a consequence of the fact (or plausible supposition) that they share the worldview of that audience, or the situation may lie somewhere in between. I do not see that the question can be decided even in principle for any individual claim that either makes. I doubt, however, that a solution is particularly important. Even if Caesar or Cicero or both are not, on some level, committed to the "justice" of the empire and of the Gallic wars, they are at least willing to play along.

We might contrast here a roughly parallel, but intratextual, strategy. Batstone has shown how, early in his Civil War commentary, Caesar develops a standard pattern ("narrative gestalt") for Caesar's advent in the various Italian cities he comes to as he invades the peninsula.[75] This pattern makes it clear that Caesar is preferred to Pompey by the people of Italy. Once the pattern is in place, even partial repetitions give the appearance of reiterating the whole, and eventually Caesar is able plausibly to draw the explicit inference that all of Italy was on his side, even though there is little supporting evidence even in his own account. This is a virtuoso performance on Caesar's part. Creating the necessary resonance between the various instances of the gestalt requires some boot-strapping. There is a problem if a neutral or hostile audience does not buy into the first instances. When *De Bello Gallico* can exploit a history on intertexts in support of the claim of a just war, that basis is already in place.

Ideology, it has been claimed, "is designed to promote the human dignity and clear conscience of a given class at the same time that it discredits their adversaries."[76] If we bracket the (unintended?) voluntarism implicit in "designed," and take "class" simply as "group," this is a fairly good description of the situation I have been describing at Rome. Consider how the notion of *fides* converts self-interest into a moral obligation. It is also specifically a good description of what Caesar and Cicero were up to. The conquest of Gaul was made out as neither treasure hunt nor military adventure but as a legitimate and even obligatory act of justice. As is often pointed out, the legitimacy of military action was rarely a matter of open debate. This cannot be attributed solely to brilliant individual rhetorical performances on the occasion of every war. It represents the effects of a collective self-image. Would-be generals who wished, for whatever reason, to start a war had a considerable head start in justifying it. All they needed to do was to play into Romans' self-image as members of a community that fights justly. Furthermore, the constant repetition of that discourse of just wars reinforced the image, re-creating the conditions under which the next *imperator* could explain the necessity of his conquests. For instance, the existence of a border creates a danger (as discussed above) that provokes conquest that results in—another border.

In this way, too, Roman imperialist ideology not only justified individual expansion, but also guaranteed the re-creation of the conditions for further "legitimate" expansion. It was in the interest, albeit indirectly, of individuals to act to reproduce this ideological climate. Individual commanders were motivated to produce "just wars," at least in narrative, to advertise themselves and advance their own careers. (They may even have felt constrained to do so in fact to avoid the repercussions if they ever happened to be defeated.) The sum of all these individually intentional acts had the unintended consequence of reproducing the expectation that wars were supposed to be just. Nor does this kind of propaganda unavoidably contradict daily experience. This was not like telling starving people that they were well-fed. Most people see no wars at all; even those who had fought in this or that war would not have seen it from the broad point of view offered by the commander's commentaries. Even senators, who over time debated whether to start numerous wars, participated in a discursive process rather than in those wars themselves. Thus letters, speeches, and commentaries could be powerful tools for shaping everyone's experience. Writing "just" wars could make them so.

What is true of the justification of the Gallic War can largely be said of the other aspects of *De Bello Gallico*'s program as well. In many respects, Caesar's self-presentation is entirely conventional. His style of command and signs of success are largely those of Scipio, Mummius, even Pompey, and others before him. His representation fulfills expectations and so gains credibility. It also reinforces those expectations and helps impose them on the next generation (cf. Augustus *RG* 8.5). When Caesar does depart from tradition, as with his reconstruction of *virtus*, he does so only partially. He does not argue with the reader so much as set up and exploit a conflict within the reader. Moreover, in all these cases, he displaces the burden of argument by intertext or by use of other characters (e.g., Gauls' doubts about their own liberty; Critognatus on *virtus*). Thus he generally avoids the imperative mode of the crudest propaganda. The absence of that mode, however, does not *remove* the propagandistic element from *De Bello Gallico;* it is what *inserts* it so skillfully.

Appendix A: Wars against "Barbarians"

Plato suggests the existence of a natural hostility between civilized states and "barbarians" (*Resp.* 5.469–470). Aristotle connects the same opposition to a theory of natural slavery and explicitly uses this to argue that wars against barbarians are by nature just (*Pol.* 1.1255–1256). It is widely held that for the Romans, too, war could justly be waged against barbarians at will.[1] There is no trace of such a doctrine in Cicero's *On Duties*.[2] That is perhaps not surprising; Cicero's main source, Panaetius, was a Stoic, and the Stoics seem to have rejected these supposedly natural distinctions between humans.[3] More to the point, no Roman I am aware of ever claims that barbarians are a special case.

Clavadetscher-Thürlemann argues that Caesar implicitly makes such a distinction, since (1) he does not use the term *bellum iustum*, (2) his justifications tend to revolve around "not defense . . . but prevention," and (3) he often describes his opposition as "barbarians."[4] Let me take these points in reverse order. Latin *barbarus*, unlike Greek βάρβαρος, is much more a substantive behavioral category than a collective, ethnic one. Thus, on the one hand, it makes sense for one Gaul to call another one a barbarian, and, on the other, the more civilized Gauls of Book 7 are not described with that term by anyone. Caesar does not call his opponents barbarians to get around just war requirements, but (at most) to invoke them. He is claiming that they are dangerous. That his justifications are not "defensive" is not relevant. Use of this criterion, as we saw in some detail in Chapter 6, misconstrues the idea of the just war. It is true that Caesar never uses the phrase *bellum iustum*, but he does claim, for instance, to have had "very just (*iustissima*) cause" for crossing the Rhine to attack the Germans. Clavadetscher-Thürlemann wants to take this as meaning "real" or "weighty." The former sense would be meaningless here (especially in the superlative), and the latter unparalleled. And, as Clavadetscher-Thürlemann points out, Caesar does use other language that fits well with, for example, Cicero's formulation of just war theory: defend, resist, avenge, extract/pay a penalty, injure. Finally, the presence or absence of such a general term is less important in a narrative work than it might have been in an argumentative one.[5]

This difference between Greek and Roman theories should not be surprising. Wars against "barbarians," especially Persians, had played a large historical role and an even larger mythical one in defining Greek identity.[6] Plato and Aristotle were elaborating a long-standing cultural distinction. Rome spent most of its early history fighting wars against similar Italic peoples. The fetial procedure presumes that the other side will have a similar college of priests.[7] It is possible that the Romans in practice treated Western "barbarians" differently from more "civilized" Eastern peoples. In particular, it has been argued that they "annexed" barbarian territory much more freely.[8] Annexation, however, has no obvious relationship to the idea of the just war. The choice of modes of control seems to have been an issue mainly within the East. Direct control of Western peoples would have been more attractive because less-developed indigenous governments could not have been counted on to maintain local order.

Appendix B: Generals' Inscriptions

Here I collect the texts of inscriptions to which I refer in Chapter 7. I give these only for the reader's convenience. I have not attempted independent solutions to the significant textual problems posed by some of these inscriptions (e.g., nos. 3, 13, 23); in no. 13 I have also printed certain *exempli gratia* supplements in double angle brackets. The "source" given in the first column is generally meant as the easiest to refer to rather than the definitive treatment. "*CIL*" abbreviates *CIL* I²; "W" abbreviates *Remains of Old Latin*, ed. E. H. Warmington, vol. 4 (1959); *GL* abbreviates H. Keil, *Grammatici Latini* (reprint 1961). Some dates are approximate, and a few (e.g., nos. 7, 9, 19) are more severely problematic. In cases of epitaphs with nonmilitary material, I have quoted only what is salient here.

No.	Source(s)	Text	Translation	Date (B.C.)
1	Livy 6.29.9	Iuppiter atque divi omnes hoc dederunt ut T. Quinctius dictator oppida novem caperet.	Jupiter and all the gods granted that T. Quinctius the dictator should capture nine towns.	380
2	Coarelli 1997, 355	M. Folvios Q. f. cosol dedet Volsinio capto.	M. Fulvius, son of Quintus, consul, gave this when Volsinium had been taken.	264
3	W128	Secestanosque … opsidioned exemet; lecionesque Cartaciniensis omnis maximosque macistratos luci palam post dies novem castreis exfociont; Macelamque opidom pucnandod cepet. Enque eodem macistratud bene rem navebos marid consol primos eset copiasque clasesque navales	The legions of Carthage and all their top leaders were put to flight from their camp in broad daylight after nine days. He took the city Macela by assault. During this magistracy he was the first consul to win with ships at sea and to gather and equip naval forces, and with these ships he	260?

No.	Source(s)	Text	Translation	Date (B.C.)
		primos ornavet paravetque, cumque eis navebos claseis Poenicas omnis item maxumas copias Cartaciniensis praesented Hanibaled dictatored olorom in altod marid pucnandod vicet, vique naveis cepet cum socieis septeresmom I quinqueresmosque triresmosque naveis XXX merset XIII Aurom captom: numei MMMDC ... Arcentom captom, praeda: numei M ... Omne captom aes MMMMM MMM ... MMMMMMMMMMM ... Primos quoque navaled praedad poplom donavet primosque Cartaciniensis incenuos duxit in triumpod.	conquered the entire Punic fleet and their greatest armies in battle on the high seas in the presence of that dictator Hannibal and seized ships with their crews: 1 septireme and 30 quinqueremes and triremes and sank 13. Of gold he took 3,600 coins, of silver 100,000 coins. Total: HS 2,100,000. He was also the first to give the people naval plunder and led free Carthaginians in triumph.	
4	W72	M. Fourio C.f. tribunos miltare de praedad Fortune dedet.	M. Furius, son of Gaius, military tribune, gave this to Fortune out of booty.	225?
5	W72	M. Fourio C.f. tribunos miltare de praedad Maurte dedet.	M. Furius, son of Gaius, military tribune, gave this to Mars out of booty.	225?
6	W76	M. Claudius M. f. consol Hinnad cepit.	M. Claudius, son of Marcus, consul, took this from Hinna.	211
7	W4	Hec cepit Corsica Aleriaque urbe, dedet Tempestatebus aide merito.	This man took Corsica and the city of Aleria; he gave the Storms a temple, rightly.	200?
8	CIL 613	L. Quinctius L.f. Leucado cepit. Eidem consol dedet.	L. Quinctius, son of Lucius, took this from Leucadus. He gave it as consul.	192
9	W2	Taurasia Cisauna Samnio cepit, subigit omne Loucanam opsidesque abdoucit.	He took Taurasia and Cisauna in? Samnium; he conquered all Lucania? and took hostages.	190?
10	GL 6.265. 29K	Fundit fugat prosternit maximas legiones.	He destroyed, put to flight, and mowed down the greatest legions.	190
11	W78	M. Folvius M. f. Ser. n. Nobilior cos. Ambracia cepit.	M. Fulvius Nobilior, son of Marcus, grandson of Servius, consul, took [this] from Ambracia.	189

No.	Source(s)	Text	Translation	Date (B.C.)
12	W78	M. Fulvius M. f. Ser. n. cos. Aetolia cepit.	M. Fulvius, son of Marcus, grandson of Servius, consul, took this from Aetolia.	189
13	Livy 40.52. 5–6	Duello magno dirimendo, regibus subigendis, patrandae paci hac pugna exeunti L. Aemilio M. Aemilii filio <<res cessit gloriose>> auspicio imperio felicitate ductuque eius inter Ephesum Samum Chiumque, inspectante eopse Antiocho, exercitu omni, equitatu elephantisque, classis regis Antiochi antea inuicta fusa contusa fugataque est, ibique eo die naues longae cum omnibus sociis captae quadraginta duae. ea pugna pugnata rex Antiochus regnumque <<eius in potestate populi Romani redactum>>. Eius rei ergo aedem Laribus permarinis uouit.	By ending a great war, subjugating kings, and achieving peace, things went well for Lucius Aemilus, son of Marcus, leaving the field of battle. Under his aegis, command, fortune, and leadership between Ephesus, Samos, and Chios, with Antiochus himself and his entire infantry, cavalry, and elephants looking on, the previously undefeated fleet of King Antiochus was overwhelmed and put to flight. Then and there, 42 warships were captured with their crews. Once this battle was fought, King Antiochus and his kingdom were left in the power of the Roman people. Thus he vowed a temple to the guardian spirits of the sea.	179
14	*ILLRP* 321a	M.' Acilius C. f. cos. Scarpea cepit.	Manius Acilius, son of Gaius, consul, took this from Scarpea.	177
15	Livy 41.28. 8–10	Ti. Semproni Gracchi consulis imperio auspicioque legio exercitusque populi Romani Sardiniam subegit. In ea prouincia hostium caesa aut capta supra octoginta milia. Re publica felicissume gesta atque liberatis <<sociis,>>uectigalibus restitutis, exercitum saluom atque incolumem plenissimum praeda domum reportauit; iterum triumphans in urbem Romam redit. Cuius rei ergo hanc tabulam donum Ioui dedit.	Under the command and auspices of the consul Tiberius Sempronius Gracchus, the legion and army of the Roman people reduced Sardinia. 80,000 enemy were killed or captured there. Once things had gone well for the state, the allies had been liberated, and the tax revenues restored, he brought the troops home alive, safe, and full of loot. He himself returned to Rome in triumph for the second time. Thus he gave this tablet as a gift to Jupiter.	174
16	W78	L. Aimilius L. f. inperator de rege Perse Macedonibusque cepet.	Lucius Aemilius, son of Lucius, commander, took this from King Perseus and the Macedonians.	167

No.	Source(s)	Text	Translation	Date (B.C.)
17	W6	Pater regem Antioco subegit.	His father conquered King Antiochus.	160?
18	CIL 625	Cornelius Scipio Carthagine capta.	Cornelius Scipio, on the capture of Carthage.	146?
19	W86	L. Mummius L. f. imp. Dedit Corintho capta vico Italicensi.	L. Mummius, son of Lucius, gave this to the vicus of Italica when Corinth had been taken.	146?
20	CIL 631	L. Mummius consul Achaea capta	Lucius Mummius, consul, on the capture of Achaea.	145
21	W84	L. Mummi L. f. cos. ductu auspicio imperioque eius Achaia capta Corinto deleto Romam redieit triumphans. Ob hasce res bene gestas quod in bello voverat hanc aedem et signum Herculis Victoris imperator dedicat.	Once Achaea was taken and Corinth destroyed by the leadership, auspices, and authority of L. Mummius, son of Lucius, consul, he returned to Rome in triumph. On account of these fine deeds, the successful commander dedicates this temple and its statue of Hercules Victor, fulfilling his vow during the war.	142
22	W144	Ser. Folvius Q. f. Flaccus cos murum locavit de manubies.	Ser. Fulvius Flaccus, son of Quintus, consul, had this wall made from the profits of war.	135
23	W132; Morgan 1973	…ex itinere et Taruiscos Carnosque et Liburnos ex maribus coactos maritumas ad oras diebus ter quineis quater fudit et fugavit. Fausteis signeis consileis praecipuos Tuditanus ita Romae egit triumpum, statuamque dedit Timavo; sacra patria ei resituit, atque magistreis tradit.	…And on the way he defeated and put to flight the Taruisci, Carni, and Liburni, driven from the sea to the shore, four times in 15 days. Thus Tuditanus, notable for planning, celebrated his triumph at Rome with blessed standards, and gave a statue at the Timavus. He restored her ancestral rites and handed them over to the supervisors.	129
24	W132	Quod neque conatus quisquanst neque post audebit noscite rem, ut famaa facta feramus virei: Auspicio Antoni Marci pro consule classis Isthmum traductast missaque per pelagus. Ipse iter eire profectus Sidam. Classem Hirrus Atheneis	Learn of a deed no one has attempted before nor will attempt hereafter, so a man's deeds may be spread by word of mouth. Under the aegis of Marcus Antonius, proconsul, the fleet was brought across the Isthmus and put to sea. Antonius had set out to	102

No.	Source(s)	Text	Translation	Date (B.C.)
		pro praetore anni e tempore constituit. Lucibus haec pauceis parvo perfecta tumultu magna quom ratione atque salute bona. Quei probus est, laudat, quei contra est invidet illum; invideant, dum quod condecet id venerent.	go to Sida. Hirrus the propraetor set up his fleet at Athens, given the time of year. These things were accomplished in a few days with little trouble and as much good order as favorable outcome. Good men praise, but those who feel otherwise envy Hirrus. Let them do so as long as they respect proper action.	
25	CIL 2954	Serveilius C. f. imperator hostibus victeis, Isaura vetere capta, captiveis venum datis, sei deus seive deast quoius in tutela oppidum vetus Isaura fuit ... votum solvit.	Servilius, son of Gaius, commander, once the enemy had been conquered, old Isaura had been taken, and captives sold, whether it is a god or goddess under whose aegis old Isaura lay, ... paid his vow.	75
26	CIL 741	P. Servilius C. f. Isauricus imperator cepit.	Publius Servilius Isauricus, commander, took this.	74
27	Plin. HN 7.97	Cn. Pompeius Magnus imperator bello XXX annorum confecto fusis fugatis occisis in deditionem acceptis hominum centiens viciens semel LXXXIII depressis aut captis navibus DCCCXLVI oppidis castellis MDXXXVIII in fidem receptis terris a Maeotis ad Rubrum mare subactis votum merito Minervae.	Gnaeus Pompey the Great, commander, once he had concluded a thirty-year war, 12,183,000 men were defeated, put to flight, killed, or taken prisoner, 846 ships taken, 1,538 towns and strong points surrendered, and the lands from the Sea of Azov to the Red Sea had been conquered, paid this vow to Minerva, deservedly.	60
28	Plin. HN 7.98	Cum oram maratimam praedonibus liberasset et imperium maris populo Romano resituisset ex Asia, Ponto, Armenia, Paphlagonia, Cappadocia, Cilicia, Syria, Scythis, Iudaeis, Albanis, Hiberia, insula Creta, Bastrensis, et super haec de rege Mithridate atque Tigrane triumphavit.	When he had freed the coast of pirates and restored Roman control of the sea, [Pompey] triumphed over Asia, Pontus, Armenia, Paphlagonia, Cappadocia, Cilicia, Syria, the Scythians, the Jews, the Albani, Hiberia, Crete, the Bastarnae, and the kings Mithradates and Tigranes.	61
29	GL 6.294.1K	Summas opes qui regum regias refregit.	Who broke the greatest, regal forces of kings.	?
30	ILLRP 318	Consoled ... -one captom ...		?
31	CIL 2930	Cosoled ... nomen ...-ctom ... arma		?

Notes

Introduction

1. The text I have generally used for Caesar *De Bello Gallico* is Du Pontet's Oxford Classical Text. All translations are my own unless otherwise noted. Classical abbreviations follow the list given in *The Oxford Classical Dictionary*, ed. Simon Hornblower and Antony Spawforth, 3d ed. (Oxford, 1996), with the exception of Caesar's *De Bello Gallico*, which is here abbreviated *BG*.

2. Riggsby 1999b.

3. All dates are B.C. unless otherwise noted.

4. Rambaud 1966; Walser 1956, 1995, 1998.

5. Balsdon 1955; Collins 1972, 925–926.

6. McDougall 1991; Erickson 2002.

7. See Allen 2000 for a survey.

8. Where I have said "constrain," many would prefer something like "create." I am sympathetic to this view, but I think my weaker claim is sufficient for the argument that follows.

9. Giddens 1984, 16–28.

10. Aquila 1981, 3.

11. Some would insist that a discourse actually constitutes its own object(s). Again (cf. note 8 above), I am sympathetic to this view, but the weaker one seems sufficient. Nor will I rely on the falsity of the construction hypothesis. Note that my definition here differs from that of Laird (1999, 3–6, 16–18), who uses the term for particular instances of discourse, not for the larger patterns.

12. I come very close here to concatenating three features that Foucault (1977, 33–39) considers and rejects as possible distinguishing features of discourses. His objections hinge to some extent on their individual incompleteness. This argument is weaker against the combined set, especially if we do not insist that every discourse be distinguished by precisely the same features. Ultimately, moreover, Foucault is simply interested in a different question ("conditions of possibility") and so resorts to defining a somewhat different entity (the "discursive formation," p. 38).

13. Bakhtin 1986. Cf. also Kurke 1991, 257–259, setting this notion in a classical context.

14. In fact, one could probably eliminate one or the other term. However, I will retain both, because their traditional associations emphasize different features. Discourse is not tied to whole

works in the same way that genre typically is (though note how Hinds [1998,
41–42] comes close to describing topoi
as genres). Genre emphasizes features of
form and occasion.

15. The easiest mechanism for
expanding discourses is probably the
intertranslation of systems that are only
partly overlapping. Davidson (1984,
195–197) illustrates how this transforms
the discourses themselves.

16. Fowler 1997.

17. A case can be made that claims of
"allusion" are very different from those
of "intertextuality" at a philosophical
level (Fowler 1997, 15), but pragmati-
cally (i.e., in terms of what arguments
can be used to support particular claims
of either sort), allusion is essentially a
subset of intertextuality. There is useful
discussion in Hinds 1998, 47–51, 144.

18. See, e.g., below on Mader 2000.

19. Conte's (1986, 31) notion of the
use of a code model is perhaps a special
case of this phenomenon, but it is not
necessary that a single instance of the
salient discourse always be privileged.

20. The quoted phrase is from
Bourdieu 1993, 29–35, though I mean
something largely different by it.

21. Depending on the precise formulation of definitions of "intertextuality,"
the coinage of "interdiscursivity" may or
may not be logically redundant. In any
case, I use it occasionally to emphasize
the breadth of the processes in question.

22. Galinsky 1994.

23. Mader 2000, 148.

24. Ebbeler 2003, 14–15.

25. Craig 1931.

26. Nisbet 1961, 58.

27. Corbeill 1996, 170–173.

28. Ibid., 162.

29. Cf. Ramage 2003, 339–341, on
Caesar's *celeritas*.

30. See Knapp and Michaels 1985, an
argument far too casually dismissed by
Hinds (1998, 48 n. 58).

31. For a summary of the issues with
extensive bibliography, see Gesche 1976,
78–83. See also Barwick 1938, 100–123;
and Lieberg 1998, 17–19.

32. There are, of course, intermediate positions, suggesting that the work
was published in, say, three installments,
or more minimally that circumstances
forced Book 5 to be published only with
Book 6 (Wiseman 1998, 5–6, a plausible
argument). For present purposes I treat
only the two basic positions.

33. Barwick (1955, 52, 68) purports to
find contradictions between 1.31.3 and
6.12.1 and between 5.24.2/5.53.2 and
6.5.6/6.7.1, but both are likely just based
on change over time.

34. Görler 1976. Ramage (2002, 146
n. 172) points to an interesting special
case. He regards the frequency of the
phrase *populus Romanus* (as a gesture
of solidarity) as an argument of this
type. But why wouldn't Caesar want to
maintain that solidarity?

35. On Lieberg's (1998, 24–31) objections to Görler, see below, Chap. 5, note
106.

36. Von Albrecht 1997, 332–333;
Mutschler 1975.

37. See Wiseman 1998, 4 and 8 n. 18.

38. More precisely, I suggest below
that the choice of genre is in part a way
of advancing those strategic aims.
Cf. Seel 1968, xlvi, for the effect of literary strategy on these questions.

39. On this topic, see Seel 1968,
lii–lxv, and, for bibliography, Gesche
1976, 83–87.

40. Klotz 1910, 26–56; Fuchs 1932.

41. This appears to be the strategy of the various contributors to Welch and Powell 1998.

42. *Pace* Klotz (1910, 146–148).

43. Robinson 1997, 107–110.

44. In none of the relevant cases is there any manuscript support for the alleged interpolation. Contrast the long phrase at 1.13.3, generally held to be a later insertion. Not only is it entirely redundant, but it is missing in several of our manuscripts.

45. Barwick 1938, 1–100; Hering 1956; Oppermann 1933. Some have even argued that the mere presence of descriptions like these in a *commentarius* violates generic rules and therefore shows interpolation. I return to this point below.

46. Some have suggested the presence of what Seel (1968, lvii) calls "primary interpolations," i.e., segments of text inserted by the author in a pre-existing, continuous narrative without much (or any) effort to integrate the new material. This may be the case, but Caesar's deliberate stylistic choices might make it appear so even if he wrote continuously.

47. For earlier discussion, see Gesche 1976, 78–83.

48. Wiseman 1998.

49. Ibid., 4.

50. *Oxford Latin Dictionary*, s.v. 3.

51. Horsfall 1996.

52. Ibid.

53. Millar 1998; Morstein-Marx 2004; Mouritsen 2001.

54. Wiseman 1998, 2–3. Ramage (2002, 132–133) also points out the frequency with which Caesar's own name is closely tied to this phrase.

55. Welch 1998, 102.

56. Harris 1989, 175–284.

57. Mouritsen 2001, 16–17; Hall 1998, 28–29.

58. The situation is perhaps further complicated by dispatches to the Senate and public supplications and triumphs, all of which would likely have served purposes similar to that of *De Bello Gallico*.

59. Hall 2000, 80.

60. For the archeological evidence, see Roymans 1990, 157, 164–165.

61. Villard 1988, 20–25. Dunbabin (1993, esp. 128–129) makes a strong case that, while Greeks tended to mix to a fixed formula, Romans normally tried to suit the taste of the individual drinker.

62. Roymans 1990, 165, 166. This identification is based on find contexts of amphorae and other drinking apparatus, not just the textual evidence. See also Dietler (1995, 68, 71), though he notes that in northern Gaul in earlier periods, wine may have been so scarce that (reusable) Mediterranean drinking apparatus may have served a similar prestige function, whatever was drunk from it.

63. Roymans (1990) notes the prohibitions, but does not make much of them. So far as I know, there has been no comment in the Celticist literature in general on this point.

64. Brun 1995; Wells 1995. Even those such as Roymans (1990, 43–45) and Haselgrove (1995), who are disinclined to see a radical change in kind, nonetheless admit to a considerable change in degree of centralization.

65. Dietler 1995, 71.

66. Appadurai 1986, 31–33, 38–39.

67. See further at fig. 9 in Chap. 2.

68. See, e.g., Wiseman 1979, 1993; Woodman 1988; Miles 1995.

69. E.g., Barton 1994, though she is right (p. 58) to point out that the mere existence of such invective would be a historically interesting phenomenon.

70. The full formulation, frequently cited by so-called New Historicists, is "the historicity of texts and the textuality of history," Montrose 1989, 20. Unfortunately, Montrose presents it at its first occurrence as an isolated slogan, without exegesis. Thornton (1997, 215 n. 66) objects that much historical evidence, such as "ancient bones or pottery sherds or ruins," is not in fact textual. Such items are certainly not linguistic, but "textual," in that the relevant sense is not synonymous with "linguistic." Rather, it simply means "requiring interpretation [which *is* inherently linguistic] to be meaningful." For the argument that "texts" and "lumps" are equivalent in this respect, see Rorty 1991, 78–92.

71. Brunt 1988, 508–510; quotation p. 508.

72. Cf. Greenblatt 1990, 15.

73. It might be objected that in fact *both* are true "on different levels," or by virtue of saying unrelated things. This strategy seems to me merely to create yet a third representation insofar as it rejects the implicit claim of both of the others to telling the "real" story. The composite version can *account for* both of the others, but only at the cost of *denying* them.

74. Brunt 1988, 508; Rorty 1991, 113–125; Lakoff 1987. For the application of such a viewpoint specifically to history, see Jenkins 1991.

75. For an account of resistance to such change, however, see Jardine 1996, 132–147.

76. Cf. Greenblatt 1989, 12: "The work of art is not itself a pure flame that

lies at the source of our speculations. Rather the work of art is itself the product of a set of manipulations, some of them our own ..., many others undertaken in the construction of the original work." For "work of art," read, in this context, "historical source."

77. Wiseman's (1994, xii–xiii) definition of a "fact" as "a hypothesis [that] seems unchallengeable" is promising in this context, but his claim that hypotheses are to be supported by "sources" and "argument" seems to beg important questions: What counts as "source" or "argument"? Whose "challenges" count?

78. Model-building: Finley 1985. Quasi-fictionalization: Schama 1991.

Chapter 1

1. This speech will be discussed at greater length in Chap. 6 below.

2. Of course, all Roman political discourse is, as is well known, highly individualized and moralized. For similar observations, see Nisbet 1961, 192–197; Earl 1967, 11–43; and, more generally, Edwards 1993 and Corbeill 1996. The interesting feature of this case is how that tendency is exaggerated and overdetermined.

3. On the prewar construction of the threat, see Steel 2001, 126–129.

4. Lakoff 1987; Alverson 1994.

5. Rambaud 1974. Bertrand (1997, 117–120) covers some of the same ground, but has little to add to Rambaud.

6. This use of "large scale" to mean "covering the largest area" (and a comparable use of "small scale") strikes me as conventional English usage, but it is the reverse of technical cartographic language. I consistently use the former.

7. Rambaud 1974, 114, 116, 119, 121.

8. See Geertz 1973 and Crosby 1997 for qualitative time.

9. The Roman hour, whose length varies by the season of the year, does not fit this pattern, but the larger units do.

10. See 3.28.2, 5.21.2, 5.52.1, 6.5.4, 6.5.7, 6.34.2, 6.35.7, 7.16.1, 7.32.2. Cf. 6.31.2.

11. At 5.37.7, the few Roman survivors from the attack at Sabinus' and Cotta's camp manage to work their way through forest back to Labienus' position. Notably they are not acting here as a military force, and, in this nonstereotypical situation, the real rather than the stereotypical effects of forest come through.

12. Surprise attacks: 2.19.7, 3.28.3, 5.19.2, 5.32.1.

13. "Hiding": 1.12.3, 2.18.1, 2.19.6, 4.18.4, 4.32.5, 4.38.5, 5.3.4, 5.9.4, 5.19.1, 7.18.3.

14. See 6.34.4, and Goldsworthy 1996, 176.

15. Rambaud 1974, 118.

16. See 1.6.1, 5.32.2 (but the word subsequently appears at 1.9.1, 1.11.1).

17. Mountains and hills: 1.24.1 ≈ 1.24.3; 4.23.2 ≈ 4.23.3; 7.36.1 ≈ 7.36.2; 7.83.2 ≈ 7.83.7.

18. Rambaud 1974, 121–123.

19. Height of a mountain: 1.2.3, 1.6.1, 1.38.5, 3.1.5, 7.36.1, 7.52.3; the only explicit height of a hill is 200 *passus* (2.18.2).

20. Slope of a hill: 2.8.3, 2.18.1–2, 7.19.1, also the *tumulus* at 1.43.1.

21. Refuge: 1.25.6, 1.26.1, 3.2.1, 4.23.2, 7.36.1, 7.62.9 (with *silvae* as well); Romans are said to hold a *mons* at 1.22.1. Also cf. below. Guillaumin (1987) demonstrates that Caesar makes a similar distinction between large *flumina* and small *rivi*.

22. Boundaries: 1.1.7, 1.2.3, 1.6.1, 1.8.1, 1.38.5, 3.1.5, 4.23.2, 7.8.2.

23. Rambaud 1974, 118.

24. The clearest case of the indefiniteness of forests is illustrated in fig. 7 (4), but the principle holds for scenes described in less detail as well. On the lack of specifics of the various *angustiae* at the strategic level, contrast Figs. 7 (3), (7), and (10), where we are given details of the width available to the army.

25. The marsh at 7.19.1 has one limited dimension, but no size in the other.

26. On the possibility (now rightly rejected) of interpolation in this passage, see Introduction; and Hering 1956.

27. Since some feel that this entire passage derives from literary sources, this phrase might be taken as a (highly vague) source reference, not an internal cross-reference. However, there is only one clear external reference of the sort in *De Bello Gallico* (6.24.2), whereas back references with phrases like *dictum est* are common.

28. E.g., 1.2.3, 1.3.7, 1.20.4, 1.30.3, 1.31.10, 1.31.16, etc. By far, the most examples are in the first book, but the rate picks up again in Books 6 and 7.

29. It is also expansive in that one of the three parts is itself "Gaul."

30. Rambaud 1974, 114–115.

31. Cisalpine: Gelzer 1968, 222. Transalpine: ibid., 299. Longer-term interest: Steel 2001, 202.

32. Cf. Leach 1988, 86.

33. See 7.7.10, 7.81.6.

34. Rambaud 1974, 126–129.

35. These works are known collectively as the *corpus agrimensorum*. I cite the texts from Thulin's (1971) edition.

36. I address the problem of the texts' illustrations below. On the manuals, see Dilke 1967, 1971; and Campbell 1996. Campbell's article has been more important to my view on these texts than is represented by references to individual points.

37. Campbell 1996, 75−80.

38. *Misurare la terra* 1983, 74−98.

39. Agenius Urbicus 43.12−15, 44.15−17.

40. Hyg. 88.5−10.

41. See Agenius Urbicus 43.20−24 on why one might prefer this situation.

42. Frontinus 18.12−19.8. I give here the standard view of the procedure. Moscatelli 1979 offers a radical alternative, which may not be philologically impossible, but it makes a unique, angled use of the *gromma* (on normal usage, Lewis 2001, 109−133) and neglects to account for Frontinus' explanation of the direction wheat grows.

43. Frontin. 18.6−11.

44. Nipsius *Fluminis variatio.*

45. Also Hyginus 89.7−13; Siculus Flaccus 102.16−17.

46. On the illustrations, see Dilke 1961, 1967.

47. *Misurare la terra* 1983, 131.

48. Carder 1978, 183.

49. It should also be noted that the other major manuscript, while itself centuries older than the one Carder studies, appears to be much more conservative in preserving the style of earlier illustrations: Carder 1978, 183, 195. This is, however, a general trend, not a rule that can be applied mechanically in any particular case.

50. Cf. 2, 14, 20, 28, 57, 64, 65, 69T.

51. Cf. 18−21T.

52. Cf. 93, 95−98, 107, 107a, 135T.

53. It would be easy to imagine (7) set in a larger plain, producing essentially the same situation as (2), but Caesar does not in fact specify this.

54. (1): mountain and river; (2): none; (3): hill, trenches; (4): hills, forest; (5): mountains; (6): Ocean and mountains; (7): swamp; (8): none; (9): river and hills; (10): river.

55. Note that the most unusual tactical space (7) is one dictated by the enemy.

56. A similar argument cannot be made for the treatment of rivers (discussed above), but there the main problem is that rivers move. Hence, utility does not determine a single best solution.

57. Although the Latin language and Roman law make available a distinction between ownership and possession, it will not be salient here.

58. Cf. Nicolet 1991, 95−122, 149−169.

59. In fact, Siculus Flaccus 103.9−10 emphasizes the importance of differing local customs.

60. Frontinus 4.7−11 lists the standard *controversiae.*

61. And compare Caesar's almost instantaneous traverse of a mountain (7.8) with, say, Hannibal's struggles in the Alps.

Chapter 2

1. On the ancient ethnographic tradition in general, see Trüdinger 1918; on Northerners, see recently Rives 1998 and Jervis 2001.

2. Williams 2001, 78−99. Surviving elements: nomadism, clientage as a central social institution, bellicosity, low technology, primitive diet.

3. The Roman historian Livy is

contemporary with the last of these, and he does treat Gauls in various places (most notably the Gallic sack of Rome in Book 5), but his formal ethnography is in portions of the work no longer extant (*Per.* 103, 104). His Gauls do, however, have the same love of wine (5.33.2–3) and fierce nature (5.36.1, 37.4) that we will see in the other authors.

4. Edelstein and Kidd 1972, 2:8–10. For more detail, see Tierney 1960 and Nash 1976.

5. Edelstein and Kidd 1972, 1:6, 10–12. In the Athenaeus citations given below, the author is quoting Posidonius.

6. On the dating and on Caesar's role in the *Bibliothēkē*, see Sacks 1990, 167–184.

7. Strabo 6.4.2. The precise history of the composition is somewhat controversial; see Aujac and Lasserre 1969, 30–34.

8. E.g., 1.1.1, 4.4.6 (Ephorus); 3.1.4, 4.4.6 (Artemidorus). Both are cited more than fifty times each. On Pytheas, see Hawkes 1977.

9. For such inconsistencies as there are over a broader time span, see Jervis 2001, 17–60.

10. Here I use the term "barbarian" to refer to the Gauls and Germans collectively.

11. In principle Caesar could also be a source for Strabo or Diodorus, but *De Bello Gallico* does not contain the details that distinguish the one from the other.

12. The other early source is Caesar. Some have suggested that there is evidence for self-identified Germans among the participants in Spartacus' revolt; see Livy *Per.* 97; Plut. *Crass.* 9.7.

13. Important views and references are summarized by Edelstein and Kidd 1972, 2:323–325.

14. There is no direct evidence for Edelstein and Kidd's (1972, 2:324, 926–927) claim that Posidonius thought of the Cimbri as Celts.

15. Jardine 1996, 1–18.

16. Greek "Galatae" is roughly equivalent to (though broader than) Latin "Galli."

17. The same is true of Livy (*Per.* 103, 104), but the summaries give us no idea of the substantive distinctions, if any.

18. He repeats virtually the same claim at the beginning of his discussion of the Germans (7.1.2).

19. Ancient astronomical techniques were capable of giving accurate latitudes, but finding longitude requires clocks of an accuracy not achieved until recent centuries; see Sobel 1996.

20. Harley et al. 1987a, 145; 1987b, 169. The idea goes back at least to Aristotle, and probably much further (Strabo 2.2.2–2.3.3).

21. Glacken 1967, 80–115.

22. There is another north-south division at the very end of 4.4.2, and (on a larger scale) with the British at 4.5.2, Irene at 4.5.4, and Thule at 4.5.5. Even if you take this all as Roman (rather than environmental) influence, this passage seems to show a north-south gradient, not genuinely distinct peoples placed in various places on the map. Cf. Diod. Sic. 5.32.3.

23. The confusion about the course of the Danube may have to do with the different names used for the river in different languages.

24. Alps as the source of some rivers: Diod. Sic. 5.24.4; Alps as the Celt/Galatae boundary, Diod. Sic. 5.32.1; unnamed mountains along unnamed rivers: Diod. Sic. 5.27.1; "Hercynian Mountain": Diod. Sic. 5.32.1 (the Hercynian Forest

sometimes seems to be the Black Forest and at others the Bohemian; it may refer to both); Pyrenees: Diod. Sic. 5.32.1.

25. The terms are not Strabo's, nor does he conventionally divide his material in this fashion.

26. The exception is the section on the Belgae (4.4.1), which is not clearly either the end of the geography or the beginning of the ethnography. Note that the ambiguity allows Strabo to violate his normal structure without having to give any justification.

27. "Navigable rivers" is a category of standing interest for Diodorus, but the emphasis here is repeated only in the account of even more exotic India (Diod. Sic. 2.37.1, 4).

28. Later they are also characterized by their levity (4.4.5), the opposite of the Romans' prized *gravitas.*

29. Note also that in Cicero's witness sociology, Greeks can be bought, Sardi are incapable of telling the truth, but it is the Gauls who take positive pride in not telling the truth; cf. Riggsby 1999c.

30. Although the behavior described here is not precisely equivalent to modern homosexuality (note Diodorus' expectation that the Gauls will all have wives), the term is not completely inappropriate. Both authors point out that, in contradistinction to our general understanding of Greco-Roman practice, object-choice is here determined largely on the grounds of sex.

31. Posidonius' Celts are also particularly interested in boys, preferably two at a time (Ath. 13.603).

32. Some have tried to emend the word (φιλόνεικοι) away for no good reason.

33. See Goldsworthy 1996, 228–235, for infantry vs. cavalry actions.

34. On the Scythians, see Hartog 1988. Strabo actually mentions nomads (e.g., 6.4.2, 7.3.9); Diodorus makes the Celts and Scythians neighbors (5.32.1, 3).

35. Hartog 1988, 18–19.

36. Ibid., 193–194, 205–206.

37. There is a considerable early literature on this topic, focusing (unfortunately) on the issue of alleged interpolations: see Beckmann 1930, with refs.; and add Klotz 1934, 1941; and Hering 1956. On the supposed interpolations, see the Introduction above.

38. Wells (1972, 311–312) considers and rightly rejects this interpretation. I would emphasize more than he does the extent both to which Caesar's construction of the Gaul/Germany distinction is an ongoing project in *De Bello Gallico* and to which Caesar also repeatedly undercuts his own distinction.

39. Shaw 1984. The Germans also refuse basic technological developments, such as wine (4.2.6) and the saddle (4.2.4–5). We might regard this extreme view of "bandits" as unfair in most cases. A colleague suggests, instead, "what we would call, according to point of view, freedom fighters, or terrorists, or guerilla fighters" (Gwyn Morgan, personal communication). Post-9/11 usage of "terrorist" seems to me a very good parallel for the extreme interpretation of *latro.*

40. This sounds extreme today, but may have been considerably less so for a Roman audience. Public speech was always supposed to be under the control of the magistrates (Livy 39.15–16), and it was in their purview to "protect" the citizenry from inappropriate information (Gruen 1990, 163–170; that the particular event Gruen discusses may have been staged is not important to the present point).

41. See 2.17.2, 2.32–33, 3.8.2–3, 4.27.2–3, 5.37.1–2, 7.37, 7.55.

42. See 1.16.5, 5.3.2–3, 5.6–7, 7.32.4–5.

43. In the previous book, representatives of the tribe of the Treviri had attempted to play up differences between mass and elite in that tribe (5.27.3).

44. Caesar also uses terms describing some less distinctively Roman institutions: *factio, princeps, servi/domini, vacatio/tributa/immunitas, magistratus.*

45. See 2.31.5, 4.15.5, 5.45.1, 6.17.5, 6.19.3, 7.4.10, 7.20.9, 7.38.9.

46. On the Senate, see Gell. *NA* 1.23.4, and Plin. *Ep.* 8.14.4. On early education in general, see Bonner 1977, 10–19.

47. Gell. *NA* 3.2; Plut. *Quaest. Rom.* 84; Plin. *HN* 2.188.

48. Morgan (1980, 154 n. 53) suggests that the point of the passage is the ease with which the great task was carried out. That is clearly the reason for the final sentence: "In ten days from when the material first began to be assembled, the work was completed and the army led across." This emphatic conclusion is required, however, precisely because the lengthy preceding description has stressed instead the enormity of the project. Contrast *BG* 7.24.1, where a much longer project (twenty-five days) is described more briefly so as to give the impression of speed.

49. On two slightly shorter parallels in *B Civ.* and *BG,* see James 1997 and Erickson 2002, respectively.

50. My reference misrepresents Caesar's narrative slightly by referring to the engineers, *fabri;* as discussed in the next chapter, Caesar in fact gives himself the credit.

51. There are several textual problems at this point, but none of them seems to put the general sense of the passage in doubt. On the principle of the "excluded middle," see Hartog 1989, 258–259.

52. Curzon 1908, 20–21.

53. The rest of this paragraph summarizes the account of Wells 1972, 15–23. Cf. Hachmann et al. 1962, 110–113, 126–128, 129–133; Todd 1975, 42–49; and Mattern 1999, 76.

54. O'Gorman 1993, 147.

55. This passage was brought to my attention by Anita Tarar.

56. The most recent and sophisticated version of this reading is O'Gorman 1993, but there is a long tradition; see her p. 151 n. 2.

57. O'Gorman 1993, 157. O'Gorman can also cite Hartog 1988, 259, to similar effect for the Greek tradition.

58. Mannetter (1995, 4–5), following a typology of Hayden White's (1978), proposes that Gauls and Germans all fit standard variations of a single northern "Other" type—"barbarian," "noble savage," and "wildman." Thus he sees them all as relatively traditional and relatively homogeneous. To describe these types as subtypes of a single category is surprisingly essentialist and begs the present question.

59. The "truth" in this matter is problematic. Williams (2001, 12–13) exposes conceptual problems with the category of "Celt." As Wells (1972, 313–314) notes, it is possible that Caesar is writing before the sound changes that made Germanic a distinctive language group. It has also been emphasized recently that categories lower than the species level (e.g., race, ethnic group) have little biological reality: see Keita 1993; and Lewis and Wigan 1997, 122–123. If, in this context, we ask, "Who were the Celts and who were the

Germans?" it is not entirely clear what we are asking.

60. Dobesch 1989, 29–30; Jantz 1995, 140, 221; Jervis 2001, 69. The sole explicit citation of other texts in *BG* (Eratosthenes and "some Greeks") is found in the German ethnography (6.24.2).

61. Williams 2001, 220–221.

62. E.g., 2.15.3, 4.20.4, 5.6.2, and perhaps 5.13.4. More often he gets his information from prisoners: 1.22.1, 1.50.4, 2.16.1, 2.17.2, 5.8.6, 5.9.1, 5.18.4, 5.48.2, 5.52.4, 6.33.2, 7.18.1, 7.72.1 (most of these cases are after the fact).

63. Syme (1964, 152–153) notes how little Sallust's account of Numidia seems to have benefited from the author's time there.

64. The overall pattern is binary (as with the Gauls), but the exchange of individual fields is much more formless.

65. As suggested in passing by Wells (1972, 30).

66. Pelikan 1997.

67. For instance, Pompey and Lucullus in Asia, Marius and Metellus in Numidia.

68. Romm 1992, 67–77.

69. Morgan 1980; Romm 1992, 135–139; Nicolet 1991, 29–56.

70. Thomas 1982, 2 and passim; and Trüdinger 1918, 77–78.

71. Comparison to what is customary occurs twenty-nine times total. I count references to the Suebi as "German" because of the equivalence discussed above (and apparently accepted by the Suebian speaker of 4.7.2). I omit a number of ambiguous cases where the custom is described as *suus*.

72. Helvetii: 1.4.1; Aedui: 7.33.3; Aremoricae: 7.75.4.

73. I count 121 German and Gallic tribes (below the level of Celts/Aquitani/Belgae) in DuPontet's OCT index.

74. Mannetter 1995, 138.

75. Questionable cases: Segni, Cautibri, Tarusates, Vocates, Ruteni, Ambarii, Condrusi, Veragri. Collection of these data has been greatly facilitated by Mannetter's (1995, 203–207) catalog of catalogs in *BG*.

76. Forty (plus possibly Segni and Condrusi) of the hapaxes appear only in lists.

77. Holliday 1997, 146–147.

78. Jantz (1995, 63) also points out that the constant use of *ethnica* undercuts the significance of the higher-level political organization in Gaul to which Caesar occasionally points.

Chapter 3

1. Lendon 1999 is an excellent approach to similar issues from a very different direction.

2. Note other Gauls' willingness to put the Suebi as well as Romans above the gods (4.7.5).

3. In fact, by the mere arrival of the devices. The effect of the arrival (*adventus*) of the great commander is common enough (see Woodman 1983, 183), but this is an unusual variation.

4. See also 7.10.2, 7.33.1–2, 7.54.2. See further in Chap. 7 below.

5. Audouze and Büchsenschütz 1992, 88.

6. On the narratological aspects of this, see Chap. 5 below.

7. Note also that the success of the Roman attack is attributed not to superior technology, but to the diligence (*diligentia*) of Crassus' men.

8. The Latin "superlative" is not infrequently used as a simple intensive (e.g., "very skilled"), but here the separate intensifier "far" (*longe*) guarantees that "most skilled" (*peritissimi*) involves a real comparison.

9. There is a fairly common topos in later writers used of enemies who have learned Roman fighting skills while previously allied with the Romans (e.g., Livy 6.32.7, 8.6.15; [Caes.] *BAlex.* 34.4, 68.2), but it is less common for them to learn by fighting against the Romans (Vell. Pat. 109.1). See Kraus 1994, 263.

10. On Sertorius, see Spann 1987 and Konrad 1993.

11. Wells 1972, 99–100; Goldsworthy 1996, 25–26, 111–113. This is true even of more permanent bases and *hiberna*, much less the daily marching camps.

12. See Chap. 1 on *paludes* ("marshes").

13. Cf. Strabo 4.4.2.

14. Audouze and Büchsenschütz 1992, 92–93.

15. The same is true of the hooks used to defeat the ships of the Veneti in 3.14. And there, too, the result is progression to real battle.

16. Caesar's visible arrival (cf. Audouze and Büchsenschütz 1992, 92–93, and see further below) is also crucial here: "Once his arrival was noticed from the color of his clothing, which mark of distinction he was wont to use in battle ..." (7.88.1).

17. This was also the case in the battle with the Veneti at 3.14–15.

18. Note the lack of technology in the second (German) attack on Cicero's camp (6.36–40).

19. Outside *De Bello Gallico* there are a few other examples of foreign troops learning from their Roman opponents; see note 9 above.

20. Eisenhut 1973, 12–13. The gendered force of the term is repeatedly exploited by Caesar; see below and Chap. 4 on Critognatus' speech; above, Introduction, on wine; and Erickson 2002.

21. Moore 1989, 5, 6; cf. Hellegouarc'h 1972, 244. The latter part of the quotation is meant to refer only to Livy, but seems to me to represent broader usage quite well. The plural tends to take on a wider range of meaning, and particularly to be attracted to the more abstract Greek ἀρετή, "excellence" (of which *virtus* eventually becomes the standard translation in technical contexts).

22. As Eisenhut (1973, 34) points out, the prototypical sense is unsurprisingly prominent in this military narrative (but note *BG* 7.6.1).

23. "Province" here refers to the Roman province of Transalpine Gaul in the south of modern France.

24. See 1.36.7, 2.4.5, 2.24.4, 6.24.1.

25. Also 2.4.8.

26. See 1.1.4; also 4.2.1, 4.2.6, 4.3.3, 6.24.5–6.

27. Wheeler (1988, 56–57, 78) sets these comments in the general context of the Roman "vocabulary of military trickery."

28. By "Caesar" in this sentence, I mean the character rather than the narrator or author.

29. Cf. also 1.39.1: *Germanos incredibili virtute atque exercitatione in armis esse praedicabant.*

30. This conforms to a general Roman tendency to see ethnic differences primarily in terms that would today be considered "cultural" and/or

"environmental," rather than "biological" (Snowden 1983, 63–65, 85–87).

31. Note, as Caesar several times points out, that the Romans fought with the Gauls from time to time (see Chap. 6). Thus it is the presence or absence of trade (not of war) that is the first determinant here.

32. Suolahti 1955. Note how Crassus, Brutus, and Volcatius Tullus, who are given command of independent detachments, are regularly described as *adulescentes*.

33. See 2.21.2, 5.48.7, 7.62.2, 7.77.5. Cf. 1.13.4, and, on the Vesontio episode in general, James 2000.

34. Büchner 1962, 2; Eisenhut 1973, 40.

35. See 2.33.4, 3.5.3, 7.20.6, 7.29.2, 7.50.1.

36. See 3.14.8, 5.35.4.

37. See 2.30.4, 3.17.5, 5.29.2, 5.49.7, 5.51.3; Mannetter 1995, 22 n. 44.

38. This term is particularly appropriate to obedience to military orders; see *OLD* s.v. 2.

39. *Magnitudo animi* is associated especially with *fortitudo*; see Hellegouarc'h 1972, 290–292.

40. Edwards 1993, 63–97.

41. The argument was also foreshadowed by Vercingetorix, who complained of *animi mollitiem* and the inability to sustain labors (7.20.5).

42. Cf. Kaster 2002.

43. Cf. Riggsby 1995 for another example of this strategy.

44. E.g., Büchner 1962, 5; Dahlmann 1970, 17–19; Hellegouarc'h 1972, 243; and Roller 1996, 320–322. Dahlmann even cites *BG* 7.50 in this context.

45. Roller 1996; and Earl 1967, 23: "The service of the state required private virtues, but in their public application.

To a purely private cultivation of personal virtue the Roman tradition was always hostile."

46. I know of no instances of excessive *virtus* before or contemporary with Caesar. There are only three later instances that even raise the possibility (Apul. *Met.* 4.8; Sil. *Pun.* 6.404; Sen. *De vita beata* 13.5). Two of them imply the same critique of the conventional usage as Caesar. That is, all point out that concentration on the self-sacrifice usually valorized as *virtus* will sometimes be disadvantageous in the broader picture. Neither of them goes on then (as Caesar does) to recuperate *virtus* by suggesting that sometimes the bravest act is not to sacrifice oneself. The third is technical. Seneca *(De vita beata* 13.5) denies the possibility even in principle of excessive *virtus*, but he uses the term in a technical philosophical sense (translating ἀρετή).

47. As in Livy's story of Manlius Torquatus (8.7), with Feldherr 1998, 105–111.

48. Lendon 1999, 304–316.

49. On the general moral viewpoint, see Riggsby 1998 and Habinek 1998, 45–59. On the theatrical consequences, see Riggsby 1997; Dupont 1985, 19–40; and esp. Roller 2004.

50. Solodow 1979; Feldherr 1998, 58, 101–102; and note the analogous phenomena in Polybius (Davidson 1991, 11–18).

51. Goldsworthy 1996, 150–163.

52. Caesar's sub-commanders call two other *consilia* in *De Bello Gallico*. At 3.3.1–3, Galba not only holds the meeting, but takes a vote (which at least opts for appropriate restraint). His troops are then fortunate to escape a close call (3.6.4). At 7.60.1, Labienus

calls a meeting simply to give orders. His troops are highly successful.

53. Legate, not legates; only Titurius is blamed.

54. Caesar twice notes the *virtus* of Cicero's troops in his after-the-fact assessment (5.52.3, 6).

55. Cf. 7.52.1; Augustus *RG* 25; Livy 7.8.7, 30.18.14, 35.5.14, 37.16.12; Cic. *Att.* 5.20.4. Note also how an *eques* is singled out among the civilians massacred at Cenabum (7.3.1).

56. James 1997, 10. Goldsworthy (1996, 253) notes Antonius Primus' use (in A.D. 69) of a battle fought by his legion a century earlier under Antony to inspire them. He argues that a legion's oral tradition was thus used as a means of generating unit cohesion.

57. Even if the phrase refers to gladiatorial training before the rebellion (which is not at all clear), the Romans are not trying to create a collective force. Romans seem to have lived very much in fear of their slaves, as the very next sentence of Caesar's speech points out. Cf. also *Digest* 29.5; Tac. *Ann.* 14.42; Plin. *Ep.* 3.14; Sen. *Clem.* 1.24.1; and the several occurrences of the proverb *quot servi, tot hostes* (Sen. *Ep.* 47.5; Festus, *Gloss. Lat.* 314L; Macrob. *Sat.* 1.11.13).

58. See 7.1.1; for the details of the history, see Ruebel 1979.

59. This massacre is very similar to those at Cirta (at the opening of the Jugurthine War in 112) and in Asia Minor (at the beginning of the Mithradatic War in 88), though there is no particular reason to doubt the veracity of the account.

60. For other parallels between Caesar and Vercingetorix, see Jervis 2001, 156–162.

61. Mannetter 1995, 37–38.

62. See 3.4.3, 7.25.1, 7.41.2; cf. 5.45.1.

63. Similarly (though on a larger scale), the narrator says that Caesar's recruitment of fresh troops in early 53 (after the losses in Ambiorix's revolt) "taught [the Gauls] what the discipline and resources of the Roman people could do" (6.1.4).

64. Cf. the strategic mobility of the Helvetii (1.5.1).

65. The problem was also foreshadowed by the Gallic *consilium* at 7.63. The authority of Vercingetorix was formally confirmed, but several tribes did not even bother to show up, and the Aedui immediately resented his position.

66. The Bellovaci did, however, send some troops out of personal *hospitium*.

67. The *summa imperi* that Vercingetorix had denied to others at 7.20.5 and 7.63.5 suddenly appears in the hands of Commius and other leaders outside Alesia at 7.79.1.

68. Mannetter (1995, 129–130) has noted that barbarians tend to swear oaths, which inevitably lead to disaster. Though these oaths are superficially a gesture of obedience, they presume that the oath-giver is legitimately a free agent in the first place. The proper attitude, according to this text, is rather, "My loyalty was never mine to give."

69. Recall O'Gorman's (1993, 147) claim in the previous chapter that "if two types of barbarianism are represented, one will be assimilated to the Roman." One might contend that, in the end, Caesar fell into this pattern of binary thinking by assimilating Gauls to Romans. Such a claim, however, misses several important points. First, although the Gauls assimilate technologically (including technologies of organization), they do not do so morally. In fact, references

to Gallic cruelty grow denser in the later parts of *De Bello Gallico*. Second, to the extent that Gauls are assimilated to Romans, the process takes place over the entire length of the work. Caesar can clearly conceive of a three-point opposition, even if he does not employ it consistently. Finally, and perhaps most important, the assimilation is thematized. Gallic character, even at the end of the work, is defined not just by where the Gauls had gotten to, but by the entire trajectory that brought them there. Thus the three-point opposition of Gauls, Germans, Romans, remains crucial to the structure of *De Bello Gallico*, even if its instantiation in real life is eventually to some extent suppressed or denied.

70. Burns 1994.

71. The only exception seems to be that the storage huts in Cicero's camp to which the Gauls are able to set fire are made *more Gallico* (5.43.1).

72. For a proposed counter-example (4.13.5–6, 4.15.4–5), see Chap. 6.

73. See 3.2.5, 4.34.5, 5.38.2, 7.64.3, 7.77.9, 7.77.16.

74. See 2.31.5, 4.15.5, 5.45.1, 6.17.5, 6.19.3, 7.4.10, 7.20.9, 7.38.9. Publilius Syrus 682 contrasts *crudelitas* to *virtus*.

75. He also never says just how he got information *ex captivis*.

76. Collins 1972, 933–935.

77. In fact, they explicitly deal well with hunger (7.17.3).

78. Inscriptions on public works show all of these forms, crediting the magistrate in charge. *Faciendum curavit*, vel sim., is perhaps the most common (e.g., *CIL* I².737, 1523, 1529, 1627, 1759, 2661), but sometimes the presiding magistrate simply announces that he built something: cf. *CIL* I².638, 1814.

79. Rosenstein 1990, 92–113.

80. Livy 35.6.9; and Rosenstein 1990, 105 n. 59.

81. Edwards 1993, 56–57, 195–198.

82. The phenomenon was hardly new; harassing the Scipios had been a favorite pastime of late-third- and early-second-century aristocrats: Gruen 1995. More generally, see Riggsby 1997, 52–53; Beard and Crawford 1985, 53–55.

Chapter 4

1. The other is at *B Civ.* 2.31–32.

2. Fabia 1889, 86–90; Holtz 1913, 30–33; Rasmussen 1963, 47–54; Schieffer 1972; Canali 1985, 57–63.

3. Fabia (1889, 86–90) offers a very similar analysis. Schieffer (1972, 480) objects to the idea of a proem since §3 already stakes out a position (against surrender). However, my analysis here supports Fabia by showing that this "position-taking" is less an argument than an ethical positioning for the sake of *captatio benevolentiae*. To the extent that there is some ambiguity here, it is another illustration of the fact that Caesar's tactics are those of real oratory, not just textbook rhetoric (see below). Rasmussen (1963, 49) reads §§6–11 and 13–16 as autonomous excurses designed to generate pathos. About pathos he is certainly correct, but below we see that it is generated in the course of the logical argument. Canali (1985, 62) sees only three parts: §§1–2, 3–7, 8–16.

4. This is recognized even by Schieffer (1972, 480), who sees only two parts to the speech.

5. Vasaly 1993.

6. G. Kennedy 1968; Hall 1998, 31 n. 38.

7. Presumably Critognatus must also justify the metaphorical (i.e., political)

application of "slavery." The features that allow this include loss of personal control and subjection to physical punishment (*securibus subiecta*). On the mechanism, see Roller 2001, 214–233.

8. Also more locally in the *copia* noted by Fabia (1889, 88) and Holtz (1913, 34–35).

9. Narducci 1997, 162–163.

10. Craig 1979, 3–4.

11. Roller 2001, 214–233.

12. For the phrase, see Anderson 1991, 6–7.

13. Holtz (1913, 35) notes this as an ornamental metaphor. Schieffer (1972, 489–490) sees that the phrase is tendentious, but says that the point is to support Caesar's own position that Gaul should be seen as a unified entity (cf. *Gallia … omnis*, 1.1.1). This is true as far as it goes, but it does not really account for the other devices Critognatus is given to construct that unity.

14. Cf. Fabia 1889, 88–89: Caesar sneaks up on the point. Note also the long gap between "bodies" and "life." Even the very phrase is dragged out abnormally.

15. On this conventional use of dilemma, see Craig 1993, 172.

16. Riggsby 1999a, 111.

17. See Chap. 3. Nor is it limited to *De Bello Gallico*; cf. Sall. *Cat.* 58.11, 60.3.

18. Especially relevant here is the fact that Roman opponents are allowed to voice very pointed criticisms of Roman imperialism; for examples, see Sall. *Hist.* 4.69; Livy 9.1; Tac. *Agr.* 30–31; and see Collins 1972, 937; Canali 1985, 51–53. It has been suggested that this is "merely" an issue of style, that a Roman author would not want to disfigure his text with a substandard speech. However, (1) that does not explain the choice of what those

opponents will talk about, nor (2) would the purported fact that style trumps patriotism be an unimportant one.

19. Critognatus, unlike the narrator, follows the general ancient pattern of collapsing three ethnic groups into an essentially binary opposition (cf. Chap. 2).

20. Thus Holtz (1913), Schieffer (1972), and (to a lesser extent) Rasmussen (1963). By contrast, Fabia (1889) thinks the speech too good to be credibly put in the mouth of a barbarian.

21. Quint. 10.1.28–36.

22. Obviously, in the absence of ancient punctuation, almost any declarative sentence in Latin could be punctuated today with an exclamation point. What this text undeniably lacks, though, are *quam* and forms of *qui/quae/quod* in their exclamatory uses. Nor does it show the accusative of exclamation.

23. For instance, see the exclamations in Cic. *Cat.* 1.2, 15; 2.4, 7, 8, 10, 14, 24, etc. These speeches also contain a multitude of rhetorical questions.

24. Schieffer 1972, 490.

25. Schieffer (ibid., 486) also argues for the Romanness of the appeal to exemplum. Cf. Livy's Cato, arguing against repeal of the *lex Oppia* and claiming to stand for fundamental Roman values (34.2.4): *ego vix statuere apud animum meum possum utrum peior ipsa res an peiore exemplo agatur.*

26. Augustus *RG* 8.5. Cf. also Plin. *Ep.* 6.21.1–2; Val. Max. praef. See now the magisterial discussion of exemplary process (and particularly its bidirectionality) in Roller 2004.

27. D. Davidson 1984.

28. Rorty 1991, 126–150; Lakoff 1987, 260–303. By "causal" here I mean simply that ongoing feedback between our experience of the world and our

linguistic descriptions of it are what lead us to assign meanings and truth values as we do.

29. Mannetter 1995, 16 n. 38.

30. I retain here Spurr's term "trope," though I would probably have used "topos" myself. I thank Shadi Bartsch for directing my attention to Spurr's book.

31. Hierarchy of races: Spurr 1993, 66–67; atavistic alien: ibid., 46, 125–128.

32. Ibid., 4.

33. As seen in *BG* 7.4, 7.20; Mannetter 1995, 4–5.

34. Spurr 1993, 92–108.

35. Ibid., 96.

36. Ibid., 13–27.

37. Ibid., 13, emphasis original.

38. It is rightly pointed out to me that the possibility of such reversal is more realistic than the unidirectional fantasy; cf., for instance, Scott 1990, 10–11, 49–50.

39. Other examples: 1.51.1, 7.45.2. Ariovistus raises the possibility of the same at 1.44.10. Cf. Welch 1998, 93.

40. Spurr 1993, 63, emphasis in original. Of course, one need not accept the general argument of *The Order of Things* to inquire into the possible existence of such classification elsewhere.

41. Gould 1985.

42. Riggsby 2004.

43. Jervis 2001, 68.

44. There is considerable room for disagreement as to whether the Social War constituted a decisive break in this respect or just aggravated a problem of long standing. The choice does not much matter for present purposes.

45. Treggiari 1969, 1–11; Balsdon 1979, 82–96.

46. Val. Max. 6.2.3; [Aur. Vict.] *De vir. ill.* 58.8; cf. Vell. Pat. 2.4.4

47. A number of Imperial poets report similar facts, but with an even more xenophobic spin: Balsdon 1979, 14.

48. Rose 1995.

49. Oniga 1995, 9–10.

50. Levine 1996, 105–120, 138–139.

51. Salmon 1970, 134–136.

52. There were failed attempts at colonies in North Africa (under C. Gracchus and Saturninus). Marius did plant one colony on Corsica, and there were a few in southern Gaul in the late second century B.C. Individual land grants overseas seem not to have been so controversial. See Salmon 1970, 119–123, 128–130, 132.

53. Sinclair 1994, 92–96.

54. Ibid., 95–96.

55. Ibid., 96.

56. On the mechanisms, see A. Cohen 1985; and Anderson 1991.

57. E.g., 3.8.3, 3.19.6, 7.3.2, 7.42.2.

58. For Mouritsen (1998, 168), the "'real' Italian issue" before the Social War was not how but whether the Italians would be incorporated into Roman hegemony. This may well have been the case then, at least from the Italian point of view, but by the time Caesar was writing, that question had been decisively settled by the war.

59. Tatum 1997. Cf. Wiseman 1985, 197, on Nepos.

60. Explicitly Sadashige 1999, but see already Skinner 1979.

61. Feldherr (1998, 112–120) discusses the passage in a similar context.

62. Habinek 1998, 88–102.

63. Toll 1997, 39, 50, 53. Vergil's distinctive spin, she argues convincingly, is not so much the "content" of these values but the importance of their reflexive consideration.

64. Syme 1939, 453.

65. Wallace-Hadrill 1997, 5. Cf. Ha-

binek 1998, 88, and A. Giardina cited at his 201 n. 40.

66. Hallet 1989.

67. Stockton 1979, 156–159.

68. Habinek 1998; Imber 1997.

Chapter 5

1. There seems to be no significance to the alternation between the masculine form, which I use throughout, and the quite common neuter commentarium. In Latin usage, the singular and plural seem generally to distinguish a single book (i.e., roll) of notes from a group of these. Note that I have not followed this usage in my text, but have used whichever form English idiom seems to demand.

2. The authorship of the Commentariolum is still controversial, but most recent (published) opinion seems to favor Quintus. For references, see Morstein-Marx 1998.

3. Görler 1976, 96–97. I am not, of course, rejecting the principle of interpreting Caesar from Caesar, merely the claim to divine tradition and innovation in the process.

4. For instance, I have very little to say about Caesar's commentary on the Civil War. Its ends appear to have been rather different than those of De Bello Gallico, and its apparent nonpublication during his lifetime perhaps suggests that he found the form, carried over from the earlier work, uncongenial to those new ends. I also do not address the rhetorical level of the commentarius (as conventionally measured by density of figurative language). Ends: Collins 1972. Publication history: Klotz 1911; Collins 1959.

5. See, respectively, Varro Ling. 6.88; Cic. Pro Rabirio Perduellionis 15; Livy 1.31.8, 1.32.2, 1.60.3; Cic. 2 Verr. 5.54;

Modestinus D. 4.6.32; Plin. Ep. 10.66.1, 10.95.1, 10.105.1; Tac. Hist. 4.40; Suet. Dom. 20.1; Frontin. Aq. 31, 33, 74; Siculus Flaccus 119.3, 125.5–6; Hyg. 81.9; Frontin. Aq. passim; CIL 11.3614.8 (Caere, A.D. 114), 9.1663 (Beneventum, n.d.), 8.2586.6 (Numidia, 3d century A.D.); Tac. Ann. 15.74; Fronto 2.7.9.

6. See, respectively, Plin. HN 18.14; Quint. 8.2.12; Cic. Brut. 55; Serv. Aen. 1.373; Festus 364L; Livy 4.3.9, 6.1.2; Serv. Aen. 1.398; Festus 420L, cf. Cic. Div. 2.42; Festus 178L; Festus 152, 160, 494L.

7. See, respectively, note 23 below; Ulp. 34.2.19.6; Gell. 1.12.18; Festus 164, 474, 476L; Gell. 1.21.2,4; Gell. 13.15.4, Valerius Messalla Rufus Aug. fr. 1; Gell. 10.6.4; Gell. 4.9.8, 14.2.1; Cic. De or. 2.224.

8. See, respectively, Gell. 3.12.1, 4.9.1, 10.4.1, etc.; Gell. 13.9.pr; Gell. 2.16.5, 6.2.1, 11.15.2, 5; Gell. 17.9.5; Gell. 16.8.2; Gell. 13.23.19; Cic. De or. 1.240; Gell. 18.5.12; Gell. 18.9.4; Varro Ling. 6.95; Gell. 2.6.1.

9. See, respectively, Vitr. 9.pr.14; Cic. Fin. 3.10; Cic. Div. 1.6; Cic. Off. 3.121; Cic. Off. 3.8; Gell. 1.26.3.

10. See Vitr. 7.pr.12–14; cf. Frontin. Aq.

11. See Cic. Dom. 136; Plin. Ep. 6.22.4.

12. See Quint. 2.11.7, 3.6.59; cf. Cic. De or. 1.5.

13. Habinek 1998, 34–68. The regal commentaries extant in the late Republic may well have been fake (or at least modernized), but there is little reason to doubt the asserted existence of early regal and pontifical records. See Cornell 1991, and contra, von Premerstein 1900, 728–729.

14. Gell. 13.20.7; Plin. *HN* 29.15; and perhaps Columella *Rust.* 1.1.3.

15. Hanno: Plin. *HN* 5.8. Greeks: see above, note 9. Foreign kings: Livy 33.11.1, 45.31.11, 39.47.3; Plin. *HN* 37.74 (though here Pliny is presumably translating the Greek ὑπόμνημα of his source Theophrastus rather than looking at Egyptian documents). Priests: Val. Max. 8.7 ext. 2.

16. Colonies: note 5 above. Construction: Frontin. *Aq.* 65; Vitr. 7.pr.12. Portents: Plin. *HN* 17.243. Prosecution: Varro *Ling.* 6.90, 92.

17. Asc. 87.10–12C.

18. Farming: Collumela *Rust.* 1.1.3. Stage-painting: Vitr. 7.pr.11. Varro's instructional pamphlet seems later to have been folded into a work called *Epistolary Questions* (Gell. 14.7.3), which seems to have been a miscellany (Gell. pr. 9).

19. Gell. pr. 3, 13, etc.; Plin. *Ep.* 3.5.17.

20. The *peculiaris commentarius* of Mithridates that recorded information on antidotes was presumably his own day book (hence *peculiaris*), rather than a treatise on poisons (Plin. *HN* 37.197).

21. Suet. *De grammaticis et rhetoribus* 4.4; Gell. 17.9.5.

22. Suet. *De grammaticis et rhetoribus* 4.4; see also Gell. 2.16.5, 6.2.1, 6.20.1.

23. Gaius 2.23, 2.145, 3.33, 3.54, with Honoré 1962, 59–60, 63.

24. Cic. *Fin.* 4.10, *De or.* 1.208.

25. Two further examples: Vitruvius (7.pr.14) reports *commentarii* on the precepts of symmetry in architecture. "Precepts" in rhetorical and philosophical contexts are conventionally individual rules of thumb, as opposed to systematic theory. Lucius Aetius Philologus' grammatical *commentarii*

are sometimes taken to be a general treatise, but their title Ὕλη (Suet. *De grammaticis et rhetoribus* 10.5) is equivalent to Latin *Silvae*, known as a title of miscellaneous collections (Gell. *NA* pr.; cf. Quint. 10.3.17).

26. Probably also the case for Varro's *commentarius* (addressed to Pompey) on senatorial procedure. Columella cites *commentarii* as a source of information for farming, but he seems to be referring to family records (*Rust.* 1.1.3).

27. On these, see Bömer 1953, 227–229.

28. Rufus: Charisius 1.120, 1.125, 1.130, 1.139K, 1.146, 2.195; Isid. *Orig.* 20.11.4; Diom. 1.374, 376K. Scaurus: Val. Max. 4.4.11; Diom. 1.374, 377, 385K.

29. Bömer 1953, 228.

30. Number: Plut. *Sull.* 37.1. Family: Gell. 1.12.16, citing a fragment of Book 2.

31. Bömer 1953, 222–223; Fornara 1983, 180–181.

32. *Res gestae:* Gell. 1.12.16, 20.6.2; *historia:* Cic. *Div.* 1.72; *res suae:* Priscian 2.476.5K. Plutarch uses πρᾶγμα, which looks like a translation of *res gestae*.

33. Chapters: Cic. *Rab. Perd.* 15; Serv. *Aen.* 1.373. *Annales:* Gell. pr. 25; Quint. 10.7.32; Cic. *Brut.* 164. *Satura:* Suet. *De grammaticis et rhetoribus* 5.1.

34. There is, in fact, a fourth book, but since it is not foreshadowed here, it would probably not be relevant to Rüpke's argument, even if it were (contrary to most opinion) authentic.

35. Rüpke 1992, 213–215. As Rüpke himself points out, Caesar's supposed introduction gives the order of the three elements twice, in two *different* orders (ibid., 213). Furthermore, when Rüpke tries to give a detailed account of the

structure of the work as a whole, a number of exceptions appear (ibid., 214). He suggests that for Caesar to write a three-part *divisio* without intending to fulfill it just shows how powerful the generic convention was. This begs the question for what Caesar is giving the *partitio*. It would also be more convincing if Rüpke could show more examples of a three-part *partitio* that is clearly carried out. He also claims that back-references like "the Belgae, which we had said to be the third part of Gaul" (2.1.1), and "Aquitania ... which, as was said before, ... must be judged a third part of Gaul" (3.20), are evidence of the overall structure. Instead, Caesar adds these precisely because Belgium and Aquitania, though equal to Gaul in the proem, are so insignificant in the main narrative that the reader needs a note. Gaul (in the narrow sense) never calls for such a back-reference.

36. Von Premerstein 1900, 726.

37. Kelsey 1905, 226, cf. 205.

38. Knoche 1951, 143.

39. Bömer 1953, 214, 243.

40. Adcock 1956, 7, 9; seconded by Cleary 1985, 346.

41. Seel 1968, xliii.

42. Richter 1977, 46–47.

43. T. Wiseman 1979, 6, 152 n. 52.

44. Rüpke 1992, 210.

45. Hence Gärtner (1975, 65 n. 8) doubts even the possibility of definition. Hall (1998, 17) is rightly less worried.

46. Kaster 1995, 101.

47. Bömer 1953, 214, 231. Additionally, it is not entirely clear in either case that the works with allegedly varying titles are in fact the same.

48. *BG* 8.pr.2, 4, 8.4.3, 8.30.1, 8.38.3.

49. On the stylistic requirements of literary history in antiquity, see Fornara

1983. For Caesar's alleged slide into history, see Schlicher 1936; Adcock 1956; Mutschler 1975, among many others.

50. Görler 1976, 95–96.

51. *BG* 8.pr.4–5.

52. On the Greek background, see Walbank 1985. On Livy, see Oakley 1997, 117–120.

53. On the historical value of such anecdotes, see Saller 1980.

54. Also *BG* 1.42.6 and 7.25.1; the former introduces indirect speech, and the latter an anecdote with no quotation at all. This suggests that "memorable action," not "direct speech," is the most salient rubric.

55. Caesar's other work could not, it is widely agreed, have been called *Bellum Civile*, so it does not provide a parallel. On the other hand, *De Bello Gallico* was written first, so Caesar would presumably not have manipulated its title so as to avoid suggesting *Bellum Civile* as a title for the other by analogy. If, however, the earlier work had "Gallic War" in its title, "Civil War" would naturally have entered the tradition for the second.

56. Kelsey 1905, 211–215, quotation from 212.

57. It can also be noted in passing that we are probably not dealing with an actual title, if there was one; the variation in order and word choice is too great. Kelsey (1905, 222–223) claims that the work must have had a title, but his arguments really apply only to the question of whether Caesar attached his name to it. On titles in general, see Horsfall 1981, though he has nothing to add on this particular point. On the date of the *Bellum Civile*, see Collins 1959.

58. Kelsey 1905, 230–232. Subsequent writers: Knoche 1951, 140; Adcock 1956, 6; and Cleary 1985, 345–346.

59. I argue in Chap. 3 above that the outrage, such as it was, was not directed at Caesar's militarism.

60. Kelsey 1905, 231.

61. Ibid., 228–230; Cic. *Prov. cons.* 19, 32, 35, 36, 47.

62. Kelsey 1905, 229–230; Suet. *Iul.* 55.1.

63. This is especially salient in the light of what book length shows about the dominance of the annual structure.

64. Suet. *Iul.* 37. For campaigns, see *BG* 3.16.1, 3.18.6, 4.21.2, 5.4.1.

65. Welch (1998, 101) points out that Caesar's governorship of Illyricum nearly disappears as well.

66. Rüpke 1992, 210.

67. Ibid., 212. Lieberg (1998, 33–34) suggests in a similar vein that Caesar's third person is a way to emphasize that the main character is Caesar the proconsul, not Caesar the individual. This theory is hard to understand, and seems to be based on his misapprehension that *De Bello Gallico*'s first-person forms refer to Caesar (p. 31).

68. Collins 1972.

69. *OLD*, s.v. *noster* (5); cf. *nos* (2b), *noster* (7). See Marincola 1997, 287–288.

70. Making nice to Pompey: 6.1.2, 7.6.1.

71. Cf. Vitr. 1.1.4; Plin. *HN* 30.4, 34.108.

72. By "public" I mean here state records, whether or not they were generally available to the broader public.

73. *Att.* 1.19.10, 2.1.1; *Fam.* 5.12.10.

74. Fantham 1996, 36–37.

75. Seel (1968, xliii) perhaps goes too far in saying that *commentarii* "pretend" (*dissimulat*) they will never be published, but later comes closer to the mark when he describes the genre

as one "intermediate between public and private" (xliv).

76. Adcock 1956, 9–13.

77. *Att.* 1.19.10, 1.20.6, 2.1.2; *Fam.* 5.12.10.

78. Suet. *De grammaticis et rhetoribus* 10.5; Sen. *Ep.* 39.1; Frontin. *Aq.* 109; Cic. *Tusc.* 3.54; Vitr. 4.pr.10.

79. Kelsey 1905, 220.

80. At a minimum: *BG* 2.35.4, 4.38.5, 7.90.8.

81. It is also suspicious that the text itself mentions the sending of these reports (see previous note).

82. Rüpke 1992, 217–218.

83. Fraenkel 1956, 192.

84. On this passage, see the fine remarks of Adcock (1956, 68).

85. Bömer 1953, 248–249.

86. Plin. *Ep.* 1.8.

87. See Bömer 1953, 246, for a clear example of a *commentarius* derived from other *commentarii*.

88. Cf. Knoche 1951, 143–144.

89. It is, for instance, one of the features picked up in Russell Baker's (1980) "translation" of Caesar's high school essay, "How I Spent My Summer Vacation."

90. Wiseman and Wiseman 1980.

91. See *BG* 2.1.1 (bis), 2.22.1, 2.24.1, 2.28.1, 2.29.1, 3.5.2, 3.15.1, 3.26.2, 4.4.1, 4.16.2, 4.17.1, 4.27.2, 5.2.2, 5.3.2, 5.6.1, 5.19.1, 5.22.1, 5.49.2, 5.56.3, 6.2.1, 6.8.9, 6.29.1, 6.34.1, 6.35.3, 6.35.6, 6.40.4, 7.17.1, 7.23.2, 7.37.1, 7.48.1, 7.58.4, 7.70.1, 7.76.1, 7.79.2, 7.83.8, 7.85.4.

92. On these passages, see also Reijgwart 1993, 27–28.

93. Kühner and Stegmann 1966, 1.87–88; more recent literature cited by Lilja 1971.

94. Reijgwart 1993, 31–33. She claims further that Caesar used the

third person lest the first person confuse the referent of idiomatic *nostri*. But the convention seems too well established to be threatened.

95. Five quasi-exceptions: 5.52.4, 6.35.7 (pejorative, but not necessarily with the specific force of *barbarus*), 3.16.4, 4.25.1, 4.25.2 (neutral, but resonant with the specific force of *barbarus*).

96. Or at least he uses it as if that were what it meant.

97. James 2000, 63–64.

98. Even at 3.10, which might at first glance appear to give the narrator's point of view, verbs like *incitabant* and *intellegeret* show we are dealing with Caesar's mental state.

99. The extant comparanda for *commentarii* in general are not really usable here.

100. Kraus (1994, 139) notes that even for historical narrators, such objectivity is the exception rather than the rule.

101. Habinek 1998, 45–59.

102. Rüpke 1992, n. 33.

103. Contrast the third person in the Scipionic epitaphs (Van Sickle 1987).

104. This is the same phenomenon as the change in *privatus*.

105. Plin. *Ep.* 10.66.1; cf. 10.95.1, 10.105.1.

106. For space, I largely follow the discussion of Görler 1976. So far as I can tell, the narrator does not have a grammatical gender; I use the masculine form here out of convenience. Lieberg (1998, 24–31) points out some small irregularities in Görler's readings, but they do not amount to much. Reijgwart (1993) nuances his theory somewhat by distinguishing perspective into (physical) point of view and (cognitive) focalization, but that is not salient here.

107. Görler 1976, 110.

108. Ibid., 112–114.

109. See *BG* 1.7.4, 1.12.5, 1.13.2, 1.33.4, 1.40.5, 2.4.2, 2.29.4, 3.20.1, 7.77.12.

110. So, e.g., it was "in time past" (*fuit antea tempus*, 6.24.1) that the Gauls were stronger than the Germans.

111. See 1.16.1, 2.1.1.

112. *BG* 1.22.1; also 2.17.2, 2.32.4, 2.33.2, 5.8.6; cf. Görler 1976.

113. Marshall 1985, 4–5. More precisely, Asconius never refers ahead in his own text. In four places, he cites a passage later in the particular Cicero text under discussion: 5.1–2, 27.17, 80.5–6, 84.5C.

Chapter 6

1. If one punctuates with a colon after *imperium* (thus making the succeeding phrase spell out the content of the "habit of peace"), my point is made even more strongly.

2. Collins 1972, 923 and passim. Similar claims are made by Brunt 1978, 182–183; Lieberg 1988, 73–74; Hall 1998, 27; and Ramage 2001, 170 n. 99, though Ramage also sees Caesar writing a *bellum iustum*. For a general assessment of this theory, see Appendix A.

3. There is no need to shy away from the word. Following Harris 1992, 4, I define "imperialism" simply as "the behavior by which a state or people takes and retains supreme power over other states or peoples or lands." Ongoing debates in the secondary literature about aggression and intention are interesting, but not definitional. The literature on the topic is enormous and includes Smethurst 1953; Badian 1968; Veyne 1975; Brunt 1978; Harris 1992; Gruen 1984; Ferrary 1988; and Rose 1995.

Most of this work, however, is concerned primarily with the second and/or third centuries B.C.

4. On folk theories, see also Chap. 7, note 35.

5. The earliest direct attestation of the phrase *bellum iustum* in the sense of "correctly waged war" is quite late. In 70 B.C., Cicero criticized Verres' lieutenant Caecilius for offering to prosecute his former superior; he described the attempt as an "unjust and impious war" *iniustum impiumque bellum* (*Div. Caec.* 62). This use of the phrase is both negative and metaphorical, suggesting that the basic notion was already well known and morally significant. Cf. Cic. *II Verr.* 5.188 for a similar usage of *impium* alone. The frequent, formulaic juxtaposition of *pium* and *iustum* to describe wars suggests that Cicero's connection of the just war to fetial procedure (or at least to religious considerations more generally) was not fanciful.

6. *De republica* appears to have been written between 54 (Cic. *Q. Fr.* 2.3.1, 2.12.1, 3.5.1) and 51 (Cic. *Att.* 5.12.2, *Fam.* 8.1.4).

7. It is often thought that the manuscripts of this work contain a number of later interpolations, though it is less clear precisely which passages are interpolated, and the section in which we are interested may well be one that is affected. Fortunately, the suspected passage in this case is largely redundant with parts that are not problematic. In any case, none of the arguments that follow will depend on disputed reconstructions of the text. On alleged interpolation, see Dyck 1996, 53–54.

8. Thus also, for instance, the objections of Gruen (1984, 276–277) at *Off.* 2.26. There, even this conflict may be

nonexistent, since the crucial phrase describing wars as *de imperio* seems just to mean "for the sake of the empire" (close to *pro salute*), not "for expansion."

9. Cf. *Off.* 1.80: "Let war be undertaken in such a way that it appears that nothing other than peace is sought." Relevant to both passages is the observation that "peace" (*pax*) is for the Romans the state that ensues when you have won a war.

10. Ziegler 1985, 51–54, 67–70.

11. Harris 1992, 167–170, esp. 168 n. 1; Kaser 1993, 30.

12. Dyck 1996, 135, 146–148.

13. Finger 1942, 9–10; Ferrary (1988, 412) reads the latter passage as a Ciceronian interpolation on these grounds.

14. See *SVF* 3.510, 516; Cic. *Fin.* 3.58–59; Long 1974, 203–204.

15. E.g., *Off.* 1.138–140, 2.55–60, with Dyck 1996, 315, 439–440.

16. Several recent discussions of just war theory have been conducted in the larger context of debates on whether Roman imperialism was "defensive": Gruen 1970, 1984; Harris 1982b; Linderski 1982; Rose 1995, among much else. The connections are clear, but they have perhaps distorted views of the former question. Historians of Roman imperialism have tried to find motivations for Rome's conquest of its empire, both in specific cases and in general. These are perfectly legitimate historical questions, but, if I am right that Cicero's just war is circumstantial rather than motivational, then it should not be forced into the just war question. That is, Roman thinking is not interested in the "why" of imperial expansion, even in theory. The resulting (seeming) gap between Roman theory and practice has thus been taken to indicate that the "just war" was either

simply irrelevant or a purely formal construct.

17. An honorable exception is Albert (1980, 17–18, 25), who gathered evidence that the substantive views put forth by Cicero were also fairly traditional.

18. E.g., Brunt 1978, 159. In somewhat weaker terms, Harris 1992, 35–36, 169–270, 174.

19. Gruen 1984, 275–278.

20. Bourdieu 1990, 25–41.

21. Syme 1939, 157; Taylor 1949, 7; Brunt 1988, 351–381.

22. Similarly, Mattern (1999, 214–215) has made the case that Romans of the empire could genuinely have viewed their wars as "just."

23. Cohen 1991, 18–24.

24. Riggsby 1997, 49.

25. On the full history of this development, see Bacot 1989.

26. Stoic thought provides a partial exception, but even that left plenty of room for inequality.

27. See Lintott 1968, and particularly Usener's 1901 account of "Italic Folk-justice," a tradition very much centered on self-help.

28. Kaser 1993, 32.

29. Schrenk 1994.

30. This example and the next are from Hausmaninger 1961, 342 n. 39. I presume the debate is historical even if most of the argument is Livian. This passage is at the very least evidence for the period in which Livy wrote (a few decades later than Caesar).

31. This claim is put in the mouths of his avowed enemies and may well not be true. For the present argument it is significant even that the claim (whether true or not) would have been used as invective at all.

32. The tendency will have been aggravated if, as Harris (1992, 255) suggests, senatorial deliberations about war were conducted in relative secrecy.

33. It has been pointed out (rightly) that this criticism is usually restricted to unsuccessful generals; we shall return to this point below.

34. Gell. *NA* 5.18.9; he puts this in contrast to annalistic writing.

35. Polyb. 36.2; Diod. Sic. 32.5.

36. Harris 1992, 269.

37. See ibid., 118–123, 265–266. Cf. Badian 1968, 4.

38. The point of Valerius Maximus' story is that the wording was changed to "that the gods may preserve them unharmed forever" in 141 by the censor Scipio Aemilianus. There is considerable dispute over the date of the change, but no good reason to doubt that the earlier was, at some point, the norm.

39. *Ludi: CIL* 6.32323, 32329. Oath: Diod. Sic. 37.11. Cf. Gruen 1984, 277, on Cicero.

40. Note the epitaphs of the Scipios, *CIL* I².7, 9, 12, and the taking of nicknames (*agnomina*) from conquered peoples: Africanus, Asiaticus, Hispanus, etc. Cf. Harris 1992, 125, on Cic. *Rep.* 3.24; and Badian 1968, 12–13.

41. Collins (1972, 938) has already noted this.

42. Cf. Gruen 1984, 1:283.

43. Rich 1993, 44–48.

44. Voting: Taylor 1966, 84–106. Office: Nicolet 1976, 20–30.

45. Note also the importance of sumptuary laws during the Republic: Baltrusch 1989, 40–131.

46. Gruen 1982, 68, cites related passages.

47. Riggsby 1998.

48. Cic. *Sest.* 19–20; Tac. *Ann.* 6.51.3.

49. Roller 2001, 108–124.

50. Caesar's justifications in Book 1 already assume total conquest. Even the opening phrase, *Gallia ... omnis* (1.1.1), starts to set the stage.

51. Albert (1980, 22) notes that Cicero's treatment of war under the rubric of *iustitia* implicitly claims the rules (or at least the general principles) should be the same for states and individuals.

52. Brunt (1988, 175) draws a similar connection.

53. Wenger 1935; Cic. *Leg.* 1.19, *Fin.* 5.65, *Tusc.* 5.63, *Nat. D.* 3.38, *Rep.* 3.24.

54. Wenger 1935.

55. Cic. *Rep.* 1.43.1; Plin. *Ep.* 2.12.5.

56. Hausmaninger 1961, 341–342; Cic. *Off.* 1.36; Varro, in Nonius 850L.

57. Livy 1.32; the fetials repeatedly call on Jupiter to hear their assertions; in general, see Watson 1993.

58. Rosenstein 1990.

59. Rosenstein 1986; Cic. *Pis.* 85, *Fin.* 3.75.

60. See Feldherr 1998, 54–56, 98–99.

61. For the background of the controversy, see Calboli 1978. I follow the numeration of the fragments in this edition.

62. Astin 1978, 125–130.

63. More precisely, Cato appears to have used a variety of arguments, both pragmatic and ethical, without perfect consistency (Gell. *NA* 6.3.52). This "kitchen-sink" approach to gathering arguments, common in Roman rhetoric, may make us more comfortable about interpreting the surviving fragments individually.

64. The former hypothetical law is not completely implausible. It parallels real laws that had from time to time limited holdings of public land; both use

500 *iugera* (a little more than 300 acres) as their limit.

65. Hutchinson 1998, 86–100; Cic. *Fam.* 2.10, 15.4; *Att.* 5.20.

66. *Infestus* connotes not merely ill will, but overtly threatening behavior; see *OLD*, s.v. The Cilicians' hostility is also implied by his use of the verb *pacare*, "pacify," twice (*Fam.* 15.4.8, 10).

67. Syme 1979, 120–126.

68. Cicero was compelled by domestic political circumstances to take this position: Gelzer 1968, 124–125.

69. Note that Cicero here not only assumes the undivided ethnicity of all Gauls, but also includes the potentially Germanic Cimbri and Teutoni among them. The same occurs at Sall. *Iug.* 114.1.

70. On Roman fear of the Gauls, see in general Bellen 1985, 9–19, 36–46; and with specific reference to Caesar, Gardner 1983.

71. Calendar: Livy 6.1.11 (and cf. Plut. *Luc.* 27.7 for a later example). Salluvii: Livy *Per.* 73.

72. Ilari (1985, 175) translates "not lacking a certain basis in justice," which seems to me to miss the emphasis; the war is almost, but not in fact, just. Cf. also Steel 2001, 48.

73. Brunt (1990, 309–314) and Albert (1980, 26–69) also consider the justificatory aspects of *BG*.

74. Ramage (2001, 149–165) discusses the first two of these passages in the light of the notion of *bellum iustum*. I have little quarrel with his account as far as it goes, but it is based on a fairly shallow version of the ideal.

75. The following account is essentially Caesar's. Although I am generally inclined to accept its truth, that is not necessary for the arguments that follow.

76. Collins 1972, 927.

77. Even if we were to adopt modern criteria here, we should note that he does not cross into Aeduan territory so as to attack the Aedui. Battle is not joined until after he has received requests for aid. Caesar may, however, open himself to the charge of violating his own *lex Iulia de repetundis* by leaving his province without permission. See Bauman 1967, 105–117.

78. *BG* 1.33.4, 1.40.5, 2.4.2, 2.29.4, 7.77.12.

79. History is also invoked in a different way in the defense of the war against the Germans. The Aedui, Caesar notes, had "often been declared brothers and kinsmen by the Senate" (1.33.2). This, of course, reinforces the claim that the Romans' war was in defense of their allies. Cf. 1.35.4: "In the consulship of Marcus Messalla and Marcus Piso the Senate had decreed that whoever should hold the province of Gaul, should defend the Aedui and the other friends of the Roman people, insofar as this was in the public interest."

80. They were going to solicit grain supplies. Again, the truth of Caesar's account is not particularly important here.

81. Caesar asserts the principle directly at 3.9.3; specific cases at 1.47.6, 4.12.1, 4.13.1, 4.27.2–3. Cf. also 5.37.2 and the attempt on Comius' life at a colloquium (8.21). It should be kept in mind that *ius gentium* means, at this period, common law that happens to have arisen serially in different cultures, not agreed-on "international law."

82. Collins (1972, 934–935) lists the examples. See also below.

83. On *iniuria*, see Gai. *Inst.* 3.220–225.

84. Twelve Tables 8.2 and 8.3 deal with major injuries. Tab. 8.4, which explicitly mentions *iniuria*, is probably the default measure, but we cannot tell on that basis how broad a category it covers.

85. Paulus (*Collatio* 2.5.1) explicitly points out the etymology.

86. Roller 2001, 228–248.

87. It is true, however, that Roman authors are willing to put well-worded anti-Roman sentiments in their enemies' mouths. Cf. above, Chap. 4, note 18.

88. More specifically, the idea is attributed to the character Caesar, but the verb *intellegere* shows that the anonymous narrator (associated by most readers with the historical author Caesar) accepts the truth of the claim he reports. Hence, it is doubly validated.

89. *Dicio* is the *vox propria* for Roman state authority over other, subject states (*TLL*, s.v. 960.33–67) and common for a magistrate's portfolio (961.7–24). It is also used of individual authority (961.24–36; though Cic. *Quinct.* 6 is quasi-magisterial), but it is rarely applied to slavery.

90. Riggsby 1999a, 21–49, esp. 24–26.

91. Q. Cicero (*Comment. Pet.* 16) points out that the definition of *amicus* is stretched for purposes of campaigning; this illustrates *per oppositionem* the normally social nature of the tie. In practice, Rome did of course acquire "friends" quickly and as needed to support various ventures.

92. In the narrative frame, Caesar is cut off when German troops move in toward the conference to attack Caesar. However, Caesar (the author) could have written himself a speech of any length at this point, and the narrator does not

claim that Caesar (the character) would
have spoken further had he been given
the chance.

93. Livy (1.38.2) strongly suggests
that you cannot perform *deditio* unless
in your own power.

94. Collins 1972, 933–935. I omit
three cases where the only objection is
lack of a *casus belli* (Morini and
Menapii, Germany, Britain) and the
individual case of Acco discussed above.

95. He could also argue that he did his
captives no harm, and in fact offered to
free them immediately after the battle.
As Collins (1972, 934) points out, we
know that there were contemporary
objections to Caesar's actions here. This
suggests that Caesar had great confi-
dence in the "they did it first" argument. *Pace* Collins, *BG* 4.11.5 does not
"admit" that Caesar had already planned
treachery before the Germans did,
though it is certainly compatible with
that hypothesis.

Chapter 7

1. Lendon 1999, 281.
2. Ramage 2003.
3. Batstone 1990, 351.
4. As in *BG* 1.46.3, 5.21.4, 7.10.2.
5. Another device with similar effect
in this respect, if not the first, is the
"surprise flashback," in which we are
told of a Caesarian contingency plan
only when it goes into effect, not when
the original orders were ostensibly
given: 2.33, 3.14.5, 7.13.1.

6. Again, I would not deny that
the hypotactic constructions Batstone
studies do this more vigorously; I simply
suggest that most explicit contrasts
give a similar sense of process to some
degree. Another device with the same

effect appears in passages in which
Caesar is given a private motive for an
action he would have taken anyway on
grounds of public policy: 1.112.7, 4.17.1.

7. Moore 1999, 33–36.
8. Bal 1985, 109–110.
9. The latter could reduce a general's
chances of a triumph: Livy 38.44.6, cf.
40.38.9.

10. On *continentia* in general, see
Edwards 1993, 78, 195–198. On its
political content, see Cramer 2000.

11. This could almost certainly be
said of the pragmatic sacrifices the Gauls
make for the sake of liberty (7.15.2,
7.29.5); in this respect, they act much as
Caesar has throughout the work.

12. *CIL* I², pp. 43–50.

13. When I say "self"-representation,
I refer both to products of the politician
and to works directly commissioned by
him.

14. Gruen 1984, 275.

15. For texts, see Appendix B; I use
the numeration there to refer to specific
examples throughout my discussion.
Inscriptions celebrating triumphs are
mentioned by Caesius Bassus (*De
metris* 8) and Atilius Fortunatianus (*Ars
27*) (though they doubtless share an
ultimate source); these were, they say,
characteristically written in Saturnian
verse and placed on the Capitol, though
at least one seems to have existed in
multiple copies (Livy 40.52.7). It is not
clear whether these are merely a special
type of "dedicatory" inscription, but the
issue is not relevant to what follows.

16. *CIL* I².609 (*Martei M. Claudius
M. f. consol dedit*) likely marks a dedica-
tion of spoils (cf. the similar wording of
my nos. 4, 5, 8) without using any such
word, but without the *cepit* of the latter
inscription, it is not clearly military.

More generally, there are probably a number of other such dedications, but if the dedicator has chosen not to represent his military experience in them, they are not relevant here. The contested distinction between *praeda* and *manubiae* is not salient either.

17. Cf. Cic. *Att.* 5.20.3; *Fam.* 2.10.3, 15.4.9, 10.

18. There are also a number of ablatives absolute, without expressed agents, but given the finite verbs in the context, it is hard to reconstruct an agent for them besides the general.

19. I omit here more allusive references, as to "captives."

20. Even though some such morphological "plurals" are individually more semantically ambiguous than this instance, they all alternate with unambiguous singular forms.

21. E.g., *CIL* I².24, 719, 737, 1511, 1523–1524, 1527, 1529, 1627–1628, 1694, 1759, among many other examples. This formulation was hardly required, but was quite common.

22. Pelikan 1997. Cf. no. 15, which addresses another such requirement— that the army has come back home (*exercitum saluom atque incolumem … domum reportauit*).

23. The surviving text shows deliberate, and often mistaken, archaisms, making its date uncertain. I assume here that our text follows a Republican original at least in outline, if not in phrasal detail.

24. The inscription is somewhat fragmentary, and some of the numerical values would be larger if we had the whole text. The "silver" total also seems to include the value of other items sold off.

25. Livy 27.16.7, 33.27.3, 34.52.5, 38.59.3–5, 39.5.14–16; Cic. *Att.* 5.20.5.

26. For a fine overview of the subject, see Holliday 1997.

27. For a similar division, cf. La Rocca 1984, 35. In fact, the only examples that confuse the distinction are from Appian, and may reflect a minor topos of his narrative style. He notes three triumphs in which were carried images of specific events of the campaigns involved (Scipio Africanus, *Pun.* 66; Pompey, *Mith.* 117; Caesar, *B Civ.* 2.101). In the second, he may have turned images of the defeated into scenes of their defeat. In the third, he has perhaps turned spoils into images of the winning of those spoils; in fact, his claim that there were images of Caesar's Roman enemies in the procession contradicts earlier accounts that assert that Caesar tried to suppress that aspect of his wars.

28. Livy 26.21, 37.59.3–5, 38.43.9.

29. Holliday 1997, 141–144.

30. Ibid., 138–139.

31. Ibid., 135–136; La Rocca 1984.

32. Holliday 1997, 146–147.

33. The two possibilities are not exclusive. Campbell (1987) and Goldsworthy (1998, 195) discuss the likely role of literary texts in shaping Roman military practice.

34. Campbell 1987, 20–21. Marius' speech at Sall. *Iug.* 85.12 objects to the practice, but thereby attests to it.

35. Campbell 1987, 15. See Ireland 1980, xxviii, on the disputed authenticity of the fourth book. The issue is not salient here.

36. The "folk" of "folk rules" or "folk theory" does not, of course, have the same force as it does in, say, "folk tale." Rather, folk theories are implicit, often metaphorical, understandings shared by any kind of group (a nation, a neighborhood, a professional group, etc.) of

how some system works. A folk theory in this sense could derive from a more explicit expert theory, as, for instance, popular notions of the unconscious mind, ultimately deriving from (though not necessarily consistent with) a much more elaborately articulated Freudian theory.

37. Lendon 1999, 295, 304.

38. Cf. Campbell 1987, 24.

39. Goldsworthy 1998, 195–204.

40. Ibid., 204–212; cf. Campbell 1987, 14.

41. Rosenstein 1990, 116–140. Cicero's narratives are brief enough that it is hard to tell exactly where he is, but the fact that he attributes all action to himself anyway certainly gives the impression of involvement.

42. See note 44 below for exceptions.

43. Cf. Oakley 1985 for single combat in the ranks.

44. Leigh (1995) collects the evidence. He tries to tie the political use of scars to a *popularis* position. As a symbol of real rather than inherited virtue, scars certainly lent themselves to this use (pp. 200–205, 209–212), but, as Leigh himself demonstrates, other aristocrats were certainly happy to display scars when they had them (205–206). Roller (2004, 12–16) points out the possibility of quite complex interactions with other value systems. Such display occurred further down in the ranks as well.

45. Rosenstein 1990, 172–173.

46. Ibid., 54–91. In a number of cases, not only was the error inadvertent, but the "rule" in question was unknown prior to the military failure.

47. Ibid., 102, 106–107.

48. Ibid., 98–99, 101, 108. Cicero worries about his own troops, but apparently does not feel compelled to take

steps to improve them: *Att.* 5.20.1; *Fam.* 2.10.2, 15.4.2.

49. Steel 2001, 131–139.

50. Collins 1972, 938–939.

51. Powell 1998, 133 n. 17; Jervis 2001, 141.

52. Cf. Chap. 5 for other examples of this mutual reinforcement of generic form and thematically important content.

53. For this whole paragraph, see Goldsworthy 1998.

54. This seems to have been a long-term interest for his image management (Suet. *Iul.* 71).

55. But see Chap. 5 above for a few exceptions.

56. E.g., his early run for *pontifex maximus,* his aggressive legislative program as consul, and suspicion that he might have been involved in the Catilinarian conspiracy.

57. Cf. Wiseman 1985.

58. Lieberg 1998.

59. Jervis (2001, 75–76, 90) shows that the narrative Gaul does not fit the moral topography of the ethnography. I take this to be another instance of the unified/partitioned distinction. The moral topography assumes a single Gaul. The (more random) distribution of strength in the narrative breaks down that unity.

60. E.g., Collins 1972; Wallace-Hadrill 1986, 67.

61. E.g., Galinsky 1996, 40.

62. Abercrombie et al. (1980) demonstrate certain difficulties of the "dominant ideology thesis," but see the qualifications of Riggsby 1997, 51 n. 68.

63. For the history of the idea, see Eagleton 1991. Though the word is somewhat earlier, modern usages descend in practice from Marx's.

64. Althusser 1971, 162.

65. Ibid., 173. Another common element in definitions of ideology is reference to the beliefs of specific classes (especially the dominant ones). The relationship of ideology to class is an important issue, but an open one, and for that reason it ought not to be written into the definition.

66. Gunderson 1996, 118.

67. It has been objected to Althusserian definitions of ideology that they are defeatist (and thereby, for some, doing the job of ideology) because they do not tell us how to escape ideology's effects. This strikes me as akin to objecting to Newton's theory of gravity on the grounds that it offers no "out."

68. This definition bears some resemblance to what Galinsky (1996, 18–20), following James MacGregor Burns, calls "transforming leadership." The "transformation" of the latter, however, seems to be defined as necessarily positive or improving, which seems arbitrary.

69. Galinsky 1996, 40. He goes on to offer a distinction between "programmatic" images on coins (symbolizing specific projects or qualities dear to the designer) and images involved in the "identification of authority." The point (the abstraction of the message conveyed) is interesting in its own right, but it does not ground a useful distinction between propaganda and nonpropaganda.

70. Cheney 1995, 15.

71. Moreover, Polybius' rationalistic interpretive framework would have made it very hard for him to see a real concern for "justice," whether or not it existed.

72. See the Introduction above on the audience.

73. Ellul 1962, 88–89. Ellul claims, without support, that this is a twentieth-century phenomenon.

74. By "extremist" I refer only to position on the contemporary political spectrum. I am not qualified to judge correctness.

75. Batstone 1991.

76. Rose 1995, 368, quoting Fredric Jameson.

Appendix A

1. See note 2 of Chap. 6 above, plus Wells 1972, 20–21; Clavadetscher-Thürlemann 1985; Badian 1968, 11–12.

2. The examples at *Off.* 1.38 seem to pick out "barbarians" as a group, but the term is not used, nor does the context allow for going to war more freely.

3. Clavadetscher-Thürlemann 1985, 44–45. I refer here only to the barbarian/civilized distinction.

4. Ibid., 129–131.

5. Ibid., 131.

6. Hartog 1988.

7. Watson 1993.

8. Badian 1968, 1–15.

Bibliography

Abercrombie, N., S. Hill, and B. Turner. 1980. *The Dominant Ideology Thesis.* London.

Adcock, F. 1956. *Caesar as Man of Letters.* Cambridge.

Albert, S. 1980. *Bellum Iustum: Die Theorie des "gerechten Krieges" und ihre praktische Bedeutung für die auswärtigen Auseinadersetzungen Roms in republikanischer Zeit.* Frankfurter Althistorische Studien 10. Kallmünz.

Allen, G. 2000. *Intertextuality.* London.

Althusser, L. 1971. "Ideology and Ideological State Apparatuses (Notes towards an Investigation)." Trans. B. Brewster. In L. Althusser, *Lenin and Philosophy and Other Essays*, pp. 127–186. New York.

Alverson, H. 1994. *Semantics and Experience.* Baltimore.

Anderson, B. 1991. *Imagined Communities: Reflections on the Origin and Spread of Nationalism.* 2d ed. London.

Appadurai, A. 1986. "Commodities and the Politics of Value." In idem, ed., *The Social Life of Things: Commodities in Cultural Perspective.* Cambridge.

Aquila, R. 1981. *Rhyme or Reason: A Limerick History of Philosophy.* Washington, D.C.

Arnold, B., and D. Gibson, eds. 1995. *Celtic Chiefdom, Celtic State: The Evolution of Complex Social Systems in Prehistoric Europe.* Cambridge.

Astin, A. 1978. *Cato the Censor.* Oxford.

Audouze, F., and O. Büchsenschütz. 1992. *Towns, Villages, and Countryside of Celtic Europe.* Bloomington, Ind.

Aujac, G., and F. Lasserre, eds. 1969. *Strabon, Géographie.* Paris.

Bacot, G. 1989. *La doctrine de la guerre juste.* Paris.

Badian, E. 1968. *Roman Imperialism in the Late Republic.* Ithaca, N.Y.

Baker, R. 1980. "Caesar's Puerile Wars." In idem, *So This Is Depravity*, pp. 27–29. New York.

Bakhtin, M. 1986. "The Problem of Speech Genres." In idem, *Speech Genres and Other Late Essays*, trans. V. McGee, pp. 60–102. Austin.

Bal, M. 1985. *Narratology: Introduction to the Theory of Narrative.* Toronto.

Balsdon, J. 1955. Review of first edition of Rambaud 1966. *Journal of Roman Studies* 45:161–164.

———. 1979. *Romans and Aliens.* London.

Baltrusch, E. 1989. *Regimen morum.* Munich.

Barton, T. 1994. "The Inventio of Nero: Suetonius." In J. Elsner and J. Masters, eds., *Reflections of Nero*, pp. 48–63. London.

Barwick, K. 1938. *Caesars Commentarii und das Corpus Caesarianum. Philologus* suppl. 31.2. Leipzig.

———. 1955. "Kleine Studien zu Caesars *Bellum Gallicum.*" *Rheinisches Museum für Philologie* 98:41–72.

Batstone, W. 1990. "Etsi: A Tendentious Hypotaxis in Caesar's Plain Style." *American Journal of Philology* 111:348–60.

———. 1991. "A Narrative Gestalt and the Force of Caesar's Style." *Mnemosyne* 44:126–136.

Bauman, R. 1967. *The* Crimen Maiestatis *in the Roman Republic and Augustan Principate.* Johannesburg.

Beard, M., and M. Crawford. 1985. *Rome in the Late Republic: Problems and Interpretations.* London.

Beckmann, F. 1930. *Geographie und Ethnographie in Caesars* Bellum Gallicum. Dortmund.

Bellen, H. 1985, *Metus Gallicus—Metus Punicus: Zum Furchtmotiv in der römischen Republik.* Akademie der Wissenschaften und der Literatur [Mainz], Abhandlungen der Geistes- und Sozialwissenschaftlichen Klasse, 1985.3. Stuttgart.

Bertrand, A. 1997. "Stumbling through Gaul: Maps, Intelligence, and Caesar's *Bellum Gallicum.*" *Ancient History Bulletin* 11:107–122.

Bömer, F. 1953. "Der Commentarius: Zur Vorgeschichte und literarischen Form der Schriften Caesars." *Hermes* 81:210–250.

Bonner, S. 1977. *Education in Ancient Rome: From the Elder Cato to the Younger Pliny.* Berkeley.

Botermann, H. 1987. "Ciceros Gedanken zum 'gerechten Krieg' in de officiis 1.34–40." *Archiv für Kulturgeschichte* 69:1–29.

Bourdieu, P. 1977. *Outline of a Theory of Practice.* Stanford.

———. 1990. *The Logic of Practice.* Trans. R. Nice. Stanford.

———. 1993. *The Field of Cultural Production.* New York.

Brun, P. 1995. "From Chiefdom to State Organization in Celtic Europe." In Arnold and Gibson 1995, 13–25.

Brunt, P. 1978, "Laus Imperii." In P. Garnsey and C. Whittaker, eds., *Imperialism in the Ancient World*, pp. 159–191. Cambridge.

———. 1988. *The Fall of the Roman Republic and Related Essays.* Oxford.

———. 1990. *Roman Imperial Themes.* Oxford.

Büchner, K. 1962. *Studien zur römischen Literatur.* Vol. 3, *Horaz.* Wiesbaden.

Burns, V. 1994. "Romanization and Acculturation: The Rhineland Matronae." Diss., University of Wisconsin-Madison.

Calboli, G., ed. 1978. *Marci Porci Catonis oratio pro rhodiensibus: Cato, l'oriente greco e gli imprenditori romani.* Bologna.

Campbell, B. 1987. "Teach Yourself How to Be a General." *Journal of Roman Studies* 77:13–29.

———. 1996. "Shaping the Rural Environment: Surveyors in Ancient Rome." *Journal of Roman Studies* 86:74–99.

Canali, L. 1985. *Giulio Cesare.* Rome.

Carder, J. 1978. *Art Historical Problems of a Roman Land Surveying Manuscript, the Codex Arcerianus A, Wolfenbuttel.* New York.

Cheney, L. 1995. *Telling the Truth.* New York.

Chevallier, R., ed. 1974. *Littérature gréco-romaine et géographie historique: Mélanges offerts à Roger Dion.* Paris.

Cheyfitz, E. 1997. *The Poetics of Imperialism: Translation and Colonization from The Tempest to Tarzan.* Philadelphia.

Cipriani, G. 1986, *Cesare e la retorica dell'assedio.* Amsterdam.

Clavadetscher-Thürlemann, S. 1985. ΠΟΛΕΜΟΣ ΔΙΚΑΙΟΣ *und Bellum iustum: Versuch einer Ideengeschichte.* Zurich.

Cleary, V. 1985. "Caesar's *Commentarii:* Writings in Search of a Genre." *Classical Journal* 80:345–350.

Coarelli, F. 1997. *Roma.* 2d ed. Guide Archeologiche Laterza 6. Rome.

Cohen, A. 1985. *The Symbolic Construction of Community.* London.

Cohen, D. 1991. *Law, Sexuality and Society: The Enforcement of Morals in Classical Athens.* Cambridge.

Collins, J. 1959. "On the Date and Interpretation of the *Bellum Civile.*" *American Journal of Philology* 70:113–132.

———. 1972. "Caesar as Political Propagandist." *Aufstieg und Niedergang der römischen Welt* 1.1:922–966.

Conley, D. 1983. "Causes of Roman Victory Presented in the *Bellum Gallicum:* Caesar the Commander vs. Other Factors." *Helios* 10:173–186.

Conte, G. 1986. *The Rhetoric of Imitation.* Ithaca, N.Y.

Corbeill, A. 1996. *Controlling Laughter: Political Humor in the Late Roman Republic.* Princeton.

———. 2004. *Nature Embodied: Gesture in Ancient Rome.* Princeton.

Cormack, M. 1992. *Ideology.* Ann Arbor.

Cornell, T. 1991. "The Tyranny of the Evidence: A Discussion of the Possible Uses of Literacy in Etruria and Latium in the Archaic Age." In *Literacy in the Roman World, Journal of Roman Archaeology* suppl. 3, pp. 7–33. Ann Arbor.

Cotton, M. 1957. "Appendix: Muri Gallici." In Wheeler and Richardson 1957, 159–216.

Craig, C. 1979. "The Role of Rational Argumentation in Selected Judicial Speeches of Cicero." Diss., University of North Carolina.

———. 1993. *Form as Argument in Cicero's Speeches: A Study of Dilemma.* Atlanta.

Craig, J. 1931. "The General Reflection in Caesar's *Commentaries.*" *Classical Review* 45:107–110.

Cramer, D. 2000. "The Power of Gender and the Gender of Power." Diss., University of Texas at Austin.

Crosby, A. 1997. *The Measure of Reality: Quantification and Western Society.* Cambridge.

Curzon, G. 1908. *Frontiers.* Oxford.

Dahlmann, H. 1970. *Kleine Schriften.* Hildesheim.

Davidson, D. 1984. "On the Very Idea of a Conceptual Scheme." In idem, *Inquiries into Truth and Interpretation,* pp. 183–198. Oxford.

Davidson, J. 1991. "The Gaze in Polybius' Histories." *Journal of Roman Studies* 81:10–24.

de Certeau, M. 1984. *The Practice of Everyday Life.* Trans. S. Rendall. Berkeley.

Dietler, M. 1995. "Early 'Celtic' Socio-political Relations: Ideological Representation and Social Competition in Dynamic Comparative Perspective." In Arnold and Gibson 1995, 64–71.

Dilke, O. 1961. "Maps in the Treatises of Roman Land Surveyors." *Geographical Journal* 127:417–426.

———. 1967. "Illustrations of Roman Surveyors' Manuals." *Imago Mundi* 21:9–29.

———. 1971. *The Roman Land Surveyors: An Introduction to the* Agrimensores. Newton Abbot.

Dobesch, G. 1989. "Caesar also Ethnograph." *Weiner humanistische Blätter* 31:16–51.

Dunbabin, K. 1993. "Wine and Water at the Roman *Convivium.*" *Journal of Roman Archaeology* 6:116–141.

Dunham, S. 1995. "Caesar's Perception of Gallic Social Structures." In Arnold and Gibson 1995, 110–115.

Dupont, F. 1985. *L'acteur-roi.* Paris.

Dyck, A. 1996. *A Commentary on Cicero* De Officis. Ann Arbor.

Eagleton, T. 1991. *Ideology: An Introduction.* London.

Earl, D. 1967. *The Moral and Political Tradition of Rome.* Ithaca, N.Y.

Ebbeler, J. 2003. "Caesar's Letters and the Ideology of Literary History." *Helios* 30:3–19.

Edelstein, L., and I. Kidd. 1972–. *Posidonius.* Cambridge.

Edwards, C. 1993. *The Politics of Immorality in Ancient Rome.* Cambridge.

Eisenhut, W. 1973. *Virtus Romana: Ihre Stellung im römischen Wertsystem.* Munich.

Ellul, J. 1962. *Propagandes.* Paris.

Erickson, B. 2002. "Falling Masts, Rising Rivers: The Ethnography of Virtue in Caesar's Account of the Veneti." *American Journal of Philology* 123:601–622.

Fabia, P. 1889. *De orationibus quae sunt in commentariis Caesaris de Bello Gallico.*
   Paris.
Fantham, E. 1996. *Roman Literary Culture from Cicero to Apuleius.* Baltimore.
Faubion, J. 1995. *Rethinking the Subject.* Boulder, Colo.
Feldherr, A. 1998. *Spectacle and Society in Livy's* History. Princeton.
Ferrary, J.-L. 1988. *Philhellénisme et impérialisme.* Bibliothèque des Écoles
   françaises d'Athénes et de Rome 271. Rome.
Finger, P. 1942. "Das stoische und das akademische Führerbild in Ciceros Schrift
   de Officiis 1. Buch." *Neue Jahrbücher für Antike und deutsche Bildung*
   5:1–20.
Finley, M. 1985. *Ancient History.* New York.
Fornara, C. 1983. *The Nature of History in Ancient Greece and Rome.* Berkeley.
Foucault, M. 1977. *The Archaeology of Knowledge.* London.
Fowler, D. 1997. "On the Shoulders of Giants: Intertextuality and Classical Studies."
   Materiali e discussioni 39:13–34.
Fraenkel, E. 1956. "Eine Form römischer Kriegsbulletins." *Eranos* 54:189–194.
Fuchs, H. 1932. "Beckmann, Geographie und Ethnographie." *Gnomon* 8:243–258.

Gabba, E. 1982. "Il consenso popolare alla politica espansionistica romana fra III e II
   sec. A.C." In Harris 1982a, 115–129.
Galinsky, K. 1994. "How to Be Philosophical about the End of the *Aeneid.*" *Illinois
   Classical Studies* 19:191–201.
———. 1996. *Augustan Culture: An Interpretive Introduction.* Princeton.
Gardner, J. 1983. "The Gallic Menace in Caesar's Propaganda." *Greece and Rome*
   30:181–189.
Gärtner, H. 1975. *Beobachtungen zu Bauelementen in der antiken Historiographie
   besonders bei Livius und Caesar.* Wiesbaden.
Geertz, C. 1973. "Person, Time, and Conduct in Bali." In idem, *The Interpretation of
   Cultures,* pp. 360–411. New York.
Gelzer, M. 1968. *Caesar: Politician and Statesman.* Trans. P. Needham. Cambridge,
   Mass.
Gesche, H. 1976. *Caesar.* Erträge der Forschung 51. Darmstadt.
Giddens, A. 1984. *The Constitution of Society.* Berkeley.
———. 1987. *The Nation-State and Violence.* Berkeley.
Glacken, C. 1967. *Traces on the Rhodian Shore: Nature and Culture in Western
   Thought from Ancient Times to the End of the Eighteenth Century.*
   Berkeley.
Goldsworthy, A. 1996. *The Roman Army at War, 100 B.C.–A.D. 200.* Oxford.
———. 1998. "'Instinctive Genius': The Depiction of Caesar the General." In Welch
   and Powell 1998, 193–219.
Görler, W. 1976. "Die Veränderung des Erzählerstandpunktes in Caesars *Bellum
   Gallicum.*" *Poetica* 8:95–119.

Gould, S. 1985. "Bound by the Great Chain." In idem, *The Flamingo's Smile,*
pp. 281–290. New York.

Greenblatt, S. 1989. "Towards a Poetics of Culture." In Veeser 1989, 1–14.

———. 1990. *Learning to Curse.* New York.

Gruen, E., ed. 1970. *Imperialism in the Roman Republic.* New York.

———. 1982. "Material Rewards and the Drive for Empire." In Harris 1982a,
59–82.

———. 1984. *The Hellenistic World and the Coming of Rome.* 2 vols. Berkeley.

———. 1990. *Studies in Greek Culture and Roman Policy.* Leiden.

———. 1995. "The 'Fall' of the Scipios." In I. Malkin and Z. Rubinsohn, eds., *Leaders and Masses in the Roman World,* pp. 59–90. Leiden.

Guillaumin, J.-Y. 1987. "Les flumina chez César." *Latomus* 46:755–761.

Gunderson, E. 1996. "The Ideology of the Arena." *Classical Antiquity* 15:113–151.

Habinek, T. 1998. *The Politics of Latin Literature.* Princeton.

Hachmann, R., G. Kossack, and H. Kuhn. 1962. *Völker zwischen Germanen und Kelten.* Neumünster.

Hall, L. 1998. "*Ratio* and *Romanitas* in the *Bellum Gallicum.*" In Welch and Powell 1998, 11–43.

———. 2000. Review of Lieberg 1998. *Classical Review* 50:78–81.

Hallet, J. 1989. "Women as 'Same' and 'Other' in the Classical Roman Elite." *Helios* 16:59–78.

Harley, J., and D. Woodward, eds. 1987. *The History of Cartography.* Vol. 1, *Cartography in Prehistoric, Ancient, and Medieval Europe and the Mediterranean.* Chicago.

Harley, J., D. Woodward, and G. Aujac. 1987a. "The Foundations of Theoretical Cartography in Archaic and Classical Greece." In Harley and Woodward 1987, 130–147.

———. 1987b. "Greek Cartography in the Early Roman World." In Harley and Woodward 1987, 161–176.

Harris, W. 1982a. *The Imperialism of Mid-Republican Rome.* Papers and Monographs of the American Academy in Rome 29. Rome.

———. 1982b. "Current Directions in the Study of Roman Imperialism." In Harris 1982a, 13–34.

———. 1989. *Ancient Literacy.* Cambridge.

———. 1992. *War and Imperialism in Republican Rome, 327–70 B.C.* Rev. ed. Oxford.

Hartog, F. 1988. *The Mirror of Herodotus: The Representation of the Other in the Writing of History.* Trans. J. Lloyd. Berkeley.

Haselberger, L. 1997. "Architectural Likenesses: Models and Plans of Architecture in Classical Antiquity." *Journal of Roman Archaeology* 10:77–94.

Haselgrove, C. 1995. "Late Iron Age Society in Britain and North-east Europe: Structural Transformation or Superficial Change." In Arnold and Gibson 1995, 81–87.

Hausmaninger, H. 1961. "Bellum iustum und iusta causa belli im älteren römischen Recht." *Österreichische Zeitschrift für Öffentliches Recht* 11:335–345.

Hawkes, C. 1977. *Pytheas: Europe and the Greek Explorers*. Oxford.

Hellegouarc'h, J. 1972. *Le vocabulaire latin des relations et des partis politiques sous la republique*. 2d ed. Paris.

Henderson, J. 1996. "XPDNC/Writing Caesar." *Classical Antiquity* 15:261–288.

Hering, W. 1956. "Die Interpolation im Prooemium des B.G." *Philologus* 100:67–99.

Hinds, S. 1998. *Allusion and Intertext*. Cambridge.

Holliday, P. 1997. "Roman Triumphal Painting: Its Function, Development, and Reception." *Art Bulletin* 79:130–147.

Holmes, T. 1911. *Caesar's Conquest of Gaul*. Oxford.

Holtz, L. 1913. "C. Iulius Caesar quo usus sit in orationibus dicendi genere." Diss., University of Jena.

Honoré, A. 1962. *Gaius*. Oxford.

Horsfall, N. 1981. "Some Problems of Titulature in Roman Literary History." *Bulletin of the Institute of Classical Studies* 28:103–114.

———. 1996. "The Cultural Horizons of the Plebs Romana." *Memoirs of the American Academy in Rome* 41:101–119.

Hough, J. 1941. "Caesar's Camp on the Aisne." *Classical Journal* 36:337–345.

Hutchinson, G. 1998. *Cicero's Correspondence: A Literary Study*. Oxford.

Ilari, V. 1985. " 'Ius belli'—'τοῦ πολέμου νόμος': Étude semantique de la terminologie du droit de la guerre." *Bulletino del Istituto di diritto romano* 88:159–179.

Imber, M. 1997. "Tyrants and Mothers: Roman Education and Ideology." Diss., Stanford University.

Ireland, R., ed. 1980. *Iulius Frontinus: Strategemata*. Leipzig.

James, B. 1997. "Persuasive Narrative: Focalization in Caesar's Account of the Siege of Massilia." Unpublished ms.

———. 2000. "Speech, Authority, and Experience in Caesar, *Bellum Gallicum* 1.39–41." *Hermes* 128:54–64.

Janni, P. 1984. *La mappa e il periplo: cartografia antica e spazio odologico*. Università di Macerata, Pubblicazioni della facoltà di lettere e filosofia 19. Rome.

Jantz, M. 1995. *Das Fremdenbild in der Literatur der Römischen Republik und der Augusteischen Zeit: Vorstellungen und Sichtweisen am Beispiel von Hispanien und Gallien*. Europäische Hochschulschriften, Riehe 3, Band 656. Frankfurt.

Jardine, L. 1996. *Reading Shakespeare Historically*. London.

Jenkins, K. 1991. *Re-thinking History*. London.

Jervis, A. 2001. "*Gallia Scripta:* Images of Gauls and Romans in Caesar's *Bellum Gallicum*." Diss., University of Pennsylvania.

Kaser, M. 1993. *Ius Gentium.* Forschungen zum römischen Recht 40. Cologne.

Kaster, R., ed. and comm. 1995. *Suetonius: De grammaticis et rhetoribus.* Oxford.

———. 2002. "The Taxonomy of Patience, or, When Is *Patientia* Not a Virtue?" *Classical Philology* 97:133–144.

Keita, S. 1993. "Black Athena: 'Race,' Bernal, and Snowden." *Arethusa* 26:295–314.

Kelsey, F. 1905. "The Title of Caesar's Work on the Gallic and Civil Wars." *Transactions of the American Philological Association* 36:211–238.

Kennedy, D. 1992. "'Augustan' and 'Anti-Augustan': Reflections on Terms of Reference." In A. Powell, ed., *Roman Poetry and Propaganda in the Age of Augustus,* pp. 26–58. London.

Kennedy, G. 1968. "The Rhetoric of Advocacy in Greece and Rome." *American Journal of Philology* 89:419–436.

Klotz, A. 1910. *Caesarstudien.* Leipzig.

———. 1911. "Zu Caesars *Bellum Civile.*" *Rheinisches Museum für Philologie* 60:80–93.

———. 1934. "Geographie und Ethnographie in Caesars *Bellum Gallicum.*" *Rheinisches Museum für Philologie* 83:66–96.

———. 1941. "Zu Caesar." *Mnemosyne* 9:218–224.

Knapp, S., and W. Michaels. 1985. "Against Theory." In W. Mitchell, ed., *Against Theory,* pp. 11–30. Chicago.

Knoche, U. 1951. "Caesars Commentarii, ihr Gegenstand und ihre Absicht." *Gymnasium* 58:139–160.

Konrad, C. 1993. *Plutarch's Sertorius: A Historical Commentary.* Chapel Hill.

Koster, S. 1978. "Certamen centurionum (Caes. *Gall.* 5, 44)." *Gymnasium* 85: 160–178.

Kraner, F., W. Dittenberger, and H. Meusel, eds. and comms. 1960. *C. Iulii Caesaris Commentarii de Bello Gallico.* 18th ed. Berlin.

Kraus, C., ed. 1994. *Livy, Ab Urbe Condita: Book VI.* Cambridge.

Kuhner, R., and C. Stegmann. 1966. *Ausfuhrliche Grammatik der lateinischen Sprache.* 2 vols. 2d ed. Hannover.

Kurke, L. 1991. *The Traffic in Praise.* Ithaca, N.Y.

Laird, A. 1999. *Powers of Expression, Expressions of Power.* Oxford.

Lakoff, G. 1987. *Women, Fire, and Dangerous Things.* Chicago.

La Rocca, E. 1984. "Fabio o Fannio: L'affresco medio-repubblicano dell'Esquilino come riflesso dell'arte 'rappresentativa' e come espressione de mobilità sociale." *Dialoghi de archeologia* 3:31–53.

Leach, E. 1988. *The Rhetoric of Space: Literary and Artistic Representations of Landscape in Republican and Augustan Rome.* Princeton.

Leigh, M. 1995. "Wounding and Popular Rhetoric at Rome." *Bulletin of the Institute of Classical Studies* 40:195–224.

Lendon, J. 1999. "The Rhetoric of Combat: Greek Military Theory and Roman Culture in Julius Caesar's Battle Descriptions." *Classical Antiquity* 18:273–329.

Levine, L. 1996. *The Opening of the American Mind.* Boston.
Lewis, M., and K. Wigen. 1997. *The Myth of Continents: A Critique of Metageography.* Berkeley.
Lewis, M. J. 2001. *Surveying Instruments of Greece and Rome.* Cambridge.
Lieberg, G. 1998. *Caesars Politik in Gallien: Interpretationen zum Bellum Gallicum.* Bochum.
Lilja, S. 1971. "The Singular Use of *Nos* in Pliny's Letters." *Eranos* 69:89–103.
Linderski, J. 1982. "*Si vis pacem, para bellum:* Concepts of Defensive Imperialism." In Harris 1982a, 133–164.
Lintott, A. 1968. *Violence in Republican Rome.* Oxford.
Long, A. 1974. *Hellenistic Philosophy: Stoics, Epicureans, Sceptics.* London.

McDougall, I. 1991. "Dio and His Sources for Caesar's Campaigns in Gaul." *Latomus* 50:616–638.
Mader, G. 2000. *Josephus and the Politics of Historiography.* Leiden.
Mannetter, D. 1995. "Narratology in Caesar." Diss., University of Wisconsin-Madison.
Marincola, J. 1997. *Authority and Tradition in Ancient Historiography.* Cambridge.
Marshall, B. 1985. *An Historical Commentary on Asconius.* Columbia.
Martin, R. 1989. *The Language of Heroes.* Ithaca, N.Y.
Mattern, S. 1999. *Rome and the Enemy.* Berkeley.
Mignolo, W. 1995. *The Darker Side of the Renaissance: Literacy, Territoriality, and Colonization.* Ann Arbor.
Miles, G. 1995. *Livy: Reconstructing Early Rome.* Ithaca, N.Y.
Millar, F. 1998. *The Crowd in Rome in the Late Republic.* Ann Arbor.
Misurare la terra: Centuriazione e coloni nel mondo romano. 1983. Modena.
Montrose, L. 1989. "The Poetics and Politics of Culture." In Veeser 1989, 15–36.
Moore, T. 1989. *Artistry and Ideology: Livy's Vocabulary of Virtue.* Athenäum Monografien, Altertumswissenschaft 192. Frankfurt.
———. 1999. *The Theater of Plautus.* Austin.
Morgan, M. 1973. "Pliny *HN* 3.129, the Roman Use of Statues, and the Elogium of C. Sempronius Tuditanus (cos. 129 B.C.)" *Philologus* 117:29–48.
———. 1980. "*Imperium sine finibus:* Romans and World Conquest in the First Century B.C." In S. Burstein and L. Okin, eds., *Panhellenica: Essays in Ancient History and Historiography in Honor of Truesdell Brown,* pp. 143–154. Lawrence, Kan.
Morstein-Marx, R. 1998. "Publicity, Popularity, and Patronage in the *Commentariolum Petitionis.*" *Classical Antiquity* 17:259–288.
———. 2004. *Mass Oratory and Political Power in the Late Roman Republic.* Cambridge.
Moscatelli, U. 1979. "Intorno ai passi di Frontino sulla cultellatio." *Rivista storica dell'antichità* 9:75–87.

Mouritsen, H. 1998. *Italian Unification: A Study in Ancient and Modern Historiography. Bulletin of the Institute of Classical Studies* suppl. 28. London.

———. 2001. *Plebs and Politics in the Late Roman Republic.* Cambridge.

Mutschler, F.-H. 1975. *Erzählstil und Propaganda in Caesars Kommentarien.* Heidelberger Forschungen 15. Heidelberg.

Narducci, E. 1997. *Cicerone e l'eloquenza romana: Retorica e progetto culturale.* Rome.

Nash, D. 1976. "Reconstructing Posidonius' Celtic Ethnography: Some Considerations." *Britannia* 7:112–126.

Nemet-Nejat, K. 1982. *Late Babylonian Field Plans in the British Museum.* Studia Pohl, Series Maior 11. Rome.

Nicolet, C. 1976. "Le cens senatorial sous la republique et sous Auguste." *Journal of Roman Studies* 66:20–38.

———. 1991. *Space, Geography, and Politics in the Early Roman Empire.* Ann Arbor.

Nisbet, R., ed. 1961. *Cicero In L. Calpurnium Pisonem Oratio.* Oxford.

Nörr, D. 1963. "Origo: Studien zur Orts-, Stadt-, und Reichszugehörigkeit in der Antike." *Zeitschrift der Savigny-Stiftung für Rechtsgeschichte, romanistische Abteilung* 31:525–600.

———. 1989. *Aspekte des römischen Völkerrechts: Die Bronzetafel von Alcántara.* Abhandlungen, Bayerische Akademie der Wissenschaften, Philosophisch-historische Klasse 101. Munich.

———. 1991. *Die Fides im römischen Völkerrecht.* Heidelberg.

Oakley, S. 1985. "Single Combat in Rome." *Classical Quarterly* 35:392–410.

———. 1997. *A Commentary on Livy Books VI–X.* Vol. 1. Oxford.

Odelman, E. 1972. *Études sur quelques reflets du style administratif chez César.* Stockholm.

O'Gorman, E. 1993. "No Place Like Rome: Identity and Difference in the Germania of Tacitus." *Ramus* 22:135–154.

Oniga, R. 1995. *Sallustio e l'etnografia.* Biblioteca di Materiali e discussioni per l'analisi dei testi classici 12. Pisa.

Oppermann, H. 1933. "Zu den geographischen Exkursen in Caesars *Bellum Gallicum.*" *Hermes* 68:182–195.

Parker, H. 1997. "The Teratogenic Grid." In J. Hallett and M. Skinner, eds., *Roman Sexualities,* pp. 47–65. Princeton.

Pelikan, M. 1997. "Home of the Brave: Aristocratic Self-fashioning in Triumph Debates from Livy 31–45 (200–167 B.C.)." Diss., University of California, Berkeley.

Perrotta, G. 1948. "Cesare scrittore." *Maia* 1:5–32.

Powell, A. 1998. "Julius Caesar and the Presentation of Massacre." In Welch and Powell 1998, 111–137.

Purcell, N. 1990. "The Creation of Provincial Landscape: The Roman Impact on Cisalpine Gaul." In T. Blagg and M. Millett, eds., *The Early Roman Empire in the West*, pp. 6–29. Oxford.

Ramage, E. 2001. "The *Bellum Iustum* in Caesar's *De Bello Gallico*." *Athenaeum* 89:145–170.

———. 2002. "The *Populus Romanus*, Imperium, and Caesar's Presence in the *De Bello Gallico*." *Athenaeum* 90:125–146.

———. 2003. "Aspects of Propaganda in the *De Bello Gallico*: Caesar's Virtues and Attributes." *Athenaeum* 91:331–372.

Rambaud, M. 1966. *L'art de la déformation historique dans les Commentaires de César*. 2d ed. Paris.

———. 1974. "L'espace dans le récit césarien." In Chevallier 1974, 111–129.

Rasmussen, D. 1963. *Caesars Commentarii: Stil und Stilwandel am Beispiel der direkten Rede*. Göttingen.

Reijgwart, E. 1993. "Zur Erzählung in Caesars Commentarii: Der 'unbekannte' Erzähler des *Bellum Gallicum*." *Philologus* 137:18–37.

Rich, J. 1976. *Declaring War in the Roman Republic in the Period of Transmarine Expansion*. Brussels.

———. 1993. "Fear, Greed, and Glory: The Causes of Roman War-Making in the Middle Republic." In J. Rich and G. Shipley, eds., *War and Society in the Roman World*, Leicester-Nottingham Studies in Ancient History 5, pp. 38–68. London.

Richlin, A. 1993. "Not before Homosexuality: The Materiality of the *Cinaedus* and the Roman Law against Love between Men." *Journal of the History of Sexuality* 3:523–572.

Richter, W. 1977. *Caesar als Darsteller seiner Taten. Eine Einführung*. Heidelberg.

Riggsby, A. 1995. "Appropriation and Reversal as a Basis for Oratorical Proof." *Classical Philology* 90:245–256.

———. 1997. "'Public' and 'Private' in Roman Culture: The Case of the *Cubiculum*." *Journal of Roman Archaeology* 10:36–56.

———. 1998. "Self and Community in the Younger Pliny." *Arethusa* 31:75–97.

———. 1999a. *Crime and Community in Ciceronian Rome*. Austin.

———. 1999b. Review of Welch and Powell 1998. *Bryn Mawr Classical Review* 99.4.16.

———. 1999c. "Iulius Victor on Cicero's Defenses *de Repetundis*." *Rheinisches Museum für Philologie* 142:427–429.

———. 2004. "Character in Roman Oratory and Rhetoric." In J. Powell and J. Paterson, eds., *Cicero the Advocate*, pp. 165–185. Oxford.

Rives, J., ed. and trans. 1998. *Tacitus: Germania*. Oxford.

Robinson, O. 1997. *The Sources of Roman Law*. London.

Roller, M. 1996. "Ethical Contradiction and the Fractured Community in Lucan's *Bellum Civile*." *Classical Antiquity* 15:319–347.

———. 2001. *Constructing Autocracy*. Princeton.

———. 2004. "Exemplarity in Roman Culture: The Cases of Horatius Cocles and Cloelia." *Classical Philology* 99:1–56.

Romm, J. S. 1992. *The Edges of the Earth in Ancient Thought: Geography, Exploration, and Fiction.* Princeton.

Rorty, R. 1991. *Objectivity, Relativism, and Truth.* Cambridge.

Rose, P. 1995. "Cicero and the Rhetoric of Imperialism: Putting the Politics Back into Political Rhetoric." *Rhetorica* 13:359–399.

Rosenstein, N. 1986. "*Imperatores Victi:* The Case of C. Hostilius Mancinus." *Classical Antiquity* 5:230–252.

———. 1990. Imperatores Victi: *Military Defeat and Aristocratic Competition in the Middle and Late Republic.* Berkeley.

Roymans, N. 1990. *Tribal Societies in Northern Gaul: An Anthropological Perspective.* Amsterdam.

Ruebel, J. 1979. "The Trial of Milo in 52 B.C.: A Chronological Study." *Transactions of the American Philological Association* 109:231–249.

Rüpke, J. 1992. "Wer las Caesars *bella* als *commentarii?*" *Gymnasium* 99:201–226.

Rutherford, W. 1895 [1961]. *Gai Iuli Caesaris de Bello Gallico commentariorum II, III.* London [New York].

Sacks, K. 1990. *Diodorus Siculus and the First Century.* Princeton.

Sadashige, J. 1999. "Catullus and the Fabric of Roman Identity." Unpublished ms.

Saller, R. 1980. "Anecdotes as Historical Evidence for the Principate." *Greece & Rome* 27:69–83.

Salmon, E. 1970. *Roman Colonization under the Republic.* Ithaca, N.Y.

Schama, S. 1991. *Dead Certainties: Unwarranted Speculations.* New York.

Schieffer, R. 1972. "Die Rede des Critognatus (*BG* VII, 77) und Caesars Urteil über den Gallischen Krieg." *Gymnasium* 79:477–494.

Schlicher, J. 1936. "The Development of Caesar's Narrative Style." *Classical Philology* 31:212–224.

Schrenk, L. 1994. "Cicero on Rhetoric and Philosophy: Tusculan Disputations I." *Ancient Philosophy* 14:355–360.

Scott, J. 1990. *Domination and the Arts of Resistance: Hidden Transcripts.* New Haven.

Seel, O., ed. 1968. *Bellum Gallicum.* 2d ed. Leipzig.

Shaw, B. 1984. "Bandits in the Roman Empire." *Past and Present* 105:3–52.

Sinclair, P. 1994. "Political Declensions in Latin Grammar and Oratory, 55 BCE–CE 39." *Ramus* 23:92–109.

Skinner, M. 1979. "Parasites and Strange Bedfellows: A Study in Catullus' Political Imagery." *Ramus* 8:137–152.

Smethurst, S. 1953. "Cicero and Roman Imperial Policy." *Transactions of the American Philological Association* 84:216–226.

Smith, P. 1988. *Discerning the Subject.* Minneapolis.

Snowden, F. 1983. *Before Color Prejudice: The Ancient View of Blacks.* Cambridge.

Sobel, D. 1996. *Longitude: The True Story of a Lone Genius Who Solved the Greatest Scientific Problem of His Time.* New York.

Solodow, J. 1979. "Livy and the Story of Horatius, 1.24–26." *Transactions of the American Philological Association* 109:21–68.

Spann, P. 1987. *Quintus Sertorius and the Legacy of Sulla.* Fayetteville.

Spurr, D. 1993. *The Rhetoric of Empire: Colonial Discourse in Journalism, Travel Writing, and Imperial Administration.* Durham, N.C.

Steel, C. 2001. *Cicero, Rhetoric, and Empire.* Oxford.

Stockton, D. 1979. *The Gracchi.* Oxford.

Suolahti, J. 1955. *The Junior Officers of the Roman Army in the Republican Period.* Annales Academiae Scientiarum Fennicae B97. Helsinki.

Swoboda, A. 1898. *P. Nigidii Figuli Operum Reliquiae . . . Quaestiones Nigidianas.* Vienna. (Photo reprint, Amsterdam, 1964.)

Syme, R. 1939. *The Roman Revolution.* Oxford.

———. 1964. *Sallust.* Berkeley.

———. 1979. "Observations on the Province of Cilicia." In E. Badian, ed., *Roman Papers I,* pp. 120–148. Oxford.

Taylor, L. 1949. *Party Politics in the Age of Caesar.* Berkeley.

———. 1966. *Roman Voting Assemblies from the Hannibalic War to the Dictatorship of Caesar.* Ann Arbor.

Thomas, R. 1982. *Lands and Peoples in Roman Poetry: The Ethnographic Tradition.* Proceedings of the Cambridge Philological Society, suppl. 7. Cambridge.

———. 1988. *Georgics.* Cambridge.

Thornton, B. 1997. "The Enemy Is Us: The 'Betrayal of the Postmodern Clerks.'" *Arion* 5:165–216.

Thulin, C., ed. 1971. *Corpus Agrimensorum Romanorum.* Stuttgart.

Tierney, J. 1960. "The Celtic Ethnography of Posidonius." *Proceedings of the Royal Irish Academy* 60:189–275.

Todd, M. 1975. *The Northern Barbarians, 100 B.C.–A.D. 300.* London.

Toll, K. 1997. "Making Roman-ness and the *Aeneid.*" *Classical Antiquity* 16:34–56.

Treggiari, S. 1969. *Roman Freedmen during the Late Republic.* Oxford.

Trüdinger, K. 1918. "Studien zur Geschich te der grieschisch-römischen Ethnographie." Diss., Basel.

Tuan, Y.-F. 1977. *Space and Place.* Minneapolis.

Usener, H. 1901. "Italische Volksjustiz." *Rheinisches Museum für Philologie* 56:1–21.

Van Sickle, J. 1987. "The Elogia of the Cornelii Scipiones and the Origin of the Epigram at Rome." *American Journal of Philology* 108:41–55.

Vasaly, A. 1993. *Representations: Images of the World in Ciceronian Oratory.* Berkeley.

Veeser, H., ed. 1989. *The New Historicism.* New York.

Veyne, P. 1975. "Y a-t-il eu un imperialisme romain?" *Mélanges d'archéologie et d'histoire de l'École française de Rome* 87:793–855.

Villard, P. 1988. "Le mélange et ses problèmes." *Revue des études anciennes* 90:19–33.

von Albrecht, M. 1971. *Meister römischen Prosa von Cato bis Apuleius.* Heidelberg.

———. 1997. *History of Roman Literature I.* Leiden.

von Premerstein, A. 1900. "Commentarii." *RE* 4:726–759.

Walbank, F. 1985. "Speeches in Greek Historians." In idem, *Selected Papers,* pp. 242–261. Cambridge.

Wallace-Hadrill, A. 1986. "Image and Authority in the Coinage of Augustus." *Journal of Roman Studies* 76:66–87.

———. 1997. "Mutatio Morum: The Idea of a Cultural Revolution." In T. Habinek and A. Schiesaro, eds., *The Roman Cultural Revolution,* pp. 3–22. Cambridge.

Walser, G. 1956. *Caesar und die Germanen. Studien zur politischen Tendenz römischer Feldzugsberichte.* Historia Einzelschriften 1. Wiesbaden.

———. 1995. "Zu Caesars tendenz in der geographischen Beschreibung Galliens." *Klio* 77:217–223.

———. 1998. *Bellum Helveticum. Studium sum Beginn der caesarischen Eroberung von Gallien.* Historia Einzelschriften 118. Stuttgart.

Walsh, P. 1963. *Livy: His Historical Aims and Methods.* Cambridge.

Warmington, E. 1959. *Remains of Old Latin.* Vol. 4. Cambridge.

Watson, A. 1968. *The Law of Property in the Later Roman Republic.* Oxford.

———. 1993. *International Law in Archaic Rome: War and Religion.* Baltimore.

Welch, K. 1998. "Caesar and His Officers in the Gallic War Commentaries." In Welch and Powell 1998, 85–110.

Welch, K., and A. Powell, eds. 1998. *Julius Caesar as Artful Reporter.* London.

Wells, C. 1972. *The German Policy of Augustus.* Oxford.

Wells, P. 1995. "Settlement and Social Systems at the End of the Iron Age." In Arnold and Gibson 1995, 88–95.

Wenger, L. 1935. "Suum cuique in antiken Urkunden." In *Aus der Geisteswelt des Mittelalters,* Beitrage zur Geschichte der Philosophie, Texte und Unter-suchungen, suppl. 3, pp. 1415–1425. Münster.

Werner, R. 1972. "Das Problem des Imperialismus und die römische Ostpolitik im zweiten Jahrhundert v. Chr." *Aufsteig und Niedergang der römischen Welt* 1.1:501–563.

Wheeler, E. 1988. *Stratagem and the Vocabulary of Military Trickery.* Mnemosyne suppl. 108. Leiden.

Wheeler, M., and K. Richardson. 1957. *Hill-Forts of Northern France.* Reports of the Research Committee of the Society of Antiquaries of London 19. Oxford.

White, H. 1978. "The Forms of Wildness: Archaeology of an Idea." In idem, *Tropics of Discourse: Essays in Cultural Criticism,* pp. 150–182. Baltimore.

Williams, J. 2001. *Beyond the Rubicon*. Oxford.

Wiseman, A., and P. Wiseman, trans. 1980. *Julius Caesar: The Battle for Gaul*. Boston.

Wiseman, T. 1979. *Clio's Cosmetics*. Leicester.

———. 1985. "Competition and Co-operation." In idem, ed., *Roman Political Life, 90 B.C.–A.D. 69*, pp. 3–19. Exeter.

———. 1993. "Lying Historians: Seven Types of Mendacity." In C. Gill and T. Wiseman, eds., *Lies and Fiction in the Ancient World*, pp. 122–146. Austin.

———. 1994. *Historiography and Imagination*. Exeter.

———. 1998. "The Publication of *De Bello Gallico*." In Welch and Powell 1998, 1–9.

Woodman, A., ed. and comm. 1983. *Velleius Paterculus: The Caesarian and Augustan Narrative*. Cambridge.

———. 1988. *Rhetoric in Classical Historiography*. London.

Ziegler, K.-H. 1982. Review of Albert 1980. *Zeitschrift der Savigny-Stiftung für Rechtsgeschichte, romanistische Abteilung* 99:389–393.

———. 1985. "Kriegsverträge im antiken römischen Recht. *Zeitschrift der Savigny-Stiftung für Rechtsgeschichte, romanistische Abteilung* 102:40–90.

Index